Episodes in the Rhetoric of Government-Indian Relations

Episodes in the Rhetoric of Government-Indian Relations

JANICE SCHUETZ

PRAEGER

Westport, Connecticut
London

Library of Congress Cataloging-in-Publication Data

Schuetz, Janice E.
  Episodes in the rhetoric of government-Indian relations / Janice Schuetz.
    p. cm.
  Includes bibliographical references.
  ISBN 0–275–97613–0 (alk. paper)
    1. Indians of North America—Government relations.   2. Indians of North
  America—Politics and government.   3. Indians of North America—History—Sources.
  I. Title.
  E93.S35   2002
  323.1'197073'09—dc21   2001051173

British Library Cataloguing in Publication Data is available.

Library of Congress Catalog Card Number: 2001051173
ISBN: 0–275–97613–0

First published in 2002

Praeger Publishers, 88 Post Road West, Westport, CT 06881
An imprint of Greenwood Publishing Group, Inc.
www.praeger.com

Printed in the United States of America

The paper used in this book complies with the
Permanent Paper Standard issued by the National
Information Standards Organization (Z39.48–1984).

10 9 8 7 6 5 4 3 2 1

I dedicate this book to my husband, Andrew J. Burgess

Contents

Acknowledgments

The author gratefully acknowledges the assistance of reference librarians and archivists from the Washington State Library in Olympia, the Minnesota State History Society in St. Paul, the Nebraska Historical Society in Lincoln, the Oklahoma History Center in Oklahoma City, the University of Oklahoma Library in Oklahoma City, the Denver Public Library, the New Mexico State Library, and the University of Kansas Library in Lawrence. I presented versions of the various chapters at a number of professional conferences, including the World History of Religions in Mexico City, two American Academy of Religion Regional Meetings, two National Communication Associations, two Western States Communication Associations, and for Southwest Intercultural Studies. The author appreciates the interviews with many students and scholars at the University of New Mexico who read and commented on the chapters, as well as the Nisqually historians who gave insight on Chief Leschi and the Puget Sound Indians. The Attorney General's Office of the State of Washington provided access to all of the trial and appeal documents for the Fishing Rights cases, and Ray Twohig's office gave me access to the documents of the Gordon House case. I am especially indebted to Kate Kopiske for translating early Spanish documents related to some of the chapters. Finally, I thank the University of New Mexico for awarding me a sabbatical so that I could complete this work.

Introduction

Even during the dark times of the Indian wars in the nineteenth century, the voice of the Indian was heard. At times the voice was only as a murmur; at other times it was a scream accompanied by a bang. But the government heard the Indian voice and reacted, sometimes by suppressing it and other times by using compassionate political action. John A. Campbell (1990) noted, "History chronicles the rhetorical emergence of peoples" (357). This book investigates several political and legal episodes that illuminate government-Indian relations, beginning with the trial of Chief Leschi in 1858 and ending with the vehicular homicide case of Gordon House during the 1990s. These episodes focus the attention of readers on the rhetorical discourse that the government and Indians employed to resolve the conflicts. Unlike a typical historical study that reconstructs all of the facts and then reports events in a narrative form, the focus of the subsequent chapters is on the rhetorical record of Indian and government spokespersons. This introduction to *Episodes in the Rhetoric of Government-Indian Relations* identifies the goal, reviews pertinent research, defines the rhetorical perspective, explains the method, and outlines each chapter.

GOAL

My goal is to provide a "rhetorical ancestry" to the history of government-Indian relations (Campbell 1990, 369). To accomplish this goal, each of the subsequent chapters makes use of historical evidence to draw inferences about the rhetorical features of the discourse and the effects that follow. Rhetorical discourse takes both verbal and nonverbal forms; it expresses what was said and done by the agents of action in a particular controversy. Treaties, letters, oral histories, speeches, ritual performances, media reports, biographical narratives, protests and demonstrations, political hearings, and legal proceedings are all rhetorical constructions that influence audiences.

PERTINENT RESEARCH

This work adopts Kenneth Burke's perspective that "every document bequeathed us by history must be treated as strategy for encompassing a situation" (Burke [1941] 1973, 109); that is, government documents and Indian responses are rejoinders to assertions made in the situations that encompass them. Each chapter is part of what Burke calls an "unending conversation" about a subject. My discussion is similar to those of previous public policy dramas. It started long before I considered the topic, and I have not retraced all of the ideas that have gone on before. But I do "put in my oar," add to the conversation, and "allow others to continue the discussion after me" as Burke suggested ([1941] 1973, 110–11). My subsequent explanations of government-Indian relations reflect my assumptions about the rhetoric of political and legal processes and forums. Mirroring Burke's concept of the unending conversation, these interpretations rely on some of the preceding conversations on government-Indian relations and add insights based on applicable rhetorical theories and idioms.

Scholarly analysis of government-Indian relations is not a new subject. Historians, anthropologists, and political and legal scholars have documented different aspects of the legacy of this long, often tumultuous relationships through discussions of the public policies of extermination, assimilation, allotment, termination, and self-determination.

Historians

For decades, historians have chronicled the events that shaped these relationships from a variety of perspectives. For example, some historians recorded the conquest of Indians from a military perspective (Limerick 1987; Smith 1990). Other histories examined the motives of both the government and the Indians and attributed responsibility to both factions for successful and failed policies (Andrist 1964; Dunn [1886] 1969; Brown 1970; Deloria [1969] 1970; Bender 1984; Prucha 1984, vols. 1–2; Churchill & Vander Wall 1988; Bordewich 1996). Still other historians criticized the policies of the government and faulted its legal system (Washburn 1971; Deloria & Lytle 1983; Wilkins 1997). Since many nineteenth-century Indians kept no written records, their perspectives are recorded through the words of government translators and in the oral traditions of tribal members.

Anthropologists

To supplement and extend the historical perspective, anthropologists added insights about Indian culture and values even though this information was often ethnocentric (Bandelier 1892; Stevenson 1904; Bunzel 1929–1930; Cushing [1882] 1990). In the last half of the twentieth century, anthropologists often offered sympathetic accounts of tribal life and values and called attention to the government's transgressions into Indian life (Underhill 1956; Grinnell [1923] 1972, [1915] 1985; Ellis 1974; Hoebel 1978). Even though these perspectives varied, anthropologists served a significant role in congressional and legal proceedings by providing ethnographic testimony about Indian culture (Lurie 1955, 1957; Manners 1957). Some contemporary Indian writers complain about the role of anthropologists in particular and non-Indian scholars in general, claiming that outside researchers lack the insight necessary to write about Indian culture (Berkhofer 1979; Biolosi & Zimmerman 1997). A rhetorical approach reveals how the cultural assumptions of participants affect their rhetorical choices of content, style, and forums.

Law and Politics

Important contributions by legal and political scholars accentuate the role of law in the history of government-Indian relations (Washburn 1971; Deloria & Lytle 1983; Wilkinson 1987; Harring 1994). Legal and political scholars provide a record of important statutes and the legal interpretations that the government has used to define and control the American Indian. For example, the development of the Office of Indian Affairs in 1834 established a structure by which the government assumed authority over treaty Indians by administering reservation systems and regulating tribal economies through annuity payments. The flaws inherent in the legal statutes and the political structures they created figure prominently in my discussions about the trials of Chief Leschi, the Sioux Uprising, the Sand Creek Massacre, the depredations and slave taking during the Navajo wars, and the treaty controversies of the eastern and western Sioux.

The government enacted dozens of laws that affected relationships with the Indians. For example, the advent of the Grant Peace Commission in 1870 changed the course of the government's relations with Indians by ending official treaty making and replacing this process with peace agreements and diplomatic missions. Under this policy, the government appointed peace commissioners to negotiate legal agreements, and it also replaced military agents with representatives of religious groups. The effects of this policy appear in my discussions of the resistance on the Southern Cheyenne and Arapaho, the diplomatic visits of Red Cloud and the reparations paid to Fanny Kelly, the return of the Navajos to their homeland, and the 1890 massacre at Wounded Knee.

Another policy, the Major Crimes Act (18 U.S.C.A., 1153, 1885), gave the federal government criminal jurisdiction over felonies committed in Indian country. This law awarded jurisdiction over hundreds of cases to the government and reduced the ability of Indians to deal with tribal legal matters. This law enters into my analyses of the trial of Zuni Bow Priests in territorial court in 1892, the trials against Indian activists resulting from the 1973 standoff, and the vehicular homicide case of Gordon House in the 1990s.

Many of these policies had such disastrous effects on Indian culture that Congress later revoked them. One such act was the Allotment Act of 1887. This act radically altered the land base of the Southern Cheyenne and Arapaho, the Santee and Oglala Sioux, and the Navajo. The act gave the government the power to divide up reservation land and redistribute surplus land to non-Indians. After the Allotment Act took effect, the government reduced Indian lands nationwide from 180 million to less than 80 million acres. The reforms of the Franklin Roosevelt administration led by Secretary of Interior John Collier reversed the policy of allotment and initiated programs for Indian independence. The Roosevelt reforms of the 1930s made possible the return of Blue Lake in 1970.

The land the government gained from treaties and agreements, and that it redistributed under the provisions of allotment, produced major controversies with Indian tribes. To resolve these disputes, Congress established the Indian Claims Commission in 1945. This quasi-legal forum allowed land claims to be filed by hundreds of Indian tribes, including the Puget Sound Indians, the Santee and Teton Sioux, the Southern Cheyenne and Arapaho, the Taos and Zuni Pueblos, and the Navajo. During its nearly thirty years of existence, the Indian Claims Commission heard 852 cases and awarded $818 million to tribes to compensate them for lands taken under various treaties, agreements, and acts.

RHETORICAL PERSPECTIVE

Even though historical, anthropological, and legal-political scholars add depth to the ongoing conversation about government-Indian relations, a rhetorical perspective often is missing from these accounts. Although some insightful work has appeared in communication journals, these essays provide only a glimpse of the potential rhetorical legacy. For example, several sources (Maestas 1976; Nabokov 1991; Moquin & Van Doren 1995) provide examples of Indian rhetoric extracted from a variety of documents, but none of this research contextualizes or analyzes the discourse. More specifically, these authors provide no explanations about rhetorical content, forms, audiences, or effects of Indian discourse. Admittedly, these works add valuable textual resources, but they offer no substantive interpretation of rhetorical processes and effects. A second type of research focuses on the rhetoric of Indian protest and gives a glimpse of a rhetorical perspective. For example, Randall Lake (1983, 1991) analyzes the rhetoric of Indian protest during the 1970s showing that the goal of this rhetoric was not "instrumental" and did not seek to persuade public audiences, but this rhetoric served a consummatory function in which Indians addressed themselves and affirmed their Indian identity. Richard Morris and Philip Wander (1990) analyze the role of the Ghost Dance at Wounded Knee and conclude that the Ghost Dance was a master trope invoked by the Wounded Knee protesters to "affirm their identity," "plan," and "dramatize" their actions in opposition to the military's response. A third kind of research represents the point of view of critical rhetoric. In one essay, for example, Robin Patric Clair (1997) examines how the Treaty of New Echota both empowered and silenced the voices of Cherokee Indians.

The eleven chapters that follow give readers a rhetorical perspective about government-Indian relations during the nineteenth and twentieth centuries. Each of the chapters focuses on the persuasive strategies of both government and Indian leaders as they surfaced in written and oral records. This perspective shows how the government and Indian spokespersons constitute and define issues; create, prolong, in some cases manage conflict; and silence and empower voices of government officials and Indian leaders. By examining a variety of episodes in the ongoing drama of government-Indian relations, this book illuminates a rhetorical legacy that evolved in the personal, political, and legal discourse of those who participated in the episodes.

METHOD

The chapters that follow provide case studies of the rhetoric of government-Indian relations. It is not intended that they be an exhaustive account of all episodes and issues. Rather the cases are merely episodes that represent issues and rhetorical strategies common to government-Indian relations in American history. A rhetorical perspective shows how the discourse and action resulting from government reports, military speeches, negotiations, political and legal proceedings, and ethnographic reports contribute to an understanding of the complex issues and processes of problem solving that have characterized government-Indian relations in the United States. It is my hope that readers will observe parallels between the cases examined here and other similar cases that have not been discussed. Like any piece of scholarship, this book relies on some of the author's assumptions about the appropriate texts, contexts, audiences, interpretation, and forums involved in rhetorical study.

Texts

Texts include written and oral discourse as well as associated nonverbal symbolic actions and reactions. The definition of texts used here follows Michael McGee's (1990) explanation that discourse is fragmentary, rhetors "make discourses from scraps and pieces of evidence," and audiences help formulate the discourse by contributing their own meanings and understanding to the fragments presented them by rhetors (280–81). The texts analyzed in the following chapters include treaties, diaries, letters, speeches, negotiations, congressional hearings, proclamations, legal proceedings, ethnographic reports, and other related documents. These texts reveal the emergences of rhetors who bring forth themes, issues, and arguments to influence audiences and affect the social, political, and legal contexts in which the controversies occur.

Contexts

The discourse constitutes and is constituted by the context. Contexts affect both definable locations in which rhetoric emerges and the explicit assumptions of rhetors in those contexts. Each context discussed in this book represents a multiplicity of places. The locations vary from places in history, such as the mid-nineteenth century, to places in geographic space, such as the accustomed fishing locations along the Puget Sound in present-day Washington. Places of religious significance, including Blue Lake near Taos Pueblo, and specific landmarks, including the sites of the Sand Creek and Wounded Knee Massacres, symbolize the actions that occurred there. Contexts also reflect the assumptions of rhetors and their audiences. For example, contexts embrace cultural beliefs, norms for acting, attitudes, and ideologies. For this reason, contexts give some clues about the knowledge and experiences of participants in situationally located controversies. For example, when the miners and settlers rushed into Colorado territory to find gold, they trespassed on Indian land and influenced the decision of Cheyenne Peace Chief Black Kettle to camp at Sand Creek near Fort Lyon just as it influenced Colonel John Chivington to order his regiment to fire on the Indians camped there.

Audience

The audience is a fluid construct that changes according to the emerging features of rhetorical controversies. In some cases the audience is a narrow construct, referring explicitly to the person to whom the rhetor addresses oral and written discourse. For example, when Indian agents wrote to the superintendent of Indian affairs, they sought an individual response from their supervisor. Nondiscursive symbolic actions also have an audience. This effect is evident when the Navajos resisted their internment at Fort Sumner and when activists at the Wounded Knee standoff refused to submit to government demands. In both cases, the Indians addressed a broad public and political audience at the same time they addressed their own ego functions. Typically, the audience refers to the recipients influenced by the discourse. For example, the readers of the opinion of Judge Boldt in 1974 and since that time are his audience. In this case his audience consisted of persons that responded to this opinion with a change of attitude, a modification of belief, or a verbal reaction. The newspaper reporter who faulted the Boldt opinion as well as the lawyer who incorporated the opinion in order to defend a new legal principle both constituted audiences.

For each episode multiple audiences exist. For example, the return of Blue Lake would not have occurred without successful persuasive appeals to Indian, religious, social, and political audiences. The forum and the physical site of an episode suggest an audience. For example, the military commission that decided the fate of the warriors participating in the Sioux Uprising was associated with a particular site and forum. Rhetors influence immediate and remote audiences. Often the content of the discourse gives clues about who the audiences are and what assumptions they hold.

Interpretation

This book combines historical explanation and rhetorical interpretation. Each chapter offers historical background to show the cultural, political, and legal circumstances in which the rhetorical discourse emerged. Additionally, the chapters offer rhetorical interpretations about the form, content, and style of the discourse under study in a given episode. The interpretations seek to enhance readers' understanding about how specified government and Indian rhetors constructed, maintained, and changed each other's minds. The book both creates theoretical models and expands existing frameworks in order to analyze the rhetorical processes and products relevant to each episode. Thus, some of the rhetorical interpretation is inductive; it is grounded in the author's conclusions and inferences and derived from the particulars of the rhetorical situation. Some chapters modify existing models in order to make deductions about rhetorical processes and practices. Other chapters utilize combinations of inductive and deductive interpretation. Some of the analysis is normative, concentrating on what was said by whom to what audience. Still other analysis utilizes critical rhetoric to call attention to the government's structures of domination and control and to acknowledge the silenced voices of the Indians. Although the kinds of rhetorical interpretation are diverse, all chapters attempt to show the impact of rhetorical practices on government-Indian relations.

CHAPTER SUMMARIES

The chapters analyze eleven episodes in government-Indian relations. An episode is a cluster of historical incidents delineated by parameters of time and space. An episode is set apart from other events by the exigent issues that define a controversy and by the rhetoric the government and the affected Indians use to try to resolve it. Each chapter examines a different episode by identifying issues that are sources of the controversy, explaining rhetorical theories that apply to the controversy, describing the rhetorical forums, and analyzing selective discourse and behaviors that illuminate how the participants resolved the controversy. In most of the episodes, compelling issues arise because the government perceived the actions of the Indians to be in conflict with its policies or laws. Some discourse expressed the resistance of the Indians; other responses demonstrated their compliance. Still other discourse showed how Indians were colonized by the government and eventually overcame this colonization. Six episodes illuminate the government's rhetorical practices in dealing with the Indians in the nineteenth century. The other five episodes show how nineteenth-century treaties and policies led to new controversies between the tribes and the government in the twentieth century. A brief summary of these chapters follow.

Chapter 1 focuses on an episode in the Puget Sound region of the state of Washington. Conflicts arose between the government, the settlers, and the Indians over the territorial provisions of the Medicine Creek Treaty of 1854. Prior to the treaty, the British-owned Hudson Bay Company had established trade relations and strong personal allegiances with the Nisqually and other Puget Sound Indians. After an influx of settlers, called "Bostons," came west on the Oregon Trail, the government decided to guarantee more land for settlement. The result was a government-initiated treaty, the 1854 Medicine Creek Treaty, executed by territorial governor Isaac I. Stevens. The treaty forced the Puget Sound Indians onto reservations, took away fertile farm land, and made the Indians compete with settlers for their aboriginal land. The Indians resisted by killing settlers and ignoring some of the treaty provisions. The chapter claims other Indian warfare followed a common dramatic scenario exemplified by the Puget Sound conflicts. This common scenario is called a representative anecdote, and it applies to other stories of government-Indian relations in the nineteenth century. In the Puget Sound, however, the government exerted control of the conflict by the capture, trial, and execution of Nisqually Chief Leschi. The chapter centers on political maneuvers that characterized two trials and influenced the eventual execution of Chief Leschi. The dramatistic theories of Kenneth Burke provide the frameworks for analyzing the actions leading to, during, and following the trial.

Chapter 2 investigates an episode occurring along the Mississippi and

Minnesota River valleys of Minnesota. In these incidents, the unfriendly Santee Sioux visited revenge on white settlers and military sites during what historians call the Sioux Uprising of 1862. The uprising consisted of eleven different raids and murders of settlers by Santee in 1862. Divergent issues sparked the hostilities. The Indians' actions violated the treaties of 1858 in which the government granted each Santee an 80-acre plot and provided annuity payments for other land the tribe had ceded to the government. According to the Santee, their raids and killing of settlers resulted from the government's failure to pay promised annuities and from settlers encroaching on Indian lands. After the hostilities, the government rounded up "unfriendly" Santee and tried nearly 400 men and women in a remarkably quick legal proceeding before a military commission. After the trials, the government honored a reprieve granted to 360 Indians by President Abraham Lincoln, executed the remaining thirty-nine "guilty" Indians, abrogated all treaties with the Santee, and removed them to North Dakota and later to Nebraska. The chapter uses the framework of genre theory to identify and analyze treaties, eyewitness narratives, accusation and defense accounts, appeals for clemency, and consolation speeches.

Chapter 3 examines an episode in the plains between 1864 and 1865, occurring near the southwest corner of Kansas and southeast corner of Colorado. The episode centered on the Sand Creek Massacre, a battle in which 700 citizen militia led by Colonel John Chivington fired on a camp of peaceful Southern Cheyenne and Arapaho Indians, killing more than 150 men, women, and children. The definition of the issues depended on the points of view of the participants and observers. From the military point of view of Colonel Chivington, the battle occurred as the result of Cheyenne-Arapaho raids and killing throughout the region. However, from the point of view of Indians and some sympathetic political leaders, the killing was an example of the ruthless massacre of innocent Indians consummated because of the political ambitions of military leader and territorial governor John Evans. The massacre created such a political furor in Washington that congressional leaders demanded an investigation of the events at Sand Creek. The political uproar produced two rancorous congressional hearings. In both cases, congressional members faulted Chivington and Evans. The chapter applies speech act and political spectacle theory to the discourse of the letters between government leaders, treaty conferences, and congressional investigations of relevance to the Sand Creek Massacre.

The setting for Chapter 4 is in the Southwest in present day New Mexico and Arizona. Historians refer to the episode as the Navajo wars and designate the time frame as 1846 to 1868. The federal government inherited the conflicts between the Navajos and the Spanish settlers when they seized power of New Mexico territory in 1846. The warfare centered on slave raids and depredations by settlers against Navajos and retribution against

the settlers by Navajos. Despite a number of treaties, the government recognized that the chiefs they had designated as leaders lacked the ability to
control large numbers of dispersed Navajo warriors. The hostilities baffled
the military and the territorial government to such an extent that it took
more than twenty years to come up with a solution. Eventually, some military leaders decided to round up and then remove 8,000 Navajos from
their homeland to a small government installation in Fort Sumner, New
Mexico. To illuminate this long and painful episode in Navajo history, the
chapter applies theories of colonial discourse to analyze expedition reports,
letters, speeches, and oral histories.

By 1870, the public had gained more knowledge of the Indian wars and
considered diverse points of view about the relationship between the government and the Indians. This knowledge produced two types of discourse,
Indian diplomatic visits to the nation's capital and dozens of published
Indian captive narratives. Chapter 5 focuses on a unique episode involving
a visit of Chief Red Cloud of the Oglala Sioux to Washington and his
rendezvous with Fanny Kelly, a captive of his Oglala tribe in Nebraska
territory. The journeys of Red Cloud and Kelly intersect when both jointly
meet with President Ulysses Grant in 1870. Red Cloud went to see the
president to get better treatment of his tribe. Kelly went to Washington to
ask Congress for reparations for her captivity, events she had documented
in her best-selling portrayal of captivity, *Narrative of My Captivity among
the Sioux Indians*. This episode shows how the government responded to
the demands of both Red Cloud and Kelly. Specifically, the chapter analyzes
the journeys of Red Cloud and of Kelly as rhetorical processes of identity
creation and transformation.

When the nineteenth century was coming to an end, the federal courts
gained jurisdiction over crimes committed by Indians. It was in 1892 that
this type of jurisdiction adversely affected the Zuni Pueblo, a small tribe
of Pueblo Indians in northeastern New Mexico. Pueblo Indians had lived
peacefully in multidwelling structures in New Mexico for centuries. The
Zuni were successful farmers that had sufficient agricultural resources to
live independently from settlers and the military. The episode centers on
accusations of witchcraft among the Zuni between 1880 and 1892. The
Zuni had experienced a period of cultural conflict brought about by intrusions from outsiders into their religious culture. Settlers and military expeditions also trespassed onto their land and sacred sites and brought
epidemics. As a result, the Zunis experienced cultural disruption marked
by accusations of witchcraft. For centuries, Zuni culture had relied on its
religious leaders to enforce the moral order of the Pueblo and ensure appropriate moral behavior by its inhabitants. Outbreaks of witchcraft, such
as the one beginning in 1889, had always been under the jurisdiction of
Bow Priests. These religious leaders held legal proceedings to decide on the
guilt and punishment for witches from the Pueblo. Chapter 6 examines the

anthropological records of the Zuni legal proceedings against witches as well as the trial proceedings of the territorial courts that convicted several Bow Priests of torturing a Zuni witch. Victor Turner's theories of ritual and redress serve as the framework for analyzing three trials related to Indian witchcraft.

Chapter 7 investigates the legacy of Sand Creek and the consequences of the Medicine Lodge Creek Treaty of 1868, a treaty that removed the Southern Cheyenne and Arapaho to a reservation in Oklahoma. The episode began with a difficult process of resettlement. After the Indians arrived in Oklahoma, they refused to become farmers, leased their land to non-Indian ranchers, and eventually gave up much of their reservation through the policy of allotment. When the Indian Claims Commission became active in 1946, the Southern Cheyenne and Arapaho filed a claim for a monetary settlement for the lands they had ceded without government compensation under their treaties. Their claim was settled in 1965. The chapter analyzes the processes leading to the treaty that eventually led to the tribe's assimilation. By applying theories of negotiation and argumentation, the chapter investigates the rhetorical features of the claims commission proceedings.

The return of Blue Lake to the Taos Indians, a tribe located in northeastern New Mexico, is the episode under discussion in Chapter 8. Even though Taos Pueblo also won a financial settlement for their land claim against the federal government in 1965, they refused the monetary award. Instead Taos Pueblo insisted the government return Blue Lake, a sacred religious site that had been taken by the federal government in 1906 and made into a national forest. In their fight for the return of Blue Lake, Taos Pueblo, along with the activists and reformers that supported their cause, took their grievance for what they considered as theft of their holy ground to the United States Congress. This rhetorical battle took the form of a sophisticated legislative campaign characterized by a publicity and lobbying effort featuring press releases, constituent letters, fact sheets, and various forms of media advocacy. The successful campaign progressed through contentious adversarial hearings in the House of Representatives and the Senate and ended with President Richard M. Nixon signing a bill to return Blue Lake to the Pueblo. The chapter applies political movement and public relations theory to the rhetorical advocacy involved in the return of Blue Lake.

A federal district court decision by Judge George Boldt in Tacoma, Washington, in 1974 is the focus of Chapter 9. This legal decision marked another important episode in the relationship between the government and the Puget Sound Indians. The episode commonly referred to as the "fishing rights case" was part of the legacy of the Medicine Creek Treaty of 1854 that guaranteed Indians the right to fish, hunt, and gather roots in their "usual and accustomed grounds." The case was the culmination of a number of fishing controversies that placed the commercial salmon fishing industry in competition with the Puget Sound Indians during the salmon harvest. This chapter analyzes the trial testimony and the Boldt opinion from the theoretical framework of legal ethnography, a method for gathering evidence and justifying complex cultural arguments.

Chapter 10 revisits the Sioux and their grievances regarding the Fort Laramie Treaty of 1868 and the loss of the Black Hills to the federal government in 1876. The setting for two battles, one in 1890 and another in 1973, is Wounded Knee, a small village on the Pine Ridge reservation in southwestern South Dakota. The first event was the Wounded Knee Massacre in 1890. Historians credit the 7th Calvary, one of the military units that retreated at the Little Big Horn, with the slaughter of unarmed Indians and the defeat of the government's powerful Sioux adversaries. The second event was the standoff between Indian activists and the government in 1973. It is no accident that both events transpired at Wounded Knee. The lamentations about the tribe's suffering in 1890 became the rallying cry for new grievances against the government that the Indians expressed in the 1970s. When Indian activists engaged in violent protests against the Pine Ridge superintendent and the agency's ruthless mixed-blood tribal chairman Dick Wilson, the government mounted a massive resistance to the activists. The chapter frames the analysis in theories of lamentation, narrative, and agitation and control.

Chapter 11 examines the political and legal reasoning in the drunk-driving case of Navajo defendant Gordon House during the period from 1992 to 2000. The episode revolves around a 1992 vehicular homicide near Albuquerque, New Mexico. The death of four people occurred after Navajo Gordon House engaged in binge drinking and then drove the wrong way on the interstate highway. The chapter first looks at the controversies and laws created by the government to restrict and suppress Indian alcohol use and then reconstructs the history of alcohol abuse among Navajos. Next, the chapter analyzes the preliminary hearing in the Gordon House case by examining four exemplars of rhetorical narratives, including formalism, rights, social relations, and political action. My analysis of the Gordon House case shows how this legal case ignited a politically explosive issue and eventually mobilized both government and Indian political leaders to act together to try to solve the state's alcohol problem.

Chapter 1

Dramatistic Analysis and the Puget Sound War, 1854–1858

On Friday, February 19, 1858, Leschi, a noted Nisqually chief, was hung in Pierce County in Washington territory. Leschi was a leader of the dissident Indians from the southern area of the Puget Sound. Along with Indians from the region, he conducted raids against white settlers occupying the land ceded in the Medicine Creek Treaty of 1854. Even though many sympathizers believed in the chief's innocence, Leschi was executed for killing settlers. J. W. Wiley and E. Furste of the *Pioneer and Democrat* described Leschi's execution in this way:

At the foot of the ladder, looking up to the rope which hung suspended, with its sliding noose, he hesitated for a moment, but instantly collecting himself, he ascended [*sic*] with a firm step, as if he desired to show the white man how fearlessly an Indian can meet death. The prisoner, evincing no desire to speak or make any confession, his arms were secured behind him; when perceiving his life was drawing to a close, he bowed himself to the spectators, and for the space of ten or fifteen minutes engaged in fervent prayer and said . . . that he had made his peace with God. . . . The rope was adjusted, the cap drawn over his eyes, and at 35 minutes past eleven o'clock the drop fell, and Leschi, the brave in battle, was launched into eternity. . . . After hanging about 25 minutes, . . . his body was cut down and delivered to his relations, by whom he was taken to the Nisqually reserve for burial. (1858, February 26, 2)

The solemn act brought to a conclusion a lengthy drama involving government-Indian relations in Washington territory. This drama began with violent skirmishes between Indians and settlers and ended with the death of a beloved Indian leader.

Using a dramatistic framework, the chapter (1) examines the conflict as a representative anecdote of the Indian wars, (2) investigates the Puget Sound violence as a dramatistic movement, (3) elaborates the political motivations associated with the legal proceedings, and (4) shows implications of this study for the other episodes of government-Indian relations discussed in this volume.

GOVERNMENT-INDIAN RELATIONS AS A REPRESENTATIVE ANECDOTE

For the Nisqually, the arrest, conviction, and death of Chief Leschi provided a dramatic story of how the government in its zeal to settle the Puget Sound conflict killed an esteemed Nisqually chief. The story of this event takes the form of a representative anecdote about how the government dealt with the Indians in the nineteenth century. Kenneth Burke ([1950] 1969) describes a representative anecdote as a "representative act" or story that sums up a prototype of a rhetorical situation. The condensed story implicitly contains the essential features of other similar stories. Moreover, the critic discovers the anecdote by finding the "bare bones" outline of the story, defining the scene, discerning the plot, identifying the protagonists and antagonists, specifying what types of actions take place, and discussing the resolution or denouement (59–61). According to Barry Brummett (1984), the anecdote focuses attention on the motives found in the other elements of similar discourses (4). A condensed version of the stories underlying the government-Indian relations has motives similar to those in the following scenario. Federal officials make treaties with the Indians to gain possession of their land, destroy their resources and power, kill or imprison Indian leaders who resist, and promote policies that guarantee the economic progress of settlers. Using simpler terminology, Patricia Limerick (1987) identifies the motive of treaties as the conquest of the Indians in the name of progress. Although the details about how the attempted conquest played out differ from one tribe to another, the story line remains the same.

The Indian Wars Anecdote

The typical scenario of this common story is well known to those who have studied the Indian wars. The story begins in a familiar way. For centuries, many Indian bands lived peaceably as a hunting and gathering culture around a river basin. They engaged in warfare with other Indians who invaded their territory. Eventually, the Indians expanded their economic base with trade to outsiders. After settlers migrated into Indian territory, they desired the fertile lands in the river basins, the same locations in which the Indians resided. The resulting conflict over resources motivated federal officials to send representatives to make treaties with the Indians. Although the stated purpose of the treaties was to make peace with the Indians, the unstated purpose was to secure lands for agricultural and economic development and place the Indians on remote and unproductive reservation land. Since many Indians lacked an understanding of the concept of trading or selling land, they often signed treaties without knowing the consequences to their traditions and life ways.

The story continues with disputed action. After the government representatives appointed leaders of Indian groups whom they thought would sign the treaties, they proceeded with a highly dramatic treaty-signing ceremony in which both sides acknowledged the power of the other and gave gifts as signs of mutual trust and friendship. Since most Indians could not read or speak English, the translators improvised methods to communicate the meaning of the treaties. The treaties permitted settlers to take up legal residence on what had been Indian land. As a result Indians sometimes raided property or killed settlers, and the military then intervened to protect settlers from Indian aggression. Since the government had superior military armaments, it usually claimed victory over the Indians and demanded punishment for the Indians they held responsible for violence against settlers. The bare bones story of the Indian wars in the Puget Sound closely resembles the story of the Sioux wars in Minnesota and on the northern plains, the Cheyenne-Arapaho wars on southern plains of Colorado and Kansas, and Navajo wars in the Southwest. The names and places are different, but the scenario of conquest is basically the same.

The Puget Sound War Scenario

In ways similar to other anecdotes of the nineteenth-century Indian wars, the specific details of the Puget Sound war feature a scene, a plot, protagonists and antagonists, action, and denouement.

Scene. In Burke's view, any drama "is enacted against a background," context, or scene that "contains the act" ([1950] 1969, 15). Leschi's death evolved out of a complex historical scene. Prior to the influx of settlers from the Oregon Trail that began in the late 1840s, the scene in the Puget Sound was one of relative peace and prosperity. The Indians had friendly relationships with their trading partners, the Hudson Bay Company. For the most part, the Indians' relationships with English, French-Canadian, and Scottish traders were positive; many of these European traders married Indian women from the area, learned the native language, and developed friendly relationships with the local tribes. Alexandra Harmon (1998) claims this relationship depended on "diplomatic protocol" that blended together indigenous norms and rituals with Hudson Bay trading policies. The diplomacy was of mutual benefit to traders who wanted the food commodities from the Indians and the Indians who wanted blankets and other material goods from the English traders (42). Until 1848, the Hudson Bay Company had jurisdiction over its employees and mediated disputes arising with the settlers and Indians of the territory (Beardsley & McDonald 1942, 59). Many Hudson Bay employees, called "foreigners," became friendly with the Indians and with the new American military officers at Fort Steilacoom. Both entities enforced legal sanctions on Indians who took traders' goods or destroyed their property. The legal system seemed to work even though the Indians had a very different understanding of law than the traders and the military did. Indians viewed homicides as disruptions of relationships and matters for the family to resolve with the offender through a mediation process. On the other hand, the colonial governments viewed homicide as a crime that was to be settled in a court of law under the jurisdiction of the colonial power (Harmon 1998, 57). Despite the differences in legal assumptions, Leschi and other Indians seemed to respect both the economic and legal scene.

After the settlers arrived from the Oregon Trail, the scene erupted into sporadic conflicts because the settlers sought the same rich farmland along water ways that the Indians claimed as their hunting and fishing land. The Oregon Land Act of 1850 to 1855 was one source of the conflict. This law allowed any settler with a patent to claim land in the territory whether or not it was inhabited by Indians (Harmon 1998, 58). In addition to the liberal land acquisition policy, American territorial officials envisioned that the title to land held by the Puget Sound Indians would be extinguished allowing additional settlement. For example, government agent E. A. Starling envisioned that the Puget Sound Indians would readily submit to the power of the new territory and obey its code of law because they would be awed by the "munificent" government's power and wisdom (Minutes of Treaty Councils 1854, 2). In 1853, the president of the United States appointed Isaac I. Stevens as the governor of the newly created Washington territory. In ways similar to agent Starling, Stevens considered it his mission to eliminate Indian title and transfer the land to the settlers.

The Stevens' treaties transformed the scene from relative tranquility to open discord. In 1854, Stevens successfully negotiated the Medicine Creek Treaty with the Nisqually and Puyallup and other small Puget Sound bands of Indians. The treaty received its name from a waterway essential to Indian traditional life and agricultural development. The water source, Medicine Creek, ran through the middle of Nisqually land and through the center of the Puget Sound Indian fishing and hunting territory. Although the treaty attempted to resolve the conflicts between Indians and settlers, it did not succeed because, at the time, the one-sided agreement benefitted the settlers more than the Indians. The treaty preserved fishing rights, but it forced the Puget Sound Indians onto three reservations, took away prime farm land, and forced the Indians to free their slaves (Marino 1990, 169). Not all Indian leaders signed the treaty. Those Indians who signed the treaty on behalf of their bands submitted to the stipulated conditions; other Indians who refused to sign resisted government control by engaging in raids, skirmishes, and warfare with settlers.

Plot. Since the government perceived Chief Leschi as one of the esteemed Puget Sound leaders, his approval of the treaty was essential to the reduction of conflict in the Puget Sound area. The unresolved question of whether Leschi did or did not sign the Medicine Creek Treaty was an issue that contributed to the plot of the Puget Sound war story. The plot refers to how story tellers relate the main point of an event to an audience. The main point of the story of the Puget Sound conflict centered on the validity and effects of the treaty.

Although Leschi's name appeared on the treaty, Nisqually tradition says that Leschi did not sign (Wickersham 1893, 4; McBride 1970, 3; Carpenter 1976, 22). For this reason, he never agreed to cede tribal lands to white settlers. In fact Chief Steilacoom reportedly said:

Leschi stood just 10 feet from Gov. Stevens. . . . Leschi said: "We want some land along this creek so our people may come in from the Sound and camp and go to our prairies for our horses." Stevens offered instead high timber lands. Leschi refused. Stevens said they must take it [the timber land]. Leschi vowed to fight and tore up the [treaty] papers. (Meeker [1905] 1980, 52)

Indian allies affirmed this conclusion, claiming Governor Stevens forged Leschi's signature (Meeker [1905] 1980, 52), and that Leschi never accepted the provisions of the treaty nor agreed to the federally designated reservations.

B. F. Shaw (1903), the treaty meeting translator, issued a strong contrasting opinion. He argued that Leschi not only signed the treaty but understood its provisions. He recalled:

The treaty was made on the 25th day of December 1854, the second day of the council. After the Governor had made his speech, all the Indians were invited to speak and tell what they believed and were willing to do about making and signing the treaty. Everything was conducted open and above board. After all the Indians had spoken, the treaty was brought out, and was explained slowly by paragraphs, and whenever there was any doubt as to the Indians' understanding of it, it was repeated until it was understood by them. . . . All the Indians of any note signed it. Quiemuth, Leschi, Stahi, Slugamas, Snow-ho-dump-shoot, and all the other Indians of any note. . . . There was no compulsion or persuasion necessary, as they all seemed anxious to sign it. (30)

Contrasting stories about whether all leaders signed the treaty created issues about whether the document was a legitimate legal agreement. If the treaty had not been signed by one of the most prominent Indian leaders, then it had not been properly consummated and the Indians were still at war with the settlers at the time the government alleged that Leschi committed murder. Since the government cannot convict parties at war with murder charges, then presumably it could not convict Leschi. For this reason the controversy over the treaty signing entered into the subsequent plot concerning the arrest, trial, and execution of Leschi. The dispute over who had signed the treaty also polarized the factions involved in the Puget Sound wars into protagonists and antagonists.

Protagonists and Antagonists. Just as in many other anecdotes about the Indian wars, this treaty controversy loomed large in the story of Leschi's life and death. For the antagonists who believed Leschi was unjustly hung for the murder of settlers, the idea that he never signed the treaty justified his warlike actions. For the protagonists who believed the treaty was valid, Leschi was a vicious killer who deserved to be hung because he violated the law. Protagonists refer to the leading actors in a government-Indian relations drama. The protagonists usually consisted of military generals, governors, peace commissioners, and congressional leaders. Antagonists were the forces who opposed or competed with the protagonists. During the Indian wars, the antagonists most likely were outspoken chiefs who refused to submit to government control. In some cases, the chiefs forged alliances with sympathetic traders and Indian agents who joined in the tribe's resistance against federal authority.

In this episode, the territorial government served the role of protagonist because its representatives believed that Leschi was a vicious warrior and a cold-blooded killer who deserved death (Longmire 1985, 185–91). Territorial government officials and their allies constituted Leschi's adversaries. The "Bostons," settlers who migrated from the east to the Puget Sound valley, Governors Stevens and Fayette McMullen, and members of the citizen militia appointed by Stevens served as protagonists. Members of this group abided by the territorial law and by its newly evolving justice system. It is not surprising that the protagonists testified against Leschi in his trial and urged his execution.

The employees of the Hudson Bay Company and regular military officers joined with the Indians to oppose the protagonists. This group believed that Leschi was innocent, a scapegoat who was sacrificed to restore the public feeling of law and order and to rebuild the credibility of its territorial government (Carpenter 1976; Meeker [1905] 1980). Historians referred to some of the antagonists collectively as "foreigners" because they worked for the Hudson Bay Company, a British operation. Additionally, since many of the men from the Hudson Bay Company married local Indian women and developed strong ties to the local Indian culture, they became natural Indian allies. In addition to the Hudson Bay employees, the antagonists included some U.S. military officers stationed at Fort Steilacoom. The antagonists eventually testified on Leschi's behalf at his trial and also wrote public appeals to stall his execution.

As subsequent chapters indicate, the government typically acted as the protagonist and the Indians as the antagonists in conflicts between the two groups in the Indian war. Both the government and the Indians claimed allies that supported their respective points of view and found adversaries that ridiculed their positions and blocked their actions. These divergent positions led to political and legal rhetorical dramas. Having the advantage of a written language, the government voices spoke loudly. During this period, the Indians were not silent. They made their positions clear through their nonverbal resistance and through the voices of their allies.

In ways similar to the Puget Sound wars, treaty controversies dominated other government and tribal stories discussed in this volume. Treaties were at issue in the Sioux Uprising, Sand Creek Massacre, Navajo Wars, Red Cloud's diplomacy, the Wounded Knee Massacre, and the Wounded Knee Standoff. Treaty disputes also figured prominently in the rhetoric of Chiefs Little Crow, Black Kettle, Left Hand, Mariano and Largo, Red Cloud, and Sitting Bull.

Action. In dramatistic analysis, rising action refers to the events that lead to the climax of a story. Indian raids and pillaging of settlements combined with settlers' encroachments onto Indian lands created a climax for the dramas of the Indian wars.

In particular, several stages of conflict escalation led to the climatic action of Leschi's trial and hanging. Stage one occurred in October 1855. At this time Governor Stevens organized the citizen militia, a group composed of local citizens whose specific purpose was to fight the Indians and protect the rights of settlers. The citizen militia of the Puget Sound called themselves the Eaton Rangers; they organized and elected officers on October 20, 1855. Later that month, observers said that Nisqually Indians killed a leader of the Rangers, James McAllister. And on that same day, the Rangers claimed that the Nisqually Indians also killed Joseph Miles and August Benton Moses (Wiley 1855, October 30, 2). After hearing this information, the governor ordered the militia to find Leschi, the leader he believed instigated the war against the settlers. During the mission to bring in Leschi, the Indians ambushed the Eaton Rangers.

Ambushes continued in stage two of the action. On October 28, the Indians killed nine settlers and set their homes on fire near White River south of Seattle. On October 31, Puget Sound warriors ambushed pony express riders. By November the situation had become so frightening that Governor Stevens ordered 600 more volunteers to fight against the Indians. The killing of settlers by Indians eventually spread to Walla Walla and other eastern sections of the territory by January 1856. Frustrated by his inability to stop the Indian hostilities, Stevens announced that "the war shall be prosecuted until the last hostile Indian is exterminated" (Meeker [1905] 1980). Stevens' personal resolution led to the denouement of the war in Washington territory.

Denouement. In the stories about the resolution of the Indian wars, the denouement took place in a variety of legal, political, and military forums. The denouement refers to the solution or resolution of the plot. One strategy for resolving conflicts was to stop the attacks through legal maneuvers. The motivation for legal action was to purge from society the person or persons deemed responsible for the evil acts. To achieve this goal, the denouement of the Puget Sound wars transpired through the trials and execution of Leschi. At the time of the murders of settlers, Leschi believed his forces had been defeated and took his warriors north. After some Oregon Indians joined in the hostilities, the last battle of the Puget Sound war took place on July 17. In November 1856, militia men appointed by Governor Stevens captured Leschi and charged him with the murder of A. B. Moses (*Territory v. Leschi* [true bill], 1856). In the first of two legal proceedings, Leschi stood trial at Fort Steilacoom in the Washington territory. After the military court failed to convict the chief, Governor Stevens ordered a second trial for Leschi in the territorial court system. The federal court convicted Leschi and sentenced him to death.

During the Indian wars, one goal of the courts was to kill or remove dissident Indians so that the government could assume primary control over the tribes as they did later in Minnesota (Chapter 2). Another legal resolution was to punish a government representative as Congress did after the Sand Creek Massacre (Chapter 3). Still another approach was to adopt a political resolution. An example of this type of resolution was the forced removal of a whole Indian tribe from the scenes of the war as occurred with the Navajos (Chapter 4). Another political solution was to invite Indian chiefs to Washington to negotiate agreements as Red Cloud did during the 1870s (Chapter 5). Military solutions, such as the annihilation of bands of Indians at Wounded Knee in 1890, were a last resort (Chapter 10).

For the reasons described here, the dramatic events of the Puget Sound wars and Leschi's trial and death construct a scenario creating a representative anecdote for the Indian wars. This story features a scene in which Indians and settlers fight for productive land, government protagonists in dispute with Indian antagonists, and violent action that results in the denouement of some form of government conquest. One way to explain how this typical story evolved into an execution drama is to adopt a broadly based theoretical framework. One useful lens is dramatistic movement theory, an approach featuring discourses that characterize the rhetoric of the government and Indians during one part of the Puget Sound war.

A DRAMATISTIC THEORY OF MOVEMENTS

Movements are rhetorical processes. Robert S. Cathcart (1978) noted that movements come into being because certain factions confront the controlling social order. Confrontation is part of an agonistic ritual between factions that sometimes tests the loyalties between oppositional groups and at other times seeks to change them. In both cases confrontation "dramatizes the symbolic separation" of some groups from the existing order (224).

Using the theories of Kenneth Burke, Leland M. Griffith (1966) explains political actions are often part of broader social or cultural reform movements. Cultural movements embody several assumptions. First, participants in the movement strive to preserve their social and cultural order. In this case, the Indians tried to preserve their culture at the same time the government wanted to impose a new political order. Second, the goals of the participants depend upon what they believe is the "good" of their order. The Indians wanted to retain traditional ways; the government wanted to impose its own political and legal policies. Third, by delineating the phases of this movement, observers can chart cultural change. Both cultures experienced *pathema* or suffering; this suffering led to *poiema* manifested in warlike action; and the action created *mathema*, a new state of affairs (460) in which the government achieved power over the Indians. The reform movement as a whole progressed through five stages—inception, crisis, consummation, redress, and redemption. This chapter shows how Leschi's trial and execution evolved out of conflicts between political factions and then emphasizes the rhetorical strategies used by both factions to resist each other's control.

Inception

When the social order is disrupted, the inception of a movement begins. Members representing the social-political order try to restore harmony by responses associated with guilt reduction, including purgation, victimage, mortification, and redemption. Griffith (1966) claims society begins in "indecision" and ends in "decision"; that is, the social order begins with guilt and ends by transforming the identity of those in conflict (461). Studying a movement necessitates investigation of a social-political drama and the analysis of the acts of transformation that result from the rhetorical actions of participants in the drama.

The conviction and execution of Leschi were the acts that transformed the meaning of the Puget Sound war. Instead of conceiving of the wars as a set of skirmishes between Indians and settlers over land rights, the government conceived of the fighting as an orchestrated event of several Puget Sound tribes led by Chief Leschi. The purpose of the war, they believed, was to overthrow Governor Stevens and the citizen militia he appointed. In contrast, the Indians and their allies perceived the war as a deliberate government political action to destroy their culture (Carpenter 1996, 73–78).

For the adversaries of Leschi, order meant a competitive system based on reason and justice. Griffith (1966) explains that a properly functioning social order creates a hierarchical system in which participants submit to authority. The authoritative resources of the social system include codes that create legal and political controls and resolve disorder and restore social harmony. A peaceful resolution of conflict takes place when the participants in a conflict adopt rhetorical practices that identify with the common needs, values, and interests of their adversaries and allies (461–62). This identification then permits opposing parties to transcend the conflict and restore peace.

Governor Stevens, the Bostons, and the citizen militia had a clear concept of the order they wanted to establish in Washington territory. Moreover, they had the power to control the legal and political system to achieve that concept of order. Governor Stevens, for example, gave orders and assumed responsibility for protecting the settlers by creating a citizen militia. Stevens and his allies also considered their actions reasonable because they believed they were upholding legally transacted treaties with the Puget Sound Indians. To enforce justice in a way that upheld settlers' property rights and bolstered regional economic progress, Stevens and his allies demanded the territorial court system enforce their vision of order.

On the other hand, the Puget Sound Indians and their allies envisioned an order based on Indian religion and traditions. A desirable social order related to the Indian's metaphysical sense of order; that is, Indians worked as partners with supernatural beings who gave earthly beings certain abilities. If the Indians failed to take advantage of their God-given abilities, then their villages experienced conflict. Evidence of Indian cooperation with the supernatural order surfaced in the natives' beliefs about their God-ordained abilities, including technical skills for hunting and for war, human relations skills to make peace and achieve goodwill with other villages and people, and economic skills permitting ownership of land, horses, and slaves. Those with the most skills belonged to the noble class. The Puget Sound Indians had a class system within each village. The upper class was born into families of talent and possessions; the middle class had some, but not all, of the abilities; and the "no-accounts" were part of the lower class that had few skills (Smith [1940] 1969, 47). Chief Leschi was of the noble class, hence his people perceived him to have many skills and significant possessions.

The trial and execution of Chief Leschi called attention to the ways the social order was disrupted by the Indian war, the different cultural factions involved in that war, and the political and legal resources the government needed to exert control.

Crisis

A period of crisis or struggle marks the beginning of a movement; it is a "time of judgment" when leaders and followers build allegiances, establish coalitions, and mobilize for action. It is also the point at which the sides to a conflict agree on strategy, pursue goals, and attribute adverse motives to each other (Griffith 1966, 466–67). This struggle places participants in a *pathema* of suffering in which each side tries to win the right to determine who will control the social order.

In this stage, the adversaries of Leschi attributed evil motives to the Indians and positive motives to themselves. Stevens, the Boston settlers, and the Indian agents claimed that the Indians had engaged in a conspiracy to raid and kill settlers. Thomas Goodnight and John Poulakos (1981) explain that people in political power often claim that their adversaries are conspirators who come from a "twisted secret world carved out by a mastermind and followed by a few loyal fanatics" (301–2).

Although little verbal or written evidence pointed to a conspiracy, Indian agents used this theory to implicate Leschi as the mastermind responsible for the war. For example, Indian agent W. B. Gosnell explained Leschi's involvement in the war as a sinister economic venture. He reasoned that in the summer of 1855 the "Indians on the Sound" got together with the Yakimas, Walla Wallas, and Klickatats to make an agreement about "exterminating the Whites." The groups used the Treaty of Medicine Creek as an excuse for their attacks on settlers, but the real reason for their warlike action was economic profit. He claimed that Leschi and his brother Quiemuth were called upon by other Indians to get the Nisquallies to engage in "open acts of hostility against the settlements on the Puget Sound" in exchange for "100 head of cattle and 150 horses." He believed the Nisqually chiefs expected the Indian tribes to the north to acquire gun powder and supplies from "discharged employees of the Hudson Bay Company and other foreigners married to Indian women" (Gosnell 1856 [1926], 294–95).

The conspiracy theory served several functions for leaders of the territorial government (Toch 1965, 53–54). First, it provided a "concrete target" or scapegoats for the war by implicating Leschi and his brother. Second, it permitted some government officials to explain the war as the result of a single causal agent. Finally, this kind of reasoning enabled the Indian agent to use his rhetorical authority to define the conflict. For these reasons, the conspiracy theory allowed Gosnell to avoid any personal responsibility for the war and permitted him to assign blame for the war to the hostile Puget Sound Indians and their Hudson Bay allies.

The government willingly accepted Gosnell's explanation since it validated its hunch that Leschi and other hostile Indians threatened settlement in the Puget Sound area. Citizens and territorial leaders probably accepted this conspiracy theory even more readily after Indians killed some Boston settlers. Stevens at least tacitly agreed with the explanation. On January 25, 1856, he publicly declared a policy of exterminating all of the Indians (Meeker [1905] 1980, 138). Shortly thereafter Stevens ordered federal troops to arrest hostile Indians and to bring them to trial. Stevens especially wanted Chief Leschi to be arrested for the murder of A. B. Moses. He offered fifty blankets to Indians as a reward for information leading to Leschi's capture. In November 1856, Sluggia [sometimes also spelled Sluggy], nephew of Leschi, delivered him to the authorities (Schmitt 1949, 31).

As a direct response to the accusations of the territorial government, the Indian allies demonized political leaders and Boston settlers for taking traditional Indian lands and destroying their way of life. They criticized territorial leaders for being oppressive, acting unreasonably, and adopting unjust policies. One prominent Indian sympathizer, Ezra Meeker, presented the Indian side of the story in his book, *Pioneer Reminiscences of Puget Sound* ([1905] 1980). Meeker explained the crisis of the Indian wars was the fault of the governor and the ill-trained superintendent of Indian affairs. He wrote:

The system as applied to these Indians was positively vicious, cruel and unnecessary. . . . If there had been a superintendent who had taken the pains to inform himself and [taken] the time to have intelligently applied his knowledge . . . [and] investigated their grievances. . . . there need not have been a difficulty. (61)

Other allies spoke in support of Leschi, pointing to his past good deeds and to his positive personal traits. For example, William F. Tolmie from the Hudson Bay Company reported that Leschi was a friend and that he was friendly to whites even though he was "dissatisfied with the treaty" ("Letter to the Editor" 1857, March 27, 2).

In addition to faulting the policies of the territorial government in general, Meeker and some military officers at Fort Steilacoom concluded that the arrest of Leschi resulted from sinister political motives; that is, Stevens arrested the Nisqually chief to enhance his personal and political credentials. Meeker explained that "Leschi must be proven guilty or else Stevens would be discredited, and the contention of the regular army officers proven" (Meeker [1905] 1980, 213).

Quite clearly many contemporary historians, after having reviewed the positions of both factions, agree with Meeker's view. For example, Marino (1990) claims the Puget Sound wars were caused by the dispossession and removal of tribes from their traditional lands, the white encroachment onto Indian fishing and hunting grounds, and government delays in ratifying treaties.

Consummation

The period of consummation is the time of sacrifice when one political faction secures its position by deciding how justice will be done. At this point in a political dispute, one side gains control and exercises its power to dominate the other side (Griffith 1966, 469). During the period of redressive action, movement leaders select a method to punish adversaries for the wrong they allegedly have committed. The anti-Leschi faction demanded territorial officials hear Leschi's case even though court was not in session at the time. In this way, federal officials took control of the consummation of the conflict. By asserting his authority in this legal matter, Stevens attempted to enforce the government's definition of social order by declaring martial law and forcing the courts under his control to hear Leschi's case (Schmitt 1949, 30–32).

The consummation phase of the movement featured the *poiema* or action. This phase occurred during the long period of time in which the arrest, trials, and appeals of Leschi took place. During this time period, the adversaries of Leschi struggled against his allies, and each side sought to outmaneuver the other in pursuit of its preferred concept of order. At the same time, the adversaries sought a literal killing of Leschi because they believed he was the perfect scapegoat. His death would show the government's power to suppress the Indians and serve as an example to other chiefs who fought against settlers that they would experience the same fate as Leschi.

Two rhetorical features led to the consummation phase of the conflict. First, territorial government leaders eagerly pursued Leschi, a course of action that would make use of him as a scapegoat to be sacrificed to restore the government's social control over the hostile Indians, Hudson Bay workers, and Fort Steilacoom employees. In the terms of Kenneth Burke ([1950] 1969, 12–13), the territorial government sought "the kill"; they wanted to literally kill Leschi, an approach they thought would also symbolically silence the resistance of Fort Steilacoom and Hudson Bay employees, destroy an economic force in the area, and break up pro-Leschi support. According to Burke, the literal kill of an enemy alters the power structure of the existing social order (13); it certifies which group of people is in charge of the situation. If Chief Leschi died, the Puget Sound Indians would lose their power to negotiate and express their grievances against territorial authority. Additionally, the execution of Leschi would produce a symbolic kill by suppressing the voices of his allies. Burke ([1950] 1969, 140) claims that the scapegoat "is dialectically appealing, since it combines in one figure contrary principles of identification and alienation." Selecting a scapegoat allows those in power to sacrifice one person, a representative of evil in a social order, and thereby "ritualistically cleanse" the entire social order. This ritualistic cleansing marked the beginning of the government's effort for building its version of a democratic social order in Washington territory.

Second, the territory employed political maneuvers to bring about the sacrificial killing of Leschi. One maneuver involved bribing Leschi's cousin to turn the chief over to federal authorities. Another maneuver was to declare martial law, thereby placing Governor Stevens in charge of the courts, the judge, and the jurisdiction that would try Leschi. Stevens also demanded Leschi's immediate trial and placed limitations on the kind of legal appeals the defense could use after the trial. All of these maneuvers asserted government control of the situation.

Legal Redress

Many of the struggles between the government and the Indians involved elaborate forms of legal or political redress. Since these forms of legal redress produced the rhetorical transformation of the social order, the chapter treats this phase separately from consummation. The legal redress in the Puget Sound conflict took place in a long sequence of events: the arrest of Leschi, his first trial in a military court that resulted in a hung jury, the second trial in a territorial court that gained a conviction, Leschi's self defense, media efforts to absolve Leschi of guilt, a cogent legal appeal, and secret legal maneuvers to free Leschi.

Leschi's Arrest. The circumstances of Leschi's arrest showed the power of the government to maneuver the legal system to its advantage. J. W. Wiley (1856, November 28) reported the arrest in this way:

Leschi . . . had for some time been secludedly encamped on the upper Nisqually; and on Thursday, the 13th [of November 1856], inst. by per arrangement, two Indians, Sluggy and Elikukah, having ascertained his whereabouts visited his camp. After remaining a short time, they decoyed him off some distance, to the place where they had secured their horses, when they suddenly pounced upon, bound him, and placed him on one of the horses, [and then] carried him that night [as] a captive to Steilacoom. (2)

The successful arrest of Leschi for committing murder was a victory for both the citizen militia and the governor because the act fulfilled Stevens' promise to exterminate unfriendly Indians. After the arrest, Stevens notified Judge Chenoweth, told him about Leschi's capture, ordered him to call a special session of the territorial court, and mandated an immediate trial.

First Trial. The first trial began and concluded on November 17 at Fort Steilacoom. J. S. Smith and Frank Clark conducted the prosecution for the territory, and H. R. Crosbie and William Wallace presented the defense. No written record of the trial exists, but the *Pioneer and Democrat* provided a detailed account of the proceedings. The short trial consisted of the testimony of Antonio Rabbeson, a member of the citizen militia, who claimed he was an eyewitness to Leschi's murder of Moses. He said he recognized Leschi because of a scar. The defense also called William Tolmie, an official of the Hudson Bay Company, who emphasized Leschi's good character and his friendliness toward whites. In a curious turn of events, Sluggy, the nephew who turned in Leschi, claimed that he was present when Moses was killed and that Leschi was far away in the Cascade mountains. Prominent members of the community served as jurors, including William M. Kincaid, Albert Balch, I. H. Wright, and Ezra Meeker. After five hours of deliberation, the jury could not reach a verdict. Meeker ([1905] 1980), a jury member, recalled that he and Kincaid held out because they felt a guilty verdict would violate the law. Meeker said that they refused to vote guilty because the judge's charge to the jury concluded if Moses was killed by Leschi as part of an act of war, then the chief could not be found guilty of murder. Since Meeker and Kincaid believed that this killing was an act of war, they reasoned this case was not a matter for the courts to decide and therefore refused to agree with the other ten members of the jury. After the trial, Leschi returned to his jail cell at Fort Steilacoom and remained there until his second trial on March 19, 1857. In the opinions of the government faction, the first trial was a failure. Not only had Leschi escaped conviction, but the legal maneuvers of the governor had not achieved his desired goal.

Second Trial. The second trial convened after Governor Stevens gained control of the legal means of redress and thereby achieved a political advantage for the territorial government. One successful effort by Stevens was to get the case transferred to Olympia, the location where the governor lived and had extensive political support. Stevens believed the new location would secure jurors favorable to the prosecution's case (Meeker [1905] 1980, 219).

In the second trial, B. F. Kendall and J. S. Smith conducted the case for the territory, and William Wallace and Frank Clark served as the defense attorneys. In the trial, one of the lawyers switched sides; twenty-five-year-old Frank Clark joined the defense in the second trial although he was a prosecutor for the territory in the first trial. Not only did Clark switch sides, he turned into a zealous advocate for Leschi. The jury consisted of Benjamin Harned, Turner R. Roundtree, Edwin Marsh, J. P. Ecler, William Woodbridge, John Henning, Thomas Dean, George Haywood, Levi Shelton, James Tullis, John B. Dickerson, and Joseph Wairaven. The trial testimony took one day, and the jurors returned a verdict of guilty on the morning following the trial. The court record (*Territory of Washington v. Leschi*, 1857) reported the entire trial even though the recorder seems to summarize rather than record word-for-word testimony. Subsequent trial references in this section come from the trial record.

The prosecutors called only two witnesses. Once again the first witness was a citizen militia member, Antonio R. Rabbeson. He argued that he was with Moses when Leschi and his brother Quiemuth abused them, but said "none [of the Indians] I knew the names of" at the time. Despite this fact, Rabbeson concluded that "Leschi was the one that fired and fired toward me and that he had killed Moses" (58). Under cross-examination, Rabbeson was unable to identify the horse Leschi was riding, the number of

Indians in the party with him, and some other relevant features of the shooting incident. Moreover in a previous trial, in which he had testified against an Indian named Winyea, Rabbeson failed to identify Leschi's mode of dress or to note the scar on his face. Although Rabbeson's testimony lacked consistency and credibility, the jury later reported they believed him. The second witness was Charles Mason, a friend and political appointee of Governor Stevens. He testified that Leschi had been to see him on October 22 prior to the murder, but he could not place him at the scene of the murder. Mason's testimony was vague and failed to implicate Leschi directly; however, the jurors appeared to overlook these deficiencies because they maintained Leschi was guilty.

The defense called a number of witnesses that directly refuted the vague and inconsistent testimony of the prosecution's witnesses. The first witness, Andrew Bradley, said he was at the scene of the alleged crime, but he did not see Leschi speaking with Rabbeson. He claimed he knew Leschi and that he helped him rescue some horses and cattle just after he had settled in Puyallup in 1854. The second witness, Indian agent A. J. Simmons, said that when he first talked to Rabbeson he had not identified Leschi as being at the crime scene. A third witness, William Tolmie from the Hudson Bay Company, reported that Leschi was a friend and never camped at Eaton's Prairie, the site of the alleged crime. A fourth witness, Indian subagent John Swan, testified that Leschi came to try to talk to him in order to reach an understanding about how he could make peace and end the Indian war. Two other witnesses, Charles Gohrich and a Mr. Benson, recalled that on the day of the crime they had seen Leschi on the Puyallup River, a location distant from the scene of the murder.

The prosecution then called three rebuttal witnesses—James Hurd, a Mr. Offut, and John Walker. Although each of these witnesses testified that he had seen Leschi on Eaton's Prairie at different times, none could place him at the scene of the crime. Additionally, the prosecution recalled several new witnesses, including A. C. Lowell, George W. Corless, and Andrew Byrd. The prosecution reemphasized the fact that Rabbeson had identified Leschi in the Winyea trial. None of the evidence against Leschi placed him at the scene of the crime he was alleged to have committed. In fact all of the evidence was circumstantial, and most was irrelevant to the murder of August Benton Moses, the alleged victim of Leschi.

No record of the closing arguments exists. The *Pioneer and Democrat* reported that Kendall made the first summation argument for the territory, was followed by separate defense arguments by William Wallace and Frank Clark, and then J. S. Smith concluded the summations for the territory. The newspaper opined, "All the speeches were well-timed, manly efforts and reflect great credit on the counsel engaged." The jury returned the verdict of guilty of first-degree murder at 10:00 A.M. the following morning. After the verdict, the defense immediately "moved that the verdict be set aside and a new trial granted" ("Evidence and Proceedings in the Case of Leschi," 1857, March 27, 2). Given the weakness of the evidence, the verdict against Leschi showed how the territory had successfully outmaneuvered the pro-Leschi forces.

The verdict's political overtones surfaced in the jurors' public commitment to Stevens' policies, the supportive testimony of the citizen militia and the Boston settlers, and in refutative testimony of Fort Steilacoom and Hudson Bay employees. All of the prosecution witnesses were members of the militia or the Bostons, adversaries of Leschi. On the other hand, all the defense witnesses had connections to the Hudson Bay Company and to Fort Steilacoom. It seems the governor achieved his goals. By transferring the case to Olympia, he obtained a judge and jury sympathetic to his position and hostile to the Indians.

Leschi's Self Defense. During the trial the defense exercised a risky persuasive option; it decided to allow Leschi to defend himself. Leschi presented a short speech in an effort to get the jurors to acquit him. He delivered the speech shortly before sentencing, after the verdict, and in front of the jury. Leschi used rhetorical strategies of image restoration to gain leverage with his supporters and to reduce animosity from his adversaries. His speech reaffirmed the supportive trial testimony and raised issues that his attorneys would use when they appealed the case. George Hines, a translator for the court, recorded Leschi's speech. Leschi told the court:

I do not see that there is any use of saying anything. My attorney has said all he could for me. I do not know anything about your laws. I have supposed the killing of armed men in wartime was not murder; it was, the soldiers who killed Indians who were guilty of murder, too. The Indians did not keep in order like the soldiers, and therefore could not fight in bodies like them, but had to resort to ambush and seek the cover of trees, logs, and everything that would hide them from the bullets. This was their model of fighting and they knew no other. Dr. Tolmie and Quatlith, and the red headed chief [Colonel Shaw] warned me against allowing my anger to get the best of my good sense, as I could not gain anything by going to war with the United States, but would be beaten and humbled and would have to hide like a wild beast in the end. I did not take this good advice, but nursed my anger until it became a furious passion, which led me like a false Ta-man-u-ous. I went to war because I believed that the Indians had been wronged by the white men, and did everything in my power to beat the Boston soldiers, but for the lack of numbers, supplies, and ammunition I have failed. I deny that I had any part in the killing of Miles and Moses. I heard that a company of soldiers was coming out of Steilacoom, and [they are] determined to lay in ambush for it; but [I] did not expect to catch anyone coming from the other way. I did not see Miles or Moses before or after they were dead, but was told by the Indians that they had been killed. As God sees me, this is the truth. Leschi then made the sign of the cross and said in his own Nisqually tongue, "ta-temons, Ta-ta lem-mas, Ta-te ha-the-hack, tu-ul-li-as sist-ah—which being interpreted, means "This is the Father, this is the Son, this is the Holy Ghost; these are all one and the same. Amen." (Meeker Papers Box 9, File 3)

In this speech, Leschi tried to avoid the "literal kill" by giving both political and personal reasons for his innocence. Even though Leschi used standard rhetorical strategies for self-defense and image restoration (Benoit 1995), he did not succeed in changing the minds of jurors about his guilt. In several respects, however, his rhetorical strategy did succeed. First, he defended himself by reinforcing a legal argument, anticipating one of the arguments to be made by his attorneys on appeal. He claimed that the charges against him were illegal since "the killing of armed men in war-time" is justified. Second, he bolstered the testimony given by Tolmie and Casey, claiming he was a warrior without sufficient resources to win a war. Furthermore, Leschi said he had not been at the scene of the crime. Finally, he identified with the Christian tradition by calling upon God and affirming his Christian belief in the Holy Trinity.

Leschi's speech featured strategies of image restoration identified by Benoit (1995). Leschi presented "multiple goals that are not completely compatible" (65). For example, denying the murder is not compatible with saying murder is not a crime in wartime. In an attempt to restore his credibility as a "good Indian," Leschi chose prayerful terms to convey his image as Christian and selected ingratiating words to affirm his faith in the legal system, saying his "attorney had done all he could." Leschi's methods of identifying with jurors' value proved insufficient to overcome the jurors' presumption that he was guilty. Even though his speech did not change the minds of the jurors, it did motivate his allies to express further dissent after the jurors rendered the verdict.

Media Refutation. Leschi's defense fueled the media conflict between the allies and adversaries of Leschi. Each side used rhetorical invective against the opposition, producing even more polarized positions between the Indian and government sympathizers than those that existed prior to the trial. Strongly worded and emotionally loaded rhetoric appeared in press reports concerning the delay of the execution of Leschi.

The *Pioneer and Democrat*, for example, frequently reported the government's view of Leschi. Typical of this newspaper's invective rhetoric was an article about Leschi's impending execution. Invective expresses anger and attempts to emotionally polarize the audience. In a response to those who tried to stall Leschi's execution, A. W. Wiley and B. Furste reported:

The execution of the sentence of the court, . . . was prevented by the baseness, knavery, or criminal ignorance of the sheriff of Pierce [c]ounty, combined with the united exertions of a few notoriety-seeking army graduates, who had but one-half the knowledge which they exhibit in pretension, [they] ought to have known better than to engage in the transactions of that day [with] a knavish pettifogging attorney, and military fawning U.S. Commission. (1858, February 26, 1)

A newspaper circulated by Lieutenant August Kautz, the *Truth Teller*, stressed the position of Leschi's Fort Steilacoom and Hudson Bay Company allies. The sole purpose of this newspaper was to vindicate Leschi prior to his execution. Through its satirical content and tone, the newspaper made this plea:

Who is it that has deprived us of this grand carnival? Who has postponed the hour of the feast, and sent away the guests, if not thirsty, at least hungry and unsatisfied? Had it been a white man whose hands were steeped in the blood of the Indian race, and whose long list of crimes qualified him for this distinguished and elevated consideration whose execution had been put off, it would not have been a matter of regret. But when a miserable Indian is to be disposed of even when there is a doubt of his guilt of this particular crime, and the one who did it is at large, there is no doubt he dared to contest our right to his land, that he opposed being placed on a small reservation to starve, and there is no doubt that he had the impudence and hardihood to array himself against the whites, and fight for what he conceived to be his rights, and for it he must and shall be hung. (1858, February 3, 2)

To refute the name calling and the racial slurs presented in the traditional press, the *Truth Teller* used a kind of satire that Kenneth Burke ([1935] 1965, 49) calls "perspectives by incongruity." This rhetorical strategy attempts to reverse the logic typically held by public audiences. By using incongruity, Kautz reported the facts in the context of opposites. In doing so, he tried to make the public see Leschi's actions in view of their own biased assumptions about what they believed constituted justifiable behavior.

The Appeal. Another positive source of support came from Leschi's defense attorney. Clark proved to be a skillful and conscientious advocate for Leschi during the postverdict appeals. On the day of the verdict, he filed a motion for a mistrial, claiming that new evidence had been discovered that was not available at the time of the trial. The new evidence was particularly interesting since it came from one of Leschi's strongest and most outspoken allies, Lieutenant Kautz. Kautz came up with a quasi-scientific type of evidence; he claimed "that the distance from the place where the Indians were discovered in Connell's [P]rairie . . . to the swamp where the attack was made is greater by the trail" than what witnesses swore to when they testified (*Territory of Washington v. Leschi*, motion for mistrial, 1858). Despite the fact the defense presented new evidence, the territorial judge rejected the motion. An observer cannot help but speculate that the judge rejected the source of the evidence more vehemently than its content.

After this temporary setback, Clark appealed Leschi's case on several grounds: the court hearing the trial was unauthorized to do so because it was not in the jurisdiction where the alleged crime had been committed; the verdict of the jury was contrary to the evidence in the case; the court erred in overruling the motion for a new trial; and the court failed to swear in the jury according to the law (*Leschi v. Territory of Washington* [appeal briefs], 1857, 2–3).

Justice Obadiah B. McFadden ruled against the cogent arguments of Clark. McFadden began his opinion by showing his sympathies with Stevens and the Boston settlers.

The prisoner has occupied a position of influence, as one of a band of Indians, who, in connection with other tribes, sacrificed the lives of so many of our citizens, in the war so cruelly waged against our people, on the waters of the Puget Sound. It speaks volumes for our people that, notwithstanding the spirit of indignation and revenge, so natural to the human heart, incited by the ruthless massacre of their families, that at the trial of the accused, deliberate impartiality has been manifested at every stage. (*Leschi v. Washington Territory* 1857, 14)

After demonstrating his loyalties to the settlers, an approach that would violate the norms of objectivity prized by contemporary judges, McFadden justified his opinion. First, he claimed that history of the territorial courts is such that certain jurisdictional and legal procedures do not explicitly apply to the Leschi case. The opinion legitimized Steven's legal maneuvers to open the territorial court and move the trial to Olympia. In doing so, McFadden indirectly approved of Governor Stevens' political manipulation of the courts.

Clemency Appeal. The appeal ruling did not end this complicated legal and political conflict between the allies and adversaries of Leschi. Not only did defense attorneys file motions to stay Leschi's execution, but his allies also petitioned the new governor of Washington territory, Fayette McMullen, to stay his execution. McMullen scheduled a hearing at Fort Steilacoom where William Tolmie and army officers Casey and White testified for clemency. Tolmie made a long and eloquent plea, saying that Leschi was "a well-disposed, peaceable Indian of superior ability, respected by his tribe and often referred to as an arbitrator in their disputes . . . [who] during the heat of war has twice interposed successfully between Kanasket and some defenceless [*sic*] white men." Tolmie claimed further that "the hanging of Leschi at this late day would under the circumstances awaken strong feelings of distrust and dissatisfaction toward the Americans, and it is not unreasonable to suppose, might leave them open to [M]ormon overtures" (Meeker [1905] 1980, 244–45). It was not a surprise to Leschi's allies when Governor McMullen denied both the stay of execution and the appeals for clemency made by Leschi's allies. Further support for the governor came from the legislature when it mandated that Leschi be hung on January 22, 1858.

On January 22, a warrant was delivered to the sheriff of Pierce County to bring forth Leschi to kill him. But the allies of Leschi interrupted this process again. They detained Sheriff Williams on grounds that he had sold liquor to Indians and appealed to Indian Commissioner Bachelder to indict him. As a result, the hanging failed to occur at the designated time because the authorities never brought Leschi to the site. Secret legal maneuvers by the defense attorneys also delayed the execution. Secrets are an effective rhetorical tool in a political or legal conflict because they "create a sense of mystery" and evoke anger in the minds of adversaries (Levin 1971, 140). For example, Leschi's attorney, Frank Clark, maneuvered the arrest of the sheriff and prohibited him from bringing Leschi to the site at which he was supposed to be hung. Clark's actions delayed the hanging, by what citizen militia leaders alleged was "the high handed outrage perpetrated by the civil authorities of Pierce County—the connivance of the military officers at Fort Steilacoom, and particularly the disgraceful conduct of one James Bachelder, U.S. Commissioner" who conspired to allow Leschi to escape "the ends of justice" ("Mass Meeting of the Citizens of Washington Territory," 1858, January 29). It was not surprising that the adversaries of Leschi condemned Clark for orchestrating the whole event that delayed the death of Leschi ("Mass Meeting of the Citizens of Washington Territory," 1858, January 29, 3).

In fact, this secret-then-public maneuver by Clark outraged the citizens of Pierce and Thurston Counties so much that leaders gathered on January 29 in a mass meeting to protest the delay of Leschi's execution. Both pro-Leschi and pro-government factions presented eloquent emotional speeches at this meeting. One important speaker, Governor McMullen, aligned his loyalties with the citizen militia and Boston settlers. He proclaimed that "the majority of the highest courts of our territory have this day been trodden under foot, by the underground machinations of the civil authorities of Pierce County . . . also by the officers of the United States Army at Fort Steilacoom. The acts of these officers, both civil and military, fellow citizens, call for your unmitigated and unqualified condemnation" ("Mass Meeting of the Citizens of Washington Territory," 1858, January 29, 3). After the speeches, the citizens drafted several resolutions condemning the actions of Sheriff Williams, J. M. Bachelder, William F. Tolmie, and Leschi attorney Frank Clark.

The delay of Leschi's execution was the last stage of a very complex phase of legal redress that led to the redemption phase of the cultural movement. This delay added intensity and drama to the hanging of Leschi on February 19, 1858. Even after the death of Leschi eventually occurred, his sympathizers believed they had temporarily been able to resist the dual powers of the political leaders and the legal administrators of the territorial government.

Redemption

The legal redress led to redemption, a stage of the movement that temporarily resolves the conflict and restores order. Redemption produces *mathema* and creates a new social order out of the *panthema* of struggle and the *poiema* of action.

For white settlers, *panthema* originated in their fights with Indians, Hudson Bay employees, and the military. The struggle surfaced in this way. After the Medicine Creek Treaty, the settlers claimed title to the land given up by the Puget Sound tribes through treaty; they built homes, cultivated the land, and established communities. They believed that the land belonged to them and that the governor and territorial laws would protect them and their property. For the Puget Sound natives, *panthema* began in the Indians' struggle to maintain their tribal communities and to hunt and fish on all of their traditional lands without being restricted by the treaty.

This struggle progressed into *poiema*, mutual hostile actions featuring Indians killing settlers and settlers killing Indians. The Indian raided, looted, and burned some settlers' property. Since the Hudson Bay "foreigners" and the military had friendly relations with the Indians, they were not victims of raids or hostile Indian aggressions. Boston settlers also provoked conflict by failing to pay Indians for their services. They also transgressed on Indian burial sites as well as fishing and hunting grounds, and spoiled Indian camping spots and potato fields (Gosnell [1856] 1926). The resolution to this struggle was to control Indians by finding a scapegoat whose death would restore the government's concept of order and subdue the Indians. The hanging of Leschi marked a temporary end to the struggle.

Mathema, a new state of affairs, came after the death of Leschi. The territorial leaders through their power over the territorial courts tried, convicted, and killed Leschi. In doing so, these forces established their authority to control hostile Indians, the Fort Steilacoom military officers, and the Hudson Bay employees. After Leschi's death, the Indians retreated, gave tacit assent to the treaty provisions, and began to reestablish their communities according to the concept of a "good" social order described by the treaties and the territorial officials. This new order changed both white and Indian culture; however, both entities found cultural accommodation to be difficult (Chapter 9). In some movements, redemption has both a comic and a tragic effect (Griffith 1966, 472). In this case, the tragic effect was the loss of an important Indian leader. The comic effect came from the sometimes absurd maneuvers of legal and political leaders who made the law seem ridiculous.

For the Puget Sound Indians, Leschi's death symbolized a terrible historical injustice. His descendants continue today to try to get the government officially to pardon Leschi (Carpenter 1996; Shanna Stevenson interview 1999). Dissatisfaction with the way the government implemented the Medicine Creek Treaty in the nineteenth century turned into a major source of twentieth-century civil litigation about fishing rights (Cohen 1986; see also Chapter 9).

IMPLICATIONS

The analysis of Chief Leschi's case has implications for the study of rhetorical theory, the history of government-Indian relations, and territorial law.

The chapter shows that in many ways the Puget Sound war serves as a representative anecdote for the stories of other Indian conflicts to be discussed later in this volume. The story contains a common scene spawned by disagreement over a treaty, has a plot in which government protagonists instigate actions to control and subdue Indian antagonists, exemplifies agonistic action exerted on behalf of pro-Indian and pro-government forces, and features a denouement that uses legal, political, and military means to resolve the struggle over land and resources. This familiar story plays out in a dramatic movement in which parties to the conflict maneuver to gain control over each other in hopes of reordering society in line with subjective cultural goals.

The chapter also points out that some legal events should be studied as part of a complex reform movement in which political factions use courts as a means to resolve conflicts. While it is unusual to study trials as parts of political movements, clearly many Indian cases developed out of long standing cultural and political conflicts. Traditional models of movement study, such as Griffith's framework, identify stages in the movement that predict the historical evolution of a case. Investigating trials as part of reform movements requires the critic to elaborate the rhetorical events and add a phase of legal redress to the stages of the movement. The crisis cannot be understood without some attention to conspiracy rhetoric, and the consummation of the action cannot be investigated without attention to media invective, image restoration, and secretive maneuvers as they relate to the parties involved in the case. Legal action, unlike congressional decision making, tends to resurface in new legal actions. For example, more than 100 years after Leschi's execution, the treaty issues that started the Indian wars reappeared in the fishing rights litigation initiated by the Puget Sound tribes (Chapter 9).

This analysis shows how political and ethnic loyalty affect government-Indian relations. The fact that many of the Fort Steilacoom military officers and Hudson Bay employees retained their loyalty to Leschi and proclaimed his innocence to the end shows that some government-Indian relationships depended on intercultural friendships and loyalty. What surprised me in this episode was that so many military officers were allies to the Indians, shattering a common myth that the military were usually the main oppressors and the perpetrators of violence against the Indians. Finally, the study shows that the government promoted treaties that invited resistance and provoked conflict. Even though the Medicine Creek Treaty attempted to place Puget Sound Indians under government control, it still provided cultural concessions for hunting and fishing. Ironically the treaty controlled the Indians while it allowed for economic subsistence.

Finally, the ability of Governor Stevens to maneuver the legal system to achieve his ends probably occurred because the territorial courts were new and operational standards by which they operated were in flux. At the time of Leschi's trial, the courts had existed for only thirty-one years. During that period, attorneys and judges created rules and procedures from precedents they had learned in the Eastern and Midwestern states where most lawyers had learned the law. A. S. Beardsley and Donald A. McDonald (1942) identify a number of problems that plagued the courts and probably permitted Stevens to exert so much pressure on the legal system. These problems included unclear delineations for jurisdictions, weather conditions that prohibited the judicial circuit riders from meeting their schedules, friendships between attorneys, judges, and federal officials, uncertainty about how to use the legal system for Indians and foreigners, and a lack of appropriate facilities for conducting trials (59–82). It is reasonable to believe that Stevens manipulated the legal system by declaring martial law, transferring jurisdiction, and putting Judge Lander in jail. His maneuvers actually motivated attorney Frank Clark and other pro-Leschi forces to be more zealous in their defense of Leschi. Unlike other Indians who received ineffective legal counsel, Leschi's attorneys defended him in a zealous manner that created public doubt about his guilt for subsequent generations of scholars.

Chapter 2

Rhetorical Genres and the Sioux Uprising, 1862

The Sioux Uprising created a reign of terror in Minnesota on a scale far exceeding that of the Puget Sound conflict. Not only did warfare result in the deaths of over 400 people, the government hanged thirty-eight Indians and imprisoned and exiled hundreds more in its effort to rid Minnesota of all Santee Sioux. Although the causes for this war fit with the representative anecdote described in Chapter 1, the effects of the war on the settlers, military, and Indians were far more severe than in Washington territory.

The execution of thirty-eight warriors in Mankato, Minnesota, marked a temporary end to the Sioux Indian war in Minnesota in 1862. The scene was especially memorable to those who observed it. Harriet E. B. Mc-Conkey ([1889] 1970) reported the execution in this dramatic way:

[All] now listened with marked attention. They [the Indians waiting to be hung] had painted their faces. . . . They shook hands with the officers, bidding each a cheerful goodbye. . . . Then they chanted their monotonous but very exciting death song. The irons being knocked off, one by one, their arms were pinioned with small cords and their wrists fastened in front, leaving their hands free. . . . They arranged themselves in a row and again sang the death song, after which they sat down for a last smoke. . . . As they commenced their ascent to the gallows, the air was made hideous by their death song. . . . Then came three slow, measured, and distinct beats on the drum by a signal officer. . . . [E]ach of the condemned clasped hands with his neighbor which remained in a firm grasp till [*sic*] taken down, and then the rope was cut. (263–66)

During the mass execution, 1,500 military troops positioned themselves around all sides of the scaffold. The execution fulfilled the need of the settlers and the military to avenge the deaths of their family members.

The Sioux Uprising began on August 17, 1862, and ended with the surrender of the Indian warriors at Camp Release on September 27 of the
same year. The total deaths in the Sioux wars are not known. Governor
Alexander Ramsey placed the number at 500, President Abraham Lincoln
claimed 800 died, and Indian Agent Galbraith claimed 737 were killed and
350 wounded with $2 million in property damage. Marion Satterlee's es-
timate of 447 fits with the assessment of other historians about fatalities
(Satterlee 1909–1914; Folwell 1961).

Embedded in the history of this war are a complex set of government
and Indian rhetorical discourses. The rhetoric of the Santee Sioux, the government, the military, and the settlers paints a picture of those who participated in the war. The goal of this chapter is to illuminate some of the
different kinds of discourse that evolved from the Sioux Uprising. Specifically, this chapter (1) explains rhetorical genres; (2) outlines the cultural
values of Sioux; (3) analyzes the genres of treaties, eyewitness histories,
trial accounts, speeches for clemency, and messages of consolation; and (4)
explains the aftermath of the trials in contrast to the episodes discussed in
other chapters.

GENRES OF DISCOURSE

Many types of speech genres emerged in the discourses about the war
and during the trials of the Sioux Uprising. In its simplest definition, genre
means kind or type of discourse. Mikhail Bakhtin (1986) explains that
genres are bundles of utterances that speakers and writers package together
through a common "thematic content, style, and compositional structure"
(60). Rhetors construct genres by combining utterances they have heard
and read from others and then reconstruct the utterances to include the
values and beliefs of those they address in a particular social, cultural, and
historical context (21). Rhetors create genres according to what Bakhtin
calls "speech plans"; that is, speakers design messages according to their
topic, the addressees to whom they are speaking, and the expectations
about how they will be understood (xvii).

Kathleen H. Jamieson and Karlyn Kohrs Campbell (1990) extend Bakhtin's concept by explaining that genres fuse together "a synthetic core" of
"significant rhetorical elements, e.g., a system of belief, lines of argument,
stylistic choices, and the perception of the situation" (336). Moreover, they
note that genres possess "an internal dynamic fusing substantive, stylistic,
and situational elements" (336). A genre then "is a classification" based
on "the fusion and interrelation of elements" that coalesce to form a unique
kind of rhetorical discourse (339). In a genre, the similarities of the discourse outweigh the differences.

Using several explanations of genre, this chapter delineates how the content, style, and structure of diverse genres coalesce to create recognizable

types of discourse. Each genre discussed in this chapter combines bundles of utterances in accordance with the textual conventions of nineteenth-century social, political, and legal culture and the demands of the multiple audiences that the rhetors addressed. The government created some of these genres to meet its colonial goals; other genres evolved out of Sioux traditions; and still other government utterances became intertwined with Sioux ceremonies.

CULTURE OF THE SANTEE SIOUX

The cultural background or social situation affects the meaning of discourse. The northeastern Santee Sioux consisted of four bands who lived along the Mississippi and Minnesota Rivers, the primary sources of fish and game for their food supply. These Mdewakanton, Wahpekute, Sisseton, and Wahpeton bands numbered about 6,000 at the time of the Sioux warfare. The Sisseton and Wahpetons lived on the upper Mississippi near the present location of St. Paul, and the Mdewakantons and Wahpekutes lived farther south and west near present-day Mankato (Anderson 1986b, 11). The bands perceived as hostile by the military and settlers consisted primarily of Mdewakantons and Wahpekutes, and therefore all but two of the people executed at Mankato came from these two bands of Santee Sioux. The eastern bands of Sioux claimed a common culture through their traditions of hunting and gathering, warfare, and public ceremonies. To some extent, these traditions affected the accounts of the massacre, the treaty ceremonies, the trials, and speeches of clemency and consolation.

Many Santee were hunters and gatherers. By setting up temporary summer and fall residences, they could gather and preserve the food needed for the tribe during winter and spring. They raised few crops and depended on wildlife for sustenance. In fact, Samuel Pond ([1908] 1986) commented that "so little corn was then raised by the Dakota that some of the bands ate all they had when it was green and some did not plant at all" (27). They lived on deer, fish, ducks, muskrats, and geese. Occasionally, they ate elk, bear, and dogs. The women gathered berries, wild turnips, roots, wild rice, and nuts. Food was shared and stored for communal use. The food supply depended on nature, and oftentimes the Santee found too little food to support tribal needs (26–31). Because the Sioux were a food-gathering culture, they resisted the treaty provisions that tried to make them farmers. The lack of food caused them to sign the treaties, but after the Sioux signed, the failure of the government to provide sufficient annuities for food was one cause of the war.

The Indians conducted warfare against settlers and the military in the same way they did against their Indian enemies. Using guns, hatchets, knives, and war clubs, the Santee scouted tribal enemies and laid in waiting to kill them. In preparing for battle, they took off most of their clothes, painted their bodies with war paint, and used a loud war hoop to differentiate themselves from their enemies. After killing an enemy, warriors took their scalps as proof they had killed someone, and then they returned to camp and sometimes used these confiscated scalps as part of an elaborate celebration of singing and dancing to ritualize their success as warriors (Pond [1906] 1986, 122). *Harper's* magazine (1863) described the "savage massacre" of Minnesota settlers during 1862 in this way: "We heard the rattle of their guns; we saw the smoke and flames, as they enveloped house after house, in which the savage had first butchered or tortured to death the inmates" (14). Many accounts of the Uprising, including the trial record, described brutal elements of Sioux warfare.

Third, the Santee celebrated social rituals in the presence of important people and for significant events. These rituals included smoking the pipe, presenting speeches, and gift giving. A single pipe served a dozen or more men, and the pipe was passed around at ceremonial occasions including the signing of treaties. The condemned warriors smoked the pipe before their mass execution. Oratory, like pipe smoking, was a feature of all important occasions. All of the treaty negotiations, councils for war, and tribal festivals featured eloquent oratorical expressions by Indian leaders (Pond [1906] 1986, 78–81). In combination with pipe smoking and speech making, the Sioux valued gift giving. As a symbol of friendship in Sioux culture, leaders gave gifts to others in exchange for receiving property or possessions. Similar kinds of celebrations occurred in treaty meetings as well as during the execution drama.

TREATIES AS GENRES

Treaties are formal agreements between two or more political entities that are negotiated by official delegations and approved with the consent of the government (Prucha 1994, 2). The eastern and western Sioux made a total of thirty-two treaties with the federal government. Chapter 5 explains the nature and effects of the treaties with the western Teton Sioux. The Santee as a distinct group made eight treaties between 1805 and the end of the treaty period in 1871. The Sioux Uprising was a direct response to the Traverse des Sioux and Mendota treaties of 1851, amended in 1858 and referred to in this chapter as the Treaty with Mdewakanton and Wahpekute and the Treaty with the Sisseton and Wahpetons. Provisions of the 1858 amended treaties illustrate the content, form, and style of treaty genres.

Situational Demands

Congress expected government delegations to execute treaties so the Indians would cede their land, agree to peace, and become civilized (DeMallie

1977, 3–5; Prucha 1994, 3–17). Before they would join the negotiations, the Santee Indians requested that their cultural ceremonies be included in the treaty process. As a result, a performance of cultural values occurred during the treaty signing ceremony when the formal written texts designed by government interacted with the oral and ceremonial culture of the Sioux. For this reason, treaty ceremonies provided occasions for Indians to show their culture to federal officials. Ralph Mayer describes the cultural performance of the Sisseton band at the time they made a grand entry to the camp of treaty makers at Traverse des Sioux. He reported:

[A] rank of horsemen . . . advanced abreast beating their drums and singing a wild war song as they approached our camp. . . . The effect was very wild, this cavalcade of savage musicians, in their wild dress and paint, mou[nted] on spirited horses and singing [a] loud shrill monotonous chaunt [*sic*]. (Heilbron 1941, 138)

Mayer further explained that after this process, the musicians came to the camp and joined with the hundreds of other assembled Indians in a "begging dance." After "they had danced for a time, the Governor presented a blanket to the chief's brother," an action that prompted the Indians to sing praises of thanks to the governor. Following this performance, the government and Indians joined in a feast, smoked tobacco, and enjoyed a party atmosphere (Heilbron 1941, 138–39). Additional speeches and pipe smoking followed the ceremonies. After the treaty was signed at Traverse des Sioux, government leaders and traders distributed presents to the Indians "consisting of blankets, cloth, powder, lead, tobacco, beads, looking glasses, knives, trinkets" (Heilbron 1941, 143). The festival-like atmosphere of the treaty signing concealed some of the duplicitous goals of both the government and the Indians.

After pretreaty festivities, Chiefs Little Crow and Wabasha held up the treaty signing. In fact, Chief Little Crow stalled the negotiations because he said the government had not made good on previous treaties. He told the council that "[w]e spoke about it last fall, but we have not yet seen the money. We desire to have it laid down to us. It is money due on the treaty, and I think it should be paid; we do not want to talk about a new treaty until it is all paid" (LeDuc 1852, 75–77). After the commissioner of Indian affairs threatened to withhold rations, the chiefs agreed to sign (LeDuc 1852, 82–85).

Hidden within this visual spectacle of the treaty celebrations were deep seeded differences between the government and the Indians. Raymond J. DeMallie (1977) argues that the goals of the government were to acquire more land, prescribe reservations, and destroy tribal identity. In contrast, the goals of the Indians were to get presents, continue trade, solidify their prestige and power, and formally relate to the government (5–7). The content of the treaties and the speeches of the Indians about these documents provides evidence of the diverse goals and the multiple audiences of this rhetorical genre. Government representatives had as their primary audience the Senate who had to ratify the treaties, but they also addressed military leaders, Indian agents, and traders by affirming each other's credibility as federal power brokers. Seeking to bolster their own power and give their people a voice, the Indians' oratory expressed tribal values, challenged government officials, and sought to impress observers. In ways typical of the other treaty meetings referred to in this volume, the written treaty served as a legal document to enforce the dependence of the Santee on the government. In many cases, however, the ceremony took precedence over the treaty content. For example, Southern Cheyenne Chief Black Kettle (Chapter 3) and Oglala Chief Red Cloud (Chapter 5) recalled the social aspects of the treaty events but claimed not to understand the legal provisions of the treaties they had signed.

Content

The content followed a formula common to many of the 400 treaties made with the various Indian nations since it dealt with a typical set of issues and strategies. Following Bakhtin (1986), the treaties are a bundle of borrowed utterances. The government borrowed the issues and strategies from other treaties and then reconstituted the content to fit with its goals for the Santee. Although the issues—cessions of land, Indian dependence on the government, placement of Indians on reservations, payment of debts, and religious, educational, and agricultural reforms—provided common content in all of the treaties, the details about the size of land cessions and the amount of government annuities differed among tribes. At Traverse des Sioux and Mendota, the Santee bands agreed to "cede, sell, or relinquish" huge tracts of their land and "remove themselves to the country set apart for them," pay off debts to the traders from the loans they had received, establish schools, begin farming, and receive annuities for their concessions. Since the U.S. Senate did not ratify the section of the treaties that specified the location of the reservations, the state of Minnesota gave the Indians a five-year lease on the treaty stipulated land. When the lease elapsed, federal officials called Indian leaders to Washington to finalize the 1858 amendments with them. This resulting treaty assigned the Indians to even smaller reservations than they had been given in 1851 and paid them thirty cents per acre for the ceded land.

Treaties contain two distinct types of rhetorical strategies—promises and threats. Promises express the goals of negotiators, state their intentions to cooperate, and emphasize the means by which these goals are to be achieved. One type of promise merely asserted the goals and established the government as the agency of power. Article 4 of the 1858 treaty emphasized that Congress regulate trade and intercourse and that only traders licensed with the secretary of interior be allowed to trade with the Indians (Treaty with the Mdewakanton and Wahpekute). Other promises stated intentions to fulfill obligations. For example, the 1858 treaty promised that a "sum not exceeding seventy-thousand dollars" would be paid to the chiefs and headmen "to satisfy their just debts and obligations" and to provide goods for them and their bands at the discretion of the superintendent of Indian affairs (Article 3, both 1858 treaties).

Each of the Santee treaties featured about an equal number of promises and threats. Two types of threats appeared in the 1858 treaties. The first type, sometimes called a veiled threat, states a preference and implies a sanction for nonadherence. For example, Article 6 states:

The Sisseeton [*sic*] and Wahpaton [*sic*] . . . do hereby pledge and bind themselves to preserve friendly relations with the citizens thereof, and to commit no injuries or depredations on their persons or property, . . . but in case of any such injury or depredation, full compensation shall . . . be made therefor [*sic*] out of their monies in the hands of the United States. (Treaty with Sisseton and Wahpeton 1858)

The second type of threat presents an ultimatum, asserting the control of one party over another and stating a punishment or cost if compliance to the provisions of the threatener is not achieved. An example of this kind of threat appeared in Article 7:

If any of the members of the said . . . band of Sioux shall drink or procure for others, intoxicating liquors, the proportion of the annuities of said bands shall at the discretion of the Secretary of the Interior, be withheld from them for a period of at least one year. (Treaty with Mdewakanton and Wahpekute, 1858)

The content of the treaties consisted of standard issues borrowed from other treaties packaged into utterances combining promises with threats.

Form and Style

Legal form and style linked the content of the treaties with the government's situational requirements for control. The resulting form and style added legal potency to the treaty discourse. Treaty content takes the form of laws set apart as articles that stipulate the different threats, promises, and sanctions. In the Santee Sioux treaties, separate articles dealt with assigned reservations, annuities, trade, intemperance, and promised buildings and tools. None of these articles had original content. Treaty makers borrowed both the structure and the language from other documents—statutes (*Trade and Intercourse Act* 1832), phrases from Supreme Court decisions, such as "domestically dependent nation" (*Cherokee Nation v. Georgia*

1831), and idioms from the remarks of congressional advocates, such as "civilization process," "moral improvement," and "annuity."

Just as utterances from others contributed to the form and content, treaties also borrowed the style and tone. The treaties imported both an archaic legal style full of whereas clauses and convoluted sentences presented in an authoritative tone. Such borrowing framed the treaties in what Bakhtin calls "verbal vestments" (1986, 89). By coding the treaty in these vestments, the document asserted legal authority and political power while at the same time it presented abstractly worded promises and threats. An example of this language appeared in the government promise to pay annuities in Article 8:

And it is further agreed, that such changes may be made in the stipulations of the former treaties which provide for the payment of particular sums for specified purposes, as to permit the chiefs and braves of said bands or any of the subdivision of said bands, with the sanction of the Secretary of Interior, to authorize such payments or expenditures of their annuities, or any portion thereof, which are to become due hereafter, as may be deemed best for the general interests and welfare of the said bands or subdivisions thereof. (Treaty with Mdewakanton and Wahpekute 1858)

This article attempted to explain the method for distribution of annuities, but the obfuscated legal jargon made the details unclear both to the trained legal eye and the untrained ear of the Indians.

Treaties are distinct genres because of the cultural ceremony accompanying the signing and the coalescence of the treaty discourse's content and style with its legal form. When the government framed the issues of the treaty as threats and promises and then imposed a legal form and language, the discourse empowered the government more than it promoted Indian sovereignty. By 1862, the Santee from the lower agency had not received the annuities guaranteed by the treaties nor had they started to farm the land. As a result, many of their members suffered from starvation, and this state of affairs motivated these Indians to raid and kill settlers in order to secure food and material goods.

EYEWITNESS ACCOUNTS

Historians reconstruct eyewitness accounts into historical records of war. One way to understand the Sioux Uprising is through the accounts of Indian warriors and settlers. As rhetorical fragments, the accounts offer insight into the rhetoric of war from the point of view of eyewitnesses. These accounts are not complete genres but are utterances with similar thematic content, style and form. Michael McGee (1990) explains: "Rhetors make discourses from scraps and pieces of evidence. . . . fashioned from 'fragments.'" The creators of the discourses then arrange the "facts, events, texts, and stylized expressions" they have gathered from others into coherent explanations serving their individual purposes (279). The fragments of eyewitnesses resemble one another because they (1) evolve from a common social-cultural situation, (2) express a similar goal, (3) represent community values, and (4) call attention to the presuppositions of the rhetor (Kamberelis 1995, 120–21). Each account exists as a rhetorical fragment until another rhetor brings its content together with other similar utterances into a coherent explanation of an event.

Common Situations

Eyewitnesses construct accounts that reflect similar definitions of a common situation. At the time of the Sioux Uprising, 6,200 Santee confined to reservations were on the annuity roles. The upper agency, located at Yellow Medicine, was inhabited by the Sissetons and Wahpetons who had about 900 warriors. The lower agency, located at Redwood, was home to the Mdewakantons and Wahpekutes who had about 2,000 warriors (Roddis 1956, 59). The fighting was instigated by warriors of the lower agency bands under the direction of Chief Little Crow. After helping white settlers to leave the area of the conflict, many Santee from the upper agency fled with their white friends during the war.

Several eyewitness accounts defined the situation as one in which treaty promises had not been kept. Accounts of Santee Sioux chiefs point to the accumulation of frustrations they felt as the result of being confined to reservations and forced to live on annuities.

Just prior to the beginning of the uprising, Chief Little Crow warned the government that trouble would ensue unless the Indians got their annuities. He told agent Thomas Galbraith:

We have waited a long time. The money is ours, but we cannot get it. We have no food, but here are these stores, filled with food. We ask that you, the agent, make some arrangement by which we can get food from the stores, or else we may take our own way to keep ourselves from starving. When men are hungry they help themselves. (Barton 1919, 48–49)

Shortly after Little Crow delivered his warning, Indians raided government warehouses and took food (Meyer 1993, 107).

Settler Marion P. Satterlee (1923) observed the treaty violations were the underlying cause of the warfare. He claimed that the Sioux at Yellow Medicine had been promised more than $495,000 for their land, but they had to give up more than $220,000 of this amount to traders for back debts. He further explained, "The payment of 1862 was held back at least two months while the Indians were on the verge of starvation" (349).

Another citizen observed that "the hordes of Indians lately assembled at the Yellow Medicine Agency" are "growing impatient from the delay of their annuities" and have shown "signs of dissension" and "threatened violence," making it necessary for a company of volunteers from Fort Ridgely to come to the agency ("Indian Massacre and War of 1862" 1863, 2).

When eyewitnesses define the situation in a common way, they reinforce a similar argument about the cause of the war. These accounts, written after the war, may have been reconstituted utterances borrowed from a single source or from many different sources. Whatever the case, common explanations help audiences to decide the meaning and evaluate the content of eyewitness accounts.

Similar Goals

Another factor that contributes to meaning is the eyewitness' point of view and theme. Point of view refers to the perspective of the account giver, and themes are the argumentative conclusions of utterances. The eyewitnesses to the 1862 Uprising attempted to construct part of the historical record of the warfare using subjective, condensed, and embellished descriptions that represented their individual perceptions and experiences of war. Eyewitnesses attributed blame to others; at the same time, they called attention to their own roles in the war. As expected, the lower agency Sioux implicated the government, the upper agency Sioux sided with the settlers, and the victims pointed to hostile Indians as the source of the conflict.

Presenting an Indian point of view, Chief Big Eagle's goal was to justify the war as an unfortunate accident motivated by unkept treaty promises. Big Eagle (1862) explained the cause of the war in this way. Four people from Shakopee's band killed white people at Acton, Minnesota. They had not intended to kill anyone but were on a hunting trip when they found some eggs. One warrior dared another to take the eggs to show his courage by stealing property from white men. This caused trouble and the Indians killed three men and two women. They returned to their camp and told their leader, Shakopee, about their deeds and their fear of warfare with whites. This led to a council with Little Crow who gave orders to kill white men (134). On the morning of August 18, the first major battle occurred at the Redwood Agency, one location where traders denied the Sioux the annuities they had been promised. The Indians were especially anxious to get revenge on trader Andrew Myrick who had refused hungry Indians credit and told them "to eat grass" (135). Just as in other accounts, Big Eagle likely condensed a complex set of causes into a simple account. His authoritative tone pinpointed a reason why the Indians attacked settlers. The chief's citation of Myrick's words became one of the most memorable phrases about the war; afterwards this phrase appeared in many historical works (Satterlee 1909–1914; Roddis 1956; Oehler 1959; Carley 1976; Anderson 1986b; Meyer 1993). A contemporary film on the Sioux Indian Wars uses the quotation as a focal point for its documentary about the Uprising (Atlas Video 1992).

The goal of the eyewitness accounts of white victims was to record the unprovoked and brutal warfare of Indian warriors. To relate their experiences of warfare, victims focused attention on their personal suffering. For example, Mrs. L. Eastlick ([1863] 1959) reported the torture she experienced during a battle near New Ulm in this way:

[An Indian] came up close beside me, stood a moment watching me, then commenced beating me on the head with the butt of a gun. He struck me a great many times, so hard that my head bounded up from the sod, at every stroke, and then he gave me three severe blows across the right shoulder. . . . [O]n trying to get up, I found that I was very weak, and that it required a great deal of painful effort to raise myself to a sitting position. . . . I now found that the blood had run down from my head and coagulated among my fingers; hence I knew my head was injured by the blows. . . . I thought my skull must be broken, and this afterwards proved to be true. (19–20)

Presenting explicit physical details of the brutality accomplished Eastlick's rhetorical goal; it showed the intensity of her suffering at the hands of a vicious warrior. Her factual style meticulously pointed out the details of her beating and its ghastly effect. This style added evidence in support of her theme that the warriors committed brutal acts against innocent victims.

Community Values

When they made public their accounts, eyewitnesses established their roles as authoritative sources about the war. They added to this authority by infusing their discourse with the language and values of the community. The war accounts used "prosaic" language and idioms familiar to the audiences they represented (Bakhtin 1986, 89). It is likely the accounts borrowed words and phrases commonly used in the community to portray important audience values. Some Indians valued independence and respect; most settlers held property and prosperity in high regard. The accounts of assimilated Indians showed they had adopted values similar to settlers.

Indians from the lower agency, however, expressed resentment of what they considered to be white ethnocentrism. For example, Chief Big Eagle (1962) reported:

The whites were always trying to make the Indians give up their life and live like white men. . . . Many of the whites also seemed to say by their manner when they saw an Indian, "I am much better than you." ... Then some of the white men abused the Indian women in a way and disgraced them. (129–30)

By making pubic long standing grievances about white prejudices, Big Eagle called attention to the values of his people. In his view, failure to appreciate Indian values provoked the conflict. Ironically, his remarks echoed a point that his former agent Thomas Galbraith emphasized in his report of the Uprising in 1863. Galbraith concluded that "the habits and customs of white men are at war with the habits and customs of Indians" (Holcombe 1894, 384).

The values of the lower agency Sioux differed from those of the assimilated Indians residing at the upper agency. For example, Wahpeton Chief Akipa emphasized the values he had acquired through assimilation in his account of the war. He lamented:

There is no bravery in killing helpless men and women, and little children, who have no means of defense. This is simply cowardness, and it is only cowards who would boast of it. ... When the sun arose that witnessed the horrors of the indiscriminate massacre of the whites in this valley of the Minnesota, regardless of sex or age, by you Lower Sioux, the upper bands were peacefully attending to their crops on their own reservation. (quoted in Diedrich 1989, 69)

Chief Akipa not only criticized the warfare of the lower bands, but he also called attention to his preference for the life of a farmer. His choice of words, such as "cowardness," "lack of bravery," and "massacre," are the same terms that settlers used when they talked about the war. Just as in other eyewitness accounts, Akipa infused his theme that the lower agency Sioux are committing atrocities against whites with the language, imagery, and tone of the assimilated Indians that he represented.

When the lower Sioux Indians moved to the upper agency at Yellow Medicine, they looted the government facilities located there. This event proved to Sarah Wakefield ([1864] 1976) that the Indians came from a different community of values than she did. Her account placed value on property, civility, and sobriety. She observed the events of August 18, 1862, in this way:

They began their work of destruction at an early hour, killing traders in their stores; when this was done they began their destruction in general. The wine and spirits found in the stores added drunken madness to the[ir] dancing wildly about the dying embers of what had lately been the stores and homes of the traders. They passed on, killing everything they met. Their savage natures were aroused, and blood-thirsty as wild beasts, raced and tore around, beating and crushing everything they had no use for. (13)

When Wakefield juxtaposed property ownership and cultural civility against images of plunder and destruction, she argued that the Indians were savages from a culture alien to her own.

Chief Big Eagle's theme, Akipa's language, and Wakefield's imagery reflected the values of the respective communities to which they belonged. Other rhetors piecing together thorough accounts of the war could create multiple community points of view from the fragments they borrowed from these eyewitnesses.

Irreconcilable Assumptions

The eyewitness accounts discussed here also contain the explicit or implicit presuppositions of the rhetor. Presuppositions refer to the observer's assumptions about what constitutes appropriate behavior. Some Indians assumed that their warfare was justified because they had been victimized by unkept treaty promises and unscrupulous agents. The Indians also believed the government started the war by starving out the lower agency Sioux. The settlers believed that the Indians intentionally started the war because they knew the Minnesota military force had been weakened by an exodus of men to the civil war battlefields.

Since eyewitnesses from one side of the conflict hold assumptions incompatible with those on the other side, understanding accounts often depends on comparisons and contrasts. Although many different presumptions appeared in the accounts, one major difference was the Indians' and settlers' assumptions about warfare.

Sioux warrior Lightning Blanket (Carley 1962a) bragged about his preparations for the war against settlers in this way:

The young men were all anxious to go, and we dressed as warriors in war paint, breech clouts and leggings, with a large sash around us to keep our food and ammunition in. . . . We did not fight like white men with an officer; we all shot as we pleased. (144–45)

For some Sioux, warfare was part ceremony and part conquest. "They camouflaged their headbands with prairie grass and flowers. They tried to set fire to the roofs with blazing arrows." There were "hours of shelling and 'demonic yells'" (Carley 1962a, 129–30). At New Ulm, the Sioux burned more than 190 buildings, killed 34 settlers, and wounded 60 others.

For the settlers, warfare involved strategy and self defense. Jacob Nix ([1887] 1994) described how he and other settlers gained material advantage over the Indians at New Ulm by superior fire power and carefully maneuvered defense strategies. He noted:

[We] quickly gathered a troop of sixty or seventy courageous men . . . plunged over the barricades, with hurrahs that would have done justice to the wildest Indian cries, and attacked that strategically important blockhouse. Here ensued a terrible and bloody struggle which meant life or death. . . . The Indians even though they outnumbered us four to one were driven out of the blockhouse. (113)

The different cultural presumptions evident in these accounts help to explain why the conflict occurred.

The Uprising came to an end after General Henry Hastings Sibley came to fight the Indians with huge numbers of troops and artillery. The surrender of white and mixed-blood prisoners took place September 26 at Camp Release with the help of two friendly Mdewakanton chiefs, Taopi and Wabasha. At the same time Little Crow and his warriors fled to the Dakota prairies. Mixed-blood captive Samuel J. Brown recalled the scene as jubilant. He noted:

When the troops suddenly appeared on an eminence a mile away and there was no doubt that they were coming to our rescue, the captives could hardly restrain themselves—some cried for joy, some went into fits or hysterics, and some fainted away. (1988, 225)

The eyewitness accounts of war are not complete genres; they are part of a bundle of utterances that others can use to create a complete genre. In ways similar to genres, these fragments evolve from a common situation, express a goal about that situation, represent community values, and point to presuppositions that underlie the discourse. For this reason, these rhetorical fragments are the building blocks for the rhetoric that others incorporate into their own discourse about the Uprising.

THE LEGAL PROCEEDINGS

In ways similar to eyewitness observations, legal proceedings are created from accounts. Two days after the surrender, Sibley appointed a military commission to try 400 Indians for their crimes during the Sioux Uprising. The role of the military commission and their conduct at the trial illuminate the legal processes of the time. The legal system was undeveloped and often responded more to the emotional climate of the times than it did to the principles of the Constitution and Bill of Rights. In contrast to Chief Leschi who had a jury and legal counsel, the military commission gave no such rights to the Santee Sioux tried in Minnesota.

The Mankato Military Trial

The Mankato trials were subject to the limitations of the court procedures and the attitudes of the government officials conducting the trials.

The courts provided a rhetorical advantage to the government and a major disadvantage to Indian defendants. Petra T. Shattuck and Jill Norgren (1990) explain that order and control was established on the frontier by "openly catering to the needs of the most powerful" and "permitting the dispossession of the least powerful" (80). General Henry Hastings Sibley represented the frontier power elites when he convened a commission to try the Indians only two days after their surrender. The military arrested and shackled the Indians before the warriors knew the charges against them (Brown 1988, 226). Then, the trials proceeded with the trappings of formality and legality. The legal proceedings convened on September 28, 1862, and ended on November 4, 1862. During this time, the military commission indicted, tried, and convicted 393 men, and of those brought to trial, 309 received the death penalty, sixteen served a prison sentence, and sixty-five gained acquittals (Roddis 1956, 156). The trial took place in La Bathe's log kitchen in Mankato, Minnesota.

Prior to the trial the government arraigned the accused with written charges based on information provided by Reverend Stephen R. Riggs, a missionary from the upper agency, who had based the indictments on hearsay information. Riggs gathered evidence from mixed-bloods and others that he had questioned including several members of his church. By reading the indictments and selecting witnesses, Riggs acted as a "one-man grand jury" (Heard 1864, 251). Isaac I. V. Heard (1864) claimed that Indian raids and killings were not war crimes since most of the warfare seemed to be acts of murder against ordinary citizens. Members of the military commission heard the cases and pronounced the settlement.[1] Lieutenant Rollin C. Olin served as judge advocate. Because he lacked legal training, a lawyer, Lieutenant Isaac I. V. Heard (subsequently referred to as Judge Heard), took over judicial responsibilities. Cullen Guards filled the role of court reporter and Reverend Riggs served as interpreter (Roddis 1956, 150).

The proceedings evidenced several problems uncharacteristic of military trials, such as the absence of defense attorneys and defense witnesses (Schuetz 1994, 35–60). As a result, the primary case for the accused consisted of the defendants' own statements; some confessed, and others tried to defend themselves. The result was the same in both cases—guilty. Clearly, the testimony given by the accused was held against them, and most of the defendants had no knowledge of English (Folwell 1961, 199). Marion P. Satterlee (1927) concluded that "the whole proceeding was a disgraceful travesty of justice. . . . Most of the witnesses were plainly biased" (79). The legal anomalies had little immediate effect on the defendants. In fact, Judge Heard (1864) reported:

The defendants ranged in age from 15 to 50, one slept during the proceeding, two were idiots, one old man was "shriveled to a mummy," and one squaw was charged but not convicted. Among the nearly 400 Indians who were tried, the court acquitted warriors from the upper agency, and convicted most of the accused men from the lower agency. (258–67)

The government designed the court procedures to create a speedy trial without the presumption of innocence. Heard's standard of proof was to convict if "it should be proven by the testimony of witnesses, unless the prisoner admitted the fact, that he had fired in battles, or acted as a commissary in supplying provisions to the combatants, or committed some separate murder" (Heard 1864, 269).

The military commission created the following court procedures: The defendants made statements consisting of confessions and denials; the witnesses were called, sworn in, and gave testimony; many pleaded guilty thinking they were prisoners of war and hence not vulnerable to execution. Since neither the defendants nor the witnesses were interrogated by opposing counsel, their testimony took the form of accounts.

Accounts in the Trials

Accounts are a genre of testimony featuring clusters of utterances used to defend or accuse persons for offensive acts. Some of these accounts justify, excuse, or apologize for alleged criminal behavior. Other accounts accuse or describe offensive and criminal acts that the witnesses attribute to others. Erving Goffman's (1971) concept of face saving partially explains the content and form of the abbreviated testimonial accounts of defendants. Goffman identifies five ways people defend themselves after they have been accused of offensive acts. Although he does not apply the strategies to legal cases, his constructs illuminate the content of the rhetoric of the Indian defendants in the Mankato trials. The first strategy is a "traverse" or "rejoinder," a method where the accused denies both that the act occurred and that he or she committed the act (109). A second strategy is to admit the act occurred, but then to define the act as not offensive or evil. A third strategy is to admit responsibility for the act but to argue that the negative consequences were not known at the time of the act. A fourth strategy is to admit carelessness in acting and to demonstrate ignorance of the consequences of the act (109). A final strategy is to apologize by splitting the self into two parts—a bad person who committed the act and a good person who is sorry for that act (113).

In contrast to the strategies used by the defendants, the accusers made attributions of guilt. Fritz Heider (1958) explains strategies similar to those adopted by the accusers. First, he argues that people likely perceive the causes of a crime by making attributions about the power and motives of the defendants who allegedly committed the evil acts. This approach assumes that the accused had full control over "the whole course of events and actions" (107). A witness' attributions of power show that the defendant had the ability to do an act; attributions of motivation show that the accused also had the intention to commit an act (97–103). Second, Heider explains that accusers can use environmental or contextual factors to show that a defendant had the opportunity to commit an offensive act. On the other hand, the situation can provide an excuse for the action. If accusers perceive the situation as the cause of the event, they then can absolve the defendant of the primary responsibility for the act and claim instead that the situation was the cause of harm to another person (169–70). Third, the witnesses observe mediating circumstances that change their perceptions of causes. For example, accused persons may have committed a crime, but because they had a good record of friendship and loyalty to the whites, their good acts would be weighed against bad acts in assessing guilt. These mediating factors change perceptions of witnesses by associating favorable and unfavorable events with the defendants in order to make them seem less culpable (78). Riggs provided the interpretations of the testimony for the court record.

Both the accounts of defendants and the accusers produced content designed to prove or disprove the indictments. In the beginning, the military commission spent considerable time on each case with several witnesses testifying, but as the proceedings continued, the cases became less and less dependant on evidence. A brief sample of the Mankato trials shows the strategic content, the abbreviated form, and the biographical style characteristic of the accounts of defendants and accusers (subsequent references are from the Transcripts of the Record of the Trials of Certain Indians Charged with Barbarities in the State of Minnesota 1862).

Trial of Mazabomdu or Iron Blower. On October 6, one of the first cases was that of Mazabomdu (sometimes spelled Mazabomdoo) and translated as Iron Blower (Case 10: 1–4). The charges against him were the murder of civilians at New Ulm. The indictment read:

Mazabomdu did on or about the 20th day of August 1862 kill an elderly woman and child in a garden near New Ulm, Minnesota. . . . [He] at various times and places on the Minnesota frontier between the 1st day of August 1862 and the 28th day of September did join with and participate in the murders and robberies committed by his tribe on the white citizens of the United States.

Iron Blower's defense strategy was a kind of rejoinder, a denial of the act accompanied by an attempt to get the military commission to think kindly of him by establishing a positive set of credentials for himself. Iron Blower began by offering the following testimony:

I am not guilty. Ever since I remember I have been a friend to the whites. An old Indian . . . gave me good advice which I have always followed. Since the Treaty of 1851, I have always lived with my family near Winona. I was coming up to get my annuity at the time of the outbreak. I waited to go to Winona again but I was afraid the Indians would take me and kill me. I called Godfrey to witness that I have not killed or shot at a white man. My father and all the family were all killed by the Chippewas, but I have heard my father say that he never killed or abused any white man.

He bolstered his self defense by offering an excuse, claiming he lacked the means for killing people because "I am short sighted and never even hunted ducks" (Case 10: 1–4).

The testimony continued by statements about his good deeds. He admitted going to the lower agency at the time of battle, but told the commission that he helped save the lives of two prominent captives who were testifying at the trials: "I was going along with a load of kinnekuic (tobacco), I saw the Indians with Mary Swan and Miss Williams—I saved their lives." Then he attempted to build credibility and establish mediating factors with the members of the commission by saying, "I have a niece who is a member of the church at the lower agency. I took Miss Swan to her and she has kept her." He admitted being at the scene where Patwell (Patoile) was killed. But he emphasized "I stopped them [the other Indians] from killing the women. I left the woman at Wacanta's house. The next morning I got her to go to the Traveler's House."

The main testimony against Iron Blower was from a mixed-blood Indian, named Otakle or Godfrey, who received a prison sentence in exchange for testimony against others. Godfrey implicated Iron Blower rather than defending him as he apparently had promised to do. He claimed the accused had the power and the opportunity to commit the alleged crimes. Godfrey recalled:

I know the prisoner. This Indian killed an old woman and two children. They were going into a garden when he fired at them. It was near the Traveler's House near New Ulm. I saw the Indian fire on the old woman and saw her fall. He then jumped into the garden and kicked the children down. I did see him kill the children. I was in the wagon at the time. This took place on the first day they committed the killing of the whites. I saw him again but he didn't say he had killed any whites. (Case 10: 1–4)

In one of the rare responses allowed defendants, Iron Blower refuted Godfrey by a follow-up rejoinder arguing he lacked opportunity to commit the crime:

What Godfrey states is not true. . . . I met Godfrey and his party near the Traveler's Home. I didn't stop with them but went up near where they killed Patwell [Patoile]. I had no whiskey. I had a . . . gun when I met the soldiers on the hedge but it didn't go off. I was in the front wagon. I crossed the hedge when the soldiers shot our foot. I was not there when the soldier was killed.

Despite his denial and the testimony of only one witness, Iron Blower was found guilty of the charges and sentenced to be hanged (Case 10: 1–4).

The testimony of Godfrey impressed Judge Heard. He explained that Godfrey "had such an honest look and spoke with such a truth of tone, that the court, though prejudiced against him in the beginning, were now unanimously inclined to believe there were possibilities as to his sincerity" (Heard 1864, 234).

Trial of Ontonkanumba. One of the outsiders tried for the crimes and one of the few acquitted was a Winnebago Indian named Ontonkanumba. On October 11, 1862 (Case 13: 1–6), he was charged with "participating in Indian murders and depredations in or about the 19th day of August 1862" of joining "a war party of the Sioux Indian in a raid against the inhabitants of New Ulm" and of "participating in the murders and robberies then committed against the white citizens of the United States killing several persons with his own hand."

Ontonkanumba defended himself by admitting his involvement in warfare, but then he argued his acts were not evil or criminal. He explained:

I have been along with the Sioux. . . . I went with them to Washington and . . . I intermarried with the Sioux and have been living with them for some time. I am a Winnebago. I lived this side of Yellow Medicine, and the day previous to the outbreak I went down without a gun to Red Pond to make hay. I was with the party when the outbreak took place and having no arms took no part in it. After the outbreak I would have been glad to go back to my tribe, but I have my wife and children here and I came back to them. . . . The soldiers would not let me go back. . . . At the time they pillaged and attacked, I went into the Roberts Store but took nothing. Since then I came up here but have done nothing. God was watching me, and it was his providence that saved me from mixing up in this affair. (Case 13: 1–2)

Henry Miller, a witness on his behalf, testified that Ontonkanumba had neither the power nor the opportunity to commit the crime, "I know the prisoner. I saw the prisoner before the trouble—didn't see him during the troubles. I was at Fort Ridgely but [he] had no gun. . . . I was at the battle of New Ulm. Didn't see the prisoner there."

After the testimony against him, Ontonkanumba offered evidence against other defendants supplying the court with a mediating factor. He claimed

Okomikah or Little Chief was there, and Wachasta, Chasta, Hakakky, Wazekali fired at whites. I saw these three with my own eyes. Ibunka, the brother of Wkyakaky, and the son of Honwekah, a chief. . . . They were at the first outbreak at Red River. Two were killed about noon. I saw them fire at whites, and I heard the residue. I recall the names of the other two—Wedukounikah and Haymundekah. (Case 13: 5)

In this three-pronged defense account, Ontonkanumba admitted involvement, denied power and opportunity, and then offered evidence against others. The commission found him "not guilty" on all counts and recommended that this prisoner be held as a witness against other Winnebagos, and then he was released.

Trial of Mephpeokenaji or Stands in the Midst of Clouds. By October 20, the court reporter resorted to paraphrasing rather than quoting the defendants and the witnesses. For this reason, the trial transcript became increasingly abbreviated as the proceedings came to an end. Stands in the Midst of Clouds was charged with "numerous outrages and robberies . . . between the 18th day of August 1862 and the 28th day of September 1862" (Case 92: 1–5).

The defendant used rejoinder, a strict denial of the crimes alleged against him. The court reporter paraphrased Mephpeokenaji's testimony in this way: "Was on the west side of Fort [Ridgely] at the battle. Was not at New Ulm nor at Birch Coulee. Was at the Big Woods. . . . Did not kill a white man any time. Fired three shots at Beaver Creek."

Mack Frazer Swan testified against Stands in the Midst of Clouds, concluding that the defendant had the power and opportunity to commit the alleged crime. He recalled, "I was standing by Forbes Store. The Indians were going by. . . . Saw prisoner level his gun at Antoine Young and shoot him dead then went with the horses and hid himself." Another witness, Lewis Thiele, claimed, "He shot one man off a wagon. I saw him strike the persons in the wagon with a knife. There were four women and eleven children. They were all killed." The commission found Stands in the Midst of Clouds to be guilty and sentenced him to hang.

Trial of Chaskaydon, Chaska or First Born Son. On October 30, 1862, the commission heard the 121st case, but provided only a sparse record of the proceedings. The record is problematic because five of the defendants had the name "Chaska" or "First Born Son" (Case 121: 1–3). The commission charged this particular man "with participation in the murderous offenses and outrages in the State of Minnesota by Sioux Indians between the 18th day of August and the 28th day of September 1862," including the murders at New Ulm, Birch Coulee, and Wood Lake. Chaskaydon's brief account shows he admitted the act occurred, but claimed this act did not result in evil. Nonetheless, the commission convicted Chaskaydon on the testimony of one witness, Lewis Theile, who argued Chaskaydon had the power and opportunity to commit the act. He said, the prisoner carried a gun and "shot a woman that was with child and then threw her over at Redwood. I have known the prisoner for a year. He has been frequently at my house."

Since several defendants confused the name of Chaska with someone else, this Chaskaydon was granted a reprieve because the court thought he had helped white captives. But this defendant was not the "good" Chaska who had protected captive Sarah Wakefield. The "good" Chaska (testifying earlier) was convicted and hung because of the court's mistake. After finding out about this error, Wakefield contacted Stephen Riggs who admitted the problem. In a letter to her, he explained: "We had forgotten that any other Chaska [by that name] was called. On that fatal morning we never thought of the third one, [and] when the name Chaska was called, your protector answered to the name and came out" [to be killed] (Wakefield [1864] 1976, 52–53).

This variety of accusations and defenses share some similarities. For example, each of the defendants offered simple reasons for their innocence that parallel Goffman's concepts of the accounts of self defense. Furthermore, each of the accusers presented attributions of responsibility based on observations of the opportunity, power, and motives of the defendants to kill victims. These examples of testimony in the trials demonstrate how the military commission accepted simplistic reasoning from defendants and accusers without substantive corroborating evidence or interrogation. Because these simplistic accounts met the presumptions of the commission about the guilt of the lower agency Sioux and about the truthfulness of white witnesses, it is not surprising that so many Indians were convicted.

Clemency Appeal

The hanging itself took place several days after it was scheduled because General Sibley had not received the needed authorization from President Abraham Lincoln. Even though Sibley, Governor Alexander Ramsey, and General John Pope wanted to execute all of the convicted prisoners, just prior to the execution, Lincoln granted clemency to most of those convicted. The clemency appeal described here provides an example of a distinct genre of legal discourse that surfaced in this episode. This genre synthesizes belief, argument, stylistic choices, and perceptions of the situation and contains an internal dynamic that fuses together the various elements (Jamieson & Campbell 1990, 336).

In an eloquent appeal written in early December, Episcopalian Bishop Henry Benjamin Whipple, a missionary to the Sioux, argued against execution (Whipple 1864, 343–48). Whipple designed the speech to respond to the court's decision to execute hundreds of Santee, a situation that demanded a persuasive response. He organized his clemency appeal according to the following topics: an acknowledgment of the evils of the warfare, an appeal for doing justice, an indictment of the treaty system, an explanation of why the treaties caused problems, a statement of the ill effects of the treaties on the Sioux, and a plea for clemency on behalf of all of the convicted Indians. His appeal addressed Lincoln, government agencies, and military and civil leaders of Minnesota, families of the victims, and citizens of the United States.

The clemency appeal began when Whipple personally identified with the white victims and with the official government audience. Then, Whipple acknowledged the horrors of the war in this way:

There are times when the Christian laborer has the right to ask for the sympathy, the prayers, and cooperation of all good men; for this reason I ask the calm attention of my fellow citizens to an appeal on behalf of one of the most wretched races of heathen men on earth. . . . The nation has heard of the most fearful Indian massacres in history; but those who live remote from the border can have no idea of the awful horror which have accompanied the desolations of two-hundred miles of the fairest country on earth. Many of these victims of savage ferocity were my friends. (343)

After identifying with the government and his citizen audience, he appealed for justice, claiming that the crimes had multiple causes. He pleaded: "I ask that the people shall lay the blame on this crime for where it belongs and rise up with one voice to demand reform of the atrocious Indian system . . . an organized system of robbery." He followed this explanation with his own definition of the causes of the Sioux Uprising by criticizing the treaties, emphasizing the government failed to pay annuities, and implicating failed assimilation policies. Whipple concluded:

It [the treaty system] has left the savage man without governmental control. . . . It has fostered savage life by wasting thousands of dollars in the purchase of paint, beads, scalping knives, and tomahawks; it has fostered a system of trade which robbed the thrifty and virtuous to pay the debts of the indolent and vicious; it has squandered the funds for civilization and for schools; it has connived at theft; it has winked at murder; . . . it has brought a harvest of blood to our door. (344)

Whipple then indicted the government system as the major cause of the war, arguing "it was under this Indian system that the fierce, warlike Sioux were fitted and trained to be actors in this bloody drama" (512).

The plea for clemency continued by blaming the United States for the war and charging that the government was more responsible for hurting the Indians than they were for hurting the slaves. He then asked President Lincoln to take into consideration the sins of the government when he decided how many of the 340 convicted prisoners should be executed. Whipple pleaded:

There are questions pressing upon us more grave than the hanging of a few hundred Indian prisoners. They concern the nation's broken faith and a reform of a crying evil. Deeply as our people feel on the questions of slavery, they may see here on the border a system [in which] the loss of manhood, home, and heaven, had worked out a degradation to Red men which slavery has never done for the African race. (348)

The themes of the suffering of the victims, the government-created condition of the perpetrators, and the need for understanding the evil of the wars combined with themes about the harm the government had done to the Indians.

To present these themes, Whipple adopted an exhortative style, making an urgent emotional appeal supported by logical reasoning. In this way, Whipple identified with American values of home, family, forgiveness, and justice, and then he condemned the government's treatment of the Indians and urged President Lincoln to act mercifully upon the prisoners so that their rights to life and liberty would not be abridged. The plea borrowed utterances from both the Bible and the Constitution. This clemency appeal effectively combined a problem-solution structure and a reasoned content with emotional pleas creating a potent persuasive appeal. This plea resulted in the pardon of 266 people. Those pardoned went to prison, later received a reprieve, and eventually settled on reservations in Dakota and Nebraska territories.

The plea had no effect on many lower band warriors since their execution took place shortly after the reprieve had been granted. Prior to the execution, the commanding officer at the Mankato prison addressed the convicted with these remarks:

Your Great Father at Washington, after carefully reading what the witnesses have testified in your several trials, has come to the conclusion that you have been guilty of wantonly and wickedly murdering white children; and, for this reason, he has directed that you each be hanged by the neck until you are dead. (Bryant 1864, 471–72)

The officer told the prisoners they could consult with their spiritual advisors who were Protestant and Catholic missionaries, and then he established December 26, 1862, as the execution day.

Execution Drama

The Indian voice emerged both during and after the trials. On the morning prior to the executions, a newspaper reporter described the scene in this way:

While Father [Augustine] Ravoux was speaking to them, Old Tazoo, broke out into a death wail, in which one after another joined until the prison room was filled with wild unearthly plaint, which was neither despair nor grief, but rather a paroxysm of savage passion, most impressive to witnesses and startling to hear even by those who understand the language. During the lulls of their death song, they would resume their pipes, . . . and [they] sat motionless and impassive until only the elders would break out into a wild wail. ("Mankato Trials" 1862, 1)

Speech of Consolation

Tazoo's leadership during the death wail is not surprising since he was a professional performer, a juggler, and a Santee medicine man. He was convicted of participating in the murder of Patville (Patoile) and of trying to rape captive Mattie Williams. At trial he denied both, and instead said that he had "sore eyes at the time of the murder" and was trying to help "save the woman" (Case 4: 1–4).

Prior to the hanging, Tazoo's speech of consolation to the prisoners illustrates yet another genre of legal rhetoric. This speech had three themes: the religious traditions of the Sioux, the Santee beliefs about eternal life, and a personal journey to the Great Spirit. This speech combined the religious themes with a prayer-like style that invoked the name of the Great Spirit, sought consolation for loved ones left behind, and solicited spiritual support for the community. The themes, style, and humorous tone evoked a feeling of hope and assurance about an afterlife. Tazoo spoke both to those soon to be executed and their grieving families:

Tell our friends that we are being removed from this world over the same path they must shortly travel. We go first, but many of our friends may follow us in a very short time. I expect to go directly to the abode of the Great Spirit, and to be happy when I get there; but we are told that the road is long and the distance great; therefore as I am slow in all my movement, it will probably take me a long time to reach the end of the journey, and I should not be surprised if some of the young active men we leave behind us will pass me on the road before I reach the place of my destination. ("Mankato Trials" 1862, 1)

Tazoo likely borrowed some of these utterances from speeches he had used in his role as medicine man. The speech contained two seemingly incompatible types of content, an eschatological prediction and self-deprecating remarks. This content coalesced in eulogistic language expressed in a prayer-like tone. The consolation speech marked the beginning of the end for the remaining prisoners.

After many of the prisoners had signed confessions and accepted baptism from the missionaries, they stepped forward to be executed. When the rope was pulled and thirty-eight Sioux fell to their death, huge crowds of settlers, government leaders, and military observed. The government buried the Indians in a mass grave along the Minnesota River. Soon after the execution, the government revoked all of the provisions of the previous treaties and urged Congress to remove the Santee from Minnesota.

THE AFTERMATH OF THE SIOUX UPRISING

The consequences of the trial also were extreme for those not executed. After the surrender, many of those who turned themselves in at Camp

Release were sent to prison camps. Nearly 350 prisoners went to Mankato, and over 1,600 were sent to Fort Snelling. After the trial, the government sent the remaining Wahkepute and Mdewakanton prisoners to Camp Mc-Clellan in Davenport, Iowa, and in 1866 relocated them to Nebraska territory. During imprisonment, many Indians died from illness and starvation. The government also exiled Minnesota prisoners to Dakota territory. The United States, realizing the extreme nature of the expulsion of all of the Sioux from Minnesota, made a new treaty in 1867 with the Sisseton and Wahpeton bands. After acknowledging the participation of these bands in rescues and recognizing their protection of whites and captives, the government agreed to restore their annuities and honor some of the previous treaty agreements. The government provided the Sisseton and Wahpetons with land in Devil's Lake in present-day North Dakota. A small number of these bands eventually returned as farmers to Minnesota (Meyer 1993, 330–36). In their new locations, some Santee along with western Sioux warriors continued to participate in raids and skirmishes. Even though they signed new treaties, many Santee continued to contest their treatment by the government. Continuing conflicts with Sioux eventually resulted in the 1890 battle at Wounded Knee.

In 1986, Minnesota Governor Rudy Perpich declared a year of reconciliation with the Sioux. This reconciliation, recalling the executions of 1862, was celebrated by a long-distance run from Fort Snelling to Mankato on December 26. Other events took place at the Minnesota sites of the major battles of the Sioux Uprising. The remains of those prisoners who died while incarcerated at Davenport, Iowa, were reburied in the region where the lower Sioux agency had been located during the Uprising. Amos Owen, a Santee Sioux, celebrated the traditions of his ancestors for many years at Indian festivals in Mankato. When he died in 1990, a memorial garden was established in his name at Mankato State University. In 1994, hereditary chiefs Ernest and Vernell Wabasha joined with Mankato city officials to dedicate a sculpture of a buffalo at Reconciliation Park, on the site where the Indians were hung.

Just as episodes in other Indian wars, the Sioux Uprising followed the story line of the representative anecdote described in Chapter 1. The Sioux Uprising and the Mankato trials resulted from a legacy of ill-conceived and broken treaties that produced open warfare between the indigenous Sioux and the white settlers. The trial, the climax to this conflict, illustrated the government's ability to exert control over the Minnesota Sioux. The events of the Sioux Uprising illuminate several genres of discourse—treaties, eyewitness histories, accusation and defense accounts, and speeches of clemency and consolation.

What is unique about this episode in government-Indian relations is the huge number of war victims, the extreme nature of the penalty in the deaths and removal of the Indians from Minnesota, and the lack of rights granted the Indians during their trials and exile. What is similar with many of the other nineteenth-century cases discussed in this book is the variety of the rhetorical actions and responses used by the government and Indians. For the Puget Sound, the Cheyenne and Arapaho, and the Navajo, treaty controversies and divergent accounts of war also illuminate their conflicts. Although small markers appear at the sites of the hanging of Leschi, the Sand Creek Massacre, and the Navajo internment, no large cultural ceremony or act of reconciliation comparable to those in Minnesota followed these episodes. Perhaps the descendants of the settlers and those of the dead and exiled Santee Sioux found a cultural way for their voices about the Sioux Uprising to reemerge more than a century after the war.

NOTE

1. Members of the military commission were Colonel William Crooks of the Sixth Regiment, Lieutenant Colonel William R. Marshall of the Seventh Regiment, Captain Hiram P. Bailey of the Sixth Regiment, and Lieutenant Rollin C. Olin of the Third Regiment.

Chapter 3

Political Spectacles and the Sand Creek Massacre, 1864–1865

The hanging of Leschi and the execution of the Santee Sioux did not suppress the Indian wars. Instead the wars spread into other western locations. However, one episode that took place on the plains of Colorado territory near Sand Creek in 1864 changed the attitudes of Congress about territorial military policy. After Colonel John Chivington's force of 700 Colorado militia killed 150 Southern Cheyenne and Arapaho[1] men, women, and children in an unprovoked ambush, public opinion swiftly turned against the militia. In fact, public opinion was so adverse that Congress conducted two separate investigations of Chivington and the militia, called the "Sand Creek Massacre" (1867) and the "Massacre of Cheyenne Indians" (1864–1865). Both investigations concluded that Colonel John Chivington acted wrongly against friendly Indians.

In his testimony, Amos D. James, a soldier from the Colorado militia, told one congressman about what he saw after the battle. James recalled:

The morning we left the battleground I rode over the field; I saw in riding over the field [a sergeant from my military unit] dismount from his horse and cut the ear from the body of an Indian, and [take the] scalp from the head of another. I saw a number of children killed: I suppose they were shot, they had bullet holes in them; one child had been cut with some instrument across the side. I saw another that both ears had been cut off. ("Sand Creek Massacre" 1867, 145)

Reports similar to this one prompted Congress to investigate. The resulting hearings created a national political spectacle calling into question military practices and demanding reform of the nation's Indian policy. This episode focuses on one of the investigations and its resulting political spectacle. Specifically, this chapter (1) defines the investigations as political spectacles, (2) identifies some of the cultural causes of the massacre, (3) shows how John Evans' correspondence encouraged the spectacle, (4) analyzes the rhetorical features of the "Massacre of Cheyenne Indians," and (5) explains the impact of this episode on government-Indian relations.

INVESTIGATIONS AS POLITICAL SPECTACLES

Spectacles can result from both legal inquiries and political investigations. First, Murray Edelman (1995) says political spectacles evolve out of events in which the broad public interest is invested in controversial events (122). In this case, the public interest in the Plains Indians resulted from their raids and depredations on the white settlers, destruction of relay and mail stations, and traumatization of parties of emigrants moving westward. Second, the dramatic nature of the controversy evolves from the way effective and ineffective leaders cope with the problem (122). Several kinds of leaders figured prominently in the Sand Creek spectacle; peaceful Indian advocates included Southern Cheyenne Chiefs Black Kettle and White Antelope and Southern Arapaho Chief Left Hand. Furthermore, the investigations scrutinized the military leadership of Colonel John Chivington, Colonel George L. Shoup, Major Scott S. Anthony, Major Edward W. Wynkoop, and Major Silas Soule. Congress also implicated Chivington's alleged collaborator, John Evans, the territorial governor. Third, spectacles take place in a setting in which authority figures have the power to transform history (122). For this reason, the U.S. Congress was an appropriate forum for making political judgments about the massacre of friendly Indians. They succeeded in making Sand Creek a black mark on the history of government-Indian relations. Fourth, from the vantage point of multiple interpreters, the discourse of the spectacle reveals moral solutions to complex problems (124). The moral judgments of the military leaders, congressional inquisitors, and political officials differed according to their ideological positions. Finally, spectacles identify the allies and adversaries within political conflicts; the Sand Creek massacre showcased the complex relationships between the territorial government and the militia, the military officers and the Indians, and Congress and territorial officials.

This political spectacle revealed several rhetorical features. One prominent feature was the use of condensation symbols to name the event (Edelman 1995, 22). The name "massacre" evoked negative feelings, signifying the event was an unprovoked and bloody attack on innocent victims. The investigating committees used "massacre" as a devil term. According to Kenneth Burke (1970), devil words are terms of repulsion; they are the "thou shalt nots" of society that portray great evil (20). By concluding a "massacre" of Indians had occurred, the committees elicited negative reactions from the public. However, a few sources sought vindication of

Colonel Chivington, the Colorado militia, and Governor Evans. For example, Reginald Craig ([1959] 1994) vehemently defended Chivington. He used the condensation symbol of "the fighting parson" to name the colonel and praise his military and religious achievements.

Once media reports infused "massacre" into the public conversation, this term repeatedly emerged through the testimony and in the opinions of congressmen. When public narratives establish a theme, Edelman (1995) explains, then other narrators create polemical stories based on this theme, featuring a clear set of heroes and villains (105), a designated enemy (88), a virtuous hero or heroine (76), and a plot resolving a problem (76). The subsequent analysis emphasizes the massacre theme as it evolved from the culture and treaties, the letters of Governor Evans, and the hearing testimony. In the spectacle, political arguers did not establish undisputed facts. Instead they rationalized divergent eyewitness accounts, presented polarized claims based on diverse ideological interests, and set the agenda for the values they wanted the public to consider in interpreting the events (Edelman 1995, 16).

CULTURAL CONTEXT

Ethnographic and historical documents situate this political spectacle in the cultural context of the Southern Cheyenne and Arapaho by highlighting social and political events that impacted on Indian life, explaining treaty commitments, and identifying military policies toward these Indians. Political spectacles place public problem solving on exhibit. An important part of any problem is its causes. One cause of Sand Creek was the incompatibility between the needs of Indian culture and the desire of the government to promote settlement. Cultural reasons for Sand Creek surfaced in the rhetoric of the spectacle when participants blamed the government officials for ignoring the social conditions of the Indians. Witnesses also described the horrors of Indian warfare and implicated government leaders for seeking personal political fortunes.

Cultural History

Some of the reasons for the conflict also evolved from the history of the Indians. The Southern Cheyenne and Arapaho lived together during most of the nineteenth century. Even though they shared common living areas, they had different ceremonies, dress, and traditions. Ethnologists (Kroeber 1955; Trenholm 1970; Grinnell [1923] 1972; Hoebel 1978) believe the two bands of Indians met in the Black Hills during the last part of the eighteenth century where they gathered berries, used dogs for transportation, and hunted antelope. After they acquired horses, they raided other tribes to get more horses, became skillful buffalo hunters, and used their horsemanship to become proficient warriors. During the early part of the nineteenth century, the Southern Cheyenne and Arapaho moved from their homes in present-day South Dakota to hunting grounds along the South Platte and Arkansas Rivers into the plains of Nebraska, Colorado, and Kansas. In their new hunting grounds, they gained easy access to buffalo herds and found additional opportunities for horse raiding in nearby New Mexico and Texas. After 1830, the Northern Cheyenne and Arapaho stayed north of the Platte River and only made occasional visits to their southern kin. Virginia Trenholm (1970) explains the close allegiance between the Southern Cheyenne and Arapaho was motivated by the Cheyenne's need of the Arapaho for war and the Arapaho's need of the Cheyenne for trade (33).

Both the Southern Cheyenne and Arapaho were buffalo hunters and warriors. In 1839, traders described the two groups as "subsisting entirely on buffalo" because they had limited guns and ammunition and relied on the bow and arrow for warfare. After they developed relationships with traders, they bartered robes for guns and ammunition (Trenholm 1970, 99). Buffalo hunting related to the success of warfare because the more abundant the buffalo kill, the more guns the Indians could procure from traders.

Just as with the Santee Sioux, the male culture of the Southern Cheyenne and Arapaho tribes revolved around warfare. George Bird Grinnell ([1915] 1985) argues that the men of the tribes fought for tribal approval and "the pure enjoyment of the struggle." For them, fighting and going to war was "a joy" evidenced by the way they took coups and then feasted and danced around the scalps of their victims (12–24). Prior to the westward migrations of white settlers, the enemies of the Southern Cheyenne and Arapaho were other Indians. The most radical of the warrior societies was the Dog Soldiers, a roving group composed primarily of Cheyenne, Arapaho, and Sioux. Even though warrior societies were prominent in the culture, prior to Sand Creek, a substantial number of Southern Cheyenne and Arapaho chiefs wanted peace and made repeated efforts to be friendly with whites.

Social and Political Events

Other causes of the war resulted from difficult living conditions. Starvation, emigration of settlers, and territorial politics preceded the war, creating conditions ripe for conflict between the government and the Indians. As early as 1853, Indian Agent Thomas Fitzpatrick reported that the Indians "are in abject want of food half of the year . . . their women are pinched with want and their children constantly crying with hunger" (Lavender 1954, 326). Starvation occurred because of the loss of the buffalo and onslaught of settlement. People from emigrant trains either killed the buffalo or scared them away (Lavender 1954, 288). The Indians themselves also shared partial responsibility for the lack of food because they depended on the diminishing resource of the buffalo and refused to farm.

The fatal blow to the Indians' resources came during the gold rush to Pikes Peak in 1859, resulting in 100,000 whites passing through the heart of Cheyenne and Arapaho hunting grounds (Hyde 1968, 107). Because the emigrants took the game and used up the cottonwood forests along the rivers, Indians suffered from a lack of food or fuel. By 1862, the number of settlers in the traditional Indian hunting grounds was ten times the number of Cheyenne and Arapaho, 30,000 whites to 3,000 Indians (Coel 1981, 162).

In addition to the starvation and emigration, the Sand Creek Massacre also resulted in part from the political struggle for Colorado statehood. Just prior to the massacre, Territorial Governor John Evans called for statehood, an astute political move that he hoped would aid his effort to become the first senator from the new state of Colorado (Hoig 1961, 55). At the same time, Colonel John Chivington, basking in the glory of his defeat of Confederate troops at Glorietta Pass in New Mexico territory, clamored for the position of the office of congressional delegate. Bob Scott (1994) argued that Evans' and Chivington's political alliances created for them "powerful enemies in the territory" (38).

As my subsequent analysis shows, the general causes identified here parallel those ascribed to the events by witnesses in the congressional hearings. These cultural causes give clues about why the Sand Creek Massacre occurred and preview some of the testimony of the witnesses.

WAR CORRESPONDENCE OF JOHN EVANS

The letters written by military leaders and government officials to one another were a main source of evidence in the hearings. Correspondence often constituted the only communication between military leaders, Indian agents, and government officials. For this reason, war correspondence provided a primary source of data about participants' attitudes, motives, and justifications. Although many leaders participated in this conflict, this chapter concentrates on the letters of John Evans that are reported in the War of Rebellion records and the transcripts of the investigative hearings. This sample correspondence indicates how Evans contributed to the political spectacle by urging the extermination and removal of Indians.

One way of examining the rhetorical content of the correspondence is to analyze it as a diverse set of political speech acts, including assertives, directives, commissives, and expressives. Even though Fran van Eemeren and Rob Grootendorst (1990) describe speech acts as part of general problem-solving discussions, my explanations here borrow their theoretical constructs and apply them to Evans' letters about the Indian problem. The evolution of Evans' speech acts points to the development of his arguments, beginning with assertives and directives about actions, moving to expressive pleas, and ending with commissive proclamations.

Assertive Speech Acts

Speech acts reveal Evans' personal perceptions and rhetorical constructions of political facts. He started his campaign against the Indians with assertions of fact in June 1864 and then moved to declarations of war at the time of the massacre in December 1864. Assertive acts express the rhetor's standpoint about an issue by establishing a conclusion, providing evidence for the facticity of that conclusion, and rebutting the standpoint of another (van Eemeren & Grootendorst 1990, 94). For this reason, political assertions of fact are not neutral. Instead political actors, such as Evans, reconstruct events to make them conform to the general beliefs of a target audience (Edelman 1977, 37). In matters concerning Sand Creek, Evans' primary audience consisted of federal military officials; territorial citizens composed his secondary audience.

In 1864, Evans' correspondence began with assertives about the threats posed by the Indians and statements about the corresponding need to exterminate or relocate them. On May 28, Evans wrote to General S. R. Curtis, head of the regional Department of War, stating that the Cheyenne were aligning themselves with the warlike factions of the Comanche, Kiowa, and noting that this alliance could only mean trouble for the citizens of Colorado. Evans asserted, "I feel confident that they will wipe out our sparse settlements in spite of any home force we could muster against them." He supported his assertion by claiming that even the traders say the Indians are revengeful. Then Evans refuted the orders of the War Department since it had refused to send additional federal troops (*War of Rebellion* 1880–1901, 35: 97–99). By connecting military needs to public fears, Evans' assertives helped him build a persuasive case for removing the Indians from the territory.

Directive Speech Acts

In contrast to assertives, directives defend a standpoint and issue guidelines for action based on that standpoint. In this way, directives take the form of orders and prohibitions, foreclose the possibility of alternate directives, and affirm the authority of the person issuing the directives (van Eemeren & Grootendorst 1990, 95). By June 28, Evans changed the speech acts in his letters from assertives to directives. This strategic change resulted from his perception that the territory was in crisis caused by the aggression of the Indians and the inaction of the federal government. At this time, Evans issued a directive to Major S. G. Colby, the military official in charge of the Fort Lyon agency:

You will immediately make necessary arrangements for the feeding and support of all the friendly Indians of the Cheyenne and Arapaho at Fort Lyon. . . . You will make a requisition on the military commander of the post for subsistence. . . . You can send word to all these to come as directed above, but do not allow the families of those at war to be introduced into the camp. ("Sand Creek Massacre" 1867, 60)

Directives, such as this one, had a twofold purpose. Evans demanded the military leadership listen to his cries for help, and he simultaneously demonstrated to the settlers that he was taking actions to protect them. Edelman (1977) emphasizes the point that "alarm about external or internal enemies . . . makes people eager for resolute action and willing to entrust wider powers to leaders so they can act effectively" (49). By showing the federal government that he was a forceful advocate for territorial citizens, Evans hoped to garner support for his recommendations.

Expressive Speech Acts

A third kind of speech act, an expressive, shows the feeling of the rhetor about the issues at hand. In some cases expressives divert attention from the problem and instead excite the audience's emotions. In other cases, expressives affirm the danger of the impending threat and inspire immediate and thorough action (van Eemeren & Grootendorst 1990, 95). One way that expressives gain political potency is by defining a problem as "a threat or emergency people must face together" in order to defeat the enemy through "unity and for common sacrifice" (Edelman 1977, 45).

For Evans, the stories about the death and mutilation of the Hungate family provided a persuasive emotional example of Indian "savagery" and a strong justification for him to take military action against the Southern Cheyenne and Arapaho who allegedly had committed this crime. On June 27, Evans' correspondence combined expressives with directives in his general letter to agents, interpreters, and traders. He told them that they must inform friendly Indians about the following:

[Indians] have attacked and killed soldiers and murdered peaceable citizens. For this, the Great Father is angry, and will certainly hunt them out and punish them; but he does not want to injure those who remain friendly to the whites. He desires to protect and take care of them. For this purpose I direct all friendly Indians to keep away from those who are at war, and go to places of safety. . . . The object of this [action] is to prevent friendly Indians from being killed through a mistake. ("Sand Creek Massacre" 1867, 61)

By telling the agents and traders what to say and do, Evans' directives mobilized them for action in the expected crisis.

Commissive Speech Acts

As the summer progressed, Evans addressed his desperate pleas to powerful federal officials. In this letter to Secretary of War John Stanton, Evans used commissive speech acts that adopted a strong protagonist role and defended a standpoint (van Eemeren & Grootendorst 1990, 95). Evans' politically persuasive commissives showed his strong commitment to subdue the Indians and also predicted doom unless the War Department agreed to his demands.

As the crisis developed, Evans used a variety of speech acts to make his argument. For example, his August letter began with assertives defining the perils of the situation followed by commissives showing his protagonist action. Evans wrote:

I am now satisfied that the tribes of the plains are nearly all combined in this terrible war, as apprehended last winter. It will be the largest Indian War this country ever had, extending from Texas to the British lines, involving nearly all the wild tribes of the plains. . . . Please bring all the force of your department to bear in favor of speedy reenforcement of our troops, and get me authority to raise a regiment of 100-days mounted men. Our militia law is inoperative, and unless this authority is given we will be destroyed. (*War of Rebellion* 1880–1901, 41: 753–54)

In this way, Evans used commissives to construct his role as a strong advocate for war against the Indians. This letter also indicated that Evans perceived himself to be the protector of the people. His political language not only described events, but he interpreted the meaning of the impending war with the Indians, providing evidence to both the public and the War Department that he had taken complete charge of the situation on behalf of the citizens of the territory.

Directive and Assertive Speech Acts

Evans' correspondence contained a complex combination of speech acts that asserted, defended, and justified his arguments for action against the Cheyenne and Arapaho. Evans believed the increasing number of Indian attacks combined with the lack of government response to his pleas were recipes for disaster. For him, the only viable alternative was for citizens to take up arms against the Indians. This reasoning informed Evans' proclamation of August 11 urging citizens to act against the Indians. This letter featured both assertive speech acts defining the Indians as enemies and directive speech acts recommending aggressive citizen action. Evans urged:

I, John Evans, governor of Colorado Territory, do issue this my proclamation, authorizing all citizens of Colorado, either individually or in such parties as they may organize, to go in pursuit of all hostile Indians on the plains, scrupulously avoiding those who have responded to my said call . . . to kill and destroy, as enemies of the country, wherever they may be found, all such hostile Indians. And further, as the only reward I am authorized to offer for such services, I hereby empower such citizens . . . to take captives, and hold . . . [for] private use and benefit, all the property of said hostile Indians that they may capture, and to receive for all stolen property recovered from said Indians such reward as maybe deemed proper and just therefore. ("Sand Creek Massacre" 1867, 47)

This letter certified Evans' authority to make Indian policy, fulfilled his need to vilify the Indians as hostile enemies, and demonstrated his political right to empower settlers to take captives, steal, and sell Indian property. This proclamation's formal political language resembled the style and tone of a military order. The certitude of this proclamation obligated the public to act according to Evans' demands.

Even though Evans had mobilized the citizens of Colorado, he had not yet persuaded the federal government about the compelling nature of the crisis. To add persuasive potency to his earlier pleas, Evans issued another letter to Secretary of War John Stanton, using expressive speech acts to emphasize the situation was a crisis. Evans pleaded, "We are in danger both from attacks of Indians and from starvation. . . . It is impossible to exaggerate our danger. We are doing everything possible for our defense" (*War of Rebellion* 1880–1901, 51: 694). Evans accomplished this goal by creating public anxiety about the impending crisis using assertives, demanding the attention of the War Department using directives, and showing his recommended actions would dispel the anxiety and protect citizens from the Indians using commissives.

This small sample of the governor's correspondence illustrates how his perceptions of the Southern Cheyenne and Arapaho prior to the battle at Sand Creek created a public hysteria about the impending war with the Indians. In other episodes discussed in this volume, regional leaders also made emotional pleas to federal military agencies for assistance in their battles with Indians. In ways similar to Evans' war correspondence, letters from Governor Isaac Stevens in Washington territory (Richards [1979] 1993), Governor Alexander Ramsey in Minnesota (Roddis 1956), and Governor Abraham Rencher in New Mexico (Chapter 4) went unanswered. For this reason all of these men encouraged the citizen militias of their territory to take up arms against the Indians.

ANALYSIS OF THE POLITICAL SPECTACLE

The record of the political spectacle of Sand Creek appears in the minutes of the treaty councils and the testimony given during the congressional hearings. Together these texts reveal the intricacies of the spectacle and the polemical quality of the argumentative discourse it promoted.

Treaties

By focusing the attention of the government and Indians on land issues, the treaties contributed to the political spectacle. The treaties also identified the issues and established the rules for how the government should respond to the Cheyenne and Arapaho and how the Indians should relate to the government. As Chapters 1 and 2 explain, treaties promoted a few mutual benefits for the signatories. The Southern Cheyenne and Arapaho made treaties to secure food for their hungry people and to protect their families from settlers. In contrast the government gained land from the Indians and paved the way for development. Additionally, treaty rhetoric promised annuities and safety if the Indians agreed to act in accordance with federal demands and, in return, the Indians promised to honor their commitments with the government. Unfortunately, neither side kept their promises.

Just as in other political spectacles of the Indian wars, Cheyenne and Arapaho treaties addressed problems by identifying who the virtuous parties were and by delineating which Indians would be rewarded and punished. Moreover, these treaties specified power relationships, determining what parties held legitimate authority and which ones had to submit to this authority.

Two treaties gave the federal government the political authority over the hunting and camping grounds of the Southern Cheyenne and Arapaho. The first, the Treaty of Fort Laramie (1851), attempted to make peace with all of the Plains Indians located south of the Missouri and east of the Rocky Mountains (Institute for the Development of Indian Law 1974, 38–44). The goal was for the Indians to "maintain peaceful relations among themselves" and to develop "good faith and friendship" with the federal government. This treaty directed the Indians to make restitution for the wrongs they had committed and identified boundaries of land on which the tribes should be located. Additionally, the treaty forced the Southern Cheyenne and Arapaho to live between the north fork of the Platte and Arkansas Rivers, awarded them $50,000 in annuities (Article 7), and restricted the various bands to designated camping and hunting grounds in an attempt to prohibit intertribal warfare (Article 5).

This treaty initiated the political spectacle by staging an event that guaranteed federal authority over the Plains Indians in exchange for relocation and material goods. In this way, the language of the political treaty discourse "constructs a problem" and gives "a rationale for vesting authority in people who claim some kind of competence" (Edelman 1995, 20). The treaty authorized the government to deal with the Indian problem and also invested the Southern Cheyenne and Arapaho peace chiefs with authority to make decisions on behalf of their tribes.

Instead of providing a viable solution, the Treaty of Fort Laramie exacerbated the problem, permitting the massive immigration of gold seekers and land developers. As a result, the government negotiated another agreement, the Treaty of Fort Wise in 1861 (later called the Treaty of Fort Lyon). This treaty exerted even more authority over the Cheyenne and Arapaho and dictated the type of life the government expected the Indians to adopt (Kappler 1904, I: 807–11). The treaty gave the Indians a fraction of the land that they had received under the 1851 Fort Laramie Treaty. It also assigned forty acres to each tribal member and demanded all able-bodied Indians become farmers (Article 2), placed all land allocation under the authority of the secretary of the interior, and awarded annuities of livestock, agricultural tools, and machinery to signatories (Article 5). The treaty further stipulated that if the tribes were unsuccessful in agricultural enterprises, then they would have to live solely on the annuities promised them under former treaties (Article 8). After a year of drought, the treaty proved unworkable for the Indians and so their subsequent dependence on the government for subsistence increased. For example, the Indians threatened the officers at Fort Wise with violence if they did not receive some food and annuities. This threat led Captain Elmer Otis to give them enough food to quiet them down (*Annual Report of the Commissioner of Indian Affairs* 1861, 709).

In ways similar to the Medicine Creek Treaty of 1854 and the Santee Sioux treaties of 1851 and 1858, this treaty awarded little to the Indians and severely limited their land and food-gathering resources. Although the government designed the treaties to solve the problems with the Southern Cheyenne and Arapaho, this solution never succeeded because the peace chiefs signing the treaty could not convince the Dog Soldiers to cease warfare against settlers. As a result the government lost its authority with the Indians; however, at the same time, it acquired respect from settlers. Edelman (1995) explains that groups create authority when they show they are able to cope with problems and lose this authority when these coping strategies fail (20). The Treaty of Fort Wise persuaded settlers that the government would force the Indians into outlying areas and restrict their interactions with citizens, but it did nothing to convince hostile Indians to cease attacks upon settlers and their property.

Congressional Investigations

Congressional investigations resemble legal proceedings in that appointed adjudicators hear evidence from many witnesses and then render an official judgment about what the evidence means. But investigations also differ significantly from legal proceedings because they produce political and symbolic proclamations rather than impose legal penalties. This section of the chapter analyzes the rhetorical content and political effect of one of the congressional inquiries about Sand Creek.

During congressional hearings, witnesses provide evidence through a questioning process resembling fact finding in a court of law, in which leading questions call for narrative responses. One of the justifications for holding hearings of this type is to build a record. Richard Reike and Malcom Sillars (1984) explain that the hearing format implies that committee members are gathering evidence, but they usually are just verifying the evidence they already have (240). A second justification is symbolic. The politically initiated ritualist forums result in little change, but they successfully show the public that elected officials are concerned about problems (Edelman 1977, 124).

In 1865, Congress held hearings to prove to the public they were concerned about the unjustified killing of friendly Indians at Sand Creek. The hearings served the political function of symbolic reassurance; that is, Congress showed the public they were concerned about Sand Creek and wanted to deal fairly with this problem. The goal of reassurance is to convince the public that political leaders are solving a complex problem (Edelman [1964] 1980, 39–40).

This segment of the chapter examines one of the hearings conducted by The Committee on the Conduct of War in the House of Representatives that resulted in the published document, "Massacre of Cheyenne Indians" (1864–1865). Subsequent citations to this document appear only as page references. The stated purpose of this investigation was "to enquire into and report all the facts connected with the late attack by the Third Regiment of Colorado Volunteers under Colonel Chivington on a village of the Cheyenne tribe of Indians, near Fort Lyon" (i). The committee took testimony between March 13 and 16 and also considered letters, documents, and written depositions from persons involved with the battle at Sand Creek. An analysis of the rhetorical features of this hearing follows.

In order to provide reassurance, political spectacles simplify issues (Edelman [1964] 1980, 40). The testimony presented in "Massacre of Cheyenne Indians" simplified three issues: the nature of the warfare, the agreements made between Governor Evans and the Indians at Fort Weld, and the role of Colonel John Chivington in the massacre. The congressmen serving on the Committee for the Conduct of War conducted the examination of witnesses and wrote the report of findings. The record does not specify which committee members asked the questions. No cross examination occurred.

This congressional report provides a unique example of how political leaders reconstruct facts in order to persuade the public to accept a political interpretation and to "live with the decision" rendered by official adjudicators (Edelman 1977, 38). In this case, the congressmen made their decision by promoting political argumentation under the guise of legal rigor. The testimony consisted of a coached narrative response that described events, defined the enemy, attributed responsibility, and criticized the actions of responsible parties. As an example of political argument, the hearing discerned "reasons for a course of action" and also interpreted the consequences of the actions in line with the public interest (Cox 1981, 126).

The Committee on the Conduct of War used long sequences of questions to reconstruct the understandings and motivations of several principal actors in the Sand Creek controversy—Governor John Evans, Colonel John Chivington, Major Edward Wynkoop, and the Southern Cheyenne and Arapaho peace chiefs. The questioning process resembled that of a direct examination during a trial because committee members asked leading questions. In this case, the congressmen asked the witnesses about the scene, circumstances in which the military killed friendly Indians, and the principal sources of responsibility. The quasi-legal procedures gave the public the impression that the politicians were prosecutors getting evidence to convict Chivington.

An example of this kind of questioning appeared in the congressmen's examination of John Smith, an interpreter who had resided in an Indian lodge with the southern Cheyenne and Arapaho on the day of the attack. The purpose of the questioning was to get the witness to describe the attack and to recollect conversations he had after the battle:

Q: Do you know whether or not Colonel Chivington knew the friendly character of these Indians before he made the attack upon them?

A: It is my opinion that he did.

Q: On what is your opinion based?

A: On this fact, that he stopped all persons from going on ahead of him. He stopped the mail and would not allow any person to go on ahead of him at the time he was on his way from Denver City to Fort Lyon. He placed a guard around Colonel [William] Bent, the old former agent there; he stopped Mr. Hagues and many men who were on their way to Fort Lyon. He took the fort by surprise, and as soon as he got there he posted pickets all around the fort, and then left at 8 o'clock that night for his Indian camp. (8)

This excerpt shows how the members of the committee coached Smith, and by doing so, helped him to characterize Chivington as an enemy. People construct enemies by associating them with negative traits (Edelman 1995, 68). Smith constructed Chivington as an enemy by indicating he was secretive, saying he plotted to kill the Indians, and noting he tried to prevent external witnesses from observing his despicable deeds.

The subsequent testimony described the battle scene that implicated Chivington in the massacre:

Q: When did you talk with him?

A: On the day of the attack. He asked me many questions about the chiefs who were there and if I could recognize them if I saw them. I told him it was possible I might recollect the principal chiefs. . . . They were so badly mutilated and covered with sand and water that it was very hard for me to tell one from another. However, I recognized some of them—among them the Chief One Eye, who was employed by our government at $125 a month and rations to remain in the village as a spy. There was another called War Bonnet, who stayed here two years ago with me. There was another by the name of Standing Water, and I supposed Black Kettle was among them, but it was not Black Kettle. . . .

Q: Did you tell Colonel Chivington the character and disposition of these Indians at any time during your interviews on this day?

A: Yes, sir.

Q: What did he say in reply?

A: He said he could not help it that his orders were positive to attack the Indians.

Q: From whom did he receive the orders?

A: I do not know; I presume from General Curtis. (8)

In addition to defining the situation and placing Chivington at the scene of the massacre, Smith validated the hearing committee's own presumptions that the colonel was guilty of killing friendly Indians and had refused to take responsibility for this evil act.

The following excerpt extends Smith's narrative by encouraging him to criticize the tactics of Chivington and his soldiers. Words such as "barbarity," "mutilation," "scalping," and "knocking out brains" created a set of horrifying images that elaborated the meaning of the word "massacre" for the investigating committee. Smith responded in this way:

Q: Were there any acts of barbarity perpetrated there that came under your own observation?

A: Yes, sir. I saw the bodies of those lying there cut all to pieces, worse mutilated than any I ever saw before, the women [were] cut all to pieces. . . .

Q: How cut?

A: With knives, scalped, their brains knocked out; children two or three months old, all ages lying there, from sucking infants up to warriors.

Q: Did you see it done?

A: Yes, sir. I saw them fall. . . .

Q: Did you see them mutilated?

A: Yes, sir.

Q: By whom were they mutilated?

A: By the United States troops. (9)

This testimony exemplified political argumentation that projects the assumptions of the federal officials into words and sentences that evoke a belief that a person is evil or harmful (Edelman 1995, 106). In this case, the congressmen coached the witness to repeat the terms of vilification that appeared in their questions. As a result, the witness reported that Chivington's militia targeted friendly Indians, killed women and children, and attacked them in a brutal manner violating the norms for the conduct of war. Other testimony showed that Chivington observed these atrocities and gave his tacit approval.

A second example of political argument reveals how the investigators assisted witnesses to identify Chivington as responsible for unacceptable conduct of war. The purpose of this questioning was to persuade the public that the colonel had evil motives. Dexter Colley, son of Indian agent Samuel G. Colley and a trader with the Cheyenne and Arapaho, attributed responsibility to Chivington in this segment of testimony:

Q: Do you know whether Colonel Chivington was informed of this arrangement (that Cheyenne and Arapahos were at Fort Lyon as prisoners of war under the protection of the government)?

A: I know that he was.

Q: How do you know that?

A: Because the Indian agent told me he had informed him. . . . When he came down there to make the attack he was told that the Indians were out there under promise of protection. They had been at the post until a short time before, when they had moved out on the Big Sandy at the request of Major Anthony. . . .

Q: Do you know what induced Colonel Chivington to attack these Indians?

A: I do not know; I have an opinion. . . .

Q: I have thought for more than a year that he was determined to have a war with these Indians. That has been the general belief of men in our part of the country. I was acquainted with all the chiefs who were there, and I know they had all tried hard to keep peace between the Indians and whites. . . . All the chiefs who were killed by Colonel Chivington have labored as hard as men could to keep peace between the whites and the Indians. (15)

This testimony extended the political argument even further. Not only was Chivington the enemy, he was responsible for ruthless conduct of war because he had a sinister plan to kill peaceful Indians. Through the process of naming Chivington's bad acts and associating his behavior with that of the hostile Indians, the congressmen added emotional connotations to their conclusion that Chivington committed war crimes.

Additional witnesses, including Major Scott Anthony, Indian Agent Samuel Colley, and Major Edward Wynkoop, also attributed responsibility to Chivington for the massacre of Indians.

Although no full-blooded Cheyenne and Arapaho testified in person before Congress, their rhetoric became evidence in the hearing through the
records of the treaty council minutes. Part of the hearing record was the
transcript of the Fort Weld Council, featuring negotiations between Governor Evans and friendly chiefs. At this council, held shortly before the
attack at Sand Creek, prominent Indian peace leaders begged the government for protection. Evans reluctantly granted them their wish. At this
council, the chiefs emphasized their desire to be peaceful in eloquent pleas
to Evans and other officials assembled at Fort Weld, Colorado.

One prominent peace chief, Black Kettle, emphasized the god term of
"peace." Kenneth Burke ([1950] 1969) notes that god terms have persuasive power because they point to goodness and subsume all other positive
terms. Moreover, god terms carry the blessings of the people who use them
as well as provide motives for cultural actions (183–89). Black Kettle's
pleas opened the council in this way:

All we ask is that we may have peace with the whites. We want to hold you by
the hand. You are our father. We have been traveling through a cloud. The day
has been dark ever since the war began. These braves who are with me are willing
to do what I say. We want to take good tidings home to our people that they may
sleep in peace. I want you to give all those chiefs of the soldiers here to understand
that we are for peace, and that we have made peace, that we may not be mistaken
by them for enemies. I have not come here with a little wolf bark, but have come
to talk plain with you. We must live near the buffalo or starve. (87)

Black Kettle's god term associated peace with the positive imagery of holding one's hand and sharing good tidings, and he contrasted his desire for
peace with the evil terms of enemies and darkness.

Despite this eloquent rhetorical plea, Evans remained unconvinced about
Black Kettle's integrity and continued to interrogate the other peace chiefs.
One such exchange occurred between the governor and Cheyenne Chief
White Antelope. Evans warned, "You understand that if you are at peace
with us, it is necessary to keep away from our enemies." To this White
Antelope responded,

I understand every word you have said, and will hold on to it. I will give you an
answer directly. The Cheyenne have their eyes wide open this way, and they will
hear what you say. He is proud to have seen the chief of all the whites in this
country. He will tell his people. (88)

Evans explained that his condition for peace was that the chiefs take their
people to a fort under the protection of the military. He emphasized that
the chiefs must not make peace with him but "with the soldiers" (89).
White Antelope agreed. Arapaho Chief Neva echoed the views of Arapaho
Chief Left Hand, saying "I know the value of the presents which we receive

from Washington; we cannot live without them. That is why I try so hard to keep peace with the whites" (90). Both White Antelope and Neva expressed their gratitude to Evans and their dependence on him for sustenance.

This record clearly showed that the attending chiefs wanted peace and were willing to submit to military protection to secure it. What must have been disconcerting to Chivington was that White Antelope and Left Hand, through the treaty minutes, spoke from their graves since both men had been killed and mutilated at Sand Creek. The retrospective words of the chiefs likely persuaded congressmen since their final report concluded:

All the testimony goes to show that the Indians, under the immediate control of Black Kettle and White Antelope of the Cheyennes, and Left Hand of the Arapahoes [sic], were and had been friends to the whites. . . . The Indians . . . placed themselves under the protection of Major Wynkoop. They were led to believe that they were regarded . . . [as] friendly Indians, and would be treated as such. (ii)

Although Colonel Chivington did not attend the hearing, he testified through an interrogative, a series of questions he answered in a written document. Even though he was not present, he knew about the charges against him from newspaper reports. However, Chivington still lacked specific information about others' testimony, and as a result, his responses contradicted some of what others had said. The multiquestion interrogatory called for specific information, but allowed for a narrative response. The commission asked seventeen different questions. The following two sample questions permitted Chivington to refute the charge that he attacked friendly Indians:

What reason had you for making the attack? What reasons, if any, had you to believe that Black Kettle or any other Indian or Indians in the camp entertained feelings of hostility toward the whites? Give in detail the names of all the Indians so believed to be hostile, with the dates and places of their hostile acts, so far as you may be able to do so. (101)

Chivington carefully adopted political strategies to defend himself against his accusers. Instead of answering the questions directly, his interrogatory adopted what Vernon Jensen (1981) calls "pseudo-reasons," arguments that at first glance seem rational but in fact are "diversionary maneuvers" that substitute for sound reasons (185). To avoid the accusations against him, Chivington shifted the argument so that he vilified the Southern Cheyenne and Arapaho.

In the first part of the defense, he shifted from the charges against him to a countercharge against the Indians. This maneuver sidestepped the original charge and diverted the attention of the audience to someone else (Jensen 1981, 186). The colonel associated the Indians camped at Sand Creek with acts of warfare against whites, implying "they are bad people who deserved to be killed." Chivington's underlying assumption was that the rights of settlers took precedence over the rights of Indians. He justified the attack by saying:

My reason for making the attack on the Indian camp was, that I believed the Indians in the camp were hostile to whites. That they were of the same tribes with those who had murdered many persons and destroyed much valuable property on the Platte and Arkansas Rivers during the previous spring, summer, and fall was beyond a doubt. (104)

He continued his defense shifting "between parts and the whole" (Jensen 1981, 187–88). Using this maneuver, Chivington argued that what is true of Indians in general is also true of the Southern Cheyenne and Arapaho. This "fallacy of composition" implies that what is good for most Indians, is also good for those camped at Sand Creek. By using this maneuver, Chivington ignored the differences between friendly and hostile Indians. Chivington reasoned:

When a tribe of Indians is at war with the whites it is impossible to determine what party or band of the tribe or the name of the Indian or Indians belonging to the tribe so at war are guilty of the acts of hostility. The most that can be ascertained is that Indians of the tribe have performed the acts. (104)

Later, the interrogatory "shifted ground inappropriately," and in doing so, Chivington tried to divert the focus from the original argument to a "more easily defended assertion" (Jensen 1981, 185–86). The colonel used this maneuver when he implied "the Indians plotted together to destroy settlers and the territorial infrastructure." He claimed:

During the spring, summer, and fall of the year 1864, the Arapaho and Cheyenne Indians, in some instances assisted or led on by Sioux, Kiowas, Comanches and Apaches, had committed many acts of hostility in the country lying between the Little Blue and the Rocky [M]ountains and the Platte and Arkansas Rivers. They had murdered many of the whites and taken others prisoners, and had destroyed valuable property, probably amounting to $200,000 and $300,000. . . . I have every reason to believe that these Indians were directly or indirectly concerned in the outrages which had been committed upon the whites. (104)

His fourth maneuver was to shift from the issue of killing innocent Indians to making personal attacks on the Indian victims, a maneuver called an *ad hominem* attack (Jensen 1981, 186–87). His defense implied that the Indians "were not very good people anyway." Specifically, Chivington adopted a satirical tone by claiming Indians had a reputation as liars and womanizers. He remarked, "[The] character of Indians in the western country for truth and veracity, like their respect for the chastity of women who may become prisoners in their hands, is not of that order which is calculated to inspire confidence in what they may say" (104).

Chivington's fifth maneuver was "an inappropriate appeal to authority" (Jensen 1981, 179). He claimed that military officials, Major Scott Anthony and Indian Agent Samuel Colley, would corroborate his testimony. In doing so, Chivington implied "what I am saying is the same thing as other important officials say." Unfortunately for Chivington, this information was not corroborated by either of the people he named. Nonetheless, Chivington concluded he "was supported by Major Anthony . . . and Samuel Colley . . . who have been in communication with these Indians, were more competent to judge their disposition toward the whites than myself. Previous to the battle, they expressed to me the opinion that the Indians should be punished" (104).

The remainder of Chivington's defense exemplified "shifting the burden of proof"(Jensen 1981, 185); that is, he challenged the congressional investigators to prove that the Indians did not commit atrocities rather than obviating himself from guilt. Chivington charged the Indians with acts of atrocity, claiming that "scalps are a sign of warfare." He ended his defense by reporting:

We found in camp the scalps of nineteen white persons. One of the surgeons informed me that one of these scalps had been taken from the victim's head not more than four days previously. I can furnish a child captured at the camp ornamented with six white women's scalps; these scalps must have been taken by Indians or furnished to them for their gratification and amusement by some of their brethren, who, like themselves, were in amity with whites. (104)

Chivington continued to try to force the congressmen to prove the innocence of the Indians in subsequent segments of his interrogatory. For example, when asked specific questions about the battle, Chivington argued the Indians were heavily armed, that five or six hundred Indians were killed, few women or children killed, and no known scalping by soldiers took place. His attempt to shift the burden of proof failed because other witnesses contradicted his conclusions about the Indians camped at Sand Creek. Since Chivington could call no witnesses to verify his testimony, his evidence turned into unpersuasive pseudoreasons. The congressmen's conclusions showed they recognized that Chivington was not providing a legitimate argumentative defense of his leadership during the battle at Sand Creek. However, this type of pseudoreasoning likely persuaded Chivington's allies to justify his actions by vilifying all Plains Indians (Craig [1959] 1994, 210–17).

The final report showed that the investigating commission was not persuaded by Chivington. Furthermore, this report exemplified several features typical of the potent symbolic effects that political officials gain when they publicly deal with a moral problem. The committee report constructed Chivington as its political enemy. This strategy is politically effective because blaming a vulnerable person "for the sufferings and guilt people experience in their daily lives is emotionally gratifying and politically popular." This type of political condemnation "makes it psychologically and ethically possible to hurt or kill" the person being vilified (Edelman 1995, 88–89).

The congressional report tried to symbolically destroy Chivington by maligning his character as a public figure in this way:

It is difficult to believe that beings in the form of men, and disgracing the uniform of the United States soldiers and officers, could commit or countenance the commission of such acts of cruelty and barbarity as are detailed in the testimony. . . . As to Colonel Chivington, our committee can hardly find fitting terms to describe his conduct. (iv)

This vitriolic attack on Chivington by the committee resembles a standard way that political actors construct enemies in spectacles. Typically, officials gain political collateral when they assign to an already weak person "evil traits, intentions, and actions" (Edelman 1995, 87). This excerpt attributed a variety of evil qualities to Chivington:

Wearing the uniform of the United States, which should be the emblem of justice and humanity, holding the important position of commander of a military district, and therefore having the honor of the government to that extent in his keeping, he deliberately planned and executed a foul and dastardly massacre which would have disgraced the veriest [*sic*] savages among those who were victims of the cruelty. (v)

Instead of considering the evidence presented by Chivington, the congressional investigators highlighted information that reinforced public opinion in order to support what they understood to be the dominant ideology of their constituents (Edelman 1995, 120–21). The report affirmed public opinions formed before the hearing ever took place. They reasoned:

Having full knowledge of their friendly character, having himself been instrumental to the extent in placing them in their position of fancied security, he took advantage of their apprehensions and defenseless condition to gratify the worst passion that ever cursed the heart of man. (v)

Additionally, the report highlighted the political tensions and allegiances between the Congress and the military, the military and the Indians, and Congress and territorial leaders. The report asserted political authority over territorial military leaders by judging Chivington in this way:

It is thought by some that desire for political preferment promoted him to this cowardly act; that he supposed that by pandering the inflamed passion of an excited population he could recommend himself to their regard and consideration [for political office]. . . . Whatever may have been his motive, it is to be hoped that the authority of this government will never again be disgraced by acts such as he and those acting with him have been guilty of committing. (v)

The congressmen could do little to punish Chivington except to attack his character and tarnish his military record since his military commission had ended prior to the time of the hearing. Additionally, the national press vilified him and Congress named his actions "a massacre." The moral outrage expressed in the opinion supposedly resulted in Congress paying reparations to some Indian widows and orphans (Scott 1994, 214).

The congressional hearing created a political spectacle by defining the moral problem of killing friendly Indians at Sand Creek, producing emotional public political argumentation about the event, and appeasing the public demand for punitive action against the perpetrators of Sand Creek. Even today, the "Massacre of Cheyenne Indians" (1864–1865) continues to be an important document for assessing the role of the military in the Indian wars and for interpreting the history of the Southern Cheyenne and Apapaho.

IMPACT

This chapter shows how the political spectacle of Sand Creek grew out of cultural conflicts, reveals Governor Evans' perceptions of the Indians' threat to settlements, notes the controversial content of the treaties, and describes the inflamed public opinion about the event. The Sand Creek spectacle culminated in a congressional hearing that vilified Chivington as a military leader.

Rhetorical Impact

The chapter identifies the relevance of the rhetoric of Governor Evans, the treaty makers, the peaceful chiefs, military leaders and soldiers, and congressmen. The chapter explains how the conflict evolved and how some rhetors tried to resolve it. The letters of Evans showed his commitments to control the Indians and protect the settlers. To suppress the Indian threat, Evans formed a citizen militia under the direction of his political ally, John Chivington. The provisions of the treaties further contributed to the Indian problem and eventuated the Colorado militia's attack on friendly Indians. The testimony presented to the congressional investigating committees made public the animosity between various territorial, military, and congressional factions. Moreover, the hearing's final report demonstrated Congress' inability to punish those who do not submit to federal authority. All of these rhetorical processes combined to create a political spectacle embodying diverse problem-solving strategies. The lasting rhetorical legacy of the episode was the definition of the event as a massacre; and the lasting political legacy was the government's publicly expressed distrust of territorial officials and militia.

What is unique about Sand Creek is that the federal government believed the Indians and their allies and disbelieved the territorial government and some of its military leaders. The chapter showed how the hearings used rhetorical strategies to frame the public perceptions about Sand Creek. The quasilegal forum of the congressional hearing gave the public the impression that the government could vilify people they found responsible for immoral actions. By characterizing this military action as "a massacre," the hearing established a phrase which placed a lasting moral judgment on the event. Congressional members were the immediate audience for the hearings; and the general public, the citizens of Colorado territory, and the citizen militia constituted an important secondary audience. The emotional consensus by many audiences then and even now was that Colonel Chivington was responsible for killing innocent Indians. These findings created a wake-up call for other military leaders on the frontier who felt killing Indians was almost always justified.

Political Impact

The chapter noted the impotence of the efforts of territorial leaders in solving the Indian problem. Although Evans did everything in his power to build an image of Colorado as a progressive western territory, Indian wars and rumors of wars impeded his effort to gain statehood. Treaties made by the federal government created rather than resolved the Indian problem. Starvation and dependency upon the government precluded Indians from peacefully removing themselves to remote reservations. The government's failure to quiet the Southern Cheyenne and Arapaho posed a significant problem because it forced federal officials to admit that Indian warfare was beyond their control. As Chapter 7 shows, these Indians did not go speedily or quietly to their assigned reservation in Oklahoma. Instead they resisted until late in the nineteenth century.

The investigation of Sand Creek established some standards for appropriate conduct, concluding the military lacked the authority to kill friendly Indians and innocent women and children, to confiscate the property of these Indians and then sell it for private gain, and to capture Indians and hold them as prisoners. However, the records of Navajo wars in New Mexico (Chapter 4) and the continuing Sioux wars north of the Platte River (Chapters 5 and 11) show little evidence that congressional investigations had substantial subsequent impact on the actions of the other military leaders fighting Indians.

At the time of these investigations, the symbolism associated with Sand Creek succeeded better at defining issues and shaping emotional attitudes than it did at changing the behavior of the Indians or the military. Additionally, the hearings damaged Colonel Chivington's prestige, took away the fame he gained by his Civil War victory at Glorietta, and tainted the reputation of Governor Evans. Even though the Congress vilified several state leaders, it never implicated General S. R. Curtis, a Department of War official who approved of Chivington's attack. Conflicts between the military and territorial officials existed in many of the Indian war episodes in this volume, a fact that complicated an effective resolution to the Indian wars.

Impact on the Military

The military did not seem to learn from the incident. For example, Colonel George Armstrong Custer in 1868, four years to the day after Sand Creek, attacked and killed the great Southern Cheyenne Chief Black Kettle and members of his band of friendly Indians at Washita in Oklahoma. Some witnesses had identified Black Kettle among the dead at Sand Creek, but later they realized he was still alive. Moreover, the military lacked control over the dissident Cheyenne Dog Soldiers, a group that continued to make war against the settlers on the northern plains. Long after the congressional investigation, judges adopted the historical symbolism of "massacre" to explain the warfare at Sand Creek.

Cultural Impact

Although the hearings about Sand Creek vilified some military officials and evoked sympathy for its Indian victims, this temporary change was short lived because the Southern Cheyenne and Arapaho, angered by Sand Creek, joined the warring Dog Soldiers north of the Platte and the Teton Sioux in a series of attacks against settlers and the territorial government. Together they destroyed stage and postal stations, stole supplies and livestock, took captives, and killed settlers (Lavender 1954, 119; Hyde 1967, 172–96; Grinnell [1915] 1985, 150–80). But the government did not force the Indians to abide by the treaties until after 1870 when the Southern Cheyenne and Arapaho finally settled on a reservation in western Oklahoma (Chapter 7).

After the massacre, the bodies of those at Sand Creek lay unburied for weeks. In 1867, army surgeons finally collected body parts to study the effects of gunshot wounds. They cut off the heads of the Sand Creek victims and shipped them to the Army medical museum in Washington, D.C. Between 1897 and 1907, the remains were transferred to the Smithsonian collections to join 4,000 other body parts from the Indian wars. In the early 1990s, the Smithsonian contacted the Cheyenne to see if they wanted the remains of their ancestors returned (Mendoza 1993, 166). In November 2000, Congress passed legislation to make the site of the Sand Creek Massacre into a national monument ("Colorado Indian Massacre Location to Become a National Historic Site," 2000, November 12).

Economic Impact

In the long run, the government and the settlers reaped few economic rewards from the aftermath of Sand Creek. Immediately following the investigations, federal troops adopted policies that escalated the hostilities. For example, after Indian raiders pillaged government supplies, the military retaliated by setting fires that burned range land and timber extending from the Platte River in present day Nebraska to the northern border of Texas. The fires created havoc on the environment by eliminating the vegetation and scattering and killing the game (Andrist 1964, 92).

Between 1865 and 1868, the government used 8,000 troops, the Indians killed dozens of settlers and over 100 soldiers, and the government spent $30 million amounting to about $1 million for every Indian they killed (Andrist 1964, 95). Although the war with Plains Indians was extremely costly in money and human lives, the government eventually succeeded in pushing Indians out of the territory and making room for settlements on the traditional Southern Cheyenne and Arapaho hunting grounds in present day Colorado and Kansas. The removal of the Indians allowed for development of ranching, mining, and lumber. Chapter 7 continues a focus on the Southern Cheyenne and Arapaho by examining the tribe's successful appeal to the Indian Claims Commission in 1961. At that time, the government paid the Indians for lands given up in the Treaty of Fort Laramie (1851) and the Treaty of Fort Wise (1861).

Even though all of the Indian wars had a spectacle quality to them, it was Sand Creek that created the most elaborate political spectacle. For this reason, it is rare for any book on government-Indian relations to ignore this episode or to underplay the significance of the massacre at Sand Creek and its political aftermath.

NOTE

1. This chapter spells "Arapaho" without an "e" on the end. Even though some sources spell the name of the tribe "Arapahoe," this chapter adopts the standard spelling used in political and legal documents regarding the tribe.

Chapter 4

Colonial Discourse and the Navajo Internment, 1846–1868

The Navajo wars began before the outbreak in the Puget Sound and raged in vast regions stretching from Utah into Mexico, involved thousands of Navajos and their Indian adversaries, took place in rough desert terrain, and continued for nearly a quarter of a century. The story of these wars provides a case study of how the rhetoric of government officials resulted in the forced relocation of thousands of Navajos. Under the orders of General James Carleton, the Indians walked hundreds of miles to an internment at Bosque Redondo located near Fort Sumner in present day New Mexico. Because the long walk in 1864 took place in the middle of winter and led to the deaths of hundreds of Navajos and to the temporary conquest of the Navajos, the event shows the consequences of harsh colonial policies. Despite the differences, the Navajo, Nisqually, Santee Sioux, and Southern Cheyenne and Arapaho shared a common fate; they were eventually colonized by the American government.

The colonial relationship between the United States and the Indians resulted from the government's ability to take control of Indian land and subjugate native people to its form of government. In its simplest sense, colonialism refers to a government policy of extending territory and designating control of property; it is the "conquest and direct control of other people's land resulting from a desire to impose capitalism" (Williams & Chrisman 1994, 3). In addition to the taking of land, David Spurr (1993) explains that colonization is an act of imperialism whereby an outside power, the colonizer, establishes domination over another culture, the colonized, that is racially different from its own (6).

The most prominent feature of the colonization during the Indian wars occurred when General James Carleton rounded up 7,000 Navajos and forced them to walk more than 200 miles to an internment center called Bosque Redondo near Fort Sumner in New Mexico territory. General Carleton expressed his satisfaction with his accomplishment in a letter to the superintendent of Indian affairs on March 5, 1964. He bragged, "By the subjugation and colonization of the Navajo tribe, we gain for civilization their whole country, which is much larger in extent than the state of Ohio; and besides being by far the best pastoral region between the two oceans, is said to abound in precious as well as useful metals" (Keleher 1952, 370).

The process of Navajo colonization took more than twenty years. The first rhetorical action to colonize the Navajos took place on August 19, 1846, when General Stephen Kearny told Santa Fe residents:

New Mexicans: We have come amongst you to take possession of New Mexico, which we do in the name of the government of the United States. We have come with peaceable intentions and kind feelings toward you all. We come as friends to better your condition and make you part of the republic of the United States. (Keleher 1952, 15)

Three days later, Kearny proclaimed that the American government would "protect the property of the church" and the "property of all quiet and peaceable inhabitants within its boundaries against their enemies, the Eutaws [sic] and the Navajoes [sic]," and preserve order by "maintaining the authority and efficiency of the laws" (Keleher 1952, 14–15). Navajo raids and depredations against New Mexican settlers as well as settlers' raids and slave taking stalled the efforts of the United States to achieve colonial rule.

This chapter examines the rhetorical strategies and tactics of the American colonizers and their Navajo subjects. Specifically, the chapter shows the complexity of American efforts to colonize the Navajos by (1) examining the discourses of the expeditions and treaty negotiations between 1846 and 1859, (2) analyzing the texts about depredations and slavery before 1863, (3) investigating the rhetorical contrasts between the ideas of General Carleton and Navajo descendants about Indian internment at Bosque Redondo, and (4) explaining the implications of the episode.

EXPEDITIONS AND TREATIES

The discourses of the Navajo wars give glimpses into the rhetoric of this period. Spurr (1993) explains that the colonizers' rhetoric that appears in written documents emphasizes their efforts to establish power and control over the "strange" and "often incomprehensible realities" of the Other. "Other" refers to native people who do not understand or value Western approaches to authority and responsibility (3–4). More specifically, this rhetoric surfaced when political, military and Indian agency leaders described the actions and interpreted the motives of the Navajos from their perspectives as colonizers. Moreover, throughout the wars, the rhetoric of Navajo leadership expressed Indian resistance to colonization. Examples of colonial rhetoric occurred both in expedition reports and treaty councils.

Expedition Reports

Military expeditions preceded the treaty-making phase of government-Navajo relations. Supported by federal money, the expeditions consisted of a journey undertaken by a government-organized group with the objective of describing the territory and resources of Navajo-inhabited land. The Secretary of War authorized Congress to appropriate the money needed for the expeditions.

Lieutenant James William Abert (1962) led the first expedition into Navajo country in 1846–1847. The stated goal of his expedition was scientific, that is, to report and map the land area taken by Kearny and to write a scientific report of this journey. The expedition served colonial interests because Abert identified expedient travel routes for the military, located economic and trade resources, and noted locations suitable for settlement. Other expeditions by George Archibald McCall, James H. Simpson, and John M. Washington followed. At the government's expense Congress published reports of the expeditions and distributed them to prospective settlers and developers.

All of the expedition reports exemplify strategies of surveillance, a key trait of colonial discourse. Spurr (1993) describes surveillance as discourse that takes a "panoramic view," shows the writer has a mastery over the unknown, acknowledges the power of the government system he represents, and conveys the visual authority of the point of view of the writer (15–20). The role of the observer, in this case the reporter of the expedition, came from a privileged position and established "knowledge of the world and authority over space" (25).

Many examples of the privileged position of expedition leaders appeared in their reports. For example, in 1846 Abert (1962) implied his own superiority to the native population when he observed:

We scarcely left camp when the signs of civilization broke upon us. . . . [W]e saw flocks of sheep, droves of horses, and large herds of cattle. These are guarded night and day by lads who . . . were miserably clad in tattered blankets, and armed with bows and arrows. . . . The houses were the most miserable we had yet seen, and the inhabitants the most abject picture of squalid poverty. (49)

Abert's discourse showed his position of privilege, his judgments about poor people, and his predictions about the economic potential of the land.

Following Abert's expedition, other federal officials provided overt jus-tifications for a conquest of the Navajos. As an example, Colonel John Marshall Washington's expedition ventured into the center of Navajo country in 1849 at the request of Indian Agent John C. Calhoun. James A. Simpson, a topographical engineer, and Calhoun reported the expedition. Their purpose was to chastise and threaten the Navajos in order to show these native inhabitants the superiority of the government's values and practices (Frazer 1968).

Ridicule, a kind of discourse that persuades subjects of the inferiority of their values, beliefs, and actions, followed the expedition's surveillance rhetoric. At each stop on the expedition, for example, Washington and Calhoun ridiculed the Navajos, telling them that their raids were immoral and that the Americans would not tolerate such action. They claimed Nav-ajos constantly broke their promises to the United States, and they warned them of military reprisals. Even though Calhoun's rhetoric warned the In-dians, he recognized that "the powers in New Mexico have neither the authority nor the means to reduce to order the chaotic mess in the Terri-tory, and the government at Washington has not thoroughly comprehended the diversity and the difficulties to be overcome" (NMS, Calhoun to Lea, 1849, October 1). What characterized Calhoun's discourse was his dual approach to ridicule. On the one hand, he extolled the vices and power-lessness of the Navajos in an effort to get them to submit to government authority. On the other hand, he preached to the superintendent of Indian affairs about the inadequate government resources in an effort to persuade them to strengthen the military force in New Mexico.

Calhoun's ridicule of the government had a stronger persuasive effect than did his indoctrination of Navajos. His pleas prompted Indian Super-intendent Luke Lea to alert the government about the inability of its au-thorities to colonize the Navajos. He wrote:

The ruinous condition of our Indian affairs in New Mexico demands the immediate attention of Congress. In no section of the country are prompt and efficient mea-sures for restraining the Indians more imperiously required than in this Territory. . . . There are over thirty-thousand Indians within its limits, the greater portion of which, having never been subject to any salutary restraint, are extremely wild and intractable. For many years they have been in the constant habit of making exten-sive forays . . . plundering and murdering the inhabitants and carrying off large quantities of stock. (Watts 1858, 25)

However, the government did not take any strong action until 1863.

After the failure of Calhoun and Washington to shame the Indians, in 1850 the government decided to sponsor more expeditions and create ad-ditional surveillance. It enlisted Colonel George Archibald McCall to find out about the geography and material resources, explain the Navajo culture, and predict problems for military actions against the Indians (Frazer 1968). Unlike Abert who just described the economic potential of what he observed and Calhoun and Washington who chastised their potential subjects, McCall proposed specific policies.

Continuing with the strategy of surveillance begun by Abert and Simpson, McCall's report called attention to the power and superiority of the government when he noted,

The whole of the Indians of the country is ignorant of the power of the United States, and also of its views as regards themselves. And it would do much to enlighten them as to the policy of our Government, if delegations from the Pueblos and principal wild tribes were called to the United States. (Frazer 1968, 108)

Specifically, McCall proposed that select Indian leaders tour the United States so that they could observe first hand its military power and material resources. He implied that if the Indians knew about the power of the United States, they would willingly submit to colonization. His plea failed; the government did not invite Navajo delegations to Washington until after their internment at Bosque Redondo.

McCall's surveillance also promoted the political vision of conquest and offered an economic rationale for the government to continue its plans to subdue and subordinate the Navajos. He observed the presence of economic potential of mining and mineral extraction, and he noted the grazing land available for cattle and sheep raising. McCall envisioned the consequences of military conquest in this way:

The future of New Mexico, it is hoped, will disclose another picture—the Indians subdued, the hill-sides white with flocks, and the neglected mines again yielding up their hoards of precious metals. And then, the cultivation of the soil, although I believe it will always supply the wants of the inhabitants, [it] will be productive of less wealth to the state than either of the other pursuits. (Frazer 1968, 90)

All of these expeditions succeeded to the extent that they informed the government about the natural resources, the economic prospects for settlement, the routes to be taken by the military, the behaviors of the Navajos, and the inadequacy of existing military forces. This valuable information served the government's colonial interests and bolstered its desire for destroying Navajo culture and controlling the resources on tribal lands. In return, the expeditions probably gave the Navajos some information about the federal government and its intentions.

Treaty Councils

Whereas the expedition reports established a rationale for conquest, the treaties tried to make this conquest legal and to mute the Navajos. Spurr

(1993) refers to mutedness as denying the power of language to the colonized, that is, not permitting them to speak on their own behalf or recognizing the group's capability of expressing a point of view. In many situations, the government encouraged mutedness by denying native people a claim to historical existence and property rights. To the colonizers, native people were a subaltern group. Gayatri C. Spivak contrasts mutedness with voice. She notes that subaltern groups lack the power to express their needs and voice strong resistance to the colonizers. She further explains that when subaltern people have a voice, they can make the unseen visible and engage in resistance toward the colonizers (Young 1990, 159).

1846 Treaty. Even though the United States tried, its treaties did not succeed in dictating rules nor did it always mute the voice of the Navajos. The Navajos signed their first treaty in November 1846 with Colonial Alexander Doniphan. The treaty was a simple peace agreement promising mutual trade and mutual restoration of captives. Zarcillos Largos and six other Navajo leaders signed the treaty (Brugge & Correll 1971, 64–65). Ralph E. Twitchell ([1909] 1963) notes that through the treaty process, federal officials claimed everything in New Mexico was theirs by right of conquest and described New Mexicans and Indians as citizens (99). However, the government granted citizenship only to New Mexico's Pueblo Indians, not to Navajos.

The treaty negotiations provided the first evidence of Navajo resistance when Zarcillos Largos spoke through an interpreter. He said:

Americans! You have a strange cause of war against the Navajos. We have waged war against the New Mexicans for several years. We have plundered their villages and killed many of their people and made them prisoners. We had just cause for all of this. You have lately commenced the war against the same people. You are powerful. You have great guns and many brave soldiers. You have therefore conquered them, the very thing we have been attempting to do for so many years. You now turn upon us for attempting to do what you have done yourselves. . . . Look how matters stand. This is our war. We have more right to complain to you for interfering in our war than you have to quarrel with us for continuing a war we had begun long before you got here. If you will act justly, you will allow us to settle our differences. (McNitt 1972, 118)

Largos' speech made use of the strategy of identification, a tactic of resistance to the colonizer. He associated the actions of his people with those of the American government, emphasized that the New Mexican settlers were a common enemy, and acknowledged the federal government had conquered the Spanish. Largos implied that both the Navajos and the United States acted justly against New Mexican settlers. Even though Largos seemed to approve of the government conquest of the Spanish settlers, he refused to acknowledge that the government also planned to conquer him and all of the other Navajos. This short speech is one example of how

Largos expressed the resistance of his subaltern people against the government's attempt to colonize them.

1848 Treaty. Navajos signed another similar peace treaty in 1848 with Colonel E.W.B. Newby. The provisions were nearly the same as in the previous treaty except that the government demanded payment for its defense of the territory with 300 sheep and 100 head of mules and horses. By demanding this indemnity, the government requests paralleled those of Spanish colonizers in the previous century who had demanded tribute from their subjects. It is unclear if the Indians gave the livestock to the government, but Brugge and Correll (1971) suggest that the payment was likely made because "it was the usual method of handling offenses within the tribe" (27). Paying indemnities was both a strategy of submission and resistance. On the one hand, material payments signified the subservience of the Navajos to the authority of the government. On the other hand, Navajo payments legitimized their tribe as a recognized political organization with formal channels of diplomacy.

1849 Treaty. The treaty of 1849 at Canyon de Chelly, negotiated between Colonel John M. Washington and government-designated Navajo leaders, featured strategies of appropriation and classification typical of colonial discourse. A strategy of appropriation designates the territory as a possession of the colonizer, affirms the negotiations as just and fair, impresses the colonized with government values, and imposes rules on them (Spurr 1993, 28–37). This treaty specified that the government had the power to determine territorial boundaries, receive indemnities for captives and missing livestock, punish Navajos who had committed crimes, and secure safe passage through Navajo territory.

Additionally, this treaty continued the strategy of ridicule, preaching to the Navajos about how they should behave, forcing them to submit to the control of Indian agents, and calling attention to government standards of law and justice. Although at first glance, some provisions of the treaty appeared to assist the Navajos, these provisions primarily served the government's interest by naming Navajos as a subservient people. For example, the government could punish New Mexicans who committed crimes against Navajos, establish military posts, and award gifts for signing the treaty. However, in ways similar to the subsequent treaties, this one-sided document granted many rights to government, gave few privileges to the Navajos, and demanded compliance from the entire tribe. For example, although this treaty promised justice for Navajo victims of crimes, the existing territorial court records show no evidence that the government brought any New Mexicans to trial for such crimes. Moreover, no effort was made to understand Navajo concepts of justice or legal principles. Taken together these treaty-making strategies succeeded in muting the legal voice of most of the Navajos.

However, at the 1849 treaty signing, Chief Mariano Martinez, in a recorded conversation with Colonel Washington, expressed the interests of the people he represented. This conversation illustrated how Washington tested Martinez's comprehension of the provisions of the treaty while he asserted the government's power. Martinez used the strategy of conciliation by agreeing with Washington. Conciliation is a method of trying to win over the trust and secure the goodwill of others by placating their needs. The problem with this approach was that the government expected Martinez to enforce the treaty provisions with the entire Navajo population of about 10,000 people. Even though Martinez likely agreed with the provisions and wanted good relations with the government, he lacked the power to bring the agreement to fruition because he only had authority over a few friendly Navajos from his own clan.

In addition to Martinez's conciliation, this conversation also captured Colonel Washington's preachy statements embedded in his strategy of appropriation. Martinez agreed with unwarranted government assumptions. For example, federal officials assumed that the Navajos had one head chief who controlled all Navajo warriors. Washington inquired, "Who is this man?" An interpreter for Martinez responded: "He is the principal chief of the Navajos" (McNitt 1972, 88–89). Clearly, Martinez knew he was not a head chief of all of the Navajos, but he placated the colonel because he recognized he was a head chief in the perception of the government.

In another case, Washington assumed that Martinez could communicate specific rules and enforce them with other Navajos. Through an interpreter, Washington said,

Tell him when a chief wishes to talk with me, by making known his intentions by a white flag, he will be conducted safely into camp; but that everybody else must keep a mile off, or else be liable to be shot. (McNitt 1964, 88)

Even though this protocol was alien to Navajos, Martinez agreed that he could do what was asked of him. Brugge and Correll (1971) conclude that the government designated head chiefs in order to fulfill its need to have official tribal representatives involved in the treaty proceedings, but "the man who was so honored functioned more as a diplomat than as a headman" (27). Nonetheless, by agreeing to the designation of head chief, Martinez used his position to express the opinions of some Navajos, benefitted from the prestige gained from his role as a diplomat, and in doing so, resisted the attempts of the government to completely mute Navajos as a subaltern group.

In a final example, Washington sought compliance with the provisions of the treaty. He emphasized:

Tell them if they are [desirous of peace] they can easily obtain it by complying with the terms of the treaty which they have made, and that the sooner they do comply with them the better it will be for them, as less of their property will be wasted and destroyed. (McNitt 1964, 89)

Through his interpreter, Martinez promised that Navajo head men would bring in all the livestock they had stolen and "comply with the treaty." Washington explained, "Tell the chief the stolen property which the nation is required to restore is 1,070 head of sheep, 34 head of mules, 19 head of horses, and 78 head of cattle." Martinez claimed his people did not steal the cattle so "the Apaches must have stolen them." However, he promised that if this charge proved to be true, Navajo leaders would replace the stolen livestock. Again Martinez's voice was not muted because he placated the demands of Washington, and, in turn, the colonel empowered him with the credibility of a trusted head chief.

Most treaties with the Navajos failed. Because the colonizers lacked understanding of Indian culture and customs, they could not enforce the rules nor achieve authority over the Navajos. Similarly, Navajo submission to authority was more than simple verbal agreement and conciliation; it required an understanding of the conditions for submission. In the previously cited conversation, neither Washington nor Martinez achieved the power each had expected because neither understood how unrealistic each other's promises were.

The government and the Navajos entered into other treaties in 1858 and 1861. Although the signers acted as if the treaties were legally binding documents, neither of the treaties was accepted by Navajo tribal assemblies nor were they ratified by the U.S. Senate. Nevertheless, these new treaties marked government progress in its efforts to deny Navajo rights. The difficulty identified here finds an explanation in the work of Albert Memmi (1965). He emphasizes that the colonizer expresses power by establishing rules and sanctions and by calling attention to the privileges of its own political and legal systems. One assertion of privilege appeared in the 1858 treaty when the government stipulated these conditions:

It is agreed that the authorities and troops of the United States shall have the right, under the direction of the commanding officer of Fort Defiance, to capture, and destroy if necessary, all stock or flocks of the tribe found east of said line, and to destroy all crops which may be planted east of the line. (Brugge & Correll 1971, 79–80)

Clearly, the language of government-Navajo treaties was unilateral rather than bilateral. The provisions served the interests of the government and ignored many of the property interests of the Navajo. For example, Navajo encroachments onto government property were subject to severe penalties. However, if government livestock or some military personnel encroached on Navajo lands, the government forbid the Navajos from destroying any of this property. Through this lopsided discourse, treaties permitted the government to colonize the Indians by taking their territory and forcing them to comply with federal laws.

Whereas the surveillance strategies of the expeditions provided the government with a rationale and a plan for colonizing the Indians, the treaties forced the Indians to abide by government rules. The early treaties failed because of the passive resistance exerted by designated head chiefs who agreed to provisions they did not understand and could not enforce. Designated Navajo leaders likely signed the treaties to placate the government and build up personal credibility with their own followers.

COLONIAL DISCOURSE ABOUT DEPREDATIONS AND SLAVERY

The expedition and treaty discourse illustrate two responses to government-Navajo conflict, and the words and actions of the Navajos show their modes of resistance. Spivak (1994) notes that colonized subjects often express their resistance without utterance, they rebel or act with hostility toward their colonizers (82). By continuing their raids and depredations on New Mexico settlers, the Navajos resisted without utterance; that is, they ignored the treaty provisions and demonstrated the powerlessness of the treaty makers.

Two unsolved issues fueled the continuing conflict between the Navajos and New Mexico settlers. These issues were Navajo depredations and raids against settlers and the livestock and slave raids by New Mexico settlers against the Navajos. Even though most theories of colonial discourse concentrate on the motives revealed in the texts, this segment of the chapter shows how the issues the government construed to promote colonialism were reconstrued by the Navajos to prevent it. Colonial goals motivated treaty negotiations and eventually caused the government to remove the Navajos from their homeland. What did not become apparent to government leaders for many years was that depredations and Indian slave raids were in fact two sides of the same problem; both caused the Navajo wars.

Depredations

Depredations refer to the stealing and the destruction of property during Navajo raids and reprisals against New Mexico settlers and Pueblo Indians. The main purpose of Navajo raids was to steal livestock; a secondary purpose was to secure slave labor. During the raids, the Navajos murdered residents and destroyed their crops and property. Even though many leaders claimed these acts were committed by only a few bad Navajos, for decades depredations continued against New Mexico residents and became the subject of extensive rhetoric from powerless Indian agents, military leaders, territorial officials, and citizens.

Navajo depredations began long before the United States claimed New Mexico territory and lasted until 1868. Records of raids against the Spanish and Mexicans date back to the late seventeenth century when the Navajos took horses from the Spanish. Since most of the raiders stole livestock from citizens who had large herds, it is possible that Navajos justified the raiding using their cultural norm that wealthy people should share their resources with those who are poor. Of course, the need for livestock as an economic commodity was also a likely motive since the Indian population was growing and some Navajos had become wealthy because of their successful raids.

The government used the strategy of debasement to explain their powerlessness in controlling Navajo depredations. Spurr (1993) defines debasement as a way of assigning qualities to the colonized that identify them as uncivilized. The government assigned several traits of savagery to Navajos, including the commission of crimes, failure to submit to social control and governance, and engagement in wild and lawless actions (79–85).

Taken together these traits provided the government with evidence that the Navajos threatened civilized society. In turn, this threat was an excuse for the government to conquer and suppress what it considered to be an inferior culture (Spurr 1993, 80–83). In his annual report of November 1854, Superintendent of Indian Affairs George Manypenny associated the threat of depredations with the savagery of the Navajos. He debased them in this way: "The Navajoes [*sic*] commit their wrongs from a pure love of rapine and plunder. . . . They must either subsist to a considerable extent by plundering the white inhabitants, or they have to be exterminated; or else they must be colonized in a suitable location" (Watts 1858, 44). In 1857, Superintendent J. W. Denver reiterated the need to colonize the Indians: "This is the only practical system for redeeming the wild, lawless, and roaming tribes within our borders." Denver added that hope for colonization existed because "the Indians of New Mexico are beginning to have some understanding and appreciation of our power and resources" (Watts 1858, 51–52). Both government leaders deplored the depredations and, at the same time, justified their colonial goals by further debasement of the Navajos.

The strategy of negation also appeared in an extensive appeal by attorney John S. Watts on behalf of settlers who had suffered at the hands of the Navajos. Watts (1858) was unwilling to wait for the colonization of the Indians. Instead he demanded that the government pay claims to his settler clients amounting to more than $100,000. Watts revealed his ideological imperative for ridding settlers of the Indian menace by negation, that is, associating settlers with the superior consciousness and values of civilized people and identifying the Navajos with an inferior consciousness and un-civilized values (Spurr 1993, 101).

Watts' ideological imperative was to protect the citizens of New Mexico against the actions of an inferior race. He reasoned that money was owed citizens of New Mexico under the 1834 Trade and Intercourse Act, an act that provided for indemnity to citizens whose property, livestock, or crops were destroyed by Indians in amity with the United States. He further con-cluded the government had a duty to protect citizens against the Indians. Watts (1858) used emotionally evocative language to negate the Navajos:

History will prove, and the records of your Department establish the fact, that as nations they are thieves and robbers, and leave behind them in their pathway des-olation and death, and in nine of ten outrages which have occurred, the Indian, not the white man, has been the aggressor. They are given to every vice, destitute of every virtue, and wanting in every good instinct but that of affection for [their] offspring. (64)

Despite Watts' invective, the government failed to pay most of the claims because the claimants had not filed on time and the treaties they cited as proof of amity had not been ratified. These conditions meant the Navajos were not in amity and the claimants had not provided sufficient evidence to get reparations. Several dozen examples of these claims are in the Indian depredation files of the New Mexico State Archives (Box 114, File 1).

By acting at cross purposes, the various representatives of colonizers con-travened their stated goals. For example, Watts sought monetary payments to citizen victims in order to restore their trust in the federal government, a trust, he said, that was lost when the government failed to protect settlers from the uncivilized actions of Navajos. At nearly the same time that Watts demanded reparations for settlers, the government appeased the Navajos with even more treaties and predicted the Navajos were on their way to being compliant subjects. An example of this appeasement appeared in a letter dated November 20, 1858, sent from Indian Agent Samuel M. Yost to Superintendent James L. Collins. Yost noted:

I told them that it was not our wish to fight them, but threatened they must obey our laws. They said they wanted to be friends forever, and would do anything I wished them to do, to bring it about. They said they knew we could take their lands, kill their women, children, and men, and destroy their stock, if war contin-ued; and that they wanted to have peace to prevent those calamities.

More specifically, Yost reasoned that "they [the Navajos] had been thor-oughly humiliated, and were fully impressed with their own insignificance" (NMS, 1824–1881, Box T21, File 3). At the same time Watts filed petitions to force the Indians to comply with treaties, Yost was negotiating with Navajos to bring in stolen cattle and sheep.

Because citizens perceived the federal government had failed to pay reparations and to stop the raids, they petitioned Governor Abraham Rencher to allow them to organize a citizen militia and act on their own behalf. Their proclamation stated:

The Navajoe [*sic*] Indians have for a series of months been at war with the citizens of this Territory, conducting their hostilities with all the unsparing relentlessness known to savage warfare, robbing and murdering defenseless men . . . and carrying terror into the heart of the communities unprepared to repulse the barbarous foes. (Proclamation of New Mexico Citizens 1860, 1)

Since the federal troops had not reacted appropriately, the proclamation continued, the citizens planned to organize their own militia "to chastise the Navajoe [*sic*]" (Proclamation of New Mexico Citizens 1860, 1). The citizens bolstered their petition with rhetorical strategies of debasement, naming Navajo depredations as savage acts committed by barbarous people.

This fragmented policy toward the Navajos impeded the efforts of the government from stopping Indian raids. Even a citizen militia with the support of Ute warriors, a traditional enemy of the Navajo, could not stop the raids. Disparate means on the part of different groups seeking to colonize the Navajos led to a confused and chaotic approach to the problem of depredations. Instead of working together with a common set of goals and coordinating plans to execute those goals, divergent goals made it impossible to deal successfully with this problem. The Navajos surely recognized the powerlessness of the colonialists and realized that the citizen militia could not stop the depredations any better than the appointed Navajo head chiefs could.

Examples of this fragmented policy among military leaders appeared in this February 25, 1860, letter from Major Henry Lane Kendrick to Superintendent James Collins (NMS, 1849–1880, Box T21, File 4). Kendrick expected to continue communication with Navajos and enforce the provisions of the 1858 treaty by demanding the return of livestock taken by the Indians. He reported that he met with Navajos and

reminded them of their promises and obligations, and impressed upon them the necessity of a serious endeavor upon their part to fulfill their duties. They listened to my remarks with grate [*sic*] attention, showing every indication of an intelligent understanding of them, and fully assented to the truth and justice of all I had said.

Then he noted the Indians turned over a small number of horses and sheep and begged to have more time to pay their indemnities. He said Brevet

Oliver L. Shepherd threatened and forbade him from communicating with Indians except with the permission of military superiors. Kendrick concluded Shepherd had impeded the peace effort by flogging and threatening Indians and killing their livestock. This incident showed how breaches in authority among the military further weakened colonial power and damaged military credibility in the eyes of both Navajos and citizens. Infighting among the colonizers gave the Navajos the impression that the government lacked the power to enforce treaties.

Eventually, this fragmented policy encouraged Agent Collins formally to abandon treaties and to declare war on the Navajos (Collins to Greenwood, 1860, September 8, NMS, 1849–1880, Box 550, File 4). He tried to force the government to act decisively when he said, "The Navajos are now in a condition that makes them the common enemy of both the whites and the [other] Indians." Again on September 16, he stressed, "They have no friends" and are "a common scourge to all," concluding that peace with the Navajos is not worth the effort that has been expended. He then urged the territorial militia, the Utes, and the federal troops to act as a unified force to defeat the Navajos. Later some of Collins' ideas surfaced in the removal policy executed by General Carleton.

For the Navajos, this policy led to the period of "Naahondzood," the fearing time, a dark period of war forecasting the destruction of the tribe's homeland and its culture. This policy produced even more slave raids against the Navajos, destruction of their crops, and starvation of their people (Brugge 1985, 160). The resolution to this chaotic cultural period came during internment at Fort Sumner. Finally, when in 1863 the military rounded up the Navajos and marched them to Bosque Redondo at Fort Sumner, the government agreed on a unified policy of forced assimilation and relocation.

Slavery in New Mexico

Slaves Taken by Navajos. Slavery was a way of life for Indians and New Mexicans prior to and during the Navajo wars. Indians procured slaves, used them for their own benefit, and sold them to other Indian groups and to settlers. L. R. Bailey (1973) argues that Indians took slaves to replace dead relatives. They absorbed the slaves into their families. After four years, slaves could be released or could choose to be part of Navajo culture (206).

In some cases, government discourse recorded incidents of Indian slavery for propaganda purposes in an effort to further debase Navajos. For example, in 1854 Major Kendrick reported that he returned a New Mexico boy to his family after captivity with the Navajos. Kendrick indicated that the boy had been in captivity for eight years after having been "taken by Utah Indians, who sold me soon after to the Navajos. . . . Most of the time [I] have been ill treated" (Kendrick to Messervy, 1854, June 22, NMS, Box

T121, File 2). Other military agents reported that Navajo head men surrendered nameless captives to pacify government demands to take possession of Navajo criminals (Yost to Collins, 1858, November 20, NMS, 1824–1881, Box T21, File 3). Military rhetoric about the negative experiences of slaves provided additional evidence against Navajos, showing that they were savage in their treatment of captives and deceitful in substituting captives for guilty Navajo warriors.

However, in a few cases, the government reported Navajo slaves had been well treated, did not wish to return to their families, and were willing to work as interpreters for the government. The fact that the government employed Indian slaves made their rhetoric against Indian slavery suspect. One example of a satisfied captive appears in Calhoun's 1849 expedition report. Calhoun mentioned that Josea Ignacia Anane (Anaya) was captured by Navajos at Tecolote. He was then living with two wives and three children with the Navajos and seemed satisfied (McNitt 1972, 90). Anaya later served as an interpreter for Major Kendrick at Fort Defiance. Another captive, Mexican Jesus Arviso, remained with his Navajo family and became the translator for the government during and after their internment at Bosque Redondo (Brugge 1985, 171–75). The government used examples of poorly treated slaves as propaganda against the Navajos, while they featured examples of satisfied captives to show slavery served a legitimate economic and political purpose for the government.

Navajo Slaves Taken by Others. Colonial governments often exert authority over other people by enslaving them. Enslavement is an example of coercive power against an inferior cultural Other. Even though official slavery was illegal under Spanish and American law, it was a commonly accepted practice in New Mexico. In fact, political leaders declared in the Otero Slave Code of 1861 that Indian slavery was not part of federal law since Indians were peons, not slaves, because their servitude was voluntary (Hunt 1958, 116–18). Naming the slaves as peons was a rhetorical tactic for legitimizing slavery. Typically, New Mexico settlers bought Indian slaves at the cost of two horses or for about $100. Slaves provided economic benefit to their owners who put them to work in the fields or in family homes as house servants.

Ruth Underhill (1956) explained that the Taos trade fairs were an opportunity for the "slave-hungry Spaniards" to meet the "horse-hungry Indians" and make deals (56). The Comanche and Utes often sold the slaves they had captured from other tribes to settlers. By far the largest number of slaves were Navajos. Brugge (1985) concluded that in New Mexico territory Navajo slaves were held by priests, governors, and prominent military leaders. Many households had four or five slaves (121–24). Underhill also reported as many as 6,000 Indian slaves in New Mexico with three-fourths of this number being Navajos (80). Moreover, Brugge also documented the existence of 800 Navajo slaves in the baptismal records of

Catholic parishes in New Mexico just during the 1860s. His records do not account for the slaves taken by non-Catholics or unbaptized captives, so this number is only a small indication of the large number of Navajo slaves.

Sparse records about Indian captives appeared in the discourse of government leaders. Although the government knew about the existence of Indian slavery, the voices of the slaves remained silent since most could not read or write and others had assimilated into the culture of the families who adopted them. The slave's only voice was through an occasional report of a Navajo head chief or a government official.

Armijo Speaks. Curiously, the government's continued contact with Navajo head men also precluded the muting of the voices of Navajo captives. In fact the chiefs' reporting of grievances was especially important because this information enabled the Navajos to defend their raids and depredations against settlers. Stating grievances is a way of complaining that expresses indignation or resentment from having been wronged by others.

After decades of abuse, Navajo Chief Armijo reported the captivity of many Navajo women and children to Indian Agent John Greiner during one negotiation. Chief Armijo reported:

My people are all crying in the same way. Three of our chiefs now sitting before you mourn the loss for their children—who have been taken from their homes by Mexicans. More than 200 of our children have been carried off and we know not where they are. The Mexicans have lost but few children in comparison with what they have stolen from us. Three years ago they took from my people nearly all their cavalladas. Two years ago my brother lost 700 animals. How shall we get them again? We leave our Great Father to decide. From the time of Colonel Newby we have been trying to get our children back again. Eleven times have we given up our captives. Only once have they given us ours. My people are yet crying for the children they have lost. Is it American justice that we must give up everything and receive nothing? (Greiner to Calhoun, 1852, January 30, NMS 1849–1853, Box 546, File 1)

Greiner acted surprised to hear this grievance: "You have never told us this before. The Great Father at Washington shall hear of it and you shall hear what he says." Greiner's remarks are surprising since Governor Calhoun's letters confirmed that he knew about slavery, chose not to act upon this information, and never accepted slavery as an explanation for Navajo warfare (Abel 1915).

Largos Speaks. In 1853, Chief Zarcillos Largos told Governor David Meriwether that some bad Navajo men were conducting raids, but these bad acts must be understood in relation to the slave raids of the Spanish who had taken hundreds of Navajo women and children. Meriwether claimed this information was a total surprise to him (Meriwether to Manypenny, 1853, September 17, NMS, Box 548, File 1). As a result of this revelation, Meriwether issued an order to Navajo agent Henry Dodge: "You will take steps to have such Navijo [*sic*] captives as may be found with our people, and may come under your observation, or to your knowledge, speedily returned to their people" (1853, September 30, NMS, Box T21, File 1). In this instance, Meriwether voiced Largos' complaint, an action no previous governor had ever taken.

In order to be heard and to force action, the Navajo voice had to be repeated and affirmed by several government officials. An important affirmation came from a military commander.

Canby Speaks. Not only did Lt. Colonel Edward Richard Canby acknowledge the presence of Navajo slaves in 1861, he named the culprits and identified the effects of slave taking. Canby, in ways similar to Greiner, refuted the government's explanation of depredations:

Parties of Mexicans from the Rio Grande and Cebyetta [*sic*] have been in pursuit of Indians . . . kidnaping Indian children and taking them to the river for sale. . . . It seems to be a thriving business for some people. Followed up, this policy exasperates the Navajoes [*sic*], and certainly tends to aggravate and complicate affairs between them and the ranch owners of the Rio Grande, causing them to rob and steal cattle and sheep and horses. (Brugge 1985, 94)

By repeating the complaints of the colonized Navajos, Canby risked losing personal credibility with his military supervisors who had no sympathy for the Indians.

Steck Speaks. In 1864, years after the Navajo had expressed grievances to the government, Agent Michael Steck stressed the legitimacy of charges made by Armijo, Largos, Greiner, and Canby. In a letter to Superintendent William Dole on January 13, 1864, he acknowledged that Navajo depredations were acts of reprisal for the slave raids conducted against the Indians by settlers. Moreover, Steck claimed that about 2000 Navajo slaves were in the hands of New Mexicans. He emphasized:

Many have been captured recently, while others have served from childhood, to old age; it is therefore an evil that has existed for many years. . . . There is no law of the Territory that legalizes the sale of Indians, yet it is done almost daily, without an effort to stop it. The system is in such direct opposition to the humane policy of the government, that I hope the Hon. Commissioner will urge . . . an efficient remedy for the evil. . . . [I] recommend that the military commander be instructed by the proper authority to proclaim the immediate and unconditional emancipation of all Indians in this department and that they be returned to their respective tribes. (NMS, 1824–1881, Box 552, File 1)

Despite all of the aforementioned records about Navajo slaves verified by Navajo leaders and government officials, their voices remained muted until extensive corroboration from government officials validated Indian complaints. After government colonizers had rounded up the Navajos to intern them at Bosque Redondo, the government finally acknowledged information about Navajo slavery. In June 1865, President Andrew Johnson declared that all government employees are "to discontinue the practice" of slavery and "to take lawful means to suppress" it (Delgado to Dole, 1865, June 19, NMS, Box T21, File 6). Because Navajo slaves had been enculturated into the families and because slave owners profited from the work of their captives, the government acted slowly to alleviate the practice of slavery.

TWO PERSPECTIVES ON THE LONG WALK

After years of wars marked by Navajo raids on other residents of territorial New Mexico and slave taking by citizens, the government under the command of General James Carleton, with the consent of the territorial legislature, rounded up all the Navajos they could find and forced them to walk from their homes in present-day western New Mexico and eastern Arizona to Bosque Redondo at Fort Sumner, New Mexico, a distance of more than 200 miles. By the Spring of 1864, more than 7,000 men, women, and children walked into four years of internment. Carleton called upon Ute Indian Agent Kit Carson to enlist Ute warriors, traditional Navajo enemies, to round up the Navajos, destroy their crops, and kill their livestock. Each Ute received bounty payments for capturing Navajos and killing livestock (Bailey 1964, 157).

Carleton promoted removal with the vigor of a skillful political propagandist. Propaganda often appears in the colonial discourse of the government and also in the resistance rhetoric of the colonized. Propaganda is a deliberate attempt to further one's own goals through communication. Propagandists use one-sided information to promote their doctrines and to enhance their own power and credibility (Brown 1963; Bartlett 1973; Altheide & Johnson 1980). More specifically, Carleton's desire for the conquest of the Navajo fits closely with David Altheide's and John Johnson's definition of bureaucratic propaganda; that is, he reacted radically in order to achieve political expediency and to maintain the legitimacy of his plan to subdue Indians by enlisting military support for those goals (1980, 18).

Carleton concluded that the only solution to the Navajo problem was to remove them. Using his military authority, he forced Navajos to take "The Long Walk" to Bosque Redondo. Once they were interned, Carleton demanded they become farmers and Christians. His policy of Navajo removal and internment was a major catastrophe, costing the government more than $1 million and costing the Navajos hundreds of lives. In 1868, the government recognized Carleton's plan had failed, so they made another treaty with the Navajos and permitted them to return to their homeland.

This section of the chapter analyzes the Bosque Redondo internment from two diverse perspectives. One perspective is that of General Carleton who enthusiastically promoted his plan in letters to the War Department. The other perspective comes from Navajo prisoners whose recollected experiences are retold by their descendants. Since most of the interned Navajos could not read or write, their children and grandchildren recorded the experiences of their elders and wrote them down. The discursive snapshots that follow illustrate Carleton's propagandist arguments in contrast to the retrospective recollections of the colonized Navajo people. Both views expressed divergent doctrines about the colonial experience. Carleton promoted his military doctrine of forced assimilation, and Navajo relatives reinforced a cultural interpretation about Bosque Redondo. Page references for Carleton's views appear as part of his letters ("Condition of Indian Tribes" 1867), and the Navajo accounts come from Ruth Roessel's *Navajo Stories of the Long Walk* (1973).

One common feature of propaganda is oversimplification (Brown 1963; Larson 1994), that is, the strategy of defining a complex problem using simple and easy to recall emotional images. Four kinds of oversimplified statements characterized Carleton's doctrine. He claimed the Bosque Redondo was (1) an ideal place for the (2) forced assimilation of the Navajos who would work (3) so that they could forever remain in their (4) permanent internment. Carleton promoted internment by emphasizing a few images and issues and then repeating them as if they were true pronouncements (Bartlett 1973, 79–81). In contrast, the descendants' recollections of Navajo experiences promoted tribal cultural doctrine that Bosque Redondo was a (1) dreadful place, where they (2) were unable to assimilate and to do their work, (3) forced into unproductive tasks, and (4) prayed to return to their homeland. Their stories also oversimplified the experience by accentuating graphic images, constructing cultural explanations, and emphasizing cultural truths.

Both Carleton and Navajo descendants used similar propaganda techniques; they dramatized the situation by using pictorial expressions, epithets, and stereotypes to arouse the audience's emotions and persuade them about the righteousness of their respective positions (Bartlett 1973, 77–79). Carleton's emotional appeals persuaded his nineteenth-century audience that his policy was workable, and Navajo relatives persuaded their twentieth-century audience that the Navajos suffered but their culture remained strong and intact and they survived colonization.

Ideal versus Dreadful Place

A propaganda appeal presents personal standpoints that audiences are expected to accept. These standpoints are based on emotion and source credibility rather than on careful argumentation. Carleton's standpoint was that the Navajo problem could be remedied by internment. He presented Bosque Redondo as an ideal place where the Navajos had to settle in as farmers. He noted that

> there is arable land enough for all the Indians of this family. . . . Now that the war is vigorously prosecuted against the Navajoes [sic], the only peace that can ever be made with them must rest on the basis that they move on these lands, and like the Pueblos, become an agricultural people and cease to be nomads. ("Condition of Indian Tribes" 1867, 134)

Part of the problem with Carleton's emotionally appealing description was that it was disputed by others who observed the site (Bailey 1964, 53). His enthusiastic portrayal of this location ignored the fact that it was too small for the Navajo population, access was severely limited, and agricultural success was improbable. Carleton's oversimplified projections typified the discourse of many military commanders during the Indian wars; they promoted their own colonial projects without the slightest insight about how their ideas would impact on Indian culture.

Experiences of the descendants of the imprisoned Indians denied Bosque Redondo was an ideal place. Instead Navajo relatives portrayed this place as a location of hardship, suffering, and cultural survival. Using emotional imagery, Navajo relatives recalled the place was cold without firewood, a fertile valley without seed to grow food, and a place where food supplies were scarce. For example, Howard Gorman, Sr. provides graphic details of the effects of Bosque Redondo on his grandparents. He recollected:

> Life became very hard for the Navajos. There was no wood for fires; there weren't enough seeds to grow their crops . . . insects ate what did come up. The White Man used to kill cattle for them, but there was not enough meat to go around, just a small piece for each person. In this way, some cow meat . . . kept the people from starvation. (Roessel 1973, 191)

In Navajo doctrine, the government failed to provide the means for subsistence and economic independence and instead created suffering and dependence.

Forced versus Voluntary Assimilation

In addition to depicting Bosque Redondo with positive and emotional imagery, Carleton urged others to accept his ideas of forced assimilation by calling attention to his military power. In a way typical of a political propagandist, Carleton belittled the Navajo culture, and then he appealed to the government's mythic belief that military force would always prevail. For example, he noted:

The purpose now is never to relax the application of force with a people that can no more be trusted than you can trust the wolves that run through their mountains, to gather them together, little by little, onto a reservation away from the haunts and hills, and hiding places of their country, and then to be kind to them. There [they will] teach their children to read and write; teach them the arts of peace; teach them the truths of Christianity. . . . And thus little by little they will become a happy and contented people. ("Condition of Indian Tribes" 1867, 134).

Carleton constructed his oversimplified argument in this way: force resulted in internment; internment subdued the Navajos' tendency toward savagery; subdued Indians accepted education; and education led to Navajo assimilation.

The Navajo stories justified their eventual assimilation by simplifying and condensing historical events and excluding explanations derogatory to the Navajos. In other words, descendants concluded that Navajo assimilation was voluntary. For example, Tom Jim recalled that his grandfather had told him how the Navajo wars started with fights from the Utes, Comanches, and Mexicans. He recalled:

Many of the Navajo people became very discouraged. . . . It came to the point that the White Men said, "Let us gather or round up all the Navajos into one place. So the Navajos were rounded up and assembled at Fort Defiance." From there they went to Fort Sumner where the White Men told them that "From here on you will not take up any more weapons. Now there will be peace. You will place your children in school and let them learn, and after they have learned English, they will in turn help you." (Roessel 1973, 182)

Moreover, Jim explained that the wars with other Indians led to discouragement, which in turn, resulted in The Long Walk. His story left out the history of Navajo depredations, ignored the painful details of slavery, and emphasized instead how Navajos voluntarily laid down their weapons and eagerly accepted education as a means to peace. This oversimplification of the assimilation process likely fit with Navajo cultural doctrine that they are peaceful and accommodating people.

Economic Dependence versus Cultural Interdependence

Carleton made emotional pleas to convince his government audience that the Indians must work so they could become economically independent. His concept of work reflected his own cultural traditions and ignored the Navajos' cultural concepts. Carleton wrote:

Every Indian—man, woman, or child—able to dig up the ground for plowing, should be kept at work every moment of the day preparing a patch, however so small. . . . The very existence of the Indians will depend upon it, and they should understand that now; for the country cannot support the number of mouths in addition to what we want for our troops. ("Condition of Indian Tribes" 1867, 164)

In a way typical of other colonizers, the general saw the needs of the Indians as unimportant and his military goals as all important. As a result, he imposed his views on the Indians without considering their interests.

In contrast to Carleton's demand for Navajo independence at Bosque Redondo, Rita Wheeler emphasized the interdependence and communal effort of her people, the Dine. She offered graphic details of the work assigned to the Navajos. Their work did not produce food. Instead it met the demands and submitted to the power of the colonizer. Wheeler recalled this story from her grandparents:

The people were given small shovels with which they built their shelters, which were just holes dug in the ground with some tree branches for shade over the top part. Besides doing daily house chores for the white leaders, my grandfather also took care of some horses that belonged to the soldiers. He would take the horses out to graze in the field. In the evenings, before he returned to his camp, he was given a small amount of flour or corn, just enough to be fixed for one meal. (Roessel 1973, 84)

Through her family's stories, Wheeler affirmed the motivations underlying Carleton's remarks—the needs of the Indians were secondary to those of the troops. Her recollection affirmed the cultural belief of her people that work was done for the benefit of the colonizers, not for the benefit of the Indians.

Permanent versus Temporary

In an effort to defend his ideas, Carleton constantly repeated them and called attention to his power to achieve his goals regardless of the cost. He emphasized, "The Navajos should never leave the Bosque, and never shall, if I can prevent it. I told them that should be their home. They have gone there with that understanding" (169). Repeating one's own goals using a coercive tone is a common technique used by both propagandists and colonialists (Brown 1963; Larson 1994; Williams & Chrisman 1994).

In contrast to the permanence demanded by Carleton, the Navajos viewed their internment as temporary, a condition that could be altered with the help of tribal medicine men. Hosteen T. Begay recalled how his grandparents talked about the experience:

Lots of people became homesick, and they wanted to go back to their land and homes. . . . Some medicine men conducted a ceremony in connection with the request to be sent back to their homes. After the ceremony was over some men went again to see the officers in charge. This time the request was considered, and a few days later, the treaty between the Navajos and the United States was signed. . . . It provided that the Navajos be freed from Fort Sumner. (Roessel 1973, 264–65)

Begay's explanation of the Navajo's return incorporated cultural doctrine; he concluded that the fate of the Navajo people at Bosque Redondo depended on their own religious leaders, not on the federal government or its military force.

In 1863, Carleton's propaganda succeeded because he persuaded the government that interning the Navajos was a viable plan. But by 1868, it was clear to his government audience that Bosque Redondo was an inadequate location with insufficient economic resources to ensure Navajo independence and assimilation and with deficient military resources to bring about permanent relocation. Carleton's ideas ultimately failed because of nature and politics. Weather conditions led to crop failures, and his previous political allies turned against him and demanded his removal for incompetence. In 1866, he transferred out of New Mexico to the Gulf War Department (Bailey 1964, 237). In 1868, General William T. Sherman and Colonel Samuel F. Tappan issued an order mandating the return of the Navajos to their reservation. On June 18, 1868, a wagon train ten miles long under the escort of four companies of calvary returned the Navajos to their land. The Navajos, throughout their internment, remained committed to their cultural doctrine that they would return to their homeland, and this doctrine prevailed after General Carleton's scheme failed. Even today the Navajos cite the prophetic words of their head chief Barboncito at Bosque Redondo when he told his people, "After we get back to our country it will brighten up again and the Navajo will be as happy as the land, black clouds will rise and there will be plenty of rain. Corn will grow in abundance and everything looks happy" (Navajo Nation Home Page 2000).

IMPACT

This chapter emphasizes how government discourse asserted its power and dominance to subjugate Navajos. By focusing on the Navajo wars and the subsequent internment and release from Bosque Redondo, the chapter illuminates many features of colonial discourse typical of the Indian wars.

Part one of the chapter shows how the government colonizers used the strategies of surveillance and appropriation to justify their conquest of New Mexico territory and to take charge of Navajo people and claim Indian land. Even though many colonizers muted their subjects in order to assume power and control over them, the expedition reports and treaty councils feature the voices of Navajo head men who verbally asserted their resistance to government conquest.

Part two of the chapter shows how the colonizers justified their military and economic actions against the Navajos by emphasizing the savagery of Indian depredations and raids on military installations and territorial settlements. Although treaty after treaty secured the promises of Navajo head men to pay indemnities for the depredations committed by members of their tribe, the government failed to recognize that the headman had little power over the warriors of their vast tribe and that many depredations were Navajo acts of reprisal against the slave raids being conducted against them by settlers and enemy tribes. The government leaders wrote of the depredations in ways characteristic of colonial discourse by using strategies of debasement, negation, and classification.

These strategies called public attention to the savage nature of Indians and gave reasons why the government could not prevent the depredations. For many years the Navajos complained that settlers held hundreds of Navajo slaves. For the most part, the government muted Navajo complaints and failed to take action against slave owners. Eventually, Indian agents and territorial leaders heard the voices of Navajo leaders Armijo and Largos and sympathized with their grievances about others taking their people as slaves. Nonetheless, little action was taken until Carleton asked that the military locate Navajo slaves and force them into internment at Bosque Redondo.

In line with other colonial practices, expedition reports documented the availability of rich resources and the potential for economic profit in Navajo lands. To secure these sources of wealth, treaties confined the Navajos to prescribed land areas and ordered federal troops to enforce these provisions. Despite these efforts, the government still could not subdue the Navajos. Finally, under the military leadership of Carleton, the military and their Indian allies rounded up the Navajos and interned them at Bosque Redondo.

Carleton's discourse about the roundup, The Long Walk, and the internment of more than 7,000 Navajos at Bosque Redondo contrasted with the discourse of Navajo family members who reported their grandparents' stories of living there. Carleton's prospective viewpoint used propaganda techniques characteristic of colonial rhetoric. He made emotional and oversimplified pleas to secure agreement of the War Department that the Navajos had to be interned. Furthermore, he bolstered these pleas with coercive threats, demanding that the Navajos submit to his authority, become educated, and assimilate to the dominant culture. The discourse of Navajo resistance shows a retrospective viewpoint in which the Navajos opposed internment, defined their work as servitude, and explained their return as the work of Navajo ceremonials and medicine men. Even in succeeding generations, some Navajos failed to acknowledge they had been involuntarily colonized by the government.

This volume demonstrates that government conquest over Indian tribes often threatened the continued existence of tribal culture, but Carleton's plan never achieved this goal. Other chapters show the government temporarily succeeded in its colonial goals when it hanged Chief Leschi, executed the Santee Sioux, forced the survivors of Sand Creek onto a reservation, paid reparations to Fanny Kelly, and imprisoned Zuni Bow Priests. In contrast to these successes for government colonizers, other chapters show how the government was forced to retract some of its colonial accomplishments in the concessions it made to the petitions of Chief Red Cloud, the successful land claims of the Southern Cheyenne and Arapaho, the return of Blue Lake to Taos Pueblo, and the granting of fishing rights to the Puget Sound tribes. Although Navajos took a long time to recover from Bosque Redondo, they now are the second largest tribe in the United States with more than 240,000 members.

Chapter 5

Identity Transformation and the Journeys of Fanny Kelly and Chief Red Cloud, 1864–1870

At the same time the government tried to subdue the Navajos, the Indian wars spread into Montana, Wyoming, and Nebraska. With the aid of disgruntled Cheyenne and Arapaho and the displaced Minnesota Sioux, Red Cloud and other Teton Sioux tried to stop settlers from moving through their land to reach gold mines in Montana and Idaho. Not only did the warriors destroy property, they killed many emigrants and took dozens of others as captives. By 1870, the government's approach to the Indian war factions had changed. Instead of making new treaties, the government created peace commissions to make diplomatic deals with Indian leaders and passed legislation permitting payment of reparations to victims of Indian warfare. This new Indian policy made it possible for the face-to-face meeting of captive Fanny Kelly and Chief Red Cloud in Washington, D.C.

When Fanny Kelly, an Oglala Sioux captive, met Red Cloud, an Oglala chief and diplomat, both had completed life-changing journeys. Kelly's journey began with her capture during an Indian rampage against emigrants along the Platte River in 1864. Prior to the time she met Red Cloud, Kelly had been released by the Oglalas, started a new life, and written a widely circulated narrative of her captivity. By chance, Kelly's visit to Congress in 1870 to seek reparations for her suffering during captivity coincided with the first diplomatic mission of Red Cloud. Prior to his visit to Washington, Red Cloud's relationship to the government was negative; he attacked settlers, refused to abide by federal mandates, complained about the government's mistreatment of his people, and made only modest overtures toward peace.

The goal of this chapter is to explain the journeys of these one-time enemies and show how they ended up supporting each other's causes. The chapter (1) places the credibility of Kelly and Red Cloud in historical context, (2) analyzes the identity transformation created by Kelly's captivity, (3) explains the identity transformation that evolved during Red Cloud's diplomacy, (4) interprets the contrasting motifs and themes used in Kelly's and Red Cloud's rhetoric, and (5) identifies the implications of these events for government-Indian relations.

CREDIBILITY AND CONTEXT

Government failure to resolve the Indian wars in one part of the country led to increased warfare in another area. Both the Minnesota Uprising and the Sand Creek Massacre indirectly affected the capture of Fanny Kelly. After 1862, many of the surviving Santee Sioux joined the Yanktonai, Yanktons, and other Tetons who had settled west of the Missouri River (Clodfelter 1988, 78). Following the Sand Creek Massacre, many angry Northern and Southern Arapaho and Cheyenne forged a war alliance with some of the Oglala and Brule bands of Teton Sioux. This combined force of more than 1,000 warriors went on the rampage against ranchers and stage stations in 1864–1865 (Larson 1997, 81). Red Cloud, a warrior chief of the Oglalas, led several of these attacks.

Both Kelly and Red Cloud were persuasive advocates for their respective roles in the Indian wars. Credibility typically has three components: expertness refers to the intellectual dimension, trustworthiness to moral characteristics, and dynamism to the social behavior (Jensen 1981, 216). Credibility is relational since audiences attribute positive qualities to advocates according to perceptions of their character in a given rhetorical situation. Expertness refers to audiences' perceptions of the competence and knowledge as well as the "qualifications, the skill, the creativity, and the innovativeness" of advocates (216). Trustworthiness includes audiences' perceptions of the advocate as a "good person," known to the audience as "dependable, honest, frank, sincere, fair, reliable, and open minded" (217). Dynamism consists of the advocate's ability for showmanship and persuasive performance. Dynamic advocates typically show their audiences charisma through their energy, tones of voice, and "general spirit and attitude" (218).

Kelly's Credibility

Kelly gained credibility from her experience as a Sioux war captive and as a writer; Red Cloud achieved his credibility from his success as a warrior and as an eloquent orator. Kelly became a spokesperson for Indian victims by evoking images of the ignoble savage for her readers; Red Cloud became an advocate for Plains Indian tribes by evoking images of the noble savage for the audience of his diplomatic mission. The government seemed to perceive both as exemplary spokespersons for their respective causes.

Through her narrative, Kelly asserted her intellectual, moral, and social credibility. By emphasizing her personal experience, Kelly demonstrated her intellectual credibility concerning Sioux warfare. When personal experience fits with the beliefs and expectations of the audience, the advocate appears competent (Jensen 1981, 217). Kelly recalled the Indian raids were sudden and brutal. She explains that with her husband and daughter, she joined a small party of emigrants from Kansas en route to Idaho. After departing from Fort Laramie, her emigrant train headed to Horseshoe Creek and was attacked by Indians. Her narrative recorded the attack in this dramatic way:

Without a sound of preparation or a word of warning, the bluffs before us were covered with a party of about two-hundred and fifty Indians, painted and equipped for war, who uttered the wild war-whoop and fired a signal volley of guns and revolvers into the air. (Kelly [1871] 1993, 22; Subsequent references to Kelly's narrative in this chapter are cited according to page numbers.)

The Indians demanded all of the supplies. Even after these demands were met, "[t]he Indians quickly sprang into our wagons, tearing off covers, breaking, crushing, and smashing all hinderstance to plunder, breaking open locks, trunks, and boxes . . . which they split up in savage recklessness. . . . They filled the air with fearful war-whoops and hideous shouts" (24–25). Soon after Oglala Chief Ottawa captured Kelly. Kelly's dramatic narrative emphasized her ability to survive a horrible attack by ruthless Indians. Not only did Kelly validate the government's existing knowledge about Indian raids, she added explicit details that pointed to her abilities as a writer and as a courageous survivor.

Second, Kelly bolstered her moral authority by the sincerity and reliability of a story that validated the moral beliefs of her audience (Jensen 1981, 215). One way Kelly developed moral authority was by giving additional evidence about an incident she had observed on the Yellowstone River during October 1864. She indicated that a large boat filled with about twenty people was coming down the river when her captors attacked them. The attack, she remembered, was an ambush of "unsuspecting travelers" at sundown. She wrote:

With a simultaneous yell, the savages dashed down upon them, dealing death and destruction in rapid strokes. The defenseless emigrants made an attempt to rush to the boat for arms, but were cut off, and their bleeding bodies dashed into the river as fast as they were slain. Then followed the torture of women and children . . . not a soul was left alive when the black day's work was done; and the unconscious river bore away a warm tide of human blood, and sinking human forms. (125–26)

By supplying additional evidence to show that her own experience resembled other unprovoked and brutal incidents of Sioux warfare, Kelly called attention to her reliability and invited her readers to judge the morality of Indian warfare.

Third, Kelly demonstrated her dynamism. Her autobiographical account showed she was a keen observer with sufficient skills to record a compelling and adventurous story of Sioux warfare. Kelly also called attention to her personal courage by contrasting the guilt of the attackers with the innocence of the victims. The former captive demonstrated her writing skill by replicating a familiar rhetorical style and content. By using vivid details of her personal experience and relating the evidence of eyewitnesses, Kelly mimicked the genre of popular adventure novels and attracted a wide reading audience for her work.

Red Cloud's Credibility

Red Cloud also showed his intellectual, moral, and social credibility. First, he established his competence through his reputation as a powerful war chief. This intellectual reputation began in 1868 when the Oglala chief initially refused to sign the Fort Laramie Treaty. During this time, Red Cloud established a reputation as a tough bargainer because he demanded that the government abandon the Powder River country and prevent emigrants from using the Bozeman Road as their main route to western gold fields. Red Cloud's perceived intellectual savvy and knowledge of the Teton Sioux was the reason the White House invited him to Washington in 1870. Audiences attribute credibility based on their understanding of the credentials of the source. In this case, the government perceived Red Cloud as a powerful war chief from his record in two battles.

One Indian victory, the Fetterman Massacre of 1866, showed Red Cloud's commitment to annihilate white settlers who dared to venture into Teton Sioux country. During this battle, the Indians attacked an emigrant train as it approached Fort Phil Kearny. In a panicked reaction, the army sent eight men, along with Colonel W. J. Fetterman, to protect the wagon train. Although Fetterman pursued the Indians as best he could, the Indians killed him and all of his men. This military defeat won Red Cloud the reputation as a significant war chief. Robert Larson (1997) explains, "There was outrage over the so-called Fetterman Massacre. . . . General Sherman called for a vigorous winter campaign against the Sioux and their allies." Instead of placing the blame on Fetterman, army leaders wanted to "prosecute Red Cloud's War" (102).

The government also credited Red Cloud with victory in the Wagon Box fight. At this battle, Red Cloud's large force of warriors attacked a group of woodcutters who were putting up hay along the Bighorn River. The Indians pursued the men on foot "shooting flaming arrows into the hay stored in the wagon boxes." When heavy gunfire eventually drove the woodcutters into a retreat, the Indians burned their camp and "forced survivors to take refuge in a makeshift corral." Both sides suffered some casualties (Larson 1997, 112–14). The Indians continued their attacks against military troops trying to build Fort Fetterman. At first glance, Red Cloud's expertise as a war chief appears to be a source of negative credibility for a peace diplomat. However, Red Cloud's warrior reputation became a positive factor because the government believed that distinguished war chiefs had the power to restrain their warriors and to make their people comply with peace agreements.

Red Cloud's moral authority evolved during the same historical time as did his competence. The government considered Red Cloud's resistance to be a sign of his tribal authority. He gained his reputation for resistance by refusing to sign the Fort Laramie Treaty unless the government abandoned the Bozeman Trail and all of its forts along the Powder River. James Olson (1965) notes that the peace commissioners

had come west with wagon-loads of presents and a treaty which conceded everything Red Cloud had demanded, and they could not even get him to come in and talk to them. Instead, they met with a group of chiefs that would sign anything. (74)

Even after the government abandoned the forts in August, Red Cloud failed to come forward until all the treaty commissioners left the area (*Annual Report of the Commissioner of Indian Affairs* 1868, 21–24). Eventually he signed the treaty on Indian terms. Ironically, Red Cloud's failure to meet with the commissioners enhanced rather than weakened his reputation because his reluctance to sign made his eventual signature even more valuable.

Reluctance to sign a treaty unfavorable to his people also showed that Red Cloud had moral authority with his tribe. Moral authority evolves in part from a "prestigious station in life" and from the trust and respect gained from others (Jensen 1981, 218). Red Cloud gained this respect by demanding a treaty that would benefit the Teton Sioux. Dee Brown notes, "For the first time in its history the United States government had negotiated a peace which conceded everything demanded by the enemy and which extracted nothing in return" (225). The net gains for the Sioux, according to Ward Churchill and Jim Vander Wall (1988), were a land base consisting of 3 percent "of what is now the continental United States" (104).

As a war chief Red Cloud forced the government to submit to his demands. He battled against settlers and failed to comply with the commissioners' requests. In this way, Red Cloud showed both the government and his own people that he was aggressive, forceful, and bold. His credibility as a dynamic negotiator further increased during his first diplomatic visit to Washington.

The historical context in which the Oglalas captured Kelly and Red Cloud fought settlers shows how treaty commissioners invest both individuals with expertness, trustworthiness, and dynamism, traits that bolstered their credentials as advocates. The remainder of this chapter examines Kelly's journey as created through her captive narrative and Red Cloud's journey as depicted through his diplomatic oratory.

IDENTITY TRANSFORMATION IN FANNY KELLY'S CAPTIVE NARRATIVE

During the nineteenth century, much of the information that Americans gathered about Indians came to them through captive narratives. Over 200 narratives still exist. Many of these stories appeared in multiple editions of books, and others surfaced in serial form in newspapers. These popular accounts showed adventurous settlers in an agonistic struggle with Indians resisting government conquest (Derounian-Stodola & Levernier 1993, 42).

The captive narrative was so popular it became a distinct autobiographical genre that juxtaposed the heroic traits of the American character against the savage life ways of the Indian. Most narratives reinforced stereotypic images of the Indian, but occasionally these stories called the readers' attention to the helpfulness and kindness of a few Indians.

This genre's unique features consisted of its adventurous themes, sentimental style, and highly embellished melodramatic language. The style featured excessive descriptive details about life-threatening events used to provoke suspense and evoke shock from the readers (Van Der Beets 1972, xxii). For readers who never left the safety of their homes, the style made the stories both exciting and persuasive. The captive stories uplifted readers, showing them the strength of the American character and the superiority of the civilized life to that of the wild Indians. Additionally, the stories reinforced the government's policy that Indians should be forced onto reservations to reduce warfare against settlers. Kelly met these literary expectations by writing her narrative in a persuasive melodramatic style that enforced the strength of the middle-class American values of her era. By showing the savage acts committed by Indians, she reinforced the government's political agenda of civilizing Indians.

A common way of looking at the adventures of important people is through the lens of archetypes. One universal theme contrasting the lives of both Kelly and Red Cloud is the death/rebirth journey archetype outlined by Joseph Campbell (1960). He explains that a person's identity transformation begins with a separation, moves to adaptation, evolves into struggle, and culminates with a return or a rebirth (50–80). These stages of a journey fit with the structure of the captive narrative, creating persuasive adventure sequences for readers. A journey refers to the movement of individual from one psychological or physical place to another, and, in doing so, focuses attention on the changes in identity experienced by those making the journey. P. W. Preston (1997) explains that identity forms and changes according to the ways in which persons "more or less self-consciously locate" themselves in the social world (4).

In each stage of her journey, Kelly located herself in a different cultural setting. Her captive narrative moved through the stages of the death/rebirth journey, beginning with separation, followed by adaptation and the experience of traumatic ordeals, and ending with her rebirth.

Separation

Kelly's separation from her family marked the first stage of her journey. For her, this separation involved "a symbolic death of the old life" (Van Der Beets 1972, 554). The Indians not only took Kelly from her husband and daughter, but they forced her to travel with them to a feared and unknown location. Kelly characterized her separation in this way: "To portray my feelings upon this separation would be impossible. The agony I suffered was indescribable" (47). In hopes someone would find her, she immediately decided to mark the path of her captors by ripping up pieces of paper and dropping them on the ground. When this scheme failed, she feared that she was on a journey to hell. She described her descent into hell in figurative terms. We moved down "the dangerous and precipitous paths among the great bluffs which we had been approaching and the dizzy, fearful heights leading over the dark abyss and the gloomy terrible gorge where only an Indian dares to venture" (50). Kelly's graphic imagery clearly contrasted this journey with distrusted and despicable Indians to familiar journeys women usually took with friends and family. Images of fear, darkness, and hell expressed the horror she felt as she entered the unfamiliar locale of her captors.

Her separation brought her into what she considered to be a dreadful culture. Kelly recalled the difficulty of the journey:

They had taken paths inaccessible to white men, and made their crossing at a point where it would be impossible for trains to pass, so they might avoid meeting emigrants. Having reached the opposite bend they separated into squads and started in every direction except southward, so as to mislead or confuse pursuers by the various trails. (51–52)

When Kelly described the journey as inaccessible, impossible, and misleading, she established symbolic barriers that she eventually overcame. Establishing these barriers and later overcoming them was a device Kelly used to emphasize her courage.

Kelly found herself both in a different cultural and physical locale. Preston (1997) explains that locale is a key feature of identity because it shows how individuals "construe their relationships to the community they inhabit and how they consider that their community relates to the wider world" (9). She feared this new culture; at the same time, she recognized she must be part of it in order to survive. One prominent aspect of the new culture was food. For example, Kelly described the horror she felt at a dog meat feast she attended. She remembered:

It is impossible to describe my feelings on that day, as I sat in the midst of those wild, savage people. . . . Each guest had a large wooden bowl placed before him with a quantity of dogs' flesh floating in a profusion of soup or rich gravy, with a large spoon resting in the dish made of buffalo horn. . . . The women signified to me that I should feel highly honored by being called to feast with chiefs and great warriors. (89)

Kelly's presence at a dog feast honoring chiefs and warriors focused on the new and frightening foreign cultural locale in which she was forced to live as a captive. By defining a locale, Preston (1997) explains, a person understands the power/authority relationships, the mundane routines of ordinary life, and the folk knowledge of the common people (58). This foreign locale caused Kelly to search for cultural reasons for the Sioux eating habits. Kelly reflected about how the dog "is sacrificed . . . to appease the offended spirits or deities, whom it is considered necessary that they should conciliate in this way, and when done, is invariably done by giving the best in the . . . kennel" (91). In addition to the uncomfortable conditions of her captivity, Kelly learned about strange Indian customs and experienced personal suffering as she adapted to the new culture. For Kelly, eating dog meat was a sign of Indian savagery, and her disgust with this custom signified her superior civilized state. When Kelly joined in the ceremony, however, she made a slight move toward cultural adaptation.

Adaptation

The second stage featured Kelly's slow adaptation to the alien culture of the Oglala Sioux, a process that demonstrated her ability to survive under difficult circumstances (Van Der Beets 1972, 556–57). The adaptation involved both suffering and womanly accomplishments. Kelly wrote:

Hunger and thirst, sorrow and fear, with unusual fatigue and labor, had weakened me in mind and body, so that after trying to realize the frightful vision that had almost deprived me of my senses, I began to waver in my knowledge of it and half determined that it was a hideous phantom, like many others that had tortured my lonely hours. (123)

At the same time she suffered, Kelly demonstrated in a melodramatic way the feminine traits associated with the "sphere of true womanhood." This social ideal, prevalent in Kelly's time, decreed that women should be pious, pure, gentle, nurturing, and sacrificing (Woloch 1984, 119). Her caring role first came to light when a "squaw" stabbed a chief in a domestic dispute. At the time, Kelly took charge of the chief's care by bathing and dressing his wounds and feeding him (127). Even though Kelly was suffering herself, she helped out with the day-to-day needs of the Indians with whom she lived. Chronicling her adaptation in this way allowed Kelly to identify with many women readers that shared similar social expectations about how a proper woman should act.

By focusing on changes in her personal appearance and communication skills, Kelly also called attention to the sphere of women. She showed her ability to sacrifice by adapting the appearance of Indian women. She focused attention on her appearance in this way. I wore a long white dress hanging below the knee. The dress was "fastened at the waist with a red scarf," and I wore moccasins embroidered with porcupine quills and a robe over my shoulder. I had brass rings on each of my arms, and I was painted "like the squaws" (205). An even more significant sign of her positive female traits was her ability to acquire the language of the captors so she could improve her relationships with them.

Kelly's adaptation did not mean she assimilated into Indian culture. Adaptation refers to one's adjustment to the expectations and norms of another culture; it does not mean assimilation by becoming part of another culture. Kelly's external signs of female adaptation hid her internal disdain for the Indians. Kelly explained this disdain in these remarks:

The Indian does everything through motives of policy. He has none of the kindlier feelings of humanity in him. He is as devoid of gratitude as he is hypocritical and treacherous. He observes a treaty, or promise, only so long as it is dangerous for him to disregard it. . . . Cruelty is inherent in them and is early manifested in the young in torturing birds, turtles, or any little animal that may fall into their hands. They seem to delight in it, while the pleasure of the adult in torturing his prisoners is most unquestionable. (189)

In the above passages and in many other parts of her story, Kelly contrasted her feminine courage with Indian cruelty. In doing so, she showed that she understood Indians through the lens of her own culture and that she viewed herself as superior to Indians.

Kelly learned about different Sioux Indian groups because she lived with Blackfeet and with Yanktons and used their tribal life as a means of social comparison for evaluating her Oglala captors. Kelly recalled the difference between the Oglalas and Blackfeet. When she entered the village of the Blackfeet, she said,

I was received with great joy, and even marks of distinction were shown me. That night there was a feast, and everything denoted a time of rejoicing. My life was now changed—instead of waiting upon others, they waited upon me. (193)

In this instance, Kelly seemed happy because the Blackfeet showed her the homage she believed she deserved. This stage of adaptation gave Kelly a glimpse of the networks of another culture, that is, the relationships between individuals in different parts of the same culture (Preston 1997, 9). The recognition of these networks permitted Kelly to understand the Oglala's folk knowledge and see how it fit with the lifestyle of other Indian groups. Understanding political-cultural networks helps to transform a person's identity because it forces individuals to move from the familiar to the unfamiliar and from risky to safe situations (Preston 1997, 62). Kelly's recognition of positive relational networks led her to reconstruct her stereotypes of Indians and to appreciate a few qualities of one band of Plains Indians.

Ordeals

In the third stage of her journey, Kelly experienced difficult ordeals that seemed beyond her human endurance. By undergoing tests of her will and character, she not only survived but gained new insights about herself. Kelly identified many episodes in which she felt her life was threatened. But her narrative cast these events in the positive light of her strong character and personal resourcefulness. For example, early in her captivity she thought she was going to be killed because she had broken and thrown away a venerated peace pipe of one of the chiefs. The warriors put her on a horse and aimed "pistols, bows, and spears" at her. But just when she felt her death was imminent, she recalled that she had $120. She used the money to bribe the men. When they saw the money, they "laid their weapons on the ground, seemingly pleased, and anxious to understand, requesting me to explain the worth of each note" (59). In this account, Kelly attributed her survival to her insight and resourcefulness, qualities related to female virtues of courage valued by her nineteenth-century society.

Her narrative also called attention to female virtues grounded in Christian faith and morals (Woloch 1984, 119). For example, Kelly expected to be sacrificed and burned at the stake because the Indians had lost so many of their warriors in a battle with General Alfred Sully. She recalled:

Soon they sent an Indian to me, who asked me if I was ready to die—to be burned at the stake. . . . He said that he had been sent from the council to warn me that it had become necessary to put me to death on account of my white brothers killing so many of their young men recently. He repeated that they were not cruel for pleasure, . . . necessity is their first law, and he and the wise chiefs, faithful to their hatred for the white race, were in their haste to satisfy vengeance. (108–9)

Kelly believed she was saved from this awful fate by her prayers to God and her compassion for the chief. By juxtaposing her heroic Christian traits against the antiheroic savage Indian qualities, Kelly further emphasized her own female virtues.

These ordeals marked character transformations; that is, Kelly changed from an inexperienced and educated white woman who feared the "savages" to a woman who acknowledged and appreciated a few qualities of Indian humanity. Undergoing the ordeals forced her to reflect on her own strengths and frailties and to recognize the humanness of others through a process of cultural comparison. But Kelly still saw herself as superior to her captors. She was strong and positively motivated by female Christian virtues; the Indians' motivation was perverted by greed and vengeance.

Rebirth

Finally, Kelly showed new knowledge and insights based on her survival of traumatic ordeals. Eventually, a white trader negotiated for her freedom, and the military paid her captors to secure her release. The time of release coincided with her rebirth and her emotional displays of happiness. She remembered:

My heart gave a wild bound of joy. Something seemed to rise in my throat and choke my breathing. Everything was changed. The torture of suspense, the agony of fear, and the dread of evil to come, all seemed to melt away like mist before the morning sunshine when I beheld the precious emblem of liberty. (210)

The flag symbolized the end of her ordeals and a return to a familiar locale. She reflected, "After a bondage lasting more than five months, during which I endured every torture, I once more stood free, among people of my own race all ready to assist me and restore me to my husband's arms" (210–11).

The knowledge she had gained from her captivity prepared Kelly for a return to the culture of her birth. When Kelly returned to her husband, she arose from the symbolic grave of her captivity and returned to the privileged life she had lost (Van Der Beets 1971, 560–62). But this return was marred by the news that her daughter Mary had been killed by Indians at the same time Kelly was captured. Nonetheless, her journey home was joyous. First, she received a heroine's welcome at Fort Sully in Dakota Territory on the Missouri River. Then she was greeted with joyous celebrating crowds in Sioux City, Council Bluffs, and St. Joe. She recalled, "We made all haste for Leavenworth, Kansas, where I was received by friends and relatives as one risen from the dead." Then she arrived at her family home in Geneva, Kansas, where she was greeted by her mother and "swallowed up in the joy of that reunion" (232).

Upon her return, Kelly experienced joy and sorrow as well as new knowledge and understanding of her identity. The growth Kelly experienced from this difficult journey gave her the strength to act politically on her own behalf. She explained, "With the ending of this chapter [of my life], I hope to lay aside forever all regretful experiences" (232). After her return, she wrote her captive narrative as a record of her journey.

The publicity she gained from the publication of the narrative earned her an audience with the president of the United States and eventually culminated in her meeting with Red Cloud. After signing a congressional affidavit verifying that Oglalas had captured her, Kelly officially certified her personal and economic losses as a justification for reparations. By this action, she became a political advocate. During her chance meeting with Red Cloud, he told the secretary of interior and the commissioner of Indian affairs that he wished that she be paid reparations. He purportedly said:

Look at that woman. She was captured by Silver Horn's party. I wish you to pay her what her captors owe her. I am a man true to what I say, and want to keep my promise. I speak for all my nation. The Indians robbed this lady there and through your influence I want her to be paid out of the first money due us. (254)

Kelly's rhetorical plea for reparations called further attention to her personal courage. During her speech to the president, she claimed she had smuggled a letter to Captain Fish during her captivity that protected a wagon train from attack and saved the lives of many soldiers (Senate Report 1872, 1). Eventually the Senate recommended that she receive $15,000 for her losses.

The captivity experience empowered Fanny Kelly, a housewife from Kansas, to lobby Congress on her own behalf. One explanation for this courage is that her captivity gave her political capital. Pierre Bourdieu (1984) claims identity transformation empowers a person to do new things. He notes that when people occupy a cultural space or *habitas*, they hold political capital gained from that space. It is likely Kelly acquired political capital from the space she occupied as a captive and then translated it into a bargaining chip with Congress. For Bourdieu (1984), a person possessing political capital in two cultures, as Kelly had done, holds more resources for gaining advantage in the social world than does a person from a single *habitas*.

The separation, adaptation, ordeals, and rebirth endured by Kelly on her journey transformed her identity. In part, Kelly created these transformations through her public rhetoric about her captivity. The readers of her autobiographical account learned that she was a strong and resourceful woman who could act on her own behalf. She used this public identity as political collateral for persuading the government that she deserved financial reparations for her suffering at the hands of the Sioux. Preston (1997) explains that identity is never stagnant. Rather, it is socially constructed and reconstructed from privately remembered and publicly expressed ideas (7). Persons construct their political-cultural identities by taking into account a locale, networks, and a memory of culture. Kelly's creatively written and socially constructed captive narrative emphasized her ability to retain her womanly Christian virtues and civility while moving through a strange locale with the unfamiliar networks of an alien culture. The next section indicates some similarities and differences between Kelly's and Red Cloud's journeys.

IDENTITY TRANSFORMATION IN RED CLOUD'S DIPLOMACY

The government designed the diplomatic journeys of Indian chiefs as means to secure compliance with federal policies. After designating certain powerful men as chiefs, the government paid for the transportation of these Indian leaders and their agents to come to Washington and meet with the president, secretary of interior, and members of the Bureau of Indian Affairs. The overt goal was diplomatic, that is, to resolve intertribal welfare, create legal agreements, encourage Indian assimilation, and force tribes onto reservations. Indian reformers also encouraged diplomatic visits as an alternative to costly wars with the Indians. However, the visits also had the covert, propagandistic goal of impressing Indians with the power and military strength of the government. Herman Viola (1981) notes that the government expected to destroy the Indians' confidence as warriors, instill beliefs of their inferiority, instruct them about the white man's world, and persuade them to accept federal policies (26).

The Indian diplomats had covert motives of their own. They likely perceived their trips to Washington as a means of embellishing their personal power and prestige among their tribes, securing material gifts for their people, and gaining authority among regional Indian leaders (16–19). The press published the details of the Indian diplomatic visits in the major newspapers, and most of the speeches of the chiefs received careful press and political scrutiny. In the view of the national press, Red Cloud was the most eloquent Indian to visit Washington.

The delegations functioned according to a prescribed set of expectations and routines. The Indians stayed in boarding houses near the Capitol, visited the Marine barracks, the Washington arsenal, the Navy yards, and also toured battleships. Some visited the Smithsonian to see George Catlin's portraits of Indian leaders, and others went to George Washington's home in Mount Vernon. During their stay, delegates sometimes performed Indian dances and songs for Washington spectators. Each delegation received gifts from the government, including military uniforms, trinkets, and presidential medals or other peace symbols (Viola 1981, 120–23). General appropriations, philanthropists, and tribal funds paid for the Indian visits. In return the Indians brought gifts for the Great Father, including personal possessions, such as buffalo robes, calumets, moccasins, war shirts, and feathered head dresses (Viola 1981, 109). When they returned home, the government gave gifts of horses to Indian delegates so they had transport to go from stage stations to their homeland.

Even though the government expected to indoctrinate Red Cloud about the superiority of white culture and force him to submit to federal demands, he converted these goals into objectives supporting his people. This segment of the chapter examines Red Cloud's 1870 diplomatic visit and explains how his speeches during this journey contributed to the transformation of his identity. Red Cloud viewed the journey as a diplomatic mission in which he could make demands and gain concessions from the government. His journey took place in the four stages of separation, accommodation, negotiation, and return.

Separation

Red Cloud's separation from his people signified a change in the nature of his leadership. Just as Kelly had done, he found himself in a cultural and physical locale that forced him to reconfigure his relationship with his people and the larger political community (Preston 1997, 9). As a diplomat, he put aside his role as war chief and accepted the position of Oglala father figure and symbolic leader of all Teton Sioux.

Unlike Kelly's, Red Cloud's separation was voluntary. His first visit to Washington came at the request of President Grant in the form of "a call to diplomacy." The government chose the chief as one of the representatives of the Sioux people because it expected to win his support for federal policies. In one sense, it was not surprising that Red Cloud should receive the call because he was one of the leaders of the Sioux, one of the largest groups of Indians in the United States at the time, and his Oglalas were a prominent faction of this group. In the perception of the government, Red Cloud's reputation suited him for a diplomatic role. For example, the *New York Times* (1870, June 1) predicted the chief's visit would be significant:

The visit of Red Cloud to Washington cannot but do well. . . . Red Cloud is undoubtedly the most celebrated warrior now living on the American continent . . . a man of brains, a good ruler, an eloquent speaker, an able general and fair diplomat. The friendship of Red Cloud is of more importance to the whites than that of any other ten chiefs on the plains. Let every care be taken of him while in the East[,] and no efforts spared to win his good will and create in his mind a favorable impression. (1)

Even though the press and the government designated Red Cloud as the main leader of the Teton Sioux, other chiefs, especially Spotted Tail and Old Man Afraid of His Horse, were equally important leaders. As his translator, Red Cloud brought with him a mixed-blood trader and able linguist, John Richards, whose translations may have contributed to Red Cloud's eloquent expression.

In ways similar to Kelly's, Red Cloud's long journey led him into an unfamiliar locale. He began on horseback in Pine Bluff, Wyoming, and then boarded a train near Cheyenne, Wyoming. With other members of the delegation, he arrived in Washington on June 1 and took up temporary residence in a boarding house. At his first meeting with government officials on June 3, Red Cloud's first words indicated both his honor at being called and his disappointment about the reception he had received. Red Cloud told Indian Commissioner Ely Parker and other assembled leaders:

My great friends, I have come a long ways to see you, but some how or other you don't look at me. I had to come to see you. When I heard the words of my Great Father permitting me to come, I was glad and came right off. I left my women and children at home and want you to give them more rations and wish you would send my people some ammunition to kill game and telegraph to them that I arrived all right. (*New York Times* 1870, June 4, 1)

Red Cloud did not begin with the diplomatic strategy of ingratiating his audience. Rather, he criticized them and demanded additional resources. This was the first sign that Red Cloud would not be an ordinary Indian delegate.

Upon his arrival, Red Cloud defined the locale as one in which the government would assert power and exert control over the Sioux. He was not concerned as much about the folk beliefs of his white political hosts as he was about his own diplomatic goals. Red Cloud quickly observed that the government was trying to impress him with white culture. He adopted the government strategy for his own benefit when his first speech tried to impress whites about his culture and its needs. In this way, Red Cloud's separation from his people turned into serious diplomatic maneuvering.

Accommodation

Through a minimal amount of ingratiation and some subtle undermining of government power, Red Cloud persuaded federal officials to make psychological and cultural accommodations to him. Unlike Kelly who was forced to adapt to the alien culture of her captors, Red Cloud made demands of the alien political culture that hosted his visit. He seemed to understand the power and authority of Washington bureaucrats so well that he could manipulate it to achieve his own goals. For example, Red

Cloud manipulated the networks of government culture in line with Preston's recommendations (1997, 193). His speeches directly addressed the networks of another culture by attributing power and credibility to the Great Father and accepting the secretary of interior and commissioner of Indian affairs as representatives of this power structure. At the same time he paid homage to those in power who wanted compliance from him, Red Cloud cultivated support from congressional leaders and social activists who lobbied for fair treatment of Indians.

Early on Red Cloud was not impressed by government propaganda. Prior to the official council with Secretary of Interior Joseph Cox, the government tried to impress the chiefs with the material wealth, the armaments, and the trappings of power of the White Father. Commissioner Parker even arranged tours to the U.S. Capitol, the Senate, the arsenal, and the Navy yard. One reason these propaganda efforts failed was that the Indians did not comprehend the weapons nor see how they could be used. In fact, they were puzzled, not frightened, by what they saw. Another reason the propaganda failed to impress Red Cloud was his sense of himself as a powerful leader from an important tribe, a belief that caused him verbally to resist government demands.

Red Cloud's first diplomatic session proceeded in an unusual way. Instead of the government gaining accommodations from the Oglala chiefs, it encountered resistance. In his beginning remarks, Cox tried to establish the norm of accommodation, that is, "persuasive talk taking place in situations whose outcome is determined by the balance of force" (Watson 1983, 54). The success of the persuasive talk depends on two factors. First, collaboration allows parties working together to achieve common ends. Second, concession-making permits parties to make mutually agreeable exchanges. The ability to force the other party to make concessions depends on the skills, wealth, resources, and location of the diplomatic encounter (Watson 1983, 54–60). In an effort to establish common ground, Cox told Red Cloud, "Red Cloud and his people . . . now know that what the President does is not because he is afraid but because he wants to do that which is right and good" (Olson 1965, 104).

Red Cloud expressed resistance to government policies early in the talks and then demanded the government provide ammunition for hunting so that his people could feed themselves. Secretary Cox responded that the Great Father would keep his promises to send food and clothing to help the Indians. Cox also emphasized that sending powder and lead for Indian guns was another matter, so he rejected Red Cloud's request alleging that the Indians would use such supplies to fight against white settlers. Cox explained:

[The settlers say that] Red Cloud and his people have been threatening them. . . . We want Red Cloud and his people to say to us here before they go that they will never do so and they will keep peace with all of our people. (*New York Times* 1870, June 8, 1)

Cox's patronizing remarks must have irritated Red Cloud because afterward the chief ignored what he said.

When Cox sought collaboration on the issue of peace, for example, Red Cloud changed the subject by calling attention to his credibility as an important chief ordained by the Great Spirit with the power to act on behalf of his people. In doing so, Red Cloud claimed the Great Spirit gave him his power, a power superior to secular government authorities. His speech began in this way:

I came from where the sun sets. You were raised on chairs. I want to sit as I sit where the sun sets. (Here the Indian warrior sat upon the floor, in Indian fashion, and proceeded.) The Great Spirit has raised me this way. He raised me naked. I run no opposition to the Great Father who sits in the White House. I don't want to fight. I have offered my prayer to the Great Spirit so that I might come here safe and well. What I have to say to you and to these men and to my Great Father is this: "Look at me. I was raised where the sun rises and I come from where it sets." Whose voice was first heard in this land? It was the red people who used the bow. The Great Father may be good and kind but I can't see it. I am good and kind to the white people and have given my lands. . . . The Great Father has sent his people out there and left me nothing but an island. Our nation is melting away like the snow on the side of the hills where the sun is warm; while your people are like the blades of grass in the summer when the sun is coming. (*New York Times* 1870, June 8, 1)

Red Cloud claimed his power came from the Great Spirit while the government's power came from a lesser source, the Great Father (the president). He explained that it was not the esteemed Great Father that pursued peace and wanted change from the Indians, it was the Indians that were good, suffered at the hands of the Great Father, and sought peace and justice. By placing himself in the offensive position, Red Cloud relegated the government to a defensive posture and enabled himself to take charge of the diplomatic exchange.

In order to strengthen his offense even further, Red Cloud sought to rectify the injustice suffered by his people at the hands of the government. He demanded the government accommodate to his objectives by closing Fort Fetterman and prohibiting road building in the Black Hills and at the Big Horn. Moreover, Red Cloud asserted that he disliked the government ordering him around. He told Cox that he did not intend to settle on a reservation on the Missouri, desired friendly traders that he himself selected, expected quality goods for his people, and wanted payments for Indian lands taken by railroad developers.

As the diplomatic meeting progressed Red Cloud became even more bold by asserting his superior moral authority. For example, he claimed his entitlement came from his family: "I was born at the forks of the Platte. My father and mother told me that the land belonged to me." He then reprimanded the government, telling its advocates to examine their consciences concerning their deceitful dealings with the Sioux. Instead of forcing the Sioux to settle on reservations and accept treaty provisions, Red Cloud said the purpose of his diplomacy was "to know the facts from our Father why the promises which have been made to us have not been kept" (*New York Times* 1870, June 8, 1). In this way Red Cloud focused attention on his power as an Indian diplomat at the same time he questioned the power of federal officials. A newspaper columnist understated Red Cloud's ability to turn the tables on the government, when he characterized the tone of the meeting as one of "frankness and firmness" on the part of Red Cloud (*New York Times* 1870, June 8, 4). Government officials likely were stunned by Red Cloud's ability to convert the diplomacy from collaboration and concession-making into his rhetorical challenges to government policies.

Red Cloud's subversion of the government's goals resulted from his understanding of the networks of the audience in the Washington locale, his view of himself as a spiritual advocate, and his ability to take control of the diplomatic meetings. Clearly, Red Cloud did not adapt the passive role that characterized the diplomacy of many other Indian delegates.

Negotiation

Negotiation marked the third stage in the identity transformation of Red Cloud's diplomatic journey. Red Cloud's negotiation was of a psychological rather than a physical order. During this phase, he did not undergo the fear and physical suffering Kelly did, but he experienced similar psychological and cultural stress and demonstrated personal courage. Negotiation centers on the divergent and convergent interests of the parties. Divergent issues are the points about which the opposing parties disagree; convergent issues are the points about which parties agree. Diplomats attempt to influence other parties to reconcile divergent issues while at the same time they emphasize the common ground underlying the convergent issues. As a result, diplomatic persuasion involves a public polemic in which parties make demands, state threats, and issue promises (Watson 1983). The negotiation phase of this diplomatic encounter occurred in the second set of formal meetings between Red Cloud and Washington officials.

After his opening session with Cox, Red Cloud met with the president and reiterated his demands. Then in a follow-up meeting, he claimed he had no idea about the different provisions of the 1868 Fort Laramie treaty saying, "I never heard of it and [I] don't mean to follow it" (Olson 1965, 107). Instead of contesting Red Cloud's point of view, Indian Commissioner Ely Parker apologized, saying he was sorry that Red Cloud and his people did not understand the treaty, but he had arranged this time to talk so that they could clarify the treaty provisions. Parker knew that Red Cloud objected to the reservation location stipulated in the treaty. In a surprise conciliatory move, the Indian commissioner told the Oglala chief that his people could stay near their hunting grounds and promised to send adequate cattle and food supplies. Finally, Parker allowed Red Cloud to recommend names for an Indian agent (*New York Times* 1870, June 12, 1).

Even though Red Cloud won so many concessions from the government, he failed to acknowledge them. Instead the chief continued to assert his grievances in the context of his prophetic vision of the Indian's place in eternity. At the end of the diplomatic meetings, Red Cloud proclaimed:

The whites think the Great Spirit has nothing to do with us, but he has. After fooling with us and taking away our property, they [the government] will have to suffer for it hereafter. The Great Spirit is now looking at us, and we offer him prayers. . . . The Great Spirit will not make me suffer because I am ignorant. He will put me in a place where I will be better off than in this world. (*New York Times* 1870, June 12, 1)

This vision exemplified Red Cloud's spiritual and transcendent identity as a leader whose life had been determined by the Great Spirit, not by the government. This prayer-like conclusion established Red Cloud as a prototype of a subjectively identified and spiritually-ordained leader. Establishing a prototype of this sort helps rhetors achieve a self-defined purpose by constructing identity in line with personal beliefs and values (McKerrow & Bruner 1997, 53).

During his final day in Washington, Red Cloud again failed to acknowledge Parker's generous concessions, and he instead continued to pursue peace issues of importance to him. Red Cloud outlined these conditions for peace:

I know you will remember what I have said for you have good memories. If I had not been for peace I should not have come to my Great Father's house. Tell your children to keep the peace. I do not say to my father, go to my country and scare the game away. Tell him to keep them away. I will not do wrong. If you had kept your peace across the Platte, you never would have had any trouble. . . . I do not want to make war with the Great Father. I want to show I go away peaceably. (*New York Times* 1870, June 14, 1)

In these concluding remarks, Red Cloud defined his power and authority as a diplomat. It was after placing himself in a morally superior position to the government that Red Cloud requested the government to pay Fanny Kelly reparations for her captivity. When Red Cloud told the government what to do, he again asserted his power over government officials.

Return/Reconciliation

This final phase of Red Cloud's journey marked his identity conversion from a war chief to a peace-seeking diplomat. Unlike Kelly who ended her journey in military custody, Red Cloud finished his diplomacy in the alien locale of New York City. Reconciliation with the government was the goal of Red Cloud's address to Indian reformers and sympathizers at Cooper Union. In this speech he explained that what appeared to be opposites were in fact reconcilable through the transcendent spiritual and peace-seeking desire of red and white men. He proclaimed:

My brothers and my friends who are before me today. God Almighty has made us all, and He is here to hear what I have to say to you today. The Great Spirit made us both. He gave me lands and He gave you lands. You came here and we received you as brothers. When the Almighty made you, He made you all white and clothed you. When He made us[,] He made us with red skins and poor. When you first came we were very many and you were few. Now you are many and we are few. You do not know who appears before you to speak. He is a representative of the original American race, and first people of this continent. We are good and not bad. The reports which you get about us are all on one side. You hear of us only as murderers and thieves. We are not so. If we had more lands to give to you we would give them, but we have no more. (Armstrong 1971, 91)

Red Cloud's conciliatory efforts continued when he asked the help of the audience in securing peace. He pleaded,

All I want is right and justice. . . . We do not want riches, we want peace and love. The riches that we have in this world . . . we cannot take with us to the next. . . . I hope you will think of what I have said to you. I bid you all an affectionate farewell. (Armstrong 1971, 92)

These remarks reinforced Red Cloud's identity as a diplomat working toward peace and friendship with whites.

Red Cloud's speaking also demonstrated his ability to share his cultural experiences with audiences from diverse political and cultural networks. In doing so, he moved from a private cultural to a public political locale (Preston 1997, 66). Through this movement, Red Cloud changed his identity from war to peace chief and in the process gained political collateral. One journalist commented on Red Cloud's address at Cooper Union in this way:

His earnest manner, his impassioned gestures, the eloquence of his hand, and the magnetism which he evidently exercises over an audience produced a vast effect on the dense throng which listened to him yesterday. . . . The solemnity of Red Cloud's manner, an impressive way which he has of throwing both his arms upwards when referring to the "Great Spirit" and the intense pathos which he threw into his tones at many parts of his speech, thoroughly enlisted the sympathies of the audience in his favor. ("Last Appeal of Red Cloud" 1870, June 17, 4)

During his journey, Red Cloud achieved rhetorical and diplomatic success by evoking his spiritual and political authority. As a diplomat, he made many demands and gained concessions from government leaders. His diplomatic journey evolved through stages of separation, accommodation, negotiation, and reconciliation. In one way, the final phase of Red Cloud's journey solidified his identity as a capable diplomat and relegated his identity as a warrior and government foe to the historical record. In another way, Red Cloud's return to his own people was not triumphant because the government did not make good on the concessions it promised the Oglalas. Washington's failure to keep promises tarnished Red Cloud's reputation with his own people. As a result, some Oglalas began to doubt Red Cloud's moral authority because they failed to reap the positive rewards he promised his diplomacy would bring to them (Price 1996, 102–6).

The journeys of Kelly and Red Cloud shared some similarities. They both traveled roads unfamiliar to them. She journeyed to a strange Indian culture; he went to a foreign political culture. Kelly and Red Cloud both gained political collateral from their intercultural experiences and changed their identity as the result of their journeys. At the temporary end to their journeys, both spoke with government officials and achieved self-serving political motives. In other ways, their journeys were quite different. Her separation from her family was coerced, but Red Cloud's was voluntary. Her adaptation required struggle and physical pain, his required psychological and cultural accommodation. Her ordeals threatened her personal life, but his negotiations affirmed his cultural heritage. Her return was a rebirth into her family and friendly surroundings, but his return was marred by controversy. In the perception of the American public, she became a public heroine, he became a diplomat. In the eyes of her people, she was a female heroine; in the eyes of his people, he was perhaps too ambitious and too trusting. Her journey showed feminine psychological courage, his demonstrated cultural diplomatic will.

THEMES AND MOTIFS

By using contrasting themes and motifs about the ignoble and noble savage, the captive's narrative and the chief's oratory created distinctive arguments about Indian identity. According to M. H. Abrahms (1971), a motif is a formula, a phrase, or an image that recurs frequently within or among discourses (101–2). Because the repetition of motifs focuses on a central theme, these verbal devices give audiences clues to the deeper meaning of the rhetorical texts. Specifically, a motif explains movement, that is,

sets forth an idea causing a thought to move forward into different meanings (Seigneuret 1988, xvi). Although motifs are sometimes confused with
themes, themes are moral arguments that state a thesis or doctrine
(Abrahms 1971, 102), and motifs are repeated words and phrases that
emphasize the meaning of the argument (Seigneuret 1988, xxi).

As advocates, Kelly and Red Cloud used contrasting motifs. Kelly repeated the motifs about the ignoble savage to develop her argument that
white culture was superior to Indian culture. On the other hand, Red Cloud
relied on the motif of the noble savage to develop his argument that Indian
culture was spiritually superior to white culture. The subsequent paragraphs identity motifs and analyze arguments, first in Kelly's narrative and
then in Red Cloud's oratory.

Kelly's Portrayals of the Ignoble Savage

Kelly's narrative emphasized the traits of the ignoble savage. Robert F.
Berkhofer (1979) says the early meaning of "savage" was someone who
lives in a natural state. Denotative meanings associating savages with cruelty and lack of civility first appeared in the eighteenth- and nineteenth-
century verbal depictions of Indians (3–31). Kelly's "ignoble savage" motifs
claimed Indians acted in a "treacherous, cruel, perverse" manner, exhibit-
ing behavior similar to beasts in the wilderness. Words and phrases that
typically appeared in nineteenth-century motifs about the ignoble savage
were "squalor," "filth," "indolence," "lack of discipline," "thievery,"
"hard heartedness," and "abuse of women" (Prucha 1984, 1: 7).

Kelly's motifs appeared early in the first chapter and she restated them
continually throughout her narrative. During the separation phase of her
journey (1–72), she described the Indians as "murderous," "terrible enemies," "possessing demonic natures," "violent," "ferocious," "greedy."
These motifs stressed that her captors' inherent evilness was the reason they
took her as prisoner.

As Kelly progressed to the adaptation phase of her journey (73–105), the
motifs in her narrative attacked all aspects of Indian character. She saw the
Indians as "filthy," "grotesque in appearance," having a "ridiculous" sense
of humor, demonstrating "barbarous ignorance," "wild," "uncivilized,"
"fiends," and "greedy plunderers." In this phase, Kelly described herself as
prayerful, refined, attractive, educated, civilized, and honest. These contrasting motifs emphasized that Kelly came from a superior culture that
permitted her to retain her civility and femininity even during the most
trying of times.

During the time she underwent ordeals (106–48), Kelly's motifs mixed
the images of the ignoble with noble savage traits. For example, she found
the Indians to be "desperate," "bitterly cruel," "terrible," but they were
also "eager to learn" and "sometimes sympathetic to my hunger." Kelly

targeted the evil traits of women perhaps in order to emphasize her superior qualities. For her, "males had absolute power," but "the women were slanderous, like vile serpents." Indian women had one redeeming quality, because they wept "expressing sorrow at the death of their children." Most of Kelly's characterizations of the Indians were negative; she saw them as "cunning," "deceitful," and "malicious." Even though her theme was that Indians as a whole were despicable, a few redeeming qualities indicated the possibility that they might be civilized.

When her return and rebirth were eminent (140–225), Kelly's motifs changed. The linguistic alterations reflected her change in locale; she moved from living with warring Oglalas to settled village life with the Blackfeet. In the village locale, Kelly found her new family "almost affectionate," "kind," "holding out a promise of freedom," "never [making] an unchaste insult," "having an air of friendliness"; however, they were also "devoid of gratitude," "hypocritical," "treacherous," "cruel," and "fond of war." In this last part of her journey, she acknowledged that the Blackfeet had a slight potential for civilization.

Kelly's motifs pointing to the theme of Indians as ignoble savages added continuity and movement to her story. These rhetorical devices also served her political purpose; that is, since she was victimized by the Indians, she deserved reparations. The narrative's propaganda-like content supported the government's views about the Indian's "shameful" and "beastly" culture and affirmed its goals concerning the need to civilize the savages.

Red Cloud's Portrayal of the Noble Savage

In the minds of his audience, Red Cloud's discourse pointed to the opposite theme. The Indians were noble savages, "natural man [and woman] living without technology and elaborate societal structures." Francis Prucha (1984) describes noble savages as persons "naked without shame, unconcerned about private ownership," undesirous of material wealth, and free from government problems. They are "handsome in appearance, dignified in manner, and brave in combat" (1: 7). Noble savages also possess characteristics similar to those described by Joseph Labat (1988); they are persons having "natural or primitive virtues, such as purity, candor, kindness and bravery, [and] someone who is free from the restraints of civilization" (918).

During the accommodation phase of his journey Red Cloud's oratorical motifs added evidence for his assumption that Indians were noble savages. He stated that he was "raised naked," came "from where the sun rises," was "good and kind," concerned "about the Red Nation," "poor and naked," "unable to read and write," and "peaceful." These motifs supported the argument that although he was poor and naked, Red Cloud was proud to represent his culture and make peace.

Red Cloud asserted his noble savage motifs even more strongly during his speeches on June 10, 11, and 13 than he did in his meetings with the commissioner of Indian affairs. Red Cloud referred to himself as "chief of the Sioux nation," "old," "a veteran warrior," "unable to read," "a victim of government fraud," "not a slave," a "red man and a child of the red nation," "born free," "raised on wild game," "poor," a person who "came naked and will go away naked," "peaceful," "kindly," and a "man of justice." Red Cloud contrasted these positive motifs about himself with negative motifs describing the government. For him, the government was "at fault," because they "killed Chief Black Bear," "gave us too little for our land," sent "cheating and thieving traders," took "gold from our land," "destroyed our livestock," "brought in whiskey," and threw "away money on dirty flour and rotten tobacco." By referring to himself using positive motifs and to the government using negative ones, two different themes emerged. The self references showed Red Cloud was uncorrupted by material possession, and his negative references identified the government as a corrupt culture whose representatives violated treaty obligations and treated the Indians in a reckless manner. From these contrasting motifs, audiences could easily recognize Red Cloud's argument that Indian culture was superior to government culture.

Red Cloud eventually came to terms with the separateness of his culture when he expressed "gratitude to the Great Father," "thankfulness to the Great Spirit," and "concern for his women and children." Some motifs are nonverbal rather than verbal. Nonverbal motifs consist of patterns of behavior expressed through demeanor and delivery. Red Cloud's nonverbal motifs showed reporters he had "respect" for white man's culture even though he was from a "dependant people," but he "dressed appropriately" and appreciated the food ("Savages at the White House" 1870, June 8, 1). Red Cloud's words in combination with reporters' descriptions suggest he was a spiritual man with manners and demeanor characteristic of other good people.

The final reconciliation phase of the journey concluded with Red Cloud's New York City speech. The speech brought together various generalizations that he had previously drawn into a simple chain of reasons: I am a noble savage; noble savages have a different culture than whites; however, our common desire for peace can overcome cultural differences. This chain of reasoning began when Red Cloud differentiated himself from the audience by defining himself as "from the west," a "representative of the original American race," part of the "first people," "good," "generous with the land," "peaceful," "poor and ignorant," and a victim of white man's greed. Repeating these traits stressed Red Cloud's identity as a noble savage and a diplomat with spiritual authority. His reasoning followed with an assertion of cultural difference. When he characterized the government as "rich and wise," "skillful in things we know nothing about," "deceitful in treaties," "rich in goods," and from the "east," he called attention to the divergent values of Indian and white cultures. The conclusion to his argument asserted the differences could be reconciled because of a common desire for peace. The chief portrayed himself, his audience, and white people in general as "children of the Great Spirit," made equal but with "white and red skins," concerned about "children," desirous of what is "right and just," and working for "peace." This last cluster of motifs directly stated his argument; that is, red and white men can reconcile differences because of their common and God-given desire for peace.

IMPLICATIONS

This chapter shows how the journeys of Fanny Kelly and Red Cloud transformed their identities and created political power and social status for them. Through her captive narrative, Fanny Kelly, an Oglala captive, transformed her identity from a Kansas housewife into an advocate for reparations for the victims of the Indian wars. Through his diplomacy, Red Cloud transformed his identify from an Oglala war chief into a skillful peace diplomat. Both Kelly's and Red Cloud's identities changed as they moved through a culture alien to their own.

Captive narratives provide a rich resource of autobiographical rhetoric from the point of view of the Indian victims. These narratives also helped the government understand Indian culture and warfare strategies. Many authors of captive narratives achieved some temporary notoriety from their readers and gained long-term financial benefits from the publication of their stories. Fanny Kelly's narrative provides a unique case of an author who used her book to convince Congress that she deserved financial reparations for her suffering. In addition to Fanny Kelly, the published records of the experiences of hundreds of other captives are available to rhetorical scholars. For nineteenth-century readers, the captive narrative was a recognizable genre featuring adventurous men and women in a struggle with their savage captors. The captive stories embraced a sentimental style and melodramatic language that captured reader attention with suspense and intrigue. Published records exist about the experience of captives from Puget Sound captives (Smith [1941] 1969, 52), Southern Cheyenne and Arapahos (White 1969, 338–45), Santee Sioux (Anderson & Woolworth, 1988), and from the Navajo (Brugge 1985). Captive narratives began in the seventeenth century and ended with the conquest of the Indians at the beginning of the twentieth century. Whether other captives' stories show identity transformations similar to those experienced by Fanny Kelly is a subject for further study.

Diplomatic missions, similar to those made by Red Cloud, provide a fruitful source for the study of Indian rhetoric. Although Chief Leschi never made a diplomatic mission to Washington, some of his predecessors from the Puget Sound did (Carpenter 1996). Black Kettle and Left Hand never went to Washington, but Chiefs Neva and Spotted Wolf of the Arapaho and Lean Bear, War Bonnet and Standing in Water of the Cheyenne visited President Lincoln in 1863 (Coel 1981, 167–68). Chief Little Crow went to Washington in 1854 (Anderson 1986b, 73). After their return from Bosque Redondo, the government asked Navajo chiefs to visit Washington. During the 1930s John Collier invited Pueblo leaders to meet with government executives in Washington, D.C. (Philp [1977] 1981). After the advent of the Peace Commission in 1868, dozens of chiefs made visits to Washington. Although many chiefs came more than once, Chief Red Cloud "was probably the most productive political leader" and "the most talented and one of the most tenacious" (Larson 1997, 304). The public rhetoric of designated chiefs who made diplomatic visits to Washington is recorded in newspapers, Indian agency reports, and transcriptions of the negotiations of delegations to Washington. Further study of this type of diplomacy promises new insights into the rhetoric of Indian advocates and sheds light on government-Indian relations in the nineteenth century.

Chapter 6

Rituals of Redress and Zuni
Witch Cases, 1880–1900

After most of the tribal participants in the Indian wars settled on reservations, the government still continued to intervene into Indian life. Federal action was not always motivated by brutal attacks, raids, or looting of settlements. In some cases, federal officials intervened because they did not approve of Indian religious practices. One noteworthy example of this type of intervention occurred at Zuni Pueblo over tribal sanctions of witchcraft.

Many southwestern Indians practiced witchcraft at the end of the nineteenth century. For example, Marc Simmons (1974) notes that "no crime loomed more heinous nor brought swifter retribution than that of witchcraft. Often mere suspicion resulted in condemnation and execution." The removal or execution of witches purged the community of an evil force and restored cultural order (70). More specifically, Florence H. Ellis (1989) notes that these cases were rampant in the late nineteenth century at Zuni and Acoma Pueblos where religious leaders blamed witches for everything from bad storms and crop failures to illness and death (192). One witch case at Zuni Pueblo in 1897 holds more significance than the others because it resulted in the arrests of the Bow Priests for the torture of a woman alleged to be a witch. Pueblo Indian Agent C. E. Nordstrom reported the case to the secretary of interior in this way:

The village of Zuni was recently the scene of an occurrence recalling all the horrors of the days when our God-fearing ancestors of New England piously devoted their neighbors and friends to the stake. A poor old woman, 75 or 80 years old, having been reported as a witch, the society of the priests of the bow ordered her torture until she should confess. The emissaries of the society accordingly went to her house in the dead of night, dragged her from her bed, and almost literally, throwing her down the five stories to the ground, carried her off to the "torture corral," where, tying her hands behind her, until unable to endure the agony longer, she confessed to—no one knows what. It was, however, sufficient to satisfy her judges, for she was let down and allowed to crawl back to her miserable abode as best she might. Here she lay for days, no one caring to go near her, or if they had any compassion for her they were afraid to display it for fear of sharing her fame as a witch, together with the infliction of the same punishment. (Fay 1982, 2: 192)

Although the torture of this witch horrified the Indian agent, this kind of practice was common in Zuni culture. What was uncommon was the government response. When the military learned of this incident of witch torture, they arrested, tried, and imprisoned the Bow Priests for their actions.

The episodes of witchcraft emphasize the controversy between the religious legal structure of these Indians and the territorial law imposed by the government. Additionally, they illustrate one kind of rhetorical emergence in which the Zuni voiced their religious views and the government took notice. This chapter investigates the religious and legal forums used in witchcraft cases during the late nineteenth century at Zuni Pueblo. More specifically, the chapter (1) explains Victor Turner's theoretical framework for looking at culture as symbolic performance, (2) describes the causes of the witch controversy as part of a cultural breach and crisis, (3) analyzes the ritualistic forms of redress sanctioned by Zuni religion, and (4) explains how interference from the territorial government initiated change in the religious practices of the Zuni.

CULTURE AS PERFORMANCE

The religious culture of indigenous people, like the Zuni, can be understood through the metaphor of performance. Victor Turner (1988) describes processes of cultural conflict as performances, that is, theatrical rituals used in response to breaches and crises. Performances arise from structured processes designed to deal with controversial events in a culture. This process evolves in stages. First, a *breach* occurs when rule infractions threaten the existence of important communal values and violate cultural norms for maintaining those values. Second, a *crisis* evolves when people take sides concerning this breach and view it as a serious conflict threatening the existence of a culture. For Turner, the crisis is a liminal phase (limen), a threshold when social harmony is broken. Third, *redressive* procedures restore communal harmony and reaffirm cultural values. In this phase, leaders of a culture use some rituals to decipher the causes of crisis and other ones to restore the social order. If the redressive phase succeeds, *legitimization* or reintegration occurs because cultural leaders successfully have dealt with the causes of the breach. However when the redressive phase fails, social conflict persists and emerges in additional breaches and more crises (38).

Turner recommends studying cultural performances by looking at frames, small segments of the performances that delineate participants, describe their roles, and ascribe meaning. Frames are separate events that center on a common controversy within an episode. This chapter looks at three different Zuni witch trials as separate frames by analyzing the rituals of redress adopted by cultural leaders to resolve the breach, stall the crisis, restore the cultural order, and change cultural practices.

CAUSES OF CONTROVERSY: CULTURAL BREACH AND CRISIS

The causes of the witchcraft controversy at Zuni are rooted in this Pueblo's history and its religious beliefs. Turner's stages of culture performance provide a framework for understanding incidences of witchcraft at Zuni Pueblo between 1880 and 1900. For him, a crisis begins with cultural breaches created by outsiders who intervene in a culture and cause such havoc they transform stable cultural conditions into unstable ones (1988, 91). In other words, a breach is a conflict with multiple causes. The breaches to Zuni culture resulted from an accumulated set of threats, including intrusions from the Spaniards, federal troops, Catholic and Protestant missionaries, social scientists, and industrial developers. These intrusions challenged traditional religious authorities and ancient cultural practices.

The causes of the controversy are rooted in the history of the Zuni, an ancient people with a strong religious tradition. T. J. Ferguson (1995) traces the inhabitation of Zuni land to 5000 B.C. By 1 A.D., the people living in present-day northwest New Mexico established agricultural patterns and domestic dwellings. By about 700 A.D., the Anasazi ancestors of the Zuni developed trade with people living on the sea coasts. After 1350 A.D., groups of immigrants from the Mogollon culture to the west assimilated into the Anasazi groups and created the dual Anasazi-Mogollon culture of the present-day Zuni (3–7). Worship and religious festivals were the centers of life for this ancient culture. Even today Pueblo religion and culture are inseparable.

The first breach to Zuni culture began with the expeditions of the Spaniards. Coronado was so impressed with the development of the Zuni villages between 1540 and 1542 that he referred to them as the "Seven Cities of Cibola" and fantasized that the streets were paved with gold and precious stones. Onatè, during his visit in 1598, learned the Zuni were an industrious group of indigenous people who had built an impressive domestic community based on cultivation of the land (Hammond & Rey 1953, sec. 1). Spanish priests followed the explorers. They occupied Zuni

Pueblo, built churches, and tried to convert the native people. Although some Zuni became nominal Catholics to avoid conflict and to please their Spanish superiors, Pueblo life continued to center on traditional religious practices and rituals. The Zuni resented intrusions from the Spaniards into their religious way of life. This resentment built up to the point in 1680 when the Zuni joined with other Pueblos to revolt against the religious oppression of their Spanish colonizers.

Religion served an important role in the Spanish conquests of the territories in North and South America. The Spanish conquistadors claimed new territories for the Pope and asked their subjects to commit their allegiance to a Christian god and to the king of Spain. In 1598, Juan de Onatè arrived at Zuni Pueblo situated in the northwest corner of present-day New Mexico. Upon his arrival Onatè demanded "acts of obedience" and "vassalage" from the Indians of Zuni, telling them he was bringing both the knowledge of God and personal salvation. Zuni leaders consulted with one another and agreed that they wanted the peace and harmony promised by Onatè so they accepted his god and his king (Hammond & Rey 1953, sec. 1).

During this period, the voices of the Zuni were not recorded, but some of their actions showed their displeasure with the Spanish incursions into their life and thereby provided early records of their resistance to the Spaniards. For example, just after the Spanish arrived in 1539, the Spanish authorities reported that the Zuni killed Estévan, a guide for one of the Franciscan expeditions. In 1662, after Fray Francisco Letrado called the Zuni Indians "idolaters" for not attending Catholic religious services, they killed him with arrows, ripped off his scalp, and exhibited the scalp in their ceremonial dances. Gregory C. Crampton (1977) speculates that the killing of both Estévan and Letrado resulted from the infractions of outsiders into Zuni religious ceremonials (33). Since these acts of violence occurred at the time of important Zuni ceremonials, what seemed to be unprovoked murder likely was an aggressive defense of religious rights of privacy. Despite the fact historians did not know the precise cause, these actions symbolized Zuni resentment toward their Spanish colonizers.

Even though the Zuni never accepted the values of Catholicism as Onatè had envisioned, their promise of allegiance to the Spanish government gave them legal standing as an independent territory until Mexican rule, a status that ended in 1846. After the United States took control of the territory, the Pueblo Indians gained some of the privileges of citizenship apparently because the government thought they lived peaceably and engaged in agriculture. Hugh N. Smith in a letter to Orlando Brown (Fay 1982, 1: 19) notes the existence of these rights. He explains that the Pueblos are "peaceable, honest, and industrious." He also observed they had a viable system of government and could sue other citizens in any territorial court. When both the governments of Mexico and the United States gave the Zuni legal standing, they also recognized their right to practice their traditional religion.

After years of moderate success in dealing with colonial governments, events out of the Zuni's control fractured their culture. A second breach occurred when federal troops arrived in 1846 at Fort Wingate, twenty miles to the south of the Pueblo. At the same time the military relied on the Zuni for provisions, they built new settlements and gave away 9 million acres of Zuni land to settlers (Hart 1995, 93). Not surprisingly, the Zuni resented the military presence and the encroachments of settlers, but they lacked the will and the military strength to fight these intruders. Since they were a religious culture, their private ceremonials were more important than the events that went on outside of the Pueblo. During this time, however, outsiders voiced alarm about Zuni religious practices concerning witchcraft. The *Annual Report of the Secretary of Interior* (1892) claims that witchcraft cases at Zuni were common. Nearly every year a witch was killed or run off from the Pueblo. Furthermore, outsiders knew about many of these tortures and killings, and they still took no legal action against the Zuni (reprinted in Fay 1982, 2: 169).

The breach widened with the entry of Protestant missionaries and anthropologists in 1879. In that year the Presbyterian Mission Society sent Taylor Ealy and his wife to Zuni as teachers for a Christian day school. At the same time, the Bureau of Ethnology from the Smithsonian Institution sent a group of social scientists to gather ethnographic and archeological data on the Zuni Indians. The Presbyterians experienced little success in converting Zuni adults and educating their children. More specifically, Norman J. Bender (1984) concludes that the Indians "disregarded the Ealys' well-meaning overtures." Although a few of the Zuni listened to the spiritual message, it does not appear that Ealy made any specific inroads against the old Indian religion (163). One reason for the missionary's lack of success was that this Christian group, just as the Catholic padres who preceded them, had condemned and ridiculed Zuni religious practices and coerced the Indians to accept Christian values.

The expedition from the Smithsonian achieved more success than the missionaries. Frank Hamilton Cushing, James and Matilda Coxe Stevenson, and others were able to "unearth the keys to the Pueblo past linking Zuni with the ancient civilizations of Mexico and Central America" (Green 1979, 427). Not only did they complete insightful research, the anthropologists learned the language and became advocates promoting the Zuni way of life and recording their history. For example, Cushing learned the Zuni language, gained admittance to secret councils, and observed rituals and private ceremonials (Crampton 1977). The writings of Cushing and others provided a second form of rhetorical emergence for the Zuni. Through the voices of anthropologists, the Indians justified their murders of Spanish colonizers and explained their religious ceremonials (Cushing

1979, [1882] 1990). Although anthropologists gave second-hand accounts of Zuni life, this information still gave the Zuni a public voice. With the goal of discovering the secrets of Zuni civilization, dozens of anthropologists followed the Smithsonian expedition (Green 1979, 229). The influx of scientists eager to study Zuni culture partially resulted from others' interests in the complexity of Zuni religion and partially from the openness and hospitality of these Pueblo people to outsiders. The Zuni seemed eager to share knowledge of their culture with others (Smith & Roberts 1954). Unlike the missionaries, some of the anthropologists appreciated the complexity of Zuni religious culture.

After the Zuni shared some of their religious practices with outsiders, these practices became the target of criticism by some anthropologists. For example, in 1892 Adolph Bandelier, a prominent anthropologist, gave this ethnocentric account of Zuni religion:

The daily life of the Pueblo Indian is a succession of performances that may be called religious, inasmuch as they are intended to keep him on good terms with the supernatural world. He craves the good will of that world for purposes of material welfare, not for his moral good, except so far as the latter is conduced to prosperity. Therefore his existence is, in reality, a miserable one, in constant dread and fear of things and forces around him, whose immediate connection with spiritual powers he exaggerates or misconceives. (Fay 1982, 2: 161).

Another anthropologist, J. Walter Fewkes, found Zuni ceremonials immoral and the moral behavior of the people to be reprehensible. He noted:

The object of their religion is . . . to provide incantations which may protect them from evil genii [*sic*] and keep them in favor with wind and water. Were I to speak of lying and thieving, they are ignorant of the moral significance of the words. They perpetually steal from each other and cannot trust their gardens and fields against each other's rapacity in harvest.

It is a religion "void of moral convictions and distinctions," and it "deifies animal appetites" (Fay 1982, 2: 163). Both Bandelier's and Fewkes' observations show that they believed their own civilized and rational Christian beliefs were more virtuous than Zuni religious practices.

The audience for anthropologists Cushing, Stevenson, and Bunzel was the academic community; they sought to inform other scholars about the religious life of the Zuni. In contrast, the target audience of Bandelier and Fewkes was likely the government since their critical remarks attempted to appease congressional politicians. Bandelier and Fewkes degraded Zuni religion to warn the government that the Pueblos did not lead as virtuous a life as other anthropologists had claimed. Further these two men asserted that the "primitive" Indian beliefs of the Zuni impeded the educational and missionary efforts of the government to reform them. Bandelier and other detractors called public attention to controversial issues underlying government-Zuni relations.

Perhaps, it is only a coincidence, but the breach reached its crisis stage about 1892, the same year Bandelier and Fewkes warned the government about Zuni religious beliefs. Turner (1988) argues that a crisis may or may not result in physical violence, but it emanates from fears, threats, and superstitions about what might happen to a culture. Sometimes this crisis produces "supernatural dangers" associated with witchcraft and evildoers. At other times, it creates perceived threats to beliefs in spirits of ancestors and the sanctity of holy places (34). For the Zuni, the crisis demanded an internal cultural response.

Repeated and continuous encroachments from outsiders due to industrial development also contributed to the crisis at Zuni Pueblo. Railroad construction occurred between 1880 and 1881; military officers from Fort Wingate started a large cattle company in 1886; and lumber production began in 1892 (Baxter 1995, 121–36). After the Dawes Act in 1887, the federal government tried to apportion land and divide community property among the Zuni. In 1894, the commissioner of Indian affairs reported that

troubles are constantly arising among these Indians as to the possession of their lands and water rights, owning to the encroachments of Mexicans and Americans. The cutting of timber on their lands and the stealing of their stock are also fruitful sources of annoyance. (Fay 1982, 2: 179)

Quite clearly, all of these events combined to create cultural havoc for the people of Zuni Pueblo. The economic interests of outsiders threatened the Zunis' way of life by forcing them to give up their ancestral land, impeding their safe passage to holy sites, and demanding they engage in economic relationships with people they did not trust or understand. These kinds of disruptions threatened the Zunis' way of life and forced them to take action to preserve their culture.

Outside influences from the federal government, Christian religious evangelists, scientists, and industrial developers certainly impacted upon Zuni culture. Simmons (1974) notes that one of the circumstances that led to accusations of sorcery at Zuni was the external events that threatened tribal welfare (76), and religion was a key component of cultural welfare. Missionaries threatened Zuni culture when they ridiculed their religion and tried to convert them. Then after anthropologists revealed Zuni religious secrets and settlers robbed their grave sites and sold their religious paraphernalia to the Smithsonian, Zuni culture experienced even a greater peril than they had in earlier times (Stevenson 1904; Green 1979, 1990). As if this was not enough to entirely destroy the culture, the military sold off Zuni lands, and industrial developers ruined their ecology (Baxter 1995, 121–36). For these reasons, it is not surprising that a major cultural crisis occurred when the "covert antagonisms" against the culture "become visible" (Turner 1982, 70).

The resulting crisis created complex cultural performances in which some affected members of the Pueblo underwent elaborate healing rituals; others suffered torture to induce them to admit sorcery; and still others died. In each of the cases, the voices of the Zuni residents and their religious leaders emerged in the ceremonies of religious redress that revealed the rituals and the underlying beliefs of the Zuni people.

ZUNI CULTURE: USES OF RELIGIOUS REDRESS

The Zuni sought to redress the crisis in their culture through the rituals of their religious leaders who enforced traditional moral law and made prayerful appeals to Zuni ancestors and their supernatural spirits. The resulting redressive rituals gave internal "feedback on the crisis" by identifying the visible manifestations of evil (Turner 1982, 75) and asserting resistance to the cultural intrusions from outsiders. By performing rituals to restore the moral code and return community members to the traditional religious way of life, the Zuni showed others their religious beliefs and revealed internal practices that enforced these beliefs.

For the Zuni, religious beliefs were synonymous with cultural law, and religious leaders enforced this law. Many primitive people look upon religion to solve problems. Robert Redfield (1967) emphasizes that "primitive peoples get along with little law. One reason why this is so is to be found in the strength of the supernatural sanctions in restraining socially disapproved conduct" (23). Cultural sanctions constitute an important part of religious redress. According to Turner (1988), ritualistic redress has several effects: it alters the cultural order, changes relationships among members, and emphasizes what rules must be followed to maintain the social order (93). Punishing witches was one method religious leaders used to restore order to their community.

Through the exercise of their traditional religious rituals, Zuni leaders tried to mend the breach created by outsiders at the same time they tried to resolve the internal cultural crisis. Anthropologists specializing in nineteenth-century Zuni culture (Stevenson 1904; Bunzel 1929–1930; Smith & Roberts 1954; Cushing 1979, [1882] 1990) agree that the Zuni were religious, life revolved around their religious observances, and rituals guided by the priests of the sun, war, and rain gave meaning to everyday experiences. For example, Ruth L. Bunzel (1929–1930) asserted that the "Zunis are one of the most thoroughly religious peoples of the world" (480).

Religious leaders enforced the moral law of their culture through a theocracy of different priestly orders—Medicine Priests, Rain Priests, and Bow/War Priests—led by the Council of Priests. Each order had different responsibilities. Bow Priests acted as "defenders of the people in times of peace," leaders of the tribe in times of war, and police for the moral and religious matters in daily affairs (Bunzel 1929–1930, 526). They were the interrogators and judges for what the United States territorial justice system called "criminal cases." The three major concerns of Bow Priests were to minister the tribal rituals and protect religious sites, to conduct war against enemies, and to deal with matters of witchcraft (Fewkes 1891, 3; Stevenson 1904; Cushing 1979, [1882] 1990). All other violations of the social order, what contemporary systems of justice call "civil cases," were settled privately or left to the tribal governor and council who acted under the supervision of two Bow Priests (Smith & Roberts 1954). During the nineteenth century, Bow Priests served their community until they died.

Criminal violations at Zuni evolved from their cultural concept of evil. Pueblo Indians did not understand the Christian idea of evil as sin, but instead their concept of evil resembled that of the Aztecs of Mexico. Marc Simmons (1974) explains, "They viewed evil as a shadowy negative force present to some degree in every man and god and an immutable part of life [that] one simply endured" (14). In ways similar to other Pueblo people, the Zuni placed the priest and witch in "antithetical roles"; the witch sought benefit and power for self whereas the priest used power to benefit the community.

Witches had two roles. One role involved personal evil; that is, witches took the heart (soul) of an individual spirit by shooting a foreign object into the victim. Cures occurred when a shaman extracted the objects from the body and thereby retrieved the missing heart of the victim (Simmons 1974, 74). The physical healing of a victim of witchcraft involved the victim's belief in the power of shamans to do magic and extract the evil (Bunzel 1929–1930, 491). In the other role, the witches caused evil and disaster for the tribe, such as storms, drought, and epidemics of illness. For this reason, Bow Priests believed the death or removal of the witches from the culture was the only reasonable solution for eliminating the causes of pervasive evil.

In many nineteenth-century cases, religious leaders assumed that witches had caused the evil to Zuni people, but they had only a vague idea about who the witches were. For this reason some family members of Zuni victims sought the help of the shamans and supernaturals who used religious ceremonies to try to restore the individuals to health. The shamans treated the victims with corn meal, water from sacred springs, yucca seeds, and ashes saved from the winter solstice celebration. The victims and their families also invoked the help of the penitent priests, called "caciques," who interceded with the supernaturals and did penance for the victims of witchcraft (Bandelier 1890–1892, 264, 275–79).

In other cases, the victims directly identified the witch and solicited the help of the Bow Priests to rid them of the evil influences of witchery by ritual forms of religious redress. First, the priests tried to affirm the charges against the witch by seeking other accusers. Next, they asked the victim and accusers to describe the acts of sorcery. Then, the Bow Priests demanded that the accused witch or members of the witch's family confess to the alleged evil action. If the accused witches refused to confess, the priests extended their arms by the elbows from beams in the plaza and forced them to hang there for hours while being interrogated. After the witches confessed, the priests asked them to repent publicly and then permitted them to go free. In cases where the accused appeared to be a continuing threat to the community, Bow Priests exiled them to a location far away from the Pueblo. Some of those who confessed but failed to make amends and most of those who did not confess to witchcraft were clubbed by Bow Priests and eventually died (Stevenson 1904, 392–406; Smith & Roberts 1954, 38–49; Cushing [1882] 1990, 340). These forms of flogging and torture also occurred at other Pueblo settlements, but the Zuni's approach to torture most closely resembled the methods used in medieval Spain. For this reason, anthropologists conclude that the Zuni likely learned their torture practices from the sixteenth-century padres who inhabited their pueblo and tortured them (Parsons 1927, 106–12, 125–28).

Torture was not the most common way of dealing with internal conflicts. Cushing ([1882] 1990) emphasized that "sorcery trials were a last resort" conceived by the Bow Priests as the only way to "eliminate evil" from the Pueblo (342). Depending on the severity of the charge and the harm done to others, the Zuni used different forms of religious ritualistic redress— torture, banishment, or killing—against witches in order to rid the community of evil, help the victims change their lives, force confessions, and justify the killing of witches.

ZUNI WITCH CASES: RITUALISTIC REDRESS

Redress is the most complex and critical phase of cultural performances. The redressive process, when used successfully by cultural leaders, repairs the breach, alleviates the crisis, and restores order in a culture. The Zuni used rituals of redress emphasizing healing, confession, torture, and death. The Bow Priests selected rituals that fit with their perceptions of the religious state of the witch and his or her victims.

The number of witch cases occurring at Zuni Pueblo remains unknown, but the first documentation of these cases occurred with the arrival of anthropologists in 1879. Watson Smith and John Roberts (1954) reported sixteen cases between 1880 and 1900. During congressional hearings in 1892–1893, the secretary of interior claimed that outsiders saw more than one killing per year (Fay 1982, 2: 169). All of this information led Simmons (1974) to conclude that the Zuni's had an "obsession" with witchcraft (110). Since the Bow Priests "secretly tried" most of the sorcery cases and then "secretly disposed of the bodies" (Cushing 1979, 141–43), outsiders probably learned about far fewer cases than actually took place. Dealing with witches and their victims was so important to Zuni religion that shamans and priests had clearly defined responsibilities for using redressive actions to purge their culture from the power of witches.

The dominant form of redress, the third stage of cultural performance, is a kind of ritual. In this stage, cultural actors seek ritualistic redress to help victims of "sickness" or "misfortune." Shamans or priests from inside the culture cause those assembled "to reflect on the causes of the evil" and to bring their priestly spiritual power to bare on a conclusion to the crisis (Turner 1988, 38). Religious rituals involve "a sacrifice, literal or moral," and "a victim" used as a scapegoat to purge evil from the community and thereby resolve cultural crisis (Turner 1982, 71). The Zuni adopted rituals associated with both the victim and the witch who perpetrated the evil. The three case studies that follow give illustrations of the complexity of ritual redress.

Redress by Ritual: A Twelve-Year-Old Zuni Girl

The first incident involved a twelve-year-old Zuni girl. Matilda Coxe Stevenson (1904, 398–406) attended the ritual healing and the trial of the young girl, and then she reported her observations in an anthropological monograph. Stevenson and other anthropologists who observed some of the witch trials served as surrogate rhetorical voices for the Zuni; that is, they reported what was said and done by people without a written language. This particular trial probably occurred in the early 1880s, but Stevenson offers no date. The incident began when a young girl's grandfather brought her to the village because she was suffering from "hysteria." The grandfather wanted to prove to the Bow Priests that the girl had been bewitched by a seventeen-year-old boy who "held hands" and "romped" with her.

When the court of Bow Priests gathered to try the young man as a witch, Stevenson (1904) observed the event and reported it in this way:

Near the end of the long room five members of the Bow priesthood formed a semicircle. The accused, a handsome youth, sat slightly back with a warrior on each side of him. The patient lay on the pallet on the opposite side of the room, every member of her body in violent motion. Her mother attempted to keep the head quiet, while the brother clung to her legs. The poor little arms were thrown wildly about until an aunt essayed to control them. (399)

The presence of the victim served important functions in the cultural performance since it allowed the accused to reflect on his evil deed and the victim to reflect on her spiritual connection to her culture. Because the young man was able to see the consequences of his transgressions against the girl in this trial performance, he could reflect about his deeds and eventually confess what he had done. This type of reflection occurs when the ritual of redress shows performers the meaning of their actions by showing "ourselves to ourselves" (Turner 1988, 42). Reflection then creates cognitive conditions that precede and inform the perpetrator's and the victim's rhetorical responses.

The Healing Ritual. This particular performance began with an elaborate set of religious rituals conducted by a shaman or theurgist. Stevenson (1904) reported the intricacies of the healing rituals used to help the victim.

He [the shaman] sprinkled a line of meal 3 feet in length before him, then placed his mili at the east end of the line, and deposited a crystal about 2 inches high midway down the line. A medicine bow and a basket of sacred meal were by his side. A woman of the household [of the victim] deposited a vase of water and a gourd at the right of the theurgist [shaman], who lifted a gourd of water as he began his prayers. . . . Six gourds of water were poured into the bow as prayers were addressed to the Beast Gods of the six regions. . . . Medicine was afterwards sprinkled into the water, six fetishes were dropped in, and a cross, signifying the four regions, and a circle, [signifying] the world symbol were formed on the surface of the water with sacred meal. After the water had been consecrated, the theurgist rose and dipped ashes from the fireplace with eagle plumes and deposited them near the meal line and north of it. In a moment he lifted some of the ashes with the two plumes and sprinkled them to the north; again dipping ashes, he sprinkled them to the west; and then continued sprinkling them to the four regions for physical purification. Then he dipped the feather ends of the eagle plumes into the medicine water and put them to his lips. Again dipping them into the water he sprinkled the invalid, she was held in a sitting poster by her father. . . . The theurgist rubbed the girl's body with medicine water and prayed. He then placed his lips to her breast, pretending to draw material from her heart; this material [the material he extracted from her body] he deposited on the floor and covered it with [corn] meal. . . . The theurgist, having completed the treatment of the patient, lifted the material supposed to have been extracted from her with his two eagle plumes, deposited it in a corn husk, and carried it from the room. (399–400)

Theories of ritualistic redress give clues about the probable persuasive effects of this healing ceremony. The rituals likely helped the Zuni to "scrutinize, portray, understand, and then act" on themselves (Turner 1982, 75). Healing ceremonies, such as this one, defined the meaning of the evil events occurring in material reality and then contrasted them with the positive and mysterious events of Zuni's spiritual world. In this way, "[t]he known world of sensorially perceptible phenomena [connects] with the unknown and invisible realms. . . . It makes intelligible what is mysterious and . . . dangerous" (Turner 1974, 15).

The healing ritual presented here shows how this Zuni victim engaged in self reflection by understanding both her suffering and her response to this suffering as part of a complex religious culture. The shaman surrounded her with objects sacred to her culture—corn meal, water from sacred springs, crystals, fetishes, eagle plumes, and ashes from sacred ceremonials. In addition to symbolizing the victim's union with her culture, the shaman used the sacred objects to symbolize her religious beliefs and to connect the girl with the shaman's supernatural healing power. Moreover, the sacred objects purified the victim's body at the time when the shaman removed the evil substance injected by the witch. Thus the process purged the victim of a consciousness and behavior characteristic of someone bewitched. In doing so, the process allowed the girl to resume her normative rhetorical role as a good person acting on behalf of community values. In this way, the Bow Priests restored her cultural role.

In ways similar to Turner's (1982) explanation, this Zuni religious ritual has several persuasive layers resembling "artwork." First, the use of ritual in performance "engages all of the senses," "communicates the deepest values of the group," and performs the cultural values (81–82). Second, these rituals affected the victim's sense of herself by transforming her experience of hysteria ("the indicative mood"), to a mood of spiritual healing ("the subjunctive mood"), back to a transformed experience in which hysteria was absent and her normal personality was restored ("a new indicative mood") (82). This ritual also had cultural importance in a third way because it symbolically changed the consciousness of the victim at the same time that it caused the other performers in the ritual to reflect on the meaning of their religious beliefs, holy objects, cultural ceremonials, and powers of spiritual leaders. In this way, the ceremonial produced a condition of liminality, that is, a scene in which society's deepest values emerge in the rhetorical performance of a sacred drama (Turner 1988, 102).

The Accusation/Confession Ritual. After the end of the healing ritual, the trial proceeded in an orderly fashion according to Stevenson. First, the grandfather spoke accusing the boy of bewitching his granddaughter. Next, the sick girl claimed that when she met the boy a short distance from her house that he grabbed her, and "as soon as he touched me, I began to tremble, and I ran home" (Stevenson 1904, 401). The grandfather claimed this made the girl crazy, and then he coaxed the boy to speak on his own behalf. The accused remained quiet until some other Zuni also demanded that he speak. Finally, the boy spoke, claiming that he had learned the secrets of witchcraft from a boy from Santa Domingo Pueblo who had given him a potion made from root medicines that could attract females. The sorcerer explained that not only could he make others crazy, but that he could make himself recover from craziness. The Bow Priests demanded proof for these claims. For this reason, the sorcerer went to his home and returned with the potion made from medicine roots, and then he dramatically described its uses to the Bow Priests. The accused then ingested the roots and ran to his victim; his body began to shake violently, and he pulled at his victim's arms. Then the accused ingested more of the medicine and became perfectly rational, took holy meal, and offered a prayer, and sprinkled the meal on the girl.

The boy's deceptive method of self defense caused the Bow Priests to release him. When he was later captured, Chief Priest Naiuchi declared the story of the boy "a lie." The boy then told a second story about how he had learned witchcraft. To validate this second story, the sorcerer took the priests to his home where he showed them witch fetishes and prayer sticks which he used for evil purposes. Afterward he carefully extracted his evil instruments from the walls of his family house. Because these artifacts were religious instruments reserved for the use of religious officials, the priests were convinced of their authenticity as witch artifacts and of the boy's ability to use them as sorcerer's instruments. After the boy was counseled and taken to the plaza, he publicly claimed he had lost his power and expressed shame for his deeds (404–6). For the priests, the hidden artifacts of his witchery were more compelling evidence than his first public deceptive story.

The redressive action used against witches differs significantly from those used for the victims. Since witches were of an evil order and acted out of self-interest, they therefore engaged in a struggle with the Bow Priests who acted on behalf of the good of the community. Instead of the shaman sacrificing sacred objects to restore the victim to health, the Bow Priests sacrificed the witch. In this case, the Bow Priests restored the community to harmony because the bewitched boy eventually confessed his evil, revealed the instruments of his sorcery, renounced his power, and regained proper allegiance to the supernaturals. The accused boy came to know himself "through participating in the performances created by others" (Turner 1988, 81). The ritual allowed the boy to reformulate the rhetorical narrative he had originally offered in order to make it fit with the material evidence. Through the ritual, the Bow Priests forced this young witch to reflect upon the meaning of his evil actions in front of religious leaders and show his allegiance to the moral code of the Zuni community.

This witch episode shows how the ritual of confession "moves from unruly contestation through ritualized procedures to the restoration of order" (Turner 1988, 36). By accepting the power of the Bow Priests and renouncing evil, the accused sorcerer restored himself to the ways of the Pueblo and thereby eliminated himself as a threat to the cultural order.

Redress by Torture and Death: An Old Zuni Man

The witch in this 1885 case was not as fortunate as the boy just described. The charges against this mature man involved digging up dead bodies, removing the valuables that were buried with the dead, and selling these valuables to outsiders. An unnamed Zuni informant reported this case, and it was recorded in the anthropological notes of Smith and Roberts (1954). The informant claimed that a woman accidently found the opening to a tunnel in a graveyard and smelled the odor of dead bodies. She felt ill and returned to tell her family about her discovery of this religious transgression. The family eventually called one of the Bow Priests to investigate.

Their investigation resulted in the discovery of a sorcerer suspect, a man others had observed entering the tunnel of the graveyard. After finding the suspect, the Bow Priests brought him to the center of the Pueblo to make him confess. The head priest and other assembled war chiefs paraded the accused before the entire gathering of priests who were dressed in war regalia and carrying their clubs. Then the priests initiated the process of getting the accused to confess to his religious transgressions against the graves of Pueblo ancestors.

The informant noted that the Bow Priests tortured the accused witch to try to get him to confess. When he refused to confess, they killed him. The process took place in this way:

They tied the suspect's arms behind his back and took him, without telling him why, to the place at the south side of the old church where witches were customarily hung. There were two posts there about 15 feet high with a horizontal pole across the top. The suspect's legs were tied together and he was pulled up, head down. Each member of the society hit him with a club. . . . But the man would not confess. He hung there from soon after dawn till [sic] about noon, and during this time was clubbed and questioned constantly. At about 5 P.M., he broke down and said that if he were cut down he would go to his house and get the things he had stolen from the dead. . . . Accompanied by a War Chief, he went home, picked up a bag and returned. . . . He added that his sister was also a witch. The War Chief then brought the sister to the plaza. . . . Members of the society clubbed her lightly and released her. Then they again tied the man upside down, and the War Priests clubbed him to death. They buried his body in the cemetery in a shallow grave with all the jewelry that had not been reclaimed by its owners. (43)

This case illustrates the presence of a dreadful category of witches, people who deserved death because they "are the anarchists of primitive life. It is their endeavor to overcome the sacred assemblies" (Cushing [1882] 1990, 341).

The redressive action used in this case reveals how a person who intentionally violates the religious law by disturbing the graves of the ancestors engages in one of the severest religious transgressions in Zuni culture. The severity of redressive action depends on the nature of the breach, the perceived crisis that results from that breach, and the values of the community where the breach occurred (Turner 1974, 39). The Bow Priests believed that this sorcerer's disturbance of the graves of his ancestors was a major cause of the disruption and turmoil the Pueblo was experiencing at the time. Killing the man responsible for the conflict would restore the traditional culture and return religious values to the Zuni.

The torture and death of this witch served the purgation function of ritual. The priests, acting on behalf of the community, sacrificed the witch as a scapegoat for the evil being suffered by the community. This action purged the culture of the evil the witch had brought to the Zuni, and it restored cultural harmony by normalizing the relations between the people of the tribe and the dead ancestors, reinforcing tribal practices of revering and fearing the dead, and giving the Bow Priests exclusive power to deal with spiritual matters. Although the killing of the witch restored internal relationships, this action failed to deal with the external forces intruding on the culture. However, the priests still believed their actions would have a restorative effect.

Religious rituals are like mirrors: they show the people to themselves; at the same time, the people show themselves to each other as members of a complex religious culture. The Bow Priests examined the deeds of this accused witch according to the "ethical standards" that all "good" persons should abide by in the Pueblo cultural moral order (Turner 1988, 38). Because he violated the sacred assumptions of his culture, the priests found the behavior of the man so reprehensible that they decreed that he must die.

The incidences of witchcraft discussed here illustrate how healing, confessions, and executions work as rituals of redress. The religious leaders chose the rituals to force the participants in the witch performances to engage in self-reflection and participate in communal reflexivity about cultural values. As a result, the accused and tribal observers engaged in personal reflections about their membership in this religious community, the meaning of Zuni sacred objects and places, cultural relationships with one another, ancestors, and supernaturals, and the good and evil roles of people within the culture. In this way, participants gained consciousness of themselves as cultural agents and knowledge of the importance of ritualistic symbolic acts for the victims, perpetrators, priests, and other community members.

ZUNI WITCH CASES: PUBLIC LEGAL REDRESS

Some Zuni religious rituals were halted, and others were altered when the territorial government started to intervene into tribal religious practices in 1897. Even though the Zuni Pueblo was a territory with sovereign rights, the passage of the Major Crimes Act (1885, 362, 385) eventually restricted some religious rituals directed at curbing witchcraft by giving the federal government jurisdiction over felony crimes committed on Indian reservations. According to Sydney Harring (1994), this act moved all tribes toward increased dependency and forced them to assimilate to the rules and practices of the United States government. Since New Mexico did not gain statehood until 1912, all Pueblos, including the Zuni, were under the legal jurisdiction of the military at Fort Wingate until the time of statehood. The federal and district courts in the territory of New Mexico operated as a federal agency for trying criminal cases.

Redress by Territorial Courts: Zuni Bow Priests

Several witch cases occurred at Zuni after the passage of the Major Crimes Act. The Zuni handled some cases in the traditional cultural way with arrest, accusation, defense, hanging, confession, torture, and sometimes death. But this tradition of redressive action changed when the territorial authorities through legal action challenged the power of the Bow Priests to punish members of Pueblo culture for witchcraft.

In this Zuni case, outsiders, who had witnessed the torture associated with a witch trial, immediately asked the military to intervene. As a result the military came to the Pueblo and arrested the Bow Priests and put them in a territorial jail miles away from the Pueblo. The government tried the Bow Priests for a felony crime under territorial law. Records of this case provide a glimpse into how secular justice replaced the religious sanctions used by the Bow Priests and forever changed the Zuni practice of redressive rituals against witches (Parsons 1936, 50–51).

This landmark case in the territorial courts involved the torture of an alleged witch named Mauriorita [also called Marita or Marlita] by the Bow Priests. The religious leaders tortured Mauriorita for causing the death of one of the most respected women of their community. At the time the priests were arrested, they were forcing the accused witch to confess to her evil deeds. A Presbyterian missionary, Mary Dissette, and a tribal visitor, George Wharton James, immediately requested the intervention of military troops from Fort Wingate to stop the torture of Mauriorita and to arrest the Bow Priests who had clubbed her. After receiving a tip from the missionary, military officers took the Bow Priests into custody and brought them to the territorial court in Valencia County, the location where the government indicted, jailed, and convicted the Bow Priests according to the federal law.

The conviction of the Zuni priests came about because of the testimony of Dissette and a former exiled witch named "Nick." The missionary claimed the priest lacked authority to punish the alleged witch and therefore the religious leaders had committed a criminal act of assault. The second witness, an exiled Zuni witch, reported how he previously had been tortured by these same Bow Priests. To the territorial judge and jury who lacked understanding of Zuni culture and embraced Christian values, this torture seemed to violate both territorial law and Christian commandments. After they were convicted by a jury, the judge sentenced the Bow

Priests to prison for eighteen months for the assault on Mauriorita. The leader of the Bow Priests, Naiuchi, died shortly after he returned from prison (James 1920, 86–91). The trial represented yet another kind of rhetorical emergence. The legal form allowed an outsider, an exiled Zuni witch, a person previously without a voice in religious matters, to present his opposition to the power of the Bow Priests. Additionally, the legal form empowered a non-Indian jury and judge to decide what constituted good and evil.

The court records (*Territory of New Mexico v. Nyuche [Naiuchi] and Priests of the Bow*, 1899) provide these details of the government charges against the priests:

That Nyuche [Naiuchi], Hatotsi, Nourmasi, Napthlu, and Keeasi . . . did unlawfully, knowingly, willfully, maliciously and feloniously . . . with the malicious intent to maim and disfigure Mauriorita, an old Indian woman, of the said Zuni tribe of Indians, tied the hands . . . behind her with a cord or strip of raw hide, and did then and there hang her with a cord or rope and suspend her from a pole for several hours until the strength . . . was gone and she was completely exhausted and unconscious, and did commit other great bodily injuries upon the person . . . and did . . . maim, bruise, beat, cut, and disfigure [her] . . . and Mauriorita did then and there become sick, sore, and disabled. (2)

The government used a public legal form to punish religious leaders for asserting traditional and secret cultural sanctions against their tribal members. Just as in other episodes, legal redress is an important form of cultural legitimization in some cases and delegitimization in other cases. In this incident, the court delegitimized the power of priests and challenged Zuni cultural values at the same time it legitimized the power of the territorial court to rule on Indian matters.

The legal redress administered by territorial law officers differed from the religious redress used at Zuni in several ways. First, the legal redress allowed adversaries from outside the culture to decide punishment for those within the culture. In the case cited above, all of the jurors were of Spanish and Mexican heritage, the judge was white, and none of the court officials knew the language or understood the cultural practices of the Zuni. Second, this form of legal redress stressed the language of the law rather than the traditions and practices of the religious culture. In this case, the court presented its formal statements of indictments in a language unknown to the accused Zuni leaders. Third, the territorial court's form of legal redress featured evaluative standards in the form of federal legal statutes that were alien to the understanding of the indicted Zuni priests. Fourth, the legal redress occurred in a place foreign to those being accused with onlookers who knew nothing about Zuni religious beliefs. The private and secret religious services now underwent scrutiny in a public territorial courthouse in the secular location of Las Lunas, New Mexico, about 100 miles south of the Zuni Pueblo. In contrast to the court, the religious rituals, known and understood by all parties, are performed within the cultural setting in which the violations occurred. Finally, the territorial courts did not permit the accused to defend themselves as was the custom in Zuni rituals of redress and in territorial courts. In fact, the records show the court did not allow the Bow Priests to give depositions, make statements, or consult with attorneys. For these reasons, it is not surprising that the Bow Priests were convicted of all of the charges in 1898. They served a total of eighteen months in the territorial jail in Valencia County. During that time, the Pueblo suffered from the absence of the Bow Priest's spiritual leadership.

Because the Major Crimes Act permitted the territorial authorities to enforce their laws against Zuni citizens, these interventions marked a near fatal blow to Zuni religious practices. These changes, according to Elsie Clews Parsons, reduced the power of the Bow Priests so that after the trial, priests resorted to nagging to extort confessions and used exile rather than death to punish confessed witches. The subsequent accommodations of Zuni leaders to American law, according to Elsie Clews Parsons (1917), fit with the cultural practice of bowing to social pressures from outsiders (244). When the government intervened into Zuni religion and law, it usurped the Zuni's power and radically changed some of their cultural practices. The consequences for Pueblo culture were disastrous because the government diminished the role of religion in Zuni culture (Pandey 1967).

CONCLUSIONS

This study illuminates three incidences of witchcraft when the Zuni and their religious leaders emerged as rhetors who acted in a religious forum to affirm and sustain cultural values. The ceremonies performed by Bow Priests placed victims and perpetrators of witchcraft in a liminal place in which they were able to reflect on their roles in Zuni culture and experience the mysterious religious power of their leaders. This chapter shows that the Zuni's understanding of witchcraft was part of their religion, and they used traditional methods of ritualistic redress to punish witches. It further reveals how the territorial government's legal redress delegitimized Zuni practices of religious redress and usurped the traditional roles that Bow Priests had exercised for centuries.

The genesis of Zuni witchcraft beliefs was in their creation stories. Eventually these beliefs assumed a central role in Zuni religious practice. Although Catholic and Protestant missionaries tried to convert the Zuni, their beliefs about witches as sources of cultural evil continued into the twentieth century. This analysis explains several forms of ritualistic redress and shows how the rituals that the Zuni adopted purged their community of evil.

Even though the Zuni do not torture and kill witches in contemporary times, one of my students indicated that many of his people still believe in the existence of witches and use ceremonies to purge evil from the Pueblo (Zuni informant, 1994, September 10, personal interview). From a fear that the Zuni will lose their religious heritage, contemporary leaders of the Pueblo now place restrictions on outsiders, particularly anthropologists and writers, who want to attend Zuni religious ceremonies. Current Zuni leaders believe that some outsiders have ridiculed their beliefs and misled the public about the meaning of their religious practices.

Witchcraft cases provide an illuminating example of Turner's theory of cultural performance by illustrating the sources of breach, crisis, redress, and legitimization. Quite clearly the government did not understand this process or its ritualistic significance for the Indians. Additionally, the government likely was embarrassed by public revelations about sorcery practices because they "revealed images of Indian life at odds with official reports of a smoothly progressing assimilation process" (Harring 1994, 268). Publicly reported episodes of witchcraft symbolized the cultural divide between Indian life and the government's ideal of what it should be.

In contemporary times, many of these methods of cultural sanctions and forums have been replaced by public trials and legal sanctions. The Zuni, just as other Indian tribes, have tribal courts to resolve nonfelony cases and employ some traditional methods of redress, such as paying retribution to the victims. Contemporary Zuni courts utilize formal methods of mediation and dispute settlement common for domestic and intracultural disputes.

The Major Crimes Act (1885), even though it has undergone modification, still places felony crimes committed on Indian land under the jurisdiction of the federal courts. Janet Reno, the former attorney general of the United States, recommended that some of the legal jurisdiction taken from the Indians in 1885 be returned to them, but Congress took no legislative action to create this change.

The legal system serves the Zuni better than it did in the late nineteenth century. The federal courts require that Indians have legal representation, interpreters be used for those who do not speak the language well, and that Indians have the right to due process as well as a court-appointed attorney. Since some Zuni men and women are now lawyers and judges, these professionals often act as legal advocates on behalf of tribal members accused of crimes.

All of the factors discussed here resulted in new legal forms replacing traditional forms of religious redress. The witch cases of the late nineteenth century chart the demise of the power of Zuni religious leaders and the rise of secular legal power. Religion is both a symbolic system and a rhetorical forum that introduces coping strategies for dealing with moral order. When government-Indian relations evolve, relationships within cultural systems change. Charles F. Wilkinson (1987) emphasizes that "societies often are forced to alter their coping strategies to meet changed environmental and social conditions" (74). In order to be citizens under federal jurisdiction, the Zuni had to modify their religious practices associated with witchcraft in order to survive as a religious people in the changing environment in which they found themselves at the turn of the century.

During the nineteenth century, many tribes believed in witches and employed the services of a shaman to rid the culture of these evil forces (Walker 1989). Incidents of witchcraft among the Pueblos, Navajo, and Apache were especially common (Simmons 1974; Ellis 1989). Religious ceremonials to purge communities of witches also exist among other tribes discussed in this volume. The Navajo neighbors of the Pueblos believe in witches, and their religious leaders even today hold elaborate rituals to rid the people of these evil forces. In a recent work about a trial in Farmington, New Mexico, Rodney Barker (1992) claimed that Navajo witches eventually got revenge on teenagers who had killed and brutalized a Navajo man. Sorcery likely held a place in Cheyenne religion, but was not dealt with by their traditional legal system (Llewellyn & Hoebel 1942). Incidents of possession by evil spirits and shamans curing Indians from illnesses caused by possession are recorded in Marian Smith's ([1941] 1969) ethnography of the Nisqually and Puyallup Indians (67–77). Although the witch "Wakanta" is part of Sioux creation stories, no substantive accounts deal with tribal beliefs in sorcery (Hassrick 1964). However, nearly all of the tribes have medicine men or shamans who use prayer and ritual to heal those who are sick or suffering from misfortune.

Since all Indian tribes hold religious beliefs about sacred objects, sites, and interventions of the Great Spirit, the issue of the government and Indian religious conflicts appear prominently in the history of government-Indian relations. Subsequent chapters in this volume look at government intervention during the time the Ghost Dance was popular among the Teton Sioux in 1890 and later when controversy arose over government control of the holy sites at Taos Pueblo in the twentieth century. In a move to counter some of the wrongs committed in the nineteenth century, Congress has created laws to protect rather than suppress the religious beliefs of American Indians.

Chapter 7

Resistance, Advocacy, and the Southern Cheyenne and Arapaho, 1868–1961

The Sand Creek Massacre ripped apart the relationships between the Southern Cheyenne and Arapaho and the government. In fact, Sand Creek symbolized the end of nineteenth-century Cheyenne-Arapaho culture. Some Indians fled north to join hostile bands of Dog Soldiers and Sioux parties; Chief Black Kettle fled south to the Washita River in order to avoid further encounters with the military. Since the conflict continued, federal officials negotiated the Treaty of the Little Arkansas in 1865 to force the Cheyenne and Arapaho along with the Kiowa, Comanches, and Kiowa-Apaches onto reservations. Specifically, this treaty required the Southern Cheyenne and Arapaho to relinquish all land from the South Platte River in Nebraska to the Little Arkansas River in Kansas and to settle on a small reservation in Oklahoma. However, the treaty lacked force because only one-sixth of the tribal leaders signed and no hostile bands participated in the negotiation. The chiefs who signed expressed regret at giving up so much land, but they seemed satisfied with provisions permitting Indian hunting and prohibiting Indian travel close to postal and freight stations (Hyde 1968, 249; Berthrong [1963] 1972, 262).

The Southern Cheyenne and Arapaho did not remove themselves to their assigned reservation in Oklahoma after the Treaty of Little Arkansas, but they continued to fight settlers and Indian enemies in various locations on the plains of Nebraska, Colorado, and Kansas. By 1868, the conditions between the government and the southern Plains Indians had deteriorated to such an extent that General William T. Sherman declared war on the Indians. Friendly chiefs and their bands gathered around military forts for security, but the promise of protection failed just as it had at Sand Creek. A decisive defeat for the Southern Cheyenne and Arapaho came at the hands of General George Custer and 700 of his men at the Battle of Washita near Fort Supply. Custer destroyed forty-one Indian lodges, captured 900 ponies, seized dozens of lodge skins and buffalo robes, killed sixty Indians including Chief Black Kettle, and took more than fifty captives. What General Philip Sheridan and Custer saw as a decisive victory provoked criticism from the Indian Affairs Commissioner Thomas Murphy and from military officials Samuel Tappan and Edward Wynkoop (Berthrong [1963] 1972, 331; Trenholm 1970, 227–29).

In 1867, just one month before the Battle of Washita, the chiefs agreed to the provisions of the Treaty of Medicine Lodge Creek, but they still did not go to their assigned reservation until 1870. After the Indian Claims Commission Act was passed in 1946, the Cheyenne and Arapaho filed claims to gain financial payments for lands seized by the government in the Treaty of Medicine Lodge Creek.

The goals of this chapter are to (1) describe Indian participation at the negotiations for the Treaty of Medicine Lodge Creek, (2) record the Southern Cheyenne and Arapaho's resistance to assimilation, (3) explain the Indian Claims Commission as a forum for advocacy of land restitution, (4) investigate the strategies of advocacy used by attorneys appearing before the commission, and (5) show the relevance of the Indian Claims Commission for the other tribes discussed in this volume.

RESISTANCE STRATEGIES AT THE MEDICINE LODGE CREEK NEGOTIATIONS

Signs of Indian resistance appeared in negotiations of the Treaty at Medicine Lodge Creek in 1867. Extensive festivities at the treaty signing resembled the celebrations of the Sioux at the Fort Laramie Treaty Council. E. Adamson Hoebel (1978) notes:

Every treaty between the Cheyenne-Arapaho was invalidated by circumstances within months of its signing. Neither the United States government nor the leaders of the Indian tribes were capable of controlling their own people. . . . Both the Cheyenne and the United States broke their treaty commitments. Which party defaulted first is not always clear. (115)

The bridges built at the treaty signing ceremony collapsed after Custer's attack at Washita. Only after the Indians faced starvation did they comply with the government's demand that they move to an Oklahoma reservation.

The long history of the failure of the treaties with the Plains Indians frustrated Congress. Their solution was to create an Indian Peace Commission rather than to negotiate treaty agreements. The Peace Commission seemed to adopt a few basic strategies of conflict management that had been absent in other treaty councils. One strategy attempted to reduce the power disparity between the negotiators. To accomplish this goal, the president created a politically appointed group of citizens, politicians, and military officials, men who supposedly were more open to Indian issues than the Indian agents and military leaders who had conducted past treaty negotiations. In fact Samuel Tappan, a friend of the Cheyenne and Arapaho since Sand Creek, served on the Peace Commission.

A second strategy for the Peace Commission was to presume that all Indians were not alike and recognize that many Indians were friends to the government. Even though the Peace Commission's primary motive still was freeing up Indian lands for white settlement, they worded the agreements so that it appeared the government wanted to benefit rather than hurt the Indians. For example, the agreements implied that the government would safeguard the tribe's rights if the Indians kept away from railroad development rather than stating that it was really protecting the railroads in order to further economic expansion. The stated goal of the Peace Commission was to conclude a permanent peace, separate friendly from hostile Indians, and place tribes on a permanent reservation away from railroad development (Prucha 1990, 105–6).

A third negotiation strategy was for the government to give up some of its objectives in order to make the Indians perceive they could achieve some of their demands. For example, after a preliminary meeting at Fort Larned, the Indians refused to meet at a military post and suggested that the treaty be held at the neutral location of Medicine Lodge Creek, sixty miles south of the present-day Kansas boundary. The Peace Commission agreed to this demand.

A fourth strategy was to accommodate the nonverbal resistance of Indians at the treaty council. The resistance of Cheyenne and Arapaho still surfaced at Medicine Lodge Creek. The largest delegation consisted of about 5,000 Arapaho along with some Kiowa and Comanche chiefs. At the beginning, only a few Cheyenne lodges of Black Kettle attended since many Cheyenne were taking part in traditional religious ceremonies. Others refused to participate because they remained hostile to the government after the Sand Creek Massacre. Some of the first tribes to sign the treaty were the Comanches and Kiowas who agreed to settle on reservations and to limit their hunting expeditions to the Texas panhandle. Midway through the treaty negotiations, Cheyenne warriors made a dramatic entry into the scene of the council by parading into the area in formations four horses wide. During this procession, the Cheyenne yelled war hoops and showed off their skills at horsemanship (Jones 1966, 28–32).

Eventually, the peace commissioners presented the treaty provisions in a language acceptable both to the Indians and federal officials. In the process of securing acceptance for treaty provisions, the peace commissioners conducted a rhetorical interchange. For example, Indian Commissioner John Henderson, a senator from Missouri, started the negotiation by indicating two sides existed in the conflict. He noted that the Great Father had sent him to have a talk with them because they had violated treaties by attacking the men building the railroads and raiding settlements. But he also acknowledged that the Indians had been mistreated by soldiers and Indian agents. After the opening speech, Arapaho Chief Little Raven said he was loyal to the Cheyenne and defended the tribe's raids on settlers. Buffalo Chief of the Cheyenne entered the debate; he interjected that he wanted no permanent houses and would continue to hunt buffalo as his ancestors had along the range between the South Platte and Arkansas Rivers. Afterward Cheyenne Chief Little Man went on a tirade against chiefs from other tribes, claiming they had spread false rumors about his people (Jones 1966, 175–77).

In his concluding remarks, Henderson acknowledged the Indians' point of view even though he concluded their views were unrealistic. Henderson responded:

You say you do not like the medicine houses but you do like the buffalo and that you wish to do as your fathers did. We say to you that the buffalo will not last forever. They are now becoming few and you must know it. When that day comes, the Indian must change the road his father trod, or he must suffer and die. (Jones 1966, 127)

In his concluding remarks, Henderson tried to show the treaty provisions served the best interests of the Indians. He concluded:

We offer you the way. . . . Before all the good lands are taken by whites we wish to set aside a part of them for your exclusive use. . . . On that land you will build your house to hold the goods we will send you when you become hungry and naked. You can go there and be fed and clothed. (Jones 1966, 127)

Just as in other treaty negotiations, the government set the rules for the Indians. However, in this signing process, the commissioners expressed concern for the Indians' views and allowed them to express their resistance. In the end, the Treaty of Medicine Lodge Creek forced Indians to give up the land they had roamed, forbid them to enter into white settlements, placed them on reservations, and paid them $1 million in cash, food, and clothing over a twenty-five-year period. In return the Indians agreed to cease raids, live in permanent settlements, become farmers, and educate their children. Although the tone of the negotiations was conciliatory, the outcome still forced Indians to assimilate.

The treaty did not succeed in getting the Indians to cease warfare against others. Instead whites settled on Indian hunting grounds, hostile tribesmen continued to kill and raid settlements, and many warriors resumed fighting against their traditional enemies, the Ute Indians. Moreover, the tribes did not remove themselves to Oklahoma as required by the treaty; they defied the agreement by camping along Pawnee and Walnut Creek in present-day Kansas. Instead of the commissioners making peace, their efforts led to more warfare. Shortly after the treaty had been signed, federal troops attacked the Indians camping at Washita. It was not until 1869 that Cheyenne Chief Little Robe and other bands surrendered at Camp Supply (Berthrong [1963] 1972, 344) and the Indians started to move to their reservations in Oklahoma.

INDIAN RESISTANCE TO RESERVATIONS

After the Indians settled in Oklahoma, the government again expected them to submit peacefully, but the Indians resisted for many years. Indian agents engaged in a long and hard struggle to make the Southern Cheyenne and Arapaho abide by the treaty because the Indians lacked interest in agriculture, education, and the Christian religion. The conflicts caused by removal occurred off and on for the next thirty years. Indian agency efforts to enforce the agreements resulted in increased resistance from the Cheyenne and Arapaho. Just as the peace commissioners had done, the Indian agents tried to appease the Indians by offering them positive incentives for assimilating rather than punishing them for failing to assimilate. In ways similar to the Teton Sioux, the Southern Cheyenne and Arapaho created problems for the government because they refused to submit to federal authority.

Agitation occurs when a group perceives that no remedies exist for their grievances to be heard, so they resist the persons and institutions they feel are responsible for the problems (Bowers et al. 1993, 6). The Indian agitation kept the reservation agents in a constant state of turmoil. Instead of overtly suppressing the Indian resistance as is typical of colonial authorities, the agents took small steps to try to coax a few Indians to assimilate. For this reason the complicated removal process took place in several distinct

Adjustment: Phase One

Phase one represented an adjustment period when Indians and agents tried to figure out how they could work together on the reservation. In the beginning, Indians expressed their dissatisfaction with the treaties through nonviolent resistance; that is, they overtly violated provisions of the treaty they perceived to be unjust or unreasonable (Bowers et al. 1993, 37). Many Southern Cheyenne and Arapaho refused to cooperate with their Indian agents who were supposed to enforce the provisions of the Treaty of Medicine Lodge Creek (1867). For example, Article 6 of the treaty made it "the duty of the agent" to compel male and female children between six and sixteen to attend school. Indians also refused to farm, a violation of Article 8, a provision that stipulated the Indians will "begin cultivating the soil for a living." A few Indians complied. For example, during the first ten years after removal, some Arapaho sent their children to school and started farming. However, most Cheyenne refused to cooperate with either the educational or agricultural provisions (Trenholm 1970, 42). Many Indians also refused to live in houses and instead set up tepees close to the agents so they could collect their annuities. These same Indians complained about the food; they refused to eat corn and demanded increased supplies of beef (Berthrong [1963] 1972, 4–6).

Together the resistance produced what Bowers et al. (1993) call "creative disorder"; that is, the Indians resisted the treaty in so many different ways that the government found it impossible to enforce most provisions. The creative disorder produced a power reversal of sorts because the Indians were dictating to the government what they should do rather than the reverse process. Instead of directly confronting the Indians and forcing them to comply with the treaty, agents adopted appeasement strategies, allowing the Indians to resist some demands without punishment, substituting new policies, and trying to motivate them to comply with some provisions. For example, the agents appeased the Indians by giving families financial incentives for sending their children to school, allowing Indians to hunt to supplement their food supply, and permitting them to live in traditional tepees. Even after implementation of these appeasement strategies, agents failed to secure enough food and clothing to meet the Indians' needs. Indian agents claimed that since most Indians refused to farm, they were unable to contribute to their own economic welfare. As a result, the government's assimilation project failed and the Indians at the reservation lived in a constant state of starvation and social turmoil.

Escalation of Conflict: Phase Two

Escalation of conflict involved overt disputes between the Indians and their agents as well as internal dissension among the different bands of Indians living on the reservation. This conflict stemmed from material and social causes. Two events in 1877 drew attention to the economic plight of the Indians and led them to petition federal officials. The last buffalo hunt for the Cheyenne and Arapaho took place with a net harvest of only 219 robes, far below tribal needs for food and trade. The disappearance of the buffalo was a powerful sign to the Indians that the prophecy of Senator Henderson about the end of the buffalo hunts was true. In that same year, the Northern Cheyenne and Arapaho came south to Indian country after the Red River War. The demise of the buffalo in combination with the influx of people strained the limited economic resources of the

Southern Cheyenne and Arapaho (Berthrong [1963] 1972, 28–46). The Indians responded to this economic crisis by petitioning their agents for more food and medicine. When the agents did nothing to solve the problem, the Indians sent letters to the Department of Interior. When both efforts failed, the Indians stole supplies from the nearby military forts in order to feed their people.

Since the agents lacked effective sanctions to use against the Indians, they tried to resolve conflicts with appeasement strategies that took the form of new economic initiatives. One initiative was to employ Indians to run the wagons to bring in food and supplies to Indian country. This strategy met with limited success since more men wanted to run freight wagons than the freight companies needed. A second initiative was to lease Indian lands for grazing and charge the white cattlemen two cents per acre. This venture also met with limited success because it brought in capital, but created dissension between Indian landlords and the white tenants over profit. Since some Indians helped themselves to the tenant's cattle in order to feed their families, the arrangement proved unworkable. The cattle leasing issue became so heated that by 1885, President Grover Cleveland intervened, ordering the cattle be removed from the reservation (Berthrong [1963] 1972, 67–92). Both economic initiatives fostered jealousy and divisiveness among those who leased the land, those who did not, and actual and potential tenants.

In 1887, the General Allotment Act caused further economic havoc for the Cheyenne and Arapaho. Since this act allowed Indians to sell off their tribal land in the Cherokee Outlet, many families did. However, fraudulent sales agreements resulted in Indian families being cheated out of land by white settlers; at the same time, legitimate sales forced Indians to pay taxes imposed by the territorial government (Berthrong [1963] 1972, 205–7). As a result, the government's economic remedies impeded rather than promoted the assimilation of the Southern Cheyenne and Arapaho.

Compliance: Phase Three

This stage did not involve swift compliance by the Indians with the edicts of the government. Although some mixed-blood and a few full-blood Indians attended eastern boarding schools, most families refused to send their children to school. Since agents could not enforce sanctions nor enhance attendance by incentives, many Indians continued their traditional modes of living.

As time passed, authoritarian agents took control of the reservations. After this occurred, more and more Indians moved out of tepees into government housing, found employment, and sent their children to school. For the Cheyenne and Arapaho, compliance was culturally painful. Agent A. E. Woodson instituted new rules and added more stringent sanctions. Beginning in 1885, he refused to let more than four families live in one place, withheld annuities for Indians who did not work, required families to live in government-built homes, denied Indians the right to visit friends, and demanded men cut their hair (*Annual Report of the Commissioner of Indian Affairs* 1895, 244). The high-handed authoritarianism of Woodson did not end there. He also appointed himself moral guardian by forbidding marriage according to Indian custom and by mandating that Indian police arrest any tribal members involved in plural marriage (Berthrong [1963] 1972, 221).

Under threats of arrest and loss of annuities, most Indians eventually complied with the rules issued by Woodson. Compliance with these edicts meant a loss of cultural identity for the Southern Cheyenne and Arapaho. Berthrong ([1963] 1972) concludes:

Every aspect of Cheyenne culture was under stress. . . . The Indian could no longer dress as he wanted or wear his hair as had the old warriors; Indian marriages were illegal (though still practiced [in secret]); wood-framed houses replaced the tipi [*sic*], and the children were in school. (295)

Forcing Indians to comply with the material features of white culture led them to try new forms of resistance, such as practicing their own forms of religious devotion. Many Arapaho engaged in the Sun Dance rituals even though this was frowned on by agents. Others took part in the Ghost Dance religion of Wovoka, the Paiute religious leader who claimed the Indians would get back their lands and the buffalo would return. Some Cheyenne and Arapaho became involved in the peyote cult and later joined the Native American Church (Trenholm 1970, 292–94; Berthrong [1963] 1972, 324).

Assimilation and Reform: Phase Four

During the decades following the treaty, the Southern Cheyenne and Arapaho experienced hardships caused by starvation, land cession, and forced cultural assimilation. In many cases Indians settled down on their allotments; in other cases they left the reservation, joined the military, took jobs in the cities, and became urban Indians. By 1930, these Southern Cheyenne and Arapaho suffered from inadequate income and poor health, intertribal crime, and family disruptions in ways similar to other tribes discussed in this volume. Berthrong ([1963] 1972) claimed the education policy was a failure, social frustrations led to alcoholism, traditional leaders lacked power, and the federal courts usurped tribal discipline and sanctions (339). After so many years of fighting against the government, Southern Cheyenne and Arapaho lost their will; the most they could do was to fight for their own personal and cultural survival. The Indians had become wards, subject to the laws of the federal government, and powerless to control their tribal destiny. During this period from 1885 to 1930, the Indians gradually gave in to the demands of the government, and federal officials responded by giving them enough food and shelter to survive.

One glimmer of hope for reservation Indians came from the efforts of government reformers to restore Indian cultural ways and pay restitution for the wrongs committed when it abrogated treaty promises. The era featured extensive lobbying on behalf of the Indians by reformers wanting to improve the tribal living conditions. John Collier, the commissioner of Indian affairs appointed by Franklin D. Roosevelt, led the reform movement. One of his most significant accomplishments was the creation of the Indian Claims Commission (1946). The initiation of this forum permitted the Cheyenne and Arapaho to convert years of resistance into productive forms of tribal advocacy.

INDIAN CLAIMS COMMISSION AS A RHETORICAL FORUM

The Indian Claims Commission evolved out of the Court of Claims, a quasi-legal forum that permitted Indians and settlers to recover economic benefits from the loss of their land during treaty times. Several reasons contributed to the evolution of this body into the Indian Claims Commission. First, the Court of Claims could not handle the large number of Indian claims after the law permitted Indians to sue in 1881. Second, public reformers demanded that the government do something to remedy the moral injustices it had committed against the Indians. Third, Congress strongly believed that they had to resolve the huge quantity of Indian legal claims against the government. Additionally, government leaders believed that paying monetary settlements to the Indians would enhance tribal economic vitality. Finally, Indians had gained credibility because many tribal members had served honorably in World War II and demonstrated their patriotism toward the government (Rosenthal 1990, 18–20, 46–53; Prucha 1994, 382–84; Lieder & Page 1997).

The Indian Claims Commission Act of 1946 created the Indian Claims Commission. Rosenthal (1990) characterizes the Claims Commission in this way: "The history of the Indian Claims Commission is laden with all the elements of melodrama: ignorance, arrogance, racism, greed, corruption, and hypocrisy. But it also reveals flashes of morality, honesty, perseverance, and justice" (xiii). The primary purpose of the act was to settle past injustices and end the special dependent status of Indians. A secondary purpose, according to Commissioner Edgar Witt, was to balance "the interests of the taxpayers against the rights of the Indians" (Lieder & Page 1997, 116). The government established the political and judicial forum to hear Indian land grievances.

The audiences for the Claims Commission consisted of a diverse set of people with different ideological perspectives. No matter what the outcome of the hearings was, they likely pleased some members of the audience and displeased others. A political audience resembles what Chaim Perelman and Lucie Olbrechts-Tyteca (1969) call a particular audience. Effective rhetorical advocacy gains the adherence of particular audiences by persuading them with strategically designed argumentation (14). In this case the audience of the Claims Commission consisted of several groups. Three commissioners who decided the applicable legal principles and made the awards to the Indian plaintiffs composed the immediate audience. An important secondary audience was Congress; they expected to have the Indian claims settled expediently. Indian reform groups constituted another secondary audience; they desired to right moral wrongs committed against the Indians. The Indians themselves made up the third audience; they wanted to make the government pay for treaty violations and admit past injustices. The claims commissioners expected Indians to abide by the settlements and use their awards to expedite assimilation. To gain adherence from the diverse audiences was difficult because each faction held disparate values. The Indians and reformers perceived the awards as reparations, and many members of Congress and the commissioners expected the awards to silence the Indian resistance.

From its inception, the Claims Commission heard cases in a partisan political environment. Passage of the act took sixteen years of political maneuvering. Highly contentious congressional debates pitted friends of Indians against defenders of the government (*House Conference Committee Creating an Indian Claims Commission*, 1946). Congress wanted the commission to pay the Indians for the lands that they had relinquished under treaties at sums far below the market value. Each of the three commissioners appointed by the president had his own political allegiances.

The partisan audience of commissioners rendered decisions with low settlements. The Cheyenne and Arapaho were one of only a few tribes that received relatively large awards. The commissioners deciding the Cheyenne-Arapaho claims included William Holt, Arthur Watkins, and T. Harold Scott. Prior to his appointment, Holt was the chief counsel for a Nebraska insurance company and a loyal Republican. He was one of the original commissioners (Lieder & Page 1997, 87). Watkins also was a Republican and a U.S. senator from Utah with a record of service on the Senate Indian Affairs Committee and credentials as a longtime advocate for the termination of Indian land claims. His decisions supported the side of the government and showed a lack of sympathy for Indians (Lieder & Page 1997, 159–60). Colorado native Scott was the only Democrat and the only pro-Indian member of the Claims Commission. Prior to his appointment, he had served on the Federal Trade Commission and actively sought an appointment to the Indian Claims Commission. As a member, he frequently dissented from Watkins and Holt (Lieder & Page 1997, 160).

The attorneys representing the Indians and those serving the government rigorously advocated on behalf of the interests of their respective clients. The lead attorney for the Cheyenne and Arapaho was Ernest Wilkinson, the most well known of the Indian advocates. Wilkinson not only helped draft the legislation for the Indian Claims Commission Act, but he also defended Indians in some of the most successful claims, including that of the California Indians (Lieder & Page 1997, 121–22). Many successful defenses of Indian cases were under the leadership of Wilkinson's law firm. For many years, Ralph Barney, representing the Department of Justice, served as the lead government attorney and had a huge staff of lawyers whose goal it was to protect government interests. Rosenthal (1990) described Barney as "a lion in defense of the federal treasury" (122). The partisanship of the commissioners in combination with the fervor of the Indians and the aggressiveness of government attorneys produced contentious and skillful argumentation.

In the Indian claims cases, the government attorneys had the advantage of political power and financial resources. Moreover, the claims commissioners often sided with the government attorneys because of a desire to protect taxpayers from paying high monetary awards. To persuade their political audiences, attorneys representing Indian claimants needed to consider the political loyalties of the claims commissioners as well as the preferences of the reformers and Indian citizens. Some critics minimized the value of the more than $800 million awarded by the commissioners during its existence. For example, Peter Matthiessen ([1980] 1991) noted that the "chief beneficiaries of this commission were not the Indians but the Washington law firms that represented them" (28).

In addition to its political nature, the commission also resembled a legal adversarial forum. The Claims Commission created a community in which attorneys and their witnesses reconstructed reality on behalf of their clients. In doing so, they established a moral standard by which the culture of the treaty era could be evaluated. The process was predictable; the attorneys for the Indians filed the claims, and the government denied most of them. Advocates for both sides grounded their arguments in legal theories. The plaintiffs argued that tribes had aboriginal land title to the territory they had ceded in treaties, concluded that the government had failed to gain the appropriate informed consent of tribal leaders for the treaties, and therefore the government owed the Indians a fair market value for their land. The contrasting position of government attorneys was that the tribes lacked title to aboriginal lands; or if they had title, federal officials had obtained Indian land in a fair, honorable, and an equitable manner. As is typical of legal civil suits, the Indian plaintiffs had to define the acts the United States had committed as violations of the law and then show that these wrongful acts warranted the recovery of monetary damages.

Evidence for both sides consisted of competing expert testimony from historians, ethnologists, and land appraisers. The claims commissioners applied precedents developed by the court of claims to decide disputed questions of law. According to longtime Justice Department Attorney Ralph Barney (1974), "Much of the 'evidence' consists of deductions made by witnesses from the frequently meager hard facts available" (15–16). Indian plaintiffs had the right to appeal to the court of claims if they believed the Claims Commission had treated them unfairly.

Although the Act was supposed to have a limited life of ten years, legislative extensions to it continued until 1978 when the Claims Commission finally dissolved. Indian tribes filed a total of 852 claims, resulting in total settlements of $818 million, a sum far below the amount petitioned by Indian tribes. The combined tribes of the Southern and Northern Cheyenne and Arapaho filed a claim with the commission in 1951; the commission heard the claim in 1955. Finally, in 1961, the Claims Commission made awards to them.

ADVOCACY BEFORE THE INDIAN CLAIMS COMMISSION

The opportunity to present their case before the Claims Commission converted the resistance of the Southern Cheyenne and Arapaho into skillful advocacy marked by sophisticated use of language, strategic case-building, and refutation.

Advocacy Language

The subsequent analysis shows rhetorical features of the language of this act and emphasizes how the attorneys for both sides strategically used terms to enhance their argumentation. Several language choices had persuasive potency, including (1) Indian identity, (2) unconscionable considerations, (3) fair and honorable dealings, and (4) just compensation. These phrases framed the legal and moral issues of the claims proceedings and contributed to the persuasiveness of arguments.

Legal texts consist of both political and legal arguments constructed according to the language of law. James Boyd White (1985) explains that law "is a discourse working within the social context of its own creation" (98). As a legal text, the Indian Claims Act was a thirty-two-year work in progress that evolved through the attorneys' arguments and the commissioners' interpretations of that reasoning according to definitions of key words. These key words function similarly to what Kenneth Burke (1986) calls "terministic screens" (44–45); that is, legal definitions that directed the attorneys, expert witnesses, and commissioners to select out certain terms and then focus the testimony on the meanings of designated legal words while ignoring other terms.

The definitions, extracted from Section 2 of the Indian Commission Claims Act, identified the parameters of the legitimate issues about which tribes could sue the government. The act stated that tribes could sue about issues involving (1) law and equity arising out of government laws, treaties, and proclamations, (2) claims of tort permitting a party to sue, (3) claims based on "fraud, duress, and unconscionable consideration, mutual or unilateral mistake" recognized by a court of equity, (4) claims for ceded lands without proper compensation, and (5) claims based "upon fair and honorable dealings" not recognized by existing law (1946, 1049).

Indian Identity. Another significant explanation concerned what it means to be a legitimate Indian group with rights to sue the government. In other words, the commission sought an answer to the question—Who has the right to sue? This act permitted "any Indian tribe, band or other identifiable group of American Indians residing within the territorial limits of the United States or Alaska" to bring their cases to the commission (Sec. 24). At first glance the issues seemed simple, but since Indian law is complex, the Claims Commission required the plaintiffs to prove through ethnologists and legal documents that they were a legitimate Indian entity. But it was the government rather than the Indian people that first had constructed the legal identity of the aboriginal entities. Kroeber (1955) emphasizes this point, saying "[i]t was we Caucasians who again and again rolled a number of related obscure bands or minute villages into the larger page of a "tribe," then we proclaimed this tribe had "sovereign power and territorial ownership which the native nationality had mostly never even claimed" (304). For this reason, tribes were forced to prove their legal identity through historical, ethnographic, and legal records. After Indian groups had established a constitution, they became a legal entity in the eyes of the government.

Several other approaches for establishing identity as a legitimate tribe are possible. Identity can be established by meeting the legal definition of a statutory group which was done by showing the Indians had a constitution and a governing body and by meeting a social-cultural definition, showing that others had recognized the people as a separate group for many decades (Lurie 1957, 61). The Cheyenne-Arapaho established their identity by using social-cultural evidence published in the *Handbook of American Indians* (1: 251–53). Their briefs quoted this evidence: "The Cheyenne have long been closely associated with their relatives, the Arapaho, although their habitat was generally north and west of the Arapaho." After becoming joint plaintiffs, the northern and southern bands of Cheyenne and Arapaho filed common briefs on behalf of all members of their confederated tribe. William Howard Payne, attorney for the southern tribes, reinforced tribal political identity by restating the language of the treaties of Fort Laramie,

Fort Wise, Little Arkansas, and Medicine Lodge Creek (Petitioner's Brief 1974, 18–26; all subsequent references to the briefs come from the 1974 microfilm copies of the Indian Claims Commission Cases 329a and 329b).

Since legal standing was often a prerequisite for filing with the Indian Claims Commission, attorneys repeated words and phrases to validate the Indians as a statutory party to previous contracts as stipulated in treaties and executive orders. The long history of treaties between the Cheyenne and Arapaho made it very easy for them to verify their identity as a legitimate legal entity. This was not the case for many tribes including the Shoshone bands of Idaho, the Mashpee of Massachusetts, and the California Indians (Sutton 1985, 3–16).

Unconscionable Consideration. The wording in the Claims Act was at the same time legal and moral. One phrase, "unconscionable consideration," was difficult both to define and to explain. The term represented the moral exigency of the Indian Claims Commission, stating that the government was to repair the damage caused by immoral economic transactions with Indians. The literal interpretation of "unconscionable" means to shock the conscience of citizens (*Sioux Tribe of Indians v. U.S.* 1956, 229). Kenneth Burke ([1941] 1973) explains that words do not just describe reality, but they call up strongly held attitudes. Words tell us who we are and prescribe how we should act within society (103). If this is the case, then these words imply that the dealings of the government had been aberrant and that we as a country had a moral obligation to make amends for bad acts. Although the commissioners tried to change the word "unconscionable" to "inadequate," they never succeeded. This phrase meant that the commissioners had to describe payments as moral reparations rather than only as adjustments of equity (*House Committee on Interior and Insular Affairs* 1967, 53–69). In this way, the government admitted to moral wrong when it gave awards to Indian tribes. At the same time, the awards enhanced the reputation of the plaintiff tribes and their attorneys, they decreased the credibility of the government and its lawyers.

To address the issue of an "unconscionable consideration," plaintiffs' attorneys alleged that the payment for lands in the Treaty of Medicine Lodge Creek was "grossly inadequate and unconscionable, being less than $1.3 million for a net cession involving more than 43 million acres . . . or less than 3.3 cents per acre" (Petitioner's Brief 14). Additionally, attorneys alleged that an 1890 executive agreement with the Southern Cheyenne and Arapaho had been illegally transacted because members of the northern bands had not signed and too few male members of the southern tribes had signed. For this reason, the government had transacted the treaties under circumstances of "fraud, duress, unconscionable consideration," forcing the southern bands to relinquish highly valued land at $1.50 per acre (Petitioner's Brief 29). For plaintiffs the payment was not just inadequate, it proved the government intentionally cheated them. The decision of the claims commissioners used the word "unconscionable" to justify giving more than $10 million in awards to the Northern Cheyenne and Arapaho (10 Ind. Cl. Comm. 106) and more than $15 million to the Southern Cheyenne and Arapaho (16 Ind. Cl. Comm. 187).

Fair and Honorable. In addition to frequent repetition of the word "unconscionable," plaintiffs' attorneys described government transactions with the Indians as "unfair and dishonorable." These terms gained rhetorical potency because they summed up the attitudes that Indians had held for many years about the government, and they legitimized a negative conception of government relationships with the tribes. Burke ([1937] 1971) explains that "names shape our relations with our fellows. They prepare us for some functions and against others, for or against the persons representing these functions" (4). The naming of relationships with Indians as "unfair and dishonorable" characterized government actions as immoral. In an effort to refute this characterization, government attorneys counter argued that federal officials had engaged in "fair and honorable dealings" with the Indian tribes.

Both the negative and positive versions of this phrase promoted moral rather than economic arguments. Sandra C. Danforth (1973) claims that since these words are not "recognized by any existing rule of law or equity," the provision allowed Indians to sue for grievances that were not always legal violations (401). Since the Cheyenne and Arapaho attorneys were able to demonstrate that the payments were unconscionably low and that the land cessions were unfair and inequitable, they demonstrated that the economic issues had moral implications. This moral part of the Claims Act was created to "reduce the bitterness of Indians" and increase the social awareness of the public about the hardships experienced by Indians (Lurie 1955, 373). The moral arguments also forced the government to accept responsibility for not honoring treaty commitments.

In the "prayer for relief," the concluding paragraph of the petitioner's brief that summarizes the grounds of the law suit, Payne "prays that defendant make a full and complete accounting" and that the petitioner be "awarded judgment" based on "just compensation for the fair and reasonable value of lands" and "for losses and damages suffered by virtue of the defendant's violations of treaties and agreements and principles of fair honorable dealings" (31). The Claims Commission did not use the terms in its decision, and instead seemed to justify the government dealings with Indians as fair. For example, the claims commissioners argued that the 1890 executive order was fair because the lands "were given to the Southern Cheyenne and Arapaho Tribes in lieu of those promised in 1865 and in previous treaties and as such must be regarded as consideration for the cession of subject tract" (10 Indian Claims 1).

Just Compensation. The government attorneys placed the term "just compensation" in the context of land values at the time of taking. According to Kenneth Burke, this rhetorical strategy "tells us what a thing is" by placing it "in terms of something else." This "idea of locating, or placing is implicit in our very word for a definition" ([1950] 1969, 24). The Claims Act stipulated that land compensation be determined by a government, not an Indian standard. For Burke, this mode of defining allows those making the definition "to cut away, to abstract, all emotional factors that complicate the objective clarity of meaning" ([1941] 1973, 145). The government's ability to restrict "just compensation" to economic and material concerns foreclosed the possibility that Indians could sue for loss of religious sites or sacred lands. In doing so, this wording precluded the plaintiffs from seeking moral and cultural compensation.

The phrase, "just compensation," also created the presumption that the federal government's method of valuing land was superior to Indians' cultural valuations. Nonetheless many tribes wanted their land returned rather than a monetary settlement. In the cases argued before the Claims Commission, this term meant paying Indians for the market value of their land at the time the land was ceded. Unlike the provisions of the other legal terms, "just compensation" applied only to economic values.

Arguing this issue often depended on flawed and incomplete evidence. Additionally, the process of establishing "just compensation" involved complex accumulation and interpretation of data by expert appraisers. Thomas LaDuc (1957) explains that the estimates of Indian land values were flawed because retrospective appraisals were just a good guess based on a hypothetical situation. Moreover, the appraisers had no way of translating the values. At first, they tried to translate values using the cost of Army rations as the standard. Later, they used government sales as an index of value. Both standards placed the value of Indian lands "artificially low" (9–12).

The defendant's brief provides an example of the complex argument about "just compensation" for farm lands. For example, the government argued: "The total area along streams in the subject area has been calculated at 495,000 acres. Deducting the 50,000 acres of farms in cultivation, there remains 445,000 acres of land which could be irrigated and put in cultivation by the construction of ditches." About 445,000 acres of land was available for sale, but since this land had no water and lacked ditches to bring water, it was not saleable at the rate of more than a few cents an acre, a sum already paid to the Indians (Defendant's Brief 47). The claims commissioners repeatedly concluded that the value of the plaintiffs' appraiser was artificially high and that the defendant's appraiser was more reasonable (1961, 32–33).

Most of the terminology of the Indian Claims Commission Act permitted moral as well as legal argumentation. The terminology of "unconscionable considerations" and "fair and honorable dealings" allowed plaintiffs to frame their case theory and present their evidence using moral issues. At the same time the legal phrases of "identifiable tribe" and "just compensation" permitted the defense to emphasize legal standing and make monetary awards according to the rule of law as interpreted by statutes and legal precedents. The wording of the Claims Act "was an inducement to action" (Burke [1937] 1971, 4) because the language allowed the Indians and the government to be brought together, to argue against one another, and to provide incentives for morally and economically based legal actions.

Case Development and Refutation

The records of the Cheyenne-Arapaho case consisted of eighty-two claims of fact stated by the plaintiffs and denied by the defense, dozens of exhibits, the testimony of the expert witnesses, the transcripts of the oral arguments of the attorneys, and the opinion of the commissioners. One interesting feature of the findings of fact was a two-page protest from plaintiffs' attorneys stating the defense had withheld "the books of account and all other records pertaining to all moneys and financial transactions" from them, and this negligence had resulted in "a failure of the government to account for its management, handling and disposition of said moneys and properties" (Petitioner's Brief 56–57). The statement implied that the government had not engaged in fair and honorable dealings with either the contemporary attorneys or the Indians of the past. This section explains how attorneys arguing before the Indian Claims Commission used expert witnesses, built their cases, and refuted the testimony of the opposition in the Cheyenne-Arapaho land claim.

Expert Witnesses. The legal nature of the Indian Claims Commission was apparent in its use of evidence. The expert testimony that constituted both sides of the case was not subject to strict rules of admissibility based on relevance, materiality, foundation, and hearsay. In contrast to these standards, Julian H. Steward (1955) explains the Claims Commission viewed Indian informants as weak since they gained their knowledge from tradition and stories rather than first-hand observations. Settlers, trappers, hunters, and missionaries kept diaries and records, but this data also was suspect since it was subjective evidence from a white point of view. However, the commissioners considered material objects, such as bills of sale and contracts, to be reasonably objective (300). Nonetheless all of the evidence presented by the Indian plaintiffs required that experts draw conclusions from secondary sources. Other evidence from the government and the Indian tribes came from experts that subconsciously included evidence that supported their side of the case and excluded evidence that did not (Barney 1955, 335; Manners 1957, 80).

A further complication in the presentation of evidence was the fact that the academic experts often held presumptions that directly opposed those of the attorneys and commissioners who had been trained in law. For example, ethnologists expressed concern about "cultural intolerance" and "social misunderstandings" in contrast to lawyers who asked witnesses to establish facts and apply them to precedents (Lurie 1955, 365). Despite these complications, the lawyers and claims commissioners seemed to accept the testimony presented as the best available and the attorneys conscientiously refuted the evidence presented by their adversaries.

Case Building. The analysis of case building applies constructs defined by Perelman and Olbrechts-Tyteca (1969) to investigate how the expert appraisers from each side of the case established their claims about the value of Indian lands. The cases developed with one mutually agreed presumption about the meaning of land ownership. A presumption, according to Perelman and Olbrechts-Tyteca (1969), is a starting point of argument that is connected with the normally held beliefs of reference groups (70–73). The commissioners adopted a concept of property that fit with American law, presuming that someone who owns property has exclusive use of the land and that the property has a transferable title protected by law. This presumption permitted the commissioners to hear arguments about boundaries, land use, and land valuations.

This concept of property at the time of treaties was alien to the tribes who now claimed ownership. Steward (1955) notes that the Indians never owned the land; they roamed and used the land for its food resources. Moreover, Indians did not claim exclusive use of the land. For example the land south of the Platte and north of the Arkansas River was used by many tribes other than the Cheyenne and Arapaho, including the Comanches, Sioux, Utes, and Kiowas, but treaties ceded it to the Cheyenne and Arapaho and so this tribe considered the territory their land, and they believed they should be paid for it.

In addition to the legal presumption about land ownership, both the plaintiffs and the defense agreed that the Indians had title to the land. To draw persuasive inferences from premises, the attorneys should use techniques for "promulgating certain texts" and "the pronouncements of certain words" (Perelman & Olbrechts-Tyteca 1969, 105). For example, historian Leroy R. Hafen provided information about the history of the land ceded by the Southern Cheyenne and Arapaho in the Treaty of Medicine Lodge Creek. Since his testimony was highly contested by the defense expert, he established the premise that Cheyenne and Arapaho lived, hunted, and established their culture in the eastern plains of Colorado and the western plains of Kansas and inferred that they therefore had aboriginal title to the land.

One technique used by plaintiffs to make the testimony persuasive was to bolster Hafen's credentials. They argued:

The testimony and report of Dr. LeRoy R. Hafen have provided the Commission with unusually well-informed information about the historical and economic background of the Cheyenne-Arapaho country. Dr. Hafen is possibly the most knowledgeable living expert on the history of this area. His Master's and Doctor's degrees were both taken in the field of Western History and for thirty years he was State Historian for the State of Colorado. This position . . . entailed lecturing, interviewing pioneers, and otherwise searching out Colorado historical material. As part of his duties he was Editor of the *Colorado Magazine*, a magazine devoted to the history and ethnology of the State. . . . Perhaps most indicative of his stature in this field is the fact that he has recently completed the article, "Colorado, the History and Resources of the State" for the *Encyclopedia Britannica*. (Petitioner's Brief 69)

In this excerpt, attorneys *entitled* certain phrases to emphasize the knowledge of their expert. Entitling refers to using verbal forms that invest speech with judgments of value (Perelman & Olbrechts-Tyteca 1969, 151). For example, plaintiffs judged the value of Hafen's testimony by saying he was "the most knowledgeable living expert" and "devoted to the history and ethnology of the state" in order to establish Hafen as a valuable witness. In doing so, plaintiffs credited him with knowing the facts and using competent research methods that were so reliable that he not only knew the reported information but that his findings would be published by a prestigious encyclopedia. After judging his credentials, plaintiffs' attorneys further argued that Hafen's testimony was reliable since it had been corroborated by the defense's historical expert (Petitioner's Brief 69).

The credibility argument was the first step in more elaborate deductive reasoning given by plaintiffs to explain land value. They reasoned: (1) The Cheyenne-Arapaho had title by treaty to all lands south of the Platte and north of the Arkansas. (2) The land was valuable for ranching and mining. (3) The Cheyenne and Arapaho did not receive government payments that reflected that value. (4) Therefore the Indian Claims Commission now should pay them fair market value for this land. After these reasons were developed one at a time, the defense strongly contested them.

Even though the defense accepted the starting premise, they ignored it in their case presentation, emphasizing instead that the government had paid the Indians a "just compensation" for the ceded land. Instead of building a deductive case as the plaintiffs had done, defense engaged in point-by-point refutation. The first line of defense refutation asserted that the Cheyenne-Arapaho lands were of little value at the time they were ceded. Moreover the government had given the Indians just compensation for their lands. This defense argument developed "liaisons between facts, premises, and conclusions" (Perelman & Olbrechts-Tyteca 1969, 460). This type of refutation did not use deductive entailments like the ones presented by the plaintiffs, but it did draw conclusions from loosely connected clusters of evidence that pointed to a common idea, a method sometimes called abduction.

Defense further claimed that Cheyenne-Arapaho lands had little economic value at the time of the treaty payments. Instead of developing this idea with expert testimony, the defense pieced together evidence from historians, agricultural specialists, and climatologists from the treaty era. For example, using agricultural maps the defense argued that the rainfall in the area was sparse and even though it was not technically a desert, the land "had been referred to by many historical writers as 'The Great American Desert',," and so the land could not have been used by settlers with their accustomed agricultural methods. Furthermore, even if the land had sufficient rainfall, and climatologists concluded this was doubtful, the lack of transportation inhibited the ability of settlers to get their crops to markets. Defense emphasized that "the value of the land for farming depends on the means to get the produce to markets at a reasonable time and cost, and the value of the western land for agriculture in 1865 would have been low, even if it had water because of lack of transportation" (Defendant's Brief 10–11).

This argument used liaisons by establishing the facts that the contested land had little rainfall and that even if it had adequate rainfall, inadequate transportation would impede the sale of crops. The defense attorneys connected these facts to the presumption that the Cheyenne and Arapaho had title to the land and to the conclusion that the government had justly paid them for the land they ceded in the Treaty of Little Arkansas in 1865.

Refutation Strategies. In addition to their common use of expert testimony and their unique approaches to case building, attorneys for both sides engaged in vigorous refutation of the testimony of each other's expert witnesses. The advocates did not impeach witnesses in the same way they would in a civil case involving a contemporary property dispute by showing bias, prejudice, self interest, inconsistent statements, or bad reputation. The attorneys, at times, presumed adversarial witnesses to be knowledgeable. The refutation by both sides did not challenge the evidence, but it refuted the inferences drawn by the experts about the evidence that had been presented.

Attorneys did not refute the expert testimony of ethnologists and historians, but instead most of the controversy centered on the appraisers' evidence concerning whether or not the government had engaged in "fair and honorable" dealing and given "just compensation" to Indians after treaties were negotiated. The refutation illustrated how attorneys used different patterns of inference about similar evidence to create different conclusions. James Jasinski (1990) identifies six types of inferences—universal, special, field-dependant, emotional, authorial, and motivational. Plaintiffs and defendants used some common inferences in their argumentation regarding the testimony of plaintiffs' appraiser Jerry Holbrook and defense's appraiser Homer Hoyt.

One argument emphasized the special form of inference that takes "the shape of statements about important values and beliefs adhered to by members of society" (Jasinski 1990, 60). A value that most legal forums prize is objectivity and impartiality. Plaintiffs refuted Homer Hoyt's testimony by showing that he confused his argument with subjective emotional imagery. For example, plaintiffs concluded:

> Mr. Hoyt is a fighter and an advocate, but he is not a dispassionate expert witness, as his method starkly demonstrates. He began the mineral section of his report by printing a picture . . . entitled, "The Road to the Mines." It is a picture of some fifty men, five burros, ten horses and three wagons toiling up a corduroy road that has a fifty percent grade and disappears into the sky itself. The terrain is precipitous, rocky and almost barren of vegetation. In the foreground a reluctant burro refuses to attempt the climb. Men are seated by the roadside, mopping their brows and seemingly wishing they had never left Vermont. Together it makes the gold adventure seem not worth the candle. No source is given for the picture—it might be Colorado, but then again it might be Nevada, California, or Peru. This is the mood-setting prologue to Mr. Hoyt's discussion of the mineral resources of the Cheyenne-Arapaho. Mr. Hoyt then proceeds for twenty pages disparaging the area. (Petitioner's Brief 101)

Plaintiffs argued that using misleading emotional imagery to make connections between mining and low quality land is a strategy for distorting the truth about the wealth that has been recovered from the Cheyenne and Arapaho lands. For them, this imagery both distorted Hoyt's appraisal and threatened to reduce the settlement value of Cheyenne-Arapaho lands.

Another plaintiffs' argument emphasized a reasoning pattern that appealed to convictions valid in the field of the appraisers. Field-dependant forms of inference apply to the issues or problems within a field and may not be applicable to other fields (Jasinski 1990, 62). For some of the testimony, attorneys allowed their expert witness to justify claims by standards of their profession.

One example involved plaintiffs' refutation of Hoyt's testimony based on misuse of standard methodology. They concluded:

> [D]efendant's witnesses have completely ignored that most valuable of appraisal tools, the use of market data. Indeed, in view of the wealth of such data and the indications from the data, they had to ignore it to arrive at such a ridiculously low estimate of value. They have deliberately misinterpreted other data and arbitrarily used evaluation methods that either (a) are not accepted or recognized in the appraisal field, or (b) cannot possibly be used at this late date when the necessary information cannot be obtained. (Petitioner's Brief 107)

Since market data is the most acceptable method for analyzing evidence, Hoyt's failure to use this method revealed a potential weakness in all of his conclusions concerning Cheyenne and Arapaho land values.

Some arguments used an emotional form of inference, that is, a connection between the evidence and the conclusion that "takes shape through the depiction of certain conditions . . . that induce an emotional response" from the audience (Jasinski 1990, 63). In cases before the Claims Commission, the strategy of assailing the credibility of the opposing witness provided an example of this emotional form of inference. One of the most contentious economic issues in the Cheyenne-Arapaho land claim concerned the value of mining securities. Plaintiffs' expert Holbrook claimed that royalties were 3 percent in 1865 in contrast to defense expert Hoyt, who concluded that these securities were worth 25 percent of the current value. Since high interest rates would detract from the value of Indian lands, both sides argued that mineral rights were considerably lower at the time than they had been a hundred years earlier.

The inferences made by experts about land values created an emotional response from attorneys on both sides. Defense argued that: "Petitioners have made some irresponsible and reckless references to Dr. Hoyt's testimony, even going so far as to accuse him of fraud in their apparent attempt to obscure the true facts which are fatal to their claim" (Defendant's Brief 86). The defense clarified the method used by their witness to calculate interest rates for the value of mines, saying: "Again we suggest that the attack on Dr. Hoyt was a desperate effort to distract attention from the ridiculous interest rate used by their witnesses" (Defendant's Brief 89). Defense's refutation concluded that at the time of the treaty the Cheyenne and Arapaho had already received just compensation for this low value property.

A final type of inference consists of authorial depictions of the character and habits of a person. Advocates use the depictions to remind the audience about the status of those presenting the evidence (Jasinski 1990, 63–64). In this case, the attorneys used inferences about their appraiser's character and about the strategies of opposing lawyers. An example of this kind of depiction appeared in this defense argument. They claimed:

[Petitioners] have combed the record in an attempt to find something to discredit the opinion of the defense's witness, Dr. Hoyt, with reference to the value of the grazing or range lands. We realize that acceptance of his opinion would be fatal to this part of their claim. We submit that this attack is grasping at straws and will not make the true unfavorable conditions go away. (Defendant's Brief 75–76)

Both the briefs of the defense and the plaintiffs show numerous instances where the arguments impugned the character of opposing counsel and called into question the credentials of opposing experts in order to show weaknesses in the conclusions drawn by their adversaries. Refutation challenging witnesses' use of special, field-dependant, emotional, and authorial inferences is common in many civil trials, but it is not usually the primary form of challenging the opposition's evidence as it was in the Cheyenne and Arapaho case. Since the attorneys accepted the government's presumption about land title and the premise that expert witnesses should use secondary sources, attorneys resorted to refutation of the inferences drawn from the opposing side's evidence. Both sides used this type of refutation throughout their briefs and presumably during their oral arguments based on these briefs.

The claims commissioners, attorneys, and witnesses reconstructed legal history through their participation in the case of the Cheyenne and Arapaho. Their rhetorical construction of legal texts depended upon the definitions in the Claims Act, the testimony of expert witnesses, and the advocate's refutation of each other's evidence.

Any case appearing before the Claims Commission evolved out of a complex history of government-Indian relations, resulted in an imperfect legal solution to a nagging moral issue, and took place in a forum unequipped to decide complex grievances on the merits of the evidence. Lieder and Page (1997) emphasize the limited success of the Claims Commission:

Congress hoped to solve an intractable social problem by having the judicial system make restitution for some of the government's actions. Unable to adjudicate the claims cases satisfactorily with established judicial doctrines, the Commission was reduced first to collecting historical and anthropological information and then to dispensing moderate sums to the tribes. (272)

The Cheyenne and Arapaho succeeded more than most tribes in getting an award; their success resulted from a long legal quest carried out on their behalf by competent counsel and experts who presented a persuasive case to politically motivated commissioners. The money they eventually received did not rectify the many years of suffering the Southern Cheyenne and Arapaho experienced on their reservation in Oklahoma, but this compensation did help provide needed services for tribal members.

Other Indian tribes discussed in this volume received some restitution from the Claims Commission and the court of claims, the forum that preceded and followed the work of the Claims Commission, as well as from congressional action. For example, the Nisqually claimed a right to land in the lower Puget Sound, and they received an award of $160 thousand in 1971 (29 Ind. Cl. Comm. 432). The Santee Sioux through appeals to the court of claims got two separate awards for annuities and lands forfeited under the treaties negotiated prior to the Minnesota Uprising. In 1907, the lower bands received more than $788,000; and in 1924, the upper bands got more than $386,000 (Meyer 1993, 334). Other Sioux tribes, including the Santee and Teton, used the Claims Commission to try to get the Black Hills of South Dakota restored to them after it was taken by the government in 1876. In 1974, the Claims Commission awarded the Sioux $17.5 million for taking the Black Hills. In 1979, the Sioux appealed to the

Court of Claims who sustained the award and added interest. In 1989, the Court of Claims awarded the Sioux $40 million for the Black Hills, but the tribe declined the money because they wanted the land returned to them, not an economic award (Lazarus, 1991). At one time the Navajo and Hopi were going to bring their case of disputed lands to the Claims Commission, but this never occurred and the land dispute between these two tribes eventually was resolved by Congress (Benedek 1992, 134–35). Many Pueblo Indians filed claims for lands lost through the Spanish Land Grants. In 1965, Taos Pueblo (*Pueblo of Taos v. United States*, 1965, 15 Ind. Cl. Comm. 666) filed, claiming 300 acres of tribal land had been taken by settlers; the Claims Commission awarded the Pueblo nearly $300,000. The more important dispute at Taos Pueblo involved the return of the sacred land at Blue Lake accomplished through congressional action rather than a case before the Claims Commission (Chapter 8). Despite these awards, most tribes continue to express regret and anger about land that they ceded to the government through nineteenth-century treaties and agreements.

Chapter 8

Legislative Movements and the Return of Blue Lake, 1922–1970

Taos Pueblo celebrated the return of Blue Lake, a sacred religious shrine in August of 1971. At the celebration, Pueblo Governor John Reyna noted:

Our people have been in sorrow for many years and now we have such a day as this. . . . It came to be by the efforts not only of our own people but of others who were interested in preserving our way of life—those who even though they don't understand what our way of life is, know it is sacred. (Loh, 1971, August 16, A1, A10)

This event ended a long struggle by Taos Indians to regain title to a traditional site of their religious worship.

In contrast to the Zuni Pueblo who lost a fight for religious freedom when the government imprisoned its Bow Priests in the late nineteenth century (Chapter 6), Taos relatives regained some of their religious autonomy when the government restored Blue Lake to them. After Taos Indians refused the financial compensation awarded them by the Indian Claims Commission in 1965, the Pueblo sought and eventually reclaimed the land they had lost to the U.S. Forest Service in 1906.

The essence of legislative movements is persuasion. The movement to return Blue Lake provides a case study of the rhetoric of legislative movements and campaigns. This chapter (1) describes the historical heritage of Taos Indians, (2) explains how land and religion defined the ideology and delineated the legislative issues, (3) investigates the strategies used in the legislative campaign to return Blue Lake, (4) analyzes the advocacy used in hearings and political debates, and (5) offers implications about other legislative movements and religious rights.

HISTORICAL HERITAGE

Observers gain a glimpse of the causes of legislative movements by understanding the historical context that created political controversy. Some New Mexico tribes got their Spanish name "pueblo" from the multistory adobe homes where they have resided for centuries. Taos Pueblo, located in the northeastern corner of present-day New Mexico, is one of nineteen Pueblos. Florence Ellis (1974) explained that the Taos people came to their present location 500 years prior to the arrival of the Spanish colonizers in 1541. For Taos Indians, Blue Lake represented their place of emergence and the location of important religious rituals.

Part of Taos Pueblo's heritage was a history of resistance toward those who tried to colonize them. The historical roots of resistance started in 1598 when the Spanish government assigned priests to Taos whom the Indians disliked (Ellis 1974). After the Indians killed their priest in 1640, they fled to an Apache village in present-day Kansas. When they returned, they took an active role in the Pueblo Revolt against their Spanish colonizers in 1680. When the Spanish continued to dictate how the Indians should behave, they revolted again in 1696. But for the next 100 years, Taos peacefully submitted to Spanish rule. In 1796, however, Taos Indians protested encroachment onto their lands by Spanish settlers (Horr 1974, 10–26).

Taos land allotments evolved out of a complicated history. Prior to the Treaty of Guadalupe Hidalgo, royal ordinances decreed by the viceroy made land grants to the Indians and required their allegiance to the government of Spain (Sando [1976] 1982, 91). Subsequent to the Treaty of Guadalupe Hidalgo of 1848, the Pueblo Indians seemed to be satisfied with the land they had been granted because the treaty had ceded to the United States millions of acres of land including New Mexico west of the Rio Grande and north of the Gadsden Purchase. From this treaty, the United States acquired 334 million acres of land once held by Indians (Sando [1976] 1982, 13). The treaty also gave Taos title to 17,000 acres, a land area far short of the 300,000 acres the Land Claims Commission decided was Taos aboriginal land in 1965 (15 Ind. Cl. Comm. 666, 347–48). The treaty also allowed Spanish settlers to purchase, occupy, and graze their cattle on Indian land, but it made no specific references to religious uses of land.

At Taos Pueblo, land rights usually were tied to religious autonomy. During the time of Spanish control, priests insisted on Catholic baptism of Taos children. After the United States asserted its rule over Pueblos, federal officials demanded the Indians discontinue their religious dances. Rather than fight the government, the Indians synchronized their traditional religious ceremonies with those of Christianity, practicing both traditions at different times. The historical heritage of Taos Pueblo accentuates the land and religious issues that created the controversy over Blue Lake.

THE EVOLUTION OF LEGISLATIVE MOVEMENTS

The legislative movement to return Blue Lake evolved over a period of more than forty-five years. Divergent political ideologies concerning religion and land polarized the Indians against the government. Polarized religion and land issues then produced legislative efforts to protect government rights. When the progovernment legislation failed, the Indians mobilized their supporters to persuade Congress to adopt pro-Indian policies.

Ideological Differences

The divergent political ideology of Taos Indians and the government split the groups into factions. Herbert Simons and Elizabeth Mechling (1981) define a political movement as "an organization or grouping of organizations whose members operate together to promote or resist social change" (418). Just as in social movements, legislative movements arise when divergent ideologies foster opposition between political units. A first stage of a legislative movement is the identification of the ideology that propels a movement forward. An ideology consists of "a whole set of beliefs that serve to hold a group together," "to justify its activities and attitudes," and to "promote its interests" (Plamenatz 1970, 31).

Until the Indian Claims Commission decision in 1965, the ideological clash over Indian land and government jurisdiction seemed to be unresolvable. The Pueblo Indians believed that to maintain their culture, they had to have title to their aboriginal lands in order to practice their religion and to retain their minimal agricultural pursuits. In contrast, the government wanted Indian land for public recreation, wildlife preservation, and economic development of the grazing, timber, and mining industries. Since ideology points to the principles and objectives that guide political action (Toch 1965, 21), the divergent goals of Taos Pueblo and the federal government made conflict inevitable.

Ideological clashes also stemmed from the government's land confiscation policy. For example in 1906, President Theodore Roosevelt wanted to set aside land for public recreation. Using executive orders, Roosevelt acquired Indian land and then designated it as a national forest. Under this confiscation policy, the government took Blue Lake away from the Indians and gave it to the public. From the Indian perspective, Roosevelt's executive order converting some Pueblo land into Carson National Forest was egregious because the Indians were not consulted or paid for the land. In a response to federal officials, Taos Pueblo stated that in 1906, the government "knew the Blue Lake area was occupied and used by Taos Indians" and a Department of Agriculture spokesman guaranteed their use of the sacred lake for religious purposes (Report of the Committee of Interior and Insular Affairs 1968, 22).

From the government's perspective, Taos land was so pristine and beautiful that it needed to be protected by the forest service. Elliot S. Barker claimed that at the time the land was taken over by the government, the Indians had use of only about 2,000 acres and never complained about the forest service's use of other lands until 1966 (House Committee of Interior and Insular Affairs 1967, 23). Since no Indian written records exist from 1906, it is difficult to know what the Indians' understanding of government policy was at that time. According to Taos leaders, they were ignorant of the takeover until forest service officials constructed trails, encouraged mining, permitted grazing, and planted fish in their sacred ceremonial area (Sando [1976] 1982, 83).

Government agreements made with Taos Indians and with many other tribes were not recorded in official government records. For this reason, the Indian rhetorical strategy for regaining lost land often resembled what Hans Toch (1964) calls "rewriting history." Long after the government's acquisition of Indian land, Taos leaders reconstructed the process by which the government violated the oral promises they had made to Pueblo Indians in 1906. Adopting an ideologically based rhetoric in the 1960s, Taos leaders defined the actions of the park service as self-serving, explained Parker as irresponsible, implied the government used sinister economic and power motives, and demanded that federal officials rectify the problem.

Religion and Land Issues

In political disputes between the government and Indians, tribal religious needs often were at odds with the government's desire for land development. One important policy initiative that activated the pro-Indian rights movement occurred in the early 1920s when New Mexico Senator Holm O. Bursum introduced a bill to permit white and Spanish settlers to prove their title to Indian land. Additionally, the Bursum Bill placed the water rights and contested Taos Indian land as well as all crimes and offenses under United States court jurisdiction (Long 1949, 13–14; Philp [1977] 1981, 32).

The controversy over the Bursum Bill was the impetus for organizing the Blue Lake legislative movement. On one side, the Bursum Bill motivated establishment leaders, Interior Secretary Albert Bacon Fall and Indian Commissioner Charles Burke, and legislators to fight against the Indian claims to public lands. On the other side, John Collier, Indian sympathizer and the secretary of interior during Franklin D. Roosevelt's administration, created an organized opposition to the government's restrictions on Indian religious practices. When the Bursum Bill was introduced, it engaged factions on both sides in a political struggle over Taos land.

In the end the pro-Indian forces defeated the bill. The defeat occurred because John Collier, together with his friend Stella Atwood, chair of the Indian Welfare Committee, organized 2,000 members of the committee to lobby against the bill, wrote articles to liberal publications claiming the bill would ruin Pueblo Indian culture, brought together the Taos writers and art community to oppose the legislation, and raised money from intellectuals in Taos and Santa Fe to defeat the Bursum Bill. Their efforts also promoted the creation of the All Indian Pueblo Council and eventuated the resignation of Interior Secretary Albert Fall (Collier Papers, 1920–1930; Philp [1977] 1981, 36–40).

Progovernment Orders and Legislation

Public attention about the Bursum Bill prompted progovernment factions to introduce more legislation. For example in 1924, the government passed the Pueblo Lands Act in an attempt to reconcile some of the disputed land issues by acknowledging the joint land rights of the Indians, the federal government, and settlers. To deal with competing interests, the act created a land board to mediate boundary disputes, provide guidelines for how Indians and settlers could establish title to land, offer rules for compensating Indians for lost land and water, and prohibit Pueblo Indians from selling their land (1924, 43: 639–42). Although the legislation attempted to solve the land ownership problem, it failed to address the Indians' religious uses of land. One result was the Taos Indians asserted their opposition to the bill on religious grounds. For example, the All Indian Pueblo Council stated their opposition in this way:

We have studied the bill and found this bill will deprive us of our happy life by taking away our lands and water and will destroy our Pueblo government and our customs which we have enjoyed for hundreds of years, and through which we have been able to be self-supporting and happy down to this day. (Sergeant 1922, November 26, 6)

Other conflicts about religious issues soon surfaced. Instead of using the legislative venue, government leaders exercised their control over Indian religion by issuing policy directives. Between 1924 and 1926, Indian Commissioner Charles Burke, with the support of Secretary of Interior Hubert Work, tried to restrict Indian dances, an important part of Pueblo religious ceremonies. Work believed that Indian ceremonies should be in "harmony with the forms of Christian religion which civilization has approved, from which our rules of life are drafted and from which our government is founded." He worried that the Indians' sex instinct would, in his words, "contribute to his spiritual and physical downfall" (Work 1924, May 31, 92). After receiving complaints from missionaries about Indian ceremonial activities, Burke issued a directive limiting Pueblo dances to one per month except during planting and harvesting season and prohibiting Indians less than fifty years of age from participating in ceremonies with "immoral or degrading" influences. The real reason for the federal official's directive was that Work and Burke had heard that Taos Indians withdrew their sons from school during ceremonials (Collier 1924a, July, 50).

These new restrictions on religious freedom angered Indians and their supporters. Only after the intervention of Collier did the pro-Indian rights movement gain legislative momentum. In a legislative movement, congressional bills draw public attention to a conflict. The impact on government action often depends on the ability of proponents and opponents to gain publicity for or against a cause. In the case of Taos Pueblo, John Collier's resistance to government actions fostered negative public reactions to government-Indian policies and eventually led to legislative reform.

The government's attacks on Taos religious ceremonies motivated John Collier to mobilize public reaction against the policies. Collier's fervent opposition helped bring the religious struggle of Taos Indians against the federal government to public attention. Moreover, his extensive rhetorical opposition to Work's and Burke's directives regarding Pueblo dances won him political notoriety as a zealous Indian advocate. In fact, Collier wrote a defense of Indian religious freedom in a pamphlet entitled "The Indian and Religious Freedom" (Collier Papers, 1924, July 2). The pamphlet claimed that religious freedom was the central factor in the continuance of Indian culture. Rules by Indian bureaus, he said, attempt to make slaves of Indians and ruin their cultural traditions. Collier noted that Pueblo Indians hold as "their treasure of the soul" a religious center which outsiders fail to understand. To gain more support for his position, Collier presented his case in the religious media. In an article published in *Christian Century* (1925, March 13), he concluded that the government should repay a debt to Indians for their spiritual and physical suffering (346–49). More than forty years after Collier's appeal for Indian religious freedom, the Indians reasserted this theme as a justification for the return of Blue Lake.

Instead of just calling attention to the issue, Collier helped the All Pueblo Indian Council formulate a statement about Indian religious autonomy. In doing so, he inspired Taos leaders to organize themselves politically and to speak out on their own behalf. Examples of the Indian political voice appeared in position papers, public statements, and press releases of Pueblo leaders who opposed government policies.

Collier also tried to solve the problem of encroachment by federal agencies and settlers on Pueblo Land. For example in 1933, Collier, now secretary of the interior, sponsored the Pueblo Relief Bill. This legislation appropriated more than $700,000 for Pueblos as financial incentives for them to drop their lawsuits against white and Spanish settlers. Moreover, with Collier's help, the Taos Indians received a permit from the Department of Agriculture to use the area around Blue Lake for religious purposes (Gordon-McCutchan 1995, 30). The government continued to try to work with Taos Pueblo in 1940 by giving the tribe exclusive use of Blue Lake for three days during their August religious ceremonies, improving Indian grazing rights, and permitting tribal members to monitor the area to prevent forest fires (Gordon-McCutchan 1995, 33). However, none of this legislation solved the problem of Blue Lake because the federal government still had control of the land. In a way typical of other rhetorical movements, unresolved problems keep legislative movements alive.

The Blue Lake legislative movement began with definitions of ideological differences, progressed into factional disputes over land and religion, and led to directives and legislation that partially managed the conflict. The resulting mixture of directives and legislation imprinted the issues of Pueblo land rights and religious freedom on the minds of the public. Many years of political attempts to resolve the conflict between the government and Taos Indians over land and religion laid the groundwork for the activist legislative campaigns that followed. Additionally, the successes and failures of the advocates in the early phase of this legislative movement provided useful lessons for campaign strategists during the period 1968 through 1970.

LEGISLATIVE CAMPAIGN STRATEGIES

The Pueblo's hope for the return of Blue Lake dimmed after 1933, but rekindled in 1951 when the tribe filed a petition with the Indians Claims Commission. The tribe won their case in 1965, receiving a financial award of more than $290,000 for Blue Lake and for other nearby aboriginal land (15 Ind. Cl. Comm. 666, 386). Although the Pueblo refused the monetary settlement, the decision renewed their hope that they would eventually secure the return of Blue Lake. This hope changed their stalled movement into an aggressive legislative campaign. This section of the chapter explains how the movement became a legislative campaign, identifies campaign strategies, and analyzes publicity tactics.

Movement Becomes a Campaign

Several rhetorical changes occurred when the Collier-led movement turned into a Taos-led campaign. The political movement's rhetorical efforts responded to grievances. In the ensuing campaign, however, a grass roots process orchestrated by two capable leaders took place (Stewart, Smith, & Denton, 1994, 4). One important leader was Paul J. Bernal, a Taos Indian, who had served in World War II, returned to the Pueblo in

1946, and dedicated his life to the return of Blue Lake. Bernal organized and unified the Pueblo position and created its messages. A second leader was Corrine Locker, a former secretary to Oliver LaFarge, an advocate in the Taos land claims case. Locker organized the coalitions, conducted the publicity, identified the attorneys, and wrote the letters to mobilize campaign support.

The campaign differed from the movement that preceded it because the leaders acted as managers rather than autocratic federal politicians; they assigned roles to others, and they designed and disseminated messages (Stewart, Smith, & Denton 1994, 4). Corrine Locker and Paul Bernal orchestrated the legislative campaign from its inception in 1965 until Blue Lake was returned in 1970. Bernal developed the Indian strategy and assisted with the Pueblo leaders' written and oral presentations. Locker coordinated supporters' messages so they fit with those of Bernal and Pueblo leaders.

The campaign had a preestablished end, but the movement existed for years (Stewart, Smith, & Denton 1994, 4). The predetermined end was a legislative vote to secure the return of Blue Lake. Campaign leaders promoted bills, initiated congressional hearings, and conducted the behind-the-scenes work. Together these efforts resulted in the passage of legislation to return Blue Lake to the Indians. After the bill was passed, President Richard Nixon signed it. Securing passage of this legislation may have surprised the Indians because very few of the bills introduced in Congress actually win approval. Moreover, this legislation returned land rather than paid the Indians a settlement, an action prohibited by the Indian Claims Commission Act (1946).

In contrast to the movement, this legislative campaign began at the grass roots and evolved into a successful pro-Indian effort. Bernal and Locker understood the process of political persuasion and developed an effective approach to advocacy. This campaign included sophisticated members of the political establishment acting together with inexperienced Blue Lake supporters. In the Blue Lake campaign, Taos leaders gained support from the chairs of congressional committees, prominent representatives and senators, local political leaders, media representatives, and influential activist organizations. Just as in other successful legislative campaigns, the pro-Taos faction's public relations effort reached out to target audiences who had a "monetary, ideological, or organizational stake" (Denton & Woodward 1985, 287).

Legislative Campaign Strategies

The campaign to return Blue Lake used a religious theme, developed coalitions of supporters, and effectively assigned tasks. These rhetorical strategies moved the legislation through the congressional process.

Religious Theme. The first strategy was to emphasize the theme of religious freedom to gain legislators' attention to the conflict under the guise of legal and patriotic values. Definitions have power because they establish fixed interpretations and perspectives for viewing a situation. Moreover, themes are persuasive to the extent that they evoke emotional feelings that fit with the values of the audience and anchor the goals of the campaign to strongly held public values (Graber 1981, 204).

Taos supporters bolstered the theme of Indian religious freedom using narratives that affirmed the theme, enunciated the context, and added recognizable characters. As a rhetorical strategy, narrative detail transforms themes into experiences understood by audiences. Narratives link people together creating an identification between the narrator and listeners and thereby establish an audience community (Carr 1986, 89). One forum for elaborating the religious freedom theme appeared in the publication, "The Blue Lake Area: An Appeal from Taos Pueblo" (Taos Pueblo Indian Council 1968). The pamphlet emphasized religious freedom by presenting narratives of tribal leaders testifying to the centrality of spiritual matters in Pueblo culture. One potent narrative came from tribal leader Severino Martinez. He explained:

Blue Lake is the most important of all our shrines because it is part of our life, it is our Indian church. We go there for good reason, like any other people would go to their denomination. Different people would go visit and give their humble words to God in any language that they speak. It is the same principle at Blue Lake. We go there and talk to our Great Spirit in our own language, and talk to nature about what is going to grow and ask God Almighty [to help us just] like anyone else would do. (2)

Severino emphasized to the non-Indian audience that religious expressions were as important to Taos Indians as they were to other citizens. The campaign leaders sent the booklet to 100 editors of major newspapers throughout the country with a cover letter by William Byler, president of the Association on American Indian Affairs. Byler's letter characterized the previous actions and rhetoric of the federal government in relation to Blue Lake as attempts at "turning shrines into campsites" (Gordon-McCutchan 1995, 91). This adverse publicity against the government appeared in dozens of newspaper articles that endorsed the return of Blue Lake (Bernal Papers, Box 7, File 112). The theme promoted in the publicity also played a central role in the 1968 and 1970 congressional hearings and the 1970 senate debates.

Coalition Creation. Another strategy in this legislative campaign was the creation of coalitions, that is, alliances of two or more parties formed to achieve a common goal. People join coalitions to get certain measures enacted (Folger, Poole, & Stutman 1993, 220). Coalitions not only influenced the return of Blue Lake, but members of the coalitions also became active lobbyists and surrogate speakers who advocated Pueblo Indian rights. In this way, the coalitions became an essential human resource for the campaign.

Several coalitions worked for the return of Blue Lake. In 1967 Consuelo LaFarge organized the National Committee for Restoration of the Blue Lake Lands and Taos Indians. Prestigious members of the committee included the Santa Fe Catholic Archbishop Peter Davis, American Jewish Congress leader Howard Squadron, and National Council of Churches leaders Dean M. Kelley and Russell Carter. Other sources offered ideological and financial support including Philadelphia merchant John Wanamaker, cartoonist Bill Mauldin, conservationist and photographer Elliot Porter, and the retired president of Sandia Corporation S. P. Schwater (Bernal Papers, Box 6, File 111). The campaign issued many press releases and position papers using the byline of the National Committee to Restore Blue Lake. Members of the committee also addressed their own personal constituencies on behalf of Blue Lake. An example of this kind of support came from Dean M. Kelley of the National Council of Churches. He wrote:

That land, morally and in justice, belongs to the Indians and is not rightfully available to the government to dispose of without the consent of its proper owners. It is typical of the white man's relationship with the Indians, however, that the government seems willing to let the Indians keep what the white man does not want, but will make trades and deals to his own advantage with the Indians' property as though it were his own. (Kelley 1967, 164)

The National Congress of American Indians and the Indian Rights Association together with their members also expressed support for the Indian cause through letters, petitions, and proclamations. Among the many letters of support is one from Robert Lewis of Zuni Pueblo. He emphasized the significance of the Pueblo religious sites of worship:

Religiously, the Pueblo tribes have always respected, and still do, those things that tie in with the carrying out of individual tribal rituals. Shrines are located in various areas where medicine fraternal groups make pilgrimages to at various times. Going through another tribe's territory to get to those sacred areas, religious groups making these pilgrimages were never molested. Why? Because in carrying out these observances, a tribe is doing so not only for their own wants but also for the well-being and requests for plants and [for the] good health of the others. (Bernal Papers, Box 5, File 89)

Lewis stressed that the religious rites benefit not just the Taos Indians but other people as well. His letter, along with those of many others from Indian leaders, became evidence in the legislative hearings and debates.

Whenever coalitions are created in support of policies, those who oppose this legislation come forward with their own resolutions and petitions. One resolution that objected to the return of Blue Lake came from the Taos County Board of Commissioners. The Taos officials voiced strong objections to "any proposed legislation which would grant ownership administration and exclusive use and benefit [of Blue Lake] to Taos Pueblo." The New Mexico Wildlife and Conservation Association put forward another anti-Blue Lake resolution, stating that this organization "firmly believes that it is to the best interest of all concerned for the United States Forest Service to retain exclusive administrative jurisdiction over the area proposed to be transferred to the Indians for the protection of the watershed and other resources" (Bernal Papers, Box 5, File 83). The coalitions supporting the return of Blue Lake had more persuasive power than the opposition because pro-Indian support came from a broad spectrum of American life rather than just from government agencies who had a stake in retaining control over Blue Lake.

Leadership Task Designation. Skillful designation of leadership tasks created a third strategy. While the attorneys for Taos Pueblo publicly managed the congressional persuasive efforts, Locker and Bernal built coalitions and designed messages at the grass roots level. The leaders managed different persuasive tasks. Paul Bernal organized the Taos Pueblo Council and helped prepare speeches, press releases, and historical background, creating hundreds of texts supporting the return of Blue Lake (Bernal Papers). Attorneys Rufus Poole and William Schaab refined the arguments for presentation to Congress. They also suggested legislative amendments, supplied information, served as witnesses for the legislative hearing, and mobilized political support from congressional leaders. Corinne Locker conducted the state and national publicity campaign by writing letters, issuing press releases, soliciting funds, and providing fact sheets for the use of advocates speaking in favor of the return of Blue Lake (Gordon-McCutchan 1995, 127). The combined effort of Taos advocates demonstrated how a model legislative campaign should work.

Publicity Tactics

The campaign's public relations strategy sought to influence target audiences. To influence Congress to return Blue Lake, leaders had to develop a complex set of messages including press releases, personal letters to influential decision makers, fact sheets, television documentaries, and fundraising appeals. Since the archival information about the legislative campaign provides hundreds of examples of these public relations messages, this chapter features a few examples to illustrate the quality of the publicity used in this campaign. The short-term goal of this publicity was to influence multiple target audiences of supporters. To accomplish this goal, campaign managers spoke and wrote to decision makers in order to win congressional support for the return of Blue Lake. The long-term goal was to accumulate responses from sympathetic audiences and then use those responses to support the official records of the hearings and the senate debates.

According to William Schaab, the publicity effort was extensive. In a letter to Jack E. Brown, Schaab wrote:

After reluctantly accepting the employment, a good working relationship naturally developed between me, Paul Bernal, the interpreter for the Council, and Mrs. Corinne Locker in Santa Fe, who was the coordinator of the National Committee for the Restoration of Blue Lake Lands. She served the important function of helping the Council through Paul Bernal to understand the legal concepts and political realities of the situation, and helped me grasp the traditions, religious needs, internal politics, and ultimate desires of the Pueblo Council. She also handled a huge volume of correspondence with Indian tribes, newspapers, journalists, television networks, and individuals and organizations supporting the Pueblo's fight. (Bernal Papers, Box 4, File 81)

Schaab recognized that Locker and Bernal possessed the skills needed to be strategists for the Blue Lake legislative campaign.

Press Releases. In a way typical of effective publicity campaigns, Locker designed press releases to secure media exposure for activities that supported the return of Blue Lake. The goal of a press release is to acquire identification with the audience, generate news that is timely and important, provide credible information, and get the story used. Press releases should answer the journalistic questions: who? what? when? where? why? (Schuetz & Shiver 2000). Locker sent a large number of press releases sponsored by the National Committee to Restore Blue Lake and the Taos Pueblo Council. The press releases charted the progress of the legislative campaign and monitored roadblocks that might impede the passage of the Blue Lake bill (Bernal Papers, Box 7, File 71).

Locker not only provided timely information, but she also linked that information to the values of the target audiences. For example, one of Locker's press releases announced a voter registration drive at Taos Pueblo. She quoted Paul J. Bernal who boasted about the large numbers of Indians who had registered. Locker then noted the voter registration drive brought tribal members into the "political arena" so they could make a difference. She further explained that in Taos County in the 1968 elections, most of the offices for major national, state, and county offices were decided by less than 200 votes. Locker's press release indicated the Indians wanted a political voice and implied they would use their vote to express grievances against the government (Bernal Papers, Box 4, File 71).

Constituent Letters. In addition to press releases, letters are an essential part of the legislative publicity. Janice Schuetz (1986) explains that U.S.

senators receive an average of 1,000 letters per week. The goal of most of this mail is to seek action on bills by recommending how Congress should vote based on the preferences of constituents. The typical structure of these letters defines a constituent problem and then supports a particular legislative remedy (229).

Paul Bernal, acting on behalf of the Taos Pueblo Council, sent many letters to Clinton P. Anderson, the senior senator from New Mexico. At the time the letters were sent, Anderson had made clear his position: he did not support, under any circumstances, the return of Blue Lake to the Indians. As a New Mexico senator, his failure to support legislation made him an enemy of the state's Blue Lake campaign leaders. In response to an article written by Anderson and published in the *Albuquerque Journal* in May 1969, Bernal challenged the truthfulness of Anderson's remarks in this way:

The article . . . stated that last year you "reached an agreement with the Taos tribal leadership only to have it fall apart because of outside pressures." In this statement is contained an erroneous interpretation to the American public of what had happened at our final meeting. (Bernal Papers, Box 4, File 71)

Moreover, Bernal claimed that the Taos delegation never accepted a compromise agreement and that the senator had withdrawn his offer. He then emphasized the effects of the misinformation on Taos Indians:

We resent the implication that the Taos Pueblo Council and its people are not able to make their own decision on this Blue Lake fight. We are reminding you that for the last 64 years the Indians have been persistent and they have never changed their position, so therefore this allegation is not true. (Bernal Papers, Box 4, File 71)

The letter also referred to other false and misleading statements made by Anderson regarding Blue Lake (Bernal Papers, Box 4, File 71). Apparently, Anderson did not respond to Bernal except through his public attacks in senate hearings on the Blue Lake bill. Bernal also actively monitored other media reports and refuted those who opposed the pro-Indian position.

Fact Sheets. The informational fact sheet, a condensed summary of essential information presented in a simple and readable form, is a third source of publicity. The purpose of the sheets is to inform other advocates, the media, and the adversaries about the facts from the point of view of campaign strategists (Schuetz & Shiver 2000). One common type of fact sheet, called a white paper, relates the historical development of important issues. Repetition of a proscribed set of facts unifies the content and attracts the audience's attention to important campaign information.

One white paper fact sheet from the Taos Pueblo Council presented Blue Lake's legislative history in a condensed chronological order. The fact sheet reported that Taos rejected the financial settlement of the Indian Claims Commission in 1965, the Senate Subcommittee on Indian Affairs took no action in 1966, and after the House passed H.R. 471 in 1968, Senator Anderson introduced entirely new legislation killing the bill in the Senate. In this fact sheet, the Taos Pueblo Council refuted Senator Anderson's proposal to continue federal trusteeship at Blue Lake. Bernal wrote, "Senator Anderson's proposal would dismember and destroy the essence of this relationship [between the Indians and the federal government] and the meaning of our lives. This prospect is torture for our people" (Bernal Papers, Box 4, File 71). In contrast to a typical fact sheet, this white paper publicly refuted Anderson, questioned his credibility, and promoted the Indian cause.

Television. Although television publicity for legislative initiatives was not as common as it is today, the Blue Lake campaign used the media to promote its goals. Because of its mass audience, television can inform and persuade large audiences about public policies. The documentary entitled "The Sacred Lake of Taos," produced by Wiley Hance in cooperation with the National Council of Churches, aired on ABC television. The documentary presented the history of the controversy, beginning with the Treaty of Guadalupe Hidalgo. After focusing "on the major issues of the conflict," the documentary showed viewers "a portrait of a people who cling to ancient Indian rites and customs" and acknowledged opposition to the return of Blue Lake through an interview with Ernest Taylor of the U.S. Forest Service. The general theme of the documentary, however, was the government should return Blue Lake to the Taos Pueblo in order to ensure Indian religious freedom. More specifically, the documentary featured an interview with Paul Bernal on the issue of Indian religious freedom and used Taos Indian guide Frank Marcus to work out production details ("Telecast Details Taos Blue Lake Fight" 1966, Clipping File, New Mexico State Library).

Network television coverage of this political issue likely reached a large public audience as well as New Mexico voters. Since cable television was not available in 1969, national networks, such as ABC, provided most of the political news coverage. However, the documentary was not the only news exposure; extensive coverage by local radio and newspaper outlets focused on the efforts of New Mexico grassroots leaders to restore Blue Lake.

Fund Raising. Press releases, letters, fact sheets, and media coverage required substantive financial resources. Consequently, money was a constant problem for the legislative campaign. For this reason, many of the mailings contained informational boxes requesting money. One example of the fund raising in legislative campaign mailings was the example listed here.

The Taos Pueblo Blue Lake Defense Fund

So long as the Federal Government continues in unjust possession of the Blue Lake Area, the sanctity of this wilderness area is threatened by those who are eager to plunder its natural beauty for commercial profit. In order to combat this threat, the Taos Pueblo Blue Lake Defense Fund has been established. Contributions would be thankfully accepted, or may be mailed direct to the fund at P.O. Box 258, Taos, New Mexico 87571. (Bernal Papers, Box 6, File 111)

This plea for money contained potent language that implicated the government as a source of threat to Indian religious freedom.

Another fund-raising plea appeared at the end of a fact sheet about the impending legislation prepared by Paul Bernal in 1970. The fund-raising plea appeared in this way:

Your Help Is Needed!

The costs of carrying the Blue Lake campaign to this hopeful stage have exhausted all funds. Without help the initiatives gained may be lost. Funds are needed to meet critical expenses for travel, legal services, and communications. Won't you please send a contribution for 1970 to the:

Taos Pueblo Blue Lake Defense Fund
P. O. Box 258
Taos, New Mexico 87571

Bernal begged for money, claiming that all of the progress so far attained would be lost unless the campaign obtained enough money to fund a final congressional effort.

Continuous fund raising was essential because the campaign had no money except that given by supporters. Gordon-McCutchan (1995) reported that $2,700 had been raised by the committee, but the tribe still needed to use money from its fire-fighting fund to support the campaign. Locker projected the senate lobbying campaign would cost $13,000. Added to this financial squeeze was the fact that the Pueblo owed their attorneys $7,000 (138–39). The names of all of the benefactors who supported the campaign are not recorded, but receipts in Bernal's Papers show that hundreds of people contributed.

Legislative campaigns succeed to the extent that they can implement their strategy using press releases, letters, fact sheets, media stories, and fund-raising requests. The efforts in each of these areas succeeded. Locker's public relations skill made the campaign work, and Bernal's passion and knowledge infused the issues with the spirit of the Taos Indians. Gordon-McCutchan (1995) credits Locker with the effectiveness of the entire publicity campaign. He notes she had a "genius for publicity," was a brilliant writer of quotable prose that was highly informative, aesthetically pleasing, . . . and provided an emotional appeal that inspired readers to action" (126). Paul Bernal's publicity on behalf of the tribe was inspired by his knowledge of tribal values and traditions and motivated by his personal desire to return Blue Lake to the Pueblo. Together the campaign leaders demonstrated the qualities needed to achieve legislative goals.

HEARINGS AND DEBATE

To be effective, campaign strategies must produce legislative results. In this case, the groundwork done prior to the final vote paved the way for the return of Blue Lake. Records of the groundwork done by Bernal and Locker surfaced in letters of support, petitions, and resolutions. The official records of the hearings and the congressional debates contained many of the messages received from supporters of the Blue Lake bill.

The legislative journey resulting in the return of Blue Lake began with conflict and ended in celebration. The journey began in 1965 at the time Senator Clinton Anderson presented legislation to establish a trust relationship over Blue Lake land. After a contentious debate, Anderson's bill died in the Senate Committee on Interior and Insular Affairs. In 1969 Representative James A. Haley's new bill, H.R. 471, passed in the House of Representatives without opposition. Under the sponsorship of Senator Fred Harris of Oklahoma, H.R. 3306, a version of H.R. 471, went to the Senate Committee on Interior and Insular Affairs. After presenting oppositional bills, S. 1624 and 1625, the Senate finally approved a version of the House's Blue Lake bill in 1970.

Two senate proceedings in 1968 and 1970 show how the advocacy used in the hearings and the senate debates eventuated the return of Blue Lake.

1968 Senate Hearing

The development of information, arguments, and evidence in the early stages of a legislative campaign typically surfaces in the rhetoric of congressional committee hearings. Legislative committees select witnesses to testify for and against proposed legislation. Most hearings consist of ten to twenty witnesses. In the 1968 Blue Lake hearings, testimony came from three sources: claimants, administrators, and experts. Taos Indians, Pueblo lawyer William Schaab, and advocates from the National Council of Churches served as the claimants. Congressional advocates joined with spokespersons from the Departments of Interior and Agriculture, the U.S. Forest Service, and New Mexico Department of Game and Fish to represent government administrators. Anthropologists along with historians and church leaders presented expert testimony.

At issue were two separate bills. The House bill returned Blue Lake and the Senate bill required federal trusteeship over Indian land. Obviously, Taos Indians supported H.R. 3306 (subsequently referred to as the Blue Lake bill), legislation that returned Blue Lake and 48,000 acres of nearby forest land to the Pueblo. The Pueblo opposed Senator Anderson's oppositional bill, Senate bills 1624, 1625 (subsequently referred to as the trust bill), that extended government trust privileges for 3,000 additional acres of Pueblo land. Some senators and most government agencies opposed the Senate bill and supported the House bill. The Pueblo supported the House bill because the legislation preserved religious privacy, promoted natural ecology, advocated the progress of the Indian community, and promised Indian religious freedom. Additionally, the bill resolved the conflict between the Pueblo and the Forest service by eliminating land use permits, restoring aboriginal land to the Pueblo, and ensuring conservation management.

Two distinct types of advocacy emerged in the 1968 hearing—proprietary and oppositional. Proprietary advocacy occurs when legislators assume ownership of a bill and do everything possible to pass it. One way to own a bill is to defend its content against the opposition. Another way is to express the righteousness of the assumptions on which the proposal is based and attack the evidence offered by opponents. Because proprietary advocates often refuse to admit weaknesses in their proposals and resist compromise, they often kill bills in committee hearings.

Proprietary Advocacy. The senate hearings featured heated exchanges between Senator Clinton Anderson and Secretary of Interior Stewart Udall. Anderson defended the trust bill, saying that government trusteeship provided the greatest good for the greatest number of his constituents. Udall's testimony defended the Blue Lake bill, emphasizing the need for Indian religious freedom. Repeating the theme established by the Blue Lake campaign literature, Udall argued:

The Taos Pueblo Indians' freedom to practice their religion depends on their being able to conduct their sacred ceremonies and religious contemplations in private. The entire watershed of the Rio Pueblo is also part of the symbolism of Blue Lake because it is the area in which the Pueblo's religious life is practiced. It plays an important role in the physical, social and political structure of the Pueblo. (Hearings Before the Subcommittee on Indian Affairs of the Committee on Interior and Insular Affairs of the United States Senate 1968, 51; subsequent references to this document appear only as Hearings, 1968)

Immediately after he had spoken, Anderson objected to Udall's support of the Blue Lake bill; in doing so, he established his proprietary rights to the trust bill, claiming the government needed to control the access to the contested land. Anderson's refutation of the Blue Lake bill began with his interrogation of Udall. First, Anderson asked Udall to admit the House had erred in its passage of past legislation regarding Taos. Udall replied that all bills "recognize a wrong was done [to Taos Pueblo] and that corrective action needs to be done." To bolster his main conclusion, Anderson responded that returning Blue Lake would result in the return of other government land to Indians. Then Anderson asked Udall to agree that this bill also would give other tribes the privilege of getting back their aboriginal land. Udall answered "No," saying that the Taos circumstances are unique. Through another series of questions, Anderson reinforced his opposition to the return of Blue Lake. He argued vehemently that passing the Blue Lake bill would lead to similar frivolous claims by other Indians, adding that Taos should have accepted the financial settlement offered to them by the Indian Claims Commission.

In addition to refuting Udall's arguments favoring the return of Blue Lake, Anderson promoted his bill, claiming that federal trusteeship of Taos land protected the interests of the public and Indian constituents. The core of Anderson's justification was that his bill served the public interest by weighing "the good of the Indians against the good of the general public." Anderson further supported his position using an odd mixture of refutation and advocacy, claiming that weighing the public good demands the government considers the rights of the Forest Service and not just caters to the exaggerated religious needs of Indians. Anderson concluded his testimony by inserting into the record more than twenty bills that he had sponsored to help Indian tribes during his thirty years in Congress. Inserting this litany about pro-Indian legislation was an attempt to buttress Anderson's wounded credibility. He wanted to show his large Indian constituency that he had righteous motives toward Indian policy in general even though he opposed the return of Blue Lake.

Oppositional Advocacy. In addition to the proprietary role adopted by Anderson, he and his longtime friend Senator Mike Metcalf of Montana engaged in oppositional advocacy that accentuated the weaknesses of evidence supporting the Blue Lake bill and impugned the motives of pro-Indian advocates. Instead of adopting the perspective of fact finders and evidence gatherers, the traditional roles for senators conducting a hearing (Schuetz, 1986), Anderson and Metcalf became inquisitors, cross-examined witnesses as adversaries, and interrupted witnesses in order to frustrate them and confuse the meaning of the testimony. For example, veteran and sometimes venerated Senators Anderson and Metcalf challenged the knowledge of Pueblo attorney Schaab. The senators used their inquisitorial role to reinforce their political power at the same time they ridiculed witnesses who opposed their position.

Part of Anderson's and Metcalf's strategy was to interrupt witnesses in order to confuse their testimony. An example of this strategy surfaced when they questioned Schaab. The Taos attorney began his testimony by saying:

[Just] as Christianity has its symbols, the cross, the altar, the chalice, the wafer, so also do the Taos Pueblo Indians have their symbols, their holy sacred symbols. The most sacred are the river, the Rio Pueblo de Taos, and the source of the river, the Blue Lake. . . . The religion as practiced in the Pueblo is conducted by religious societies called kivas. (Hearings 1968, 98–99)

Immediately, Metcalf interrupted: "Why don't you tell us more about the kivas?" Schaab continued by explaining the location of kivas and then used a map to describe the area the Pueblos needed for their sacred ceremonies. Metcalf again interrupted Schaab, asking him to show the map to Senator Anderson. When Schaab showed Anderson the map, Anderson arrogantly responded that he knew the map very well and flippantly told Schaab not to expect the map would be included in the record of the hearing. Presumably the purpose of this interruption was twofold: to suggest that Schaab lacked knowledge of the religious issues and to demonstrate that the senators controlled the information presented at the hearing.

Shortly after this exchange, Anderson interrupted Schaab again by asking if the attorney knew about the Bursum Bill. When Schaab said "Yes," Anderson went on a tirade explaining the good intentions of Bursum and expressing his admiration for him, noting that the Taos Indians had wrongfully maligned Bursum. This irrelevant line of questioning attempted to discredit both Schaab and his Taos Indian clients.

The typical goal of hearings is to discover policy options after gathering sufficient evidence from witnesses to define legislative issues. When Anderson and Metcalf conducted the 1968 hearings using proprietary and oppositional advocacy, they impeded the information-gathering process. Both the hostility of the two senators and the large quantity of the testimony opposing the Blue Lake bill ensured that the legislation would never make it out of the committee.

1970 Hearings

With little opposition in 1969, the House of Representatives passed another Blue Lake bill. After passage, this bill was sent to the Senate Subcommittee on Indian Affairs and the Committee on Interior and Insular Affairs. Although the membership on the committees was nearly the same as in 1968, the witnesses and the senators offering support had changed. Administrators, Senator Fred Harris of Oklahoma and Secretary of the Interior Walter Hickel, supported the Blue Lake bill. New claimant witnesses also appeared, including LaDonna Harris, Chairman of the Americans for Indian Opportunity Action Council; Sue Lallmang, Indian Advisor to the Republican National Committee; Taos Cacique Juan de Jesus Romero, and Thomas V. O'Leary from the Indian Rights Association. Myra Ellen Jenkins, New Mexico historian, also provided expert testimony.

In ways similar to the 1968 hearings, the climate of this hearing was defensive, particularly when Senators Anderson and Metcalf interrogated witnesses. However, the climate turned supportive when Senators Harris, Quentin Burdick of North Dakota, Ted Kennedy of Massachusetts and Barry Goldwater of Arizona spoke in favor of the return of Blue Lake. These senators also defended some of the witnesses after they had undergone grueling cross-examination from Metcalf and Anderson. The bipartisan sponsorship of the Blue Lake bill favorably impressed President Richard Nixon.

Although the senate committee reformulated much of the testimony from the 1968 hearing, new testimony especially from Senator Clifford Hansen and Taos Cacique Romero provided additional religious justifications for the return of Blue Lake. These witnesses offered two types of advocacy missing in the 1968 hearing—pragmatic and prophetic. Pragmatic advocacy provides legitimacy through the support of issues bound to the political ideology and legislative principles of the party in power. Pragmatic advocacy calls attention to party loyalties that justify passage of legislation. In contrast, prophetic advocates epitomize the values and beliefs of the affected culture. Prophetic advocates are revered persons who have achieved their credibility by keeping the secrets and embodying the visions of culture. These advocates believe they have a duty to represent the most deeply held values of those in their culture; they perform this duty using language and imagery that reinforce cultural values.

Pragmatic Advocacy. An example of pragmatic advocacy surfaced in the testimony of Senator Hansen. He explained:

On assuming office, President Nixon recognized the need to revise and reform the country's policies toward the American Indians. Yesterday, the President announced a broad program designed to improve the quality of life for these natives of America, and I congratulate the President on his message. That message is of particular interest to us here today, because it contains the President's endorsement of the legislation now being considered by this subcommittee. The President believes that enactment of this legislation will provide justice to the Taos Pueblo Indians and will serve as a much needed symbol of this Government's responsiveness to the just grievances of the American Indians. (Hearings 1970, 16)

Hansen's message justified passage of the bill because the legislation had the support of the president and reflected the ideology of the Republican Party. Pragmatic leadership stems from partisan political argumentation that justifies decisions based on appeasing party loyalties (Edelman [1964] 1980, 17). Even though this type of advocacy sounds sinister, pragmatic advocates frequently depend on partisanship to achieve legislative goals.

Prophetic Advocacy. An old and revered holy man, Taos Cacique Juan Jesus de Romero, assumed the role of the prophetic advocate. At the 1970 hearing, Paul Bernal introduced Romero as "our religious and spiritual leader." Bernal then translated Romero's remarks in this way:

I came here because I recognize the dispute and the struggle, and the torture that I have experienced with my people done by the U.S. Government. I came here to tell you in a friendly way. I came here to tell you that we are supposed to be in a good relationship. We are supposed to act like brothers. We are supposed to act like one, not like an enemy.

He was interrupted by Metcalf who seemed to be mystified by the prophetic charisma of Romero. Metcalf interjected: "I want to tell your distinguished friend and you that this is a committee of justice, too, and we are going to listen with care and consideration, and with deliberation, to the presentation you make. The committee is dedicated to the interests of the American Indian." Romero then concluded:

My people are living poor, and that is the way of our nature. But we believe in worship. We believe in prayers. We believe in God's commandments. We are under His Commandments that we are going to intend to live in this country. I am the leader of the tribe of Taos Pueblo, and I am the spiritual leader. . . . I came here before you . . . to carry on the principles set forth by the American Government in this country, love and care, sympathetic, equal dividing of the bread that you have, an equal share of what you have. (Hearings 1970, 107)

These remarks illustrated the essence of prophetic advocacy. They revealed Romero's spiritual leadership, emphasized the religious values of his culture, and expressed the tribe's vision for cooperation and brotherhood.

Both pragmatic and prophetic advocates added persuasive potency to the testimony presented at the legislative hearing. Since neither type of advocacy appeared in the 1968 hearing, pragmatic and prophetic advocacy seemed to be instrumental in the Senate's passage of the Blue Lake bill. Proprietary and oppositional advocates often kill legislation, but pragmatic and prophetic advocates give life to bills and motivate legislators to support them.

Legislative Debate

During the debate over a bill, legislators typically emphasize controversial issues, restate testimony, and introduce evidence from previous hearings. The chairman and hearing committee members often introduce the legislation for debate. Senate debates occur under rules of etiquette and decorum. By selecting evidence gathered from previous stages of the legislative campaign, the debates accentuate the most persuasive information.

After Senate Majority Leader Harry Byrd read the bill, Senator Fred Harris from Oklahoma presented the opening argument supporting the Blue Lake bill and opposing the trust bill (all quotations in this section come from the *Congressional Record*, Senate, 1970, December 1, 19157–58). Most of the political speakers, including Harris, used the motivated sequence structure: attention, need, satisfaction, visualization, and action (Ehninger, Gronbeck, McKerrow, & Monroe 1986).

In the motivated sequence, an advocate gains attention by creating audience interest and fostering a desire to listen to the speaker. In addition to gaining attention, senators address one another according to the decorum of the Senate. For example, Harris began with ingratiating remarks directed to those who opposed the bills saying, "Senators who are on opposing sides of this matter are all honorable men who happen to differ on this issue." He followed by emphasizing the importance of the bill, "Support for the Taos Indians in their struggle to reclaim Blue Lake and the surrounding land has spread far beyond the Taos Pueblo. Millions await our decision." Although his introduction did not use novelty or suspense, he called attention to the need for urgent action and the public's interest in this action; both were appropriate appeals since the legislation had been pending for two years and public support had grown.

The need stage of the motivated sequence usually gives examples of the problem, provides evidence about the need for a new policy, and points to the seriousness of the issues. After introducing the bill, Harris accentuated the need, using a series of claims supported by evidence from Taos Pueblo representatives and the government agencies drawn from the 1968 and 1970 hearings. Harris' argument developed several claims supporting the return of Blue Lake:

1. Justice for the Taos Indians will mean that Congress really . . . recognizes the unique worth of American Indian culture and American Indian heritage (supported with historical evidence from Florence Ellis).

2. Many people deplore the past and support the Taos Indians in their struggle to secure their claim to these sacred lands (supported by evidence from National Council of Churches and Indian groups).

3. Blue Lake and surrounding lands were wrongfully taken from the Taos Indians in 1906 (supported by government documents).

4. Conflicts have occurred over the years with the Forest Service, with tourists, and with others (supported by statements of Pueblo leaders and the forest service).

5. The American Indian has been wronged by the use and misuse of his land, water, and natural resources (example of Cuyahoga Indians in Ohio).

Speakers typically satisfy the need by explaining a proposed action that rectifies a problem. Harris stressed how the return of Blue Lake would be a symbolic act to resolve evils done by the government in the early part of the century. He argued that the Blue Lake bill was superior to the federal trust bill because receiving title to the land is preferable to dependence on the government. Then Harris bolstered his solution with statements from the Taos delegation and from President Nixon.

Visualization means the speaker constructs word pictures to show the consequences for adopting or failing to adopt the speaker's proposal. Harris visualized the negative consequences that would result if senators failed to return Blue Lake. He predicted "that the long struggle will continue and the representatives of Taos Pueblo will be back here next session and succeeding sessions until at last the provisions of H.R. 471 [the Blue Lake bill] have been enacted into law."

The final phase of the motivated sequence features a plea for action. Harris explained the opposition's argument—that the return of Blue Lake created a bad precedent—was incorrect. Using the rhetorical strategy of turning the tables, he concluded: "If the Senate wishes to dwell on precedents, then it should be reminded of the precedents for destroying the culture, heritage, and religion and pride of the American Indian—a precedent for this is plentiful."

Subsequent testimony from Senators George McGovern of South Dakota, Robert Griffin of Michigan, Ted Kennedy of Massachusetts, and Barry Goldwater of Arizona repeated claims and evidence from Harris' opening argument. Despite subsequent refutation from Senators Metcalf, Anderson, Henry Jackson of Washington, and George Allott of Colorado, the Blue Lake bill passed with a significant majority. President Nixon signed the bill into law on July 8, 1970, noting that this "is an important symbol of the government's responsiveness to the just grievances of the American Indians (Reprinted in the *Quarterly of the Southwestern Association on Indian Affairs* and available in the Bernal Papers, Box 7, File 113). When the bill was signed, the political campaign achieved its intended goal.

A final footnote to the legislative action occurred in 1996 when Congress passed the Bottleneck Bill, a law that returned 764.5 more acres of land to Taos Pueblo. The government returned the land so the Indians could complete their path of life trail to their religious ceremonial sites at Blue Lake (Ferry 1996, May 2, B4).

IMPLICATIONS

The chapter demonstrates how legislative movements succeed after they have been activated by a strongly organized campaign. Effective campaigns mobilize support and execute publicity to gain the attention of the public, special interest groups, and legislators. The Blue Lake case study shows that legislative movements sometimes stall and even die because grassroots supporters cannot maintain sufficient public and political interest or financial backing to continue. For Taos Pueblo, winning a financial settlement from the Indian Claims Commission affirmed the Indians' aboriginal right to Blue Lake. This action became a rallying point for the subsequent legislative campaign. Even though Pueblo leaders declined the financial settlement, they gained hope that the government wanted to right historical wrongs, and for this reason, the Indians thought they had a chance to regain control of Blue Lake.

The efforts of Corrine Locker and Paul Bernal produced a carefully organized legislative campaign that resulted in the passage of the Blue Lake bill. The rhetorical savvy of these leaders exemplify effective organization and planning and masterful public relations skills. Had the campaign not attracted the public support, the legislative interest, and the financial resources, the hearings would not have occurred and Blue Lake likely would still be part of federal forest land.

Congressional hearings respond to constituents' demands and attain political visibility. The hearings of 1968 demonstrate how senators can block the progress of a bill by their proprietary and oppositional advocacy. In contrast the hearings of 1970 demonstrate the power of pragmatic and prophetic advocacy. The themes, arguments, and evidence gathered in the legislative campaign resurface in the hearings and evolve into the core arguments of the legislative debate. This chapter shows how skillful political campaigns energize legislative movements and promote political action.

The Blue Lake legislation prompted the passage of the American Indian Religious Freedom Act in 1978. This legislation protected Indian religious rights. When President Jimmy Carter signed the legislation in August 1978, he emphasized the importance of Indian religious rites and sites: "In the past government agencies have . . . denied Native Americans access to particular sites and interfered with practices and customs." It would now be "the policy of the United States to protect and preserve the inherent right of American Indian, Eskimo, Aleut, and Native Hawaiian people to believe, express, and exercise their traditional religion" (O'Brian 1996, 30). A task force appointed by Carter gave "thirty-seven pages of recommendations for administrative and legislative changes." To date, federal agencies have made few of the recommended accommodations to tribal religious needs (O'Brian 1996, 30). In an attempt to clarify the provisions of the Indian Religious Freedom Act, numerous cases followed in the courts. Most of the cases failed to guarantee Indian access to the land they used for ceremonial purposes. Sharon O'Brian (1996) claims that the judicial system is unable "to understand and properly assess Indian religious beliefs, especially regarding the importance of land" (42). An exception to this conclusion occurred in 1992 after Zuni Pueblo successfully used the courts to force a rancher to provide an easement for the Zunis so they could carry out an ancient religious pilgrimage (Hart 1995). Very few other legislative efforts favorable to a single tribe ever made it on the congressional agenda. Despite this fact, Blue Lake campaign leaders appeared to have made an effective choice when they decided to ask Congress rather than the courts to return their sacred site to them.

Only a few tribes petitioned Congress to resolve land and religious disputes. Although the Puget Sound Indians accepted awards from the Land Claims Commission, these tribes continue to rely on court decisions to gain rights to traditional Indian fishing, food gathering, and ceremonial sites (Chapter 9). In the early part of the twentieth century, the Santee Sioux accepted some awards from the Court of Claims in payment for federal land acquisitions and unpaid annuities. After years of opposition to their Indian agent missionaries, the Southern Cheyenne and Arapaho openly rebelled against Christian evangelists by participating in the Ghost Dance, the Sun Dance, and the peyote rights of the Native American church. After a century of legislative and legal fights, the Teton Sioux refused payment from the Court of Claims for their sacred sites in the Black Hills. After the restoration of Blue Lake to Taos Pueblo, the Teton Sioux gained a glimmer of hope that the government might return the Black Hills to them. Such legislative action never materialized. After the government placed the Navajos on reservations, tribal members encroached on Hopi land and Hopis encroached on their land. A long legislative movement concerning the resulting Navajo-Hopi land disputes eventually resulted in the passage of legislation to remove and resettle some of the Navajo and Hopi.

Chapter 9

Ethnography and Puget Sound Indian Fishing Rights, 1973–1974

On December 26, 1854, Governor Isaac I. Stevens of Washington Territory negotiated the *Treaty of Medicine Creek* (10 Stat. 1132) with the Nisqually, Puyallup, and seven other bands of Indians. One-hundred and twenty years later, the treaty had still not resolved the conflicts between Indians and non-Indians in the Puget Sound area of Washington state. In the late 1960s and early 1970s, the right to fish for salmon and steelhead brought the commercial and sports fishermen into open conflict with Indians. The controversy over fishing rights, gear, and conservation created dozens of legal cases in the Northwest. The most famous of these cases, *U.S. v. Washington* (384 F. Supp. 312), decided in 1974 by Judge George Boldt of the Federal District Court in Tacoma, Washington, is the subject of this chapter.

At the first reading the language of the treaties with the Puget Sound Indians seems to set forth clearly the provisions for Indian fishing. Article 3 states:

The right of taking fish, at all usual and accustomed grounds and stations, is further secured to said Indians in common with all citizens of the Territory, and of erecting temporary houses for the purpose of curing, together with the privilege of hunting, gathering roots and berries, and pasturing their horses on open and unclaimed lands: Provided, however, that they shall not take shell-fish from any beds staked or cultivated by citizens, and that they shall alter all stallions not intended for breeding-horses, and shall keep up and confine the latter. (10 Stat. 1132)

Fourteen Indian tribes from the Puget Sound fishing area, including the Nisqually, brought a federal civil suit against the fish and game officials and the reef net commercial fishermen in the state of Washington in an effort to interpret the treaties and decide the fishing rights of Indians. The case featured issues about treaty making, cultural history, and states' rights, resulting in one of the most complicated civil actions in recent history. The trial culminated with a 110-page opinion by Judge Boldt. The decision sparks controversy even today. The goal of this chapter is to investigate the Boldt decision by examining the cultural lessons presented at the trial and in the legal opinion. To accomplish this purpose, the chapter (1) describes the rhetorical action associated with the creation of the Treaty of Medicine Creek, (2) identifies the political and legal forces that led to the trial, (3) explains how trial participants used ethnographic evidence, (4) shows how Judge Boldt's opinion emphasized ethnography, and (5) discusses the complex implications of this landmark case.

THE RHETORIC CREATING MEDICINE CREEK

The treaties with Indians had similar content and form. Francis Prucha (1994) explains that they were written in a "clear and legible" manuscript form delineating the expectations of behavior and action to be adopted by treaty signers. The last lines of the treaty provided a space for Indians and government officials to sign (435). As rhetorical documents, the treaties set forth the joint obligations, rights, and responsibilities of the Indians and the government. One of the problems with the Puget Sound treaties was that many of the Indians could not understand English even after interpreters read it in Chinook jargon, a simple 300-word trading language.

In the 1973 trial, many of the written documents and most of the anthropologists' oral testimony attempted to reconstruct what the treaties had meant at the time they were signed in 1854–1855. One way to reconstruct the issues of the trial and decipher the meaning of the Medicine Creek Treaty is to observe it using Kenneth Burke's dramatistic pentad. Burke ([1950] 1969) explains the components of dramatistic analysis in this way:

In any rounded statement about motives, you must have some word that names the act (names what took place in thought or deed), and another that names the scene (the background of the act, the situation in which it occurred); also, you must indicate what person or kind of persons (agents) performed the act, what means or instruments he used (agency) and the purpose. (xv)

The elements of Burke's pentad resemble a group of discussants using five different perspectives to come to a consensus about the meaning of a discourse. In this case, the elements of the pentad show how government officials constructed the Treaty of Medicine Creek.

The act refers to what was done in thought and deed (Burke [1950] 1969, 14). Hazard Stevens (1901, vol. 1), who accompanied his father Isaac I. Stevens at the treaties, explained the act of treaty making progressed through several stages. According to the son, after he was appointed governor of Washington Territory, Stevens put together his treaty-making team of secretary James Doty, ethnologist and surveyor George Gibbs, Commissioner of Indian Affairs representative H. A. Goldsborough, interpreter B. F. Shaw, and Indian agent Colonel M. T. Simmons. The treaty ceded more than 2.4 million acres for a price of $32,500 with payment promised over a twenty-year period. The treaty gave nine tribes fewer than 4,000 acres each, but it allowed the Indians to continue fishing and hunting berries. As typical of most treaties discussed so far in this volume, this one required the Indians to abstain from selling alcohol, free slaves, and cease trade with foreign Indians. In return the federal government promised to establish schools, provide a carpenter's shop, instruct Indians in smithing, carpentry, and farming (Treaty of Medicine Creek 1854). In ways similar to other treaties, the government's purpose was to force the Indians onto reservations so that settlers could cultivate the land and developers could exploit the natural resources. A secondary goal was to convert the Indians to Christianity, require them to attend school, and civilize them into white cultural life ways.

Acts occur in settings, what Burke calls scenes. The scene consists of where and when the act took place ([1950] 1969, 20). The scene for the treaty was Medicine Creek, also known as McAllister Creek, an area inhabited by a band of Nisqually who shared their fishing and hunting grounds with the neighboring Puyallup and other small Puget Sound Indian bands. At this campsite for the treaty signing, more than 600 Indians dressed in formal festival attire joined Governor Stevens wearing a top hat and a long black dress coat. In a ceremonial atmosphere, the Indians and government officials appeared ready to celebrate an important event. Sixty-two Indians, nineteen witnesses, and the official U.S. representatives constituted the members of the treaty council. Since it rained all day, the signing took place in a tent. The Indians signed with an X and authenticated their signatures with a thumb print. Following the signing, the government distributed gifts to the Indian signatories (Minutes of the Treaty Councils 1854, 3). As indicated in Chapter 1, Chief Leschi probably did not sign (Meeker [1905] 1980, 38; American Friends Service 1970, 28). In line with Burke's explanation, this scene encapsulated the act and predicted the rhetorical discourse that followed. The festive gathering, the formal speeches, and the gift-giving rituals created a scene that affirmed the importance of the treaty and called attention to the proposed friendly relationships between government officials and the tribes. At the same time, however, the treaty asserted the federal government's power over Indian land and behavior. For most Indian signatories, the rituals of the scene overshadowed the content and potential effects the discourse would have on tribal life.

The agency emphasizes the means or instruments used to produce the action (Burke [1950] 1969, 235–320). The words of the treaty served as the agency for the treaty council's action. After Doty had studied the language and form of the recent Missouri and Oto Indian treaties, he learned how the government acquired land from other Indians. Using this treaty as a model, he constructed the Medicine Creek Treaty. According to the Minutes of the Treaty Councils (1854), all the government representatives read Doty's draft of the treaty and approved it. Doty then ordered the final draft "to be engrossed" with a government seal before presenting it to the Indians. Additionally, the treaty council minutes report that James Doty "thought it necessary to allow them [the Puget Sound Indians] to fish at all accustomed places, since this provision would not in any manner interfere with the rights of citizens and was necessary for the Indians to obtain subsistence" (4). In this way, Doty's addition to the treaty became the disputed text for the 1973 fishing trial.

Prior to the reading of the treaty, Governor Stevens gave a speech that outlined the government's goals and delineated the conditions for Indian compliance with those goals. He told the assembled Indians:

This is a great day for you and for us, a day of peace and friendship between you and the whites for all time to come. You are about to be paid for your lands, and the Great Father has sent me today to treaty with you concerning the payment. . . . The Great Father . . . has sent me here today to express these feelings, and make a treaty for your benefit. The Great Father has many white children who come here; some to build mills, some to make farms, and some to fish. And the Great Father wishes you to learn to farm and for your children to go to a good school; and he now wants me to make a bargain with you, in which you sell your lands. . . . All this is written down in this paper which will be read to you. If it is good, you will sign it, and I will send it to the Great Father. (Minutes of the Treaty Councils 1854, 2)

Stevens' remarks typified those of other government officials at other treaty celebrations; that is, he emphasized the power and the peaceful motives of the government at the same time that he noted the deficiencies of Indian life that the treaties sought to remedy. By emphasizing the power of the agency of the treaty and the importance of its language, the government consummated the treaty. The treaty coded land acquisition goals in language implying lofty government moral objectives.

Government officials read aloud one article at a time and then translated the treaty into Chinook jargon. Stevens (1901) explained, "The governor would utter a sentence in simple and clear language, and Colonel Shaw would interpret it in Chinook jargon" (1: 458). After the treaty was read, the Indians engaged in a vigorous discussion about its provisions, but none of the provisions accommodated the objections of the Indians.

In a dramatic scene that reinforced government authority and the Indians' willingness to be friends with federal officials, the treaty became law. The agency, consisting of ceremonial speeches and the treaty itself, revealed several motives of Stevens and his territorial government. They wanted to free land from Indian title so that settlers could cultivate the land, force Indians to assimilate to white culture, and officially certify government control over the Indians. Even though the treaty set forth the government's goals in a direct way, it is unlikely that the Indians understood the provisions or recognized the motives of the territorial government. Because of their positive trading history with British traders in the Hudson Bay Company, the Indians believed the scene symbolized official friendship. But because they likely misunderstood the language of the treaty and misperceived the colonial motives of the United States government, many Indians signed the document. For this reason, the ritualistic scene, a celebration of friendship, overshadowed the treaty's language and its life altering consequences.

Just as in other socially constructed actions, the agents serve an important role as instruments of the action. The primary agent was Isaac I. Stevens. According to biographer Kent D. Richards (1991), Governor Stevens was "a highly intelligent military man who was also an astute politician." He believed it was essential to make treaties with the Indians before whites could settle the territory according to the Oregon Donation Land Act of 1850 (92–93). Other important agents in the treaties were George Gibbs, an ethnologist and surveyor, and B. F. Shaw, a trader who knew the Chinook language. Purportedly, Gibbs' ethnographic knowledge of the social and economic features of the Puget Sound Indians persuaded others that the treaty article on fishing was needed to protect the economic subsistence of the tribes.

The Indian agents were passive recipients of the treaty rather than active agents in its construction. Ezra Meeker ([1905] 1980) claims that the treaty primarily was designed for the Nisqually and Puyallup who represented 800 to 900 of the Puget Sound Indians. Moreover, he claimed the territorial leaders selected only friendly Indians to sign the treaty; these signatories represented small bands rather than the Indian political leaders of the Nisquallys and Puyallups. The government agents influenced the act by giving input into special treaty provisions, such as the article on fishing. From the standpoint of the Puget Sound Indian signatories, it appears that the treaty was a good faith promise for peace that many signers assumed would not affect their lives in a significant way (*U.S. v. Washington* 1974, treaty notes in appendix). Leschi and some other leaders seemed to perceive the meaning and consequences of the treaty because they apparently refused to sign and then during the Indian wars failed to comply with treaty provisions. From the standpoint of the government agents, however, the treaty succeeded in removing the Indians from fertile lands and paved the way for settlement and economic development.

The purpose, according to Burke ([1950] 1969), is an explanation of why an act was done (275–320). Francis Prucha (1984) summarizes what he considered the purpose of the Medicine Creek Treaty. He explains, "This was not to be a 'negotiation' between two political powers, of course, but an imposition upon the Indians of the treaty provisions Stevens brought with him, for he held a highly paternalistic view of his relations with the tribes" (404).

Despite the general purpose of relinquishing land, Stevens also wanted the Indians to retain "fishing, hunting, and berry picking" rights off the reservation. He felt these activities would allow the Indians to remain self sufficient without hindering settlement (Richards [1979] 1993, 201). Although Stevens could not have envisioned the legal and economic consequences of guaranteeing Indians the right to fish "in the usual and accustomed ground," this secondary provision of the treaty became the key feature of the 1973 civil case against the state of Washington.

Since this treaty was socially constructed, these five perspectives show how the meaning of the treaty emerges from the different standpoints. The meaning of the treaty and the motives of the agents who constructed it are the focus of the 1973 fishing trial. In the trial, the scene moves from Medicine Creek to a Tacoma courtroom; the act changes from treaty persuasion to treaty interpretation; the agency changes from a formalistic contract to a scholarly explanation of one provision; the agents change from treaty council representatives to anthropologists, tribal leaders, and legal personnel; and the purpose changes from gaining Indian compliance to extending Indians rights.

Before moving to a discussion of the twentieth-century legal drama that focused on interpreting the treaty, readers need to understand what events gave rise to the trial. The Puget Sound Indians expressed resistance to treaty provisions that took their land and campsites away after the treaty had been signed. However, it was not until the twentieth century that the fishing provisions transformed the issues into a legal conflict.

THE CONTEXT FOR THE TRIAL

Civil trials take place because individuals or groups believe they have not received the rights or economic benefits to which they are entitled. Plaintiffs initiate a civil suit in order to get a judge or jury to make a ruling about a controversy they believe has created adversity for them. Civil suits are ways of resolving private and public controversies. The Puget Sound Indians brought a civil suit against the state of Washington because they believed that the fishing rights they had been granted in federal treaties had been denied them by the state. Fights between commercial and Indian fishermen fueled the controversy that resulted in the 1973 civil trial and Boldt's opinion. Indian dissent and decisions of the lower courts failed to resolve the controversy over what rights the Treaty of Medicine Creek (and other Northwest Indian treaties) had extended to the Indians.

Indian Dissent

Several political actions led to this trial. The dissent about fishing rights took place in a historical period in which the rights of women and minorities had become a national issue. American Indian groups had organized for political action. The National Indian Youth Council formed in 1960 and the American Indian Movement organized in 1968. Many Indian activist organizations wanted to determine their own futures. Vine Deloria Jr. (1973) explained the activism as a way for Indians to "gain power over our own lives. . . . We simply want the power, the political and economic power, to run our lives in our own way" (29). The need to express economic power was not unique to the Indian fishermen in the Puget Sound; it was a consciousness that pervaded Indian Americans and instigated many different forms of protest. While most Indian dissent concerned government violations of treaty rights, the protests of the Puget Sound Indians, particularly the Nisqually, focused political attention on one treaty provision—fishing rights.

The Puget Sound dissent commenced as a reaction to local legal orders. Late in 1963, Pierce County Superior Court closed part of the Nisqually River to fishing. In that same year the American Indians' Association formed a pro-Indian rights organization. Members of this organization and disgruntled Indian fishermen participated in demonstrations that called attention to their right to fish at traditional sites. As a result of the protests, the state authorities arrested Indians along with their movie star advocate Marlon Brando who had joined in the protests (Wilkinson 2000).

The problem grew worse in 1964 and 1965. Washington Senator Warren Magnuson tried to introduce a bill to clarify fishing rights in Indian treaties. Although the legislation died in committee, Magnuson's action infuriated Indians because they believed he wanted to further limit their fishing rights. During this same period, an adverse legal judgment from Judge John D. Cochran ruled that the Puyallup Indians were not a tribe, and therefore they had no fishing rights in the Puyallup River. In late 1965, several contentious incidents occurred; for example, state officials arrested Indians at a traditional fishing site called "Frank's Landing," near Olympia, Washington. At that time officers arrested seven Indians and charged them with interfering with police officers. The Indians stood trial in 1969, but were acquitted of the charges. Their defense attorneys argued that they intended to demonstrate in a peaceful manner but the state officers threatened the demonstrators' safety by an extensive and unnecessary show of force (American Friends Service 1970, 110; Wilkinson 2000, 42–47).

Later on Indians protested at the federal courthouse in Seattle. Faye Cohen (1986) explains the impact of the protest: "The drama of the fish-ins, the encampment, and the burning of railway trestles appeared to be the catalyst for a significantly higher level of federal assistance which entailed a significantly higher cost and commitment." He believes the protests led the justice department to file a complaint against the state of Washington which in turn resulted in the civil trial and the subsequent opinion of Judge Boldt (80).

Legal Jurisdiction

A factor adding to the conflict was the disagreement over whether the state or the federal courts had jurisdiction over fishing rights. The state courts affirmed the right of the state to regulate off-reservation fishing, and the federal courts denied that the state had jurisdiction over any Indian fishing.

Prior to the 1973 trial, three decisions indicated a strong difference of opinion about federal and state jurisdiction in fishing cases. In the first case, called Puyallup I (*Puyallup Tribe of Indians v. Department of Game* 1968, 392), the issue was whether the state could force Indians to obey state regulations. The state trial court said they could, and the U.S. Supreme Court said that the state could not limit the Puyallups' and Nisquallys' off-reservation fishing. Additionally, the state claimed they had a right to regulate Indian fishing in the interest of conservation. In a second case, *Sohappy v. Smith* (1969, 899), the federal court noted that the fishing rights of tribes were separate and different from nontreaty fishermen and that Oregon should manage fisheries to provide an appropriate share of fish for tribal fishermen. In the third case in 1973, the U.S. Supreme Court reviewed the Puyallup I decision and agreed that a complete ban on Puyallup net fishing by the state created discrimination against the Indians (Puyallup II, *Department of Game v. Puyallup Tribe, Inc.* 44).

Even though the courts defined the controversial issues between the tribes and the government, both the legal and political attempts to solve the conflicts between the state and tribal fishermen failed. While preparations were underway for the 1973 trial, new appellate court decisions and new political conflicts continued.

The Trial

In 1973 the federal government, representing fourteen Washington tribes, brought a civil suit against the state of Washington (Transcripts of Trial Record 1973, Case 9213) in the Federal District Court in Tacoma, Washington. The trial began September 18 and ended December 10, 1973. The plaintiffs presented thirty-six witnesses, including elders from each of the tribes being represented, and the defense presented seven witnesses, including one anthropologist. The trial records include 4,600 pages of testimony, 500 pages of findings of facts and conclusions of law, and 350 exhibits.

The primary attorneys for the federal government were George Dysart and Stuart Pierson, and David H. Getches and Alvin J. Ziontz represented the majority of the Indian tribes. The defense lawyers included Joseph Larry Coniff representing the Department of Game, Carol Crose and Earl M. McGimpsey representing the Department of Fisheries, and Thor Tollefson and David E. Rhea representing the Washington Reef Net Owners Association. Judge George H. Boldt presented the opinion of the court in 1974. The most controversial rulings in the opinion were that Indians were entitled to one-half of all the available fish, excluding that used for subsistence and ceremonies, and that the state lacked jurisdiction over Indians fishing off the reservation.

Even before the case began, Boldt characterized it as unique. He said that "never before in the entire history of litigation affecting Indian treaty rights has the Court had before it both extensive anthropological data and exposition of the means of state regulation" (*U.S. v. Washington* 1974, 114). After the opinion was issued, the controversy continued. A League of Women Voters' educational pamphlet (1980) claimed that the citizens and commercial and sports fishermen were so angry they hung effigies of Judge Boldt and called for his impeachment. From 1974 until the present, the Indians and the other fishermen have struggled to make the legal rulings work.

LESSONS IN ETHNOGRAPHY IN THE 1973 TRIAL

Culture offers many clues about how language is understood in rhetorical texts. Reconstructing cultural meaning requires ethnographic information. For this reason, it is not surprising that the judge in the Puget Sound fishing trials encouraged the use of ethnographic evidence. Ethnography refers to "the art and science of describing a group or culture" (Fetterman 1989, 8). In legal settings, the language of the legal texts becomes the focus of the ethnographic analysis (Conley & O'Barr 1990, xi). The word "ethnography" literally means the written and oral recording of racial or cultural observations. Legal proceedings and ethnographic research share the common process of gathering evidence and recording what observers say.

Although most trials and opinions are not specifically about culture, *U.S. v. Washington* (1974) focused almost entirely on Indian culture as it related to the fishing industry. Not only did the trial lawyers and witnesses take an ethnographic approach, Judge George Boldt's opinion embodied many features of an ethnographic report. He viewed the conflict as a cultural one and the trial as a means of facilitating intercultural communication between dissenting groups who rarely talked with one other. In this excerpt, for example, Judge Boldt called attention to the Indian cultural perspective:

The right to fish for all species available in the waters from which, for so many ages, their ancestors derived most of their subsistence is the single most highly cherished interest and concern of the present members of the plaintiff tribes, with rare exceptions even among tribal members who personally do not fish or derive there from any substantial amount of their subsistence. (*U.S. v. Washington* 1974, 340)

The case is worthy of study because it broke new legal ground, but it is also an intriguing way to examine how the legal rhetoric of the attorneys, witnesses, and the judge used ethnographic evidence. Since most of this case consisted of the testimony of Indian elders and anthropologists, it provides a window for showing how cultural testimony affects legal outcomes. Furthermore, it shows how the legal system used ethnographic information to resolve the cultural conflicts. This excerpt from Boldt's 1974 opinion shows his reliance on ethnographic evidence:

To this court the evidence clearly shows that, in the past, the root causes of treaty rights dissension have been an almost total lack of meaningful communication on problems of treaty rights fighting between state, commercial and sport fishing officials and non-Indian fishermen on one side and tribal representatives on the other side, and the failure of many of them to speak to each other and act as fellow citizens of equal standing as far as treaty rights are concerned. (*U.S. v. Washington* 1974, 329)

Attorneys and witnesses used several ethnographic approaches, such as the presentation of ideational perspectives by insiders, solicitation of insiders' inductive narratives, and demonstration of the ethnographers' method of triangulation.

Ideational Approaches by Insiders

Both plaintiffs and defense attorneys used ethnographic approaches in their presentation of witnesses and case development. In general, the role of ethnographer is to discover cultural values and practices from the insiders, that is, from an emic point of view. In ways similar to the ethnographer, trial attorneys selected witnesses to present the point of view of insiders. The insiders for plaintiffs consisted of tribal elders, Indian fishermen, and anthropologists; and for the defense, the insiders included biologists, economists, and one anthropologist.

Just as other ethnologists, the attorneys in this trial chose witnesses who could answer key questions or solve problems (Fetterman 1989, 15) regarding the cultural conflict between Indians and sports and commercial fishermen. Among the questions presented were the following: (1) Are the rights to fish governed by Indian tribal treaties or by the state? (2) Can the state prohibit off-reservation fishing by Indians in order to conserve the species? (3) Does the state have the right to dictate to Indians what type of fishing equipment they can use? (4) Are Indians entitled to the fish raised in state fisheries? (5) Do state officials have the right to confiscate Indian fishing gear? (6) How many fish are Indians entitled to catch? To answer these questions, both the plaintiffs and the defense selected witnesses who could testify from an insider's point of view.

Ethnologists use theories as the basis for their research in ways similar to how attorneys construct theories to guide their case presentation. Ethnologists typically rely on ideational and materialist theories. The ethnologist seeks information from informants in contrast to attorneys who gather information from the testimony of witnesses. An ideational theory examines the thoughts, ideas, and behaviors of its informants in order to find out how they view the world. The process permits informants to talk about "ideas, cognitive maps, beliefs, and ideas" (Fetterman 1989, 16). In contrast, ethnographers using materialistic theories emphasize the material conditions that affect cultures—"ecological resources, money, and modes of production." Materialist theory describes how "economic forces, class consciousness, class conflict, and various forms of social organization drive social and cultural change" (Fetterman 1989, 16).

The plaintiffs chose primarily witnesses who could support an ideational position, that is, people who could establish the traditions, patterns, and knowledge of the importance of fishing to the tribes involved in the lawsuit. Many of the tribal elders presented their testimony in a narrated form, allowing them to respond to a few questions from their attorneys without being interrupted by the judge or opposing counsel. For example, Lena Cultee Hillaire, an elder of the Nisqually-Puyallup tribes, recalled the historical role of women in fishing. She said that her tribe used canoes carrying five people. Women went along on the boats to pick the little fish out and throw them back. After the fish were caught, they were put on big Indian blankets, divided among the fishermen into equal shares, and some fish were given to the old people who could no longer fish (Transcripts of Trial Record 1973, 2857–58).

In addition to her recollections about the fishing industry, Hillaire told stories about the abuse of her people at the hands of leaders of the Bureau of Indian Affairs. This elderly woman freely gave her opinion, just as a cultural interviewee would respond to an ethnographer. She explained that "I eat a lot of Indian food, but I got no more. All of the white people took our food. We have got nothing in the woods now, not even Indian medicine" (2863). Hillaire concluded her testimony by condemning the Indian agents who had harmed her ancestors years ago. She emphasized, "The first agents was really mean to our Indian people. They used whips on them, because they couldn't understand Christian work. They start licking them, slapping the old Indians in the face. . . . I seen them whipped, and I would jump up and cry. I felt so bad, you know the way they would treat them" (Transcripts of Trial Record 1973, 2868).

The state called few witnesses. One insider witness, Henry Wendler, representing the Department of Fisheries, testified from a materialist perspective. Using scientific data, he documented the life of the salmon, charted the runs, and indicated the types of salmon catches that occurred in the different streams. His testimony focused on the quantity of salmon and the role of the fisheries in the hatching and planting of fish (Transcripts of Trial Record 1973, Exhibit JX, 2a). Wendler presented statistical data to explain the ecology and economics of fishing in Washington State.

In this case, the ideational assumptions of the plaintiffs and the materialist ones of the defense fit legal theories. The plaintiffs claimed that Indians' rights to fish on and off the reservation were guaranteed by the treaties they had signed with Territorial Governor Isaac I. Stevens. They argued that the state had no right to regulate Indian fishing or to confiscate Indian fishing gear. In contrast, the defense used scientific and legal reasons, claiming the state could regulate Indian off-reservation fishing of both salmon and steelhead in order to guarantee supplies of fish, to exercise the state's legitimate rights over business interests, and to provide for the needs of sports and commercial fishermen.

Inductive Narratives

Ethnologists survey basic ideas, including "the native language, kinship ties, census information, historical data, and the basic structure and function of the culture under study," (Fetterman 1989, 18). The information follows an inductive process in which the ethnologist (represented by the attorneys) draws out particular details of witnesses' narratives prior to forming general conclusions.

Ethnographers also select their informants to provide inductive narrative information. Informants usually are members of the mainstream who have a special "vantage point" and "objectivity" about their culture and act in some way as formal leaders (Fetterman 1989, 59). They tell their stories in the same way they would speak outside of court, relating their troubles and their personal assumptions about culture and justice (Conley & O'Barr 1990, 56). More specifically, ethnologists provide detailed autobiographical data that "tells much about the fabric of the social group" (Fetterman 1989, 61) and contributes a part to the cultural puzzle the ethnographer tries to piece together.

Ethnographers construct their theories through the direct examination of their own witnesses. For example, during direct examination, plaintiffs' attorneys sought information from tribal elders about the traditional conservation practices of Indians. Instead of eliciting information from witnesses by a structured and chronological series of questions typical of direct examination, plaintiffs' attorneys allowed their Indian witnesses to relate their personal point of view in a nonsequential narrative, a strategy characteristic of ethnographic interviews but atypical of formal witness examination procedures.

Elder Johnson Meninick of the Yakima tribe provided the vantage point of a religious leader who advocated the traditional spiritual values of unity between his people and the earth. He preached the spiritual message of the Yakimas in this way: "I said, this earth, this land, the water, the sunlight, and all of the food that is here for my people is going to be retained in my law by the creator and [it] shall never be destroyed by anyone (Transcripts of Trial Record 1973, 3368). Meninick suggested to the court that the religious law mandated conservation, and therefore tribal law superseded that of the state.

An elder and a fisherman, Horton Capoerman of the Quinault tribe, explained that fish provided the staple food of his tribe. He continued, "It helps them along in the way they have to live in this day and age. . . . I don't think they are going to deplete fish if they can help it" (Transcripts of Trial Record 1973, 3446–47). He implied that because natural conservation occurred among his people, no need existed for the state to intervene in traditionally sound Indian conservation practices.

In ways similar to other types of ethnographic interviewing, the responses of the trial witnesses varied according to the way the questioner emphasized either rules or relationships. Relational witnesses viewed the law as part of the values and traditions of their tribe. The witnesses expected legal officials to take an interest in their problems and find appropriate solutions. In contrast, rule-oriented witnesses, such as the biologists and economists testifying for the defense, viewed the law as providing specific remedies for problems that fit with a narrowly defined set of laws. Conley and O'Barr (1990) conclude that the relational style often comes from witnesses who lack power and authority (173), and a rule-like style characterizes the discourse of bureaucrats holding authority.

When used in the courtroom, ethnographic interviewing has unique features that seem to conflict with standard legal practices. First, the witnesses often focused their answers on what they thought the questioner wanted rather than just relating verifiable facts. Second, the witnesses volunteered information that was legally irrelevant but personally important. Third, witnesses speculated about the causes of historical events and gave personal interpretations of consequences of events. Fourth, witnesses typically presented their feelings and beliefs about events. Finally, the witnesses cited their understanding, often based on second- and third-hand knowledge (hearsay) rather than on direct observation. These practices convey discursive content similar to that given by lay witnesses who testify in small claims courts (Conley & Barr 1990, 13).

The law prefers information gained from visual observation rather than from oral traditions. Elders relating their oral traditions testified on behalf of the fourteen plaintiff Indian tribes and presented evidence inductively by recollecting names, places, and behaviors in a personal and self-interested narrative unrestricted by standard legal procedures. In contrast witnesses using a visual perspective usually convey ideas deductively, recalling specific details in the sequence in which they occurred by using records to verify their information. Attorneys and judges show discretion when they give latitude to witnesses from oral cultures and allow them to present their stories without imposing strict legal rules. When trial lawyers and judges allow traditional narratives, they function as ethnographers more than as traditional legal officials.

Ethnography sometimes clashes with legal rules. The defense recognized additional problems with cultural testimony about the "usual and accustomed" fishing sites, claiming this testimony was not reliable, was molded to fit with the issues of this litigation, and was entirely reconstructed because aboriginal culture had declined at the time of the treaties (Transcripts of Trial Record 1973, Pretrial Order, 145–48). What is clear is that an ethnographic approach in the courtroom allowed for speculation and hearsay evidence that usually would be excluded in a civil litigation. However, this approach permitted the Indians to express their cultural voice, a trend that continued in most subsequent judicial proceedings involving treaty rights over the next twenty-five years.

Triangulation Methods

Triangulation means comparing and contrasting sources of information against one another, excluding information that is not reliable, and selecting the remaining reliable information to understand or define a problem and suggest a solution (Fetterman 1989, 89). Ethnographers assess reliability by finding patterns of repeated thoughts and behaviors by "comparing, contrasting, and sorting" data to discern fact patterns among the responses of cultural informants. Fetterman (1989) concludes that this process "aids the ethnographer in grasping a community's fundamental ideas and values" (92).

In the 1973 fishing trial, the defense's cross-examination of the plaintiffs' expert, anthropologist Barbara Lane, demonstrates this method of triangulation. In order for Lane to provide triangulated evidence for her findings, attorneys on both sides of the case functioned as ethnographers, encouraging her to contrast evidence, exclude unreliable evidence, and select cultural data that would help define Indian fishing rights. Lane's testimony presented complex cultural lessons that she had learned from reading historical documents and others' ethnographies. She used this information to reconstruct Indian culture and beliefs at the time of the Treaty of Medicine Creek. The defense's goal was to triangulate the evidence she presented in her testimony. Several features of Lane's testimony illuminate the method of triangulation.

First, Lane provided long narratives about her findings, comparing and contrasting her evidence with that of other ethnologists and historians. One example of her defense of sources occurred when Lawrence Coniff cross-examined her:

Coniff: My question is this: given the rather general nature of the contemporaneous treaty documents, and the fact that sophisticated anthropologists did not commence their studies of these people to any great extent until the 1920s, do you feel that it is possible to discuss social and economic institutions in a clear-cut manner? . . .

Lane: The answer is yes, I think it's possible to make such statements, but I would like to be very explicit upon what these statements are based. They are based partly on historical reconstruction, as you suggest, and the results of analyses of anthropologists who did not begin serious study, except for early people like Gibbs and Swan, who did not begin this type of analysis until the 1920s. Now, their analyses are not based solely upon information collected at that time, and subsequently from living people and also from their research. . . . I would suggest to you that while we do not have as complete a record as we would like, contemporaneous documents like the diaries of James Swan, which he kept for over a decade and made daily records on where the Indians were moving and what they were doing and so on where he lived, and records of diaries left by pioneers . . . provide partial corroboration for the materials collected much later and the analyses of contemporary anthropologists. (Transcripts of Trial Record 1973, 1794–95)

Lane specifically compared and contrasted her evidence with other anthropologists, and Coniff's cross-examination questions aided her in completing the first step of triangulation.

Second, Coniff's cross-examination of Lane encouraged her to accomplish the second step of triangulation, excluding evidence from the defense expert Carroll Riley whom she sometimes considered unreliable. To facilitate this step of triangulation, Coniff read huge segments of Riley's written reports, and then he asked Lane to agree or disagree with his findings. Typically, the cross-examiner seeks to impeach the witness, point out inconsistencies of testimony, and show the testimony is flawed. In this case, however, the cross-examiner encouraged Lane to bolster her own conclusions by challenging those presented by the defense's anthropologist, Carroll Riley. Coniff explained to Judge Boldt that he was going to use Riley's testimony to contrast it with the testimony of Lane.

Coniff: (Reading defense's anthropology expert Carroll Riley's written testimony) Political authority was on [the] village level and was very weak. The leaders were those who, by reason of birth and wealth, had prestige in the community.

Lane: I agree, except for my earlier qualification that I don't tie political entity to the village, so that political authority on the village level in one way is an acceptable statement in that villages were the form of residence in this area. But if we are talking about a one-to-one relationship, again, I have to disagree on the same basis as before.

Coniff: Is your disagreement predicated upon a concept that there was a political authority over all of the villages in a given watershed?

Lane: No.

Coniff: (Still reading from Riley) The land-using unit was the village. This group made intensive use of fishing, hunting and gathering lands in the vicinity of the actual settlement. Other territory was used sporadically in hunting and collecting.

Lane: I have to disagree with this . . . because I do not agree that the land-using unit was the village. The village . . . was a group of people living together in the wintertime when subsistence activities were being carried on at a much reduced level than at other seasons of the year and where people from a village dispersed in the Spring and Summer and early Fall into most of the area. (Transcripts of Trial Record 1973, 1773–75)

In this segment of the testimony, the defense cross-examined in ways similar to an ethnographer using "a mixture of conversation and embedded questions" and the "questions emerged from the conversation" and resulted "from the comments of the interviewee" (Fetterman 1989). Unlike a standard cross-examination, Coniff did not try to impeach the testimony of Lane nor show the logical inconsistencies in what she said. In effect, Coniff aided Lane, allowing her to triangulate the evidence and thereby strengthen her position; in doing so Coniff discredited the testimony of his own anthropology expert. An observer cannot help but wonder why he used this strategy since it helped defeat the major argument of the defense. Perhaps he was not prepared to deal with the ethnographic testimony presented from an adversarial perspective.

Third, Lane defined the legal terms of the treaty, using anthropological information that defined the problem. Just as in other triangulation, the definition of the problem suggests a solution. In this case, Lane's definition of "usual and accustomed" fishing sites was the basis for a recommendation that Judge Boldt should forbid state regulation of off-reservation fishing. In this segment of cross-examination, defense attorney McGimpsey encouraged Lane to define the meaning of the treaty provisions.

McGimpsey: My question is: When the treaty drafters use the term 'at usual and accustomed places and stations,' did they by that language mean any limitation on the places where the Indians were secured in their taking of the fish?

Lane: Well, I think they meant what they said, usual and accustomed places, and I think perhaps they understood it at that time since they were on the scene, that the Indian moved around freely, that they took fish wherever they chose to do so, wherever they happened to be for some other purpose. . . .

McGimpsey: If the Nisqually Indians were to make a trip by canoe at treaty time to Cape Flattery or Neah Bay, it is your understanding the term 'usual and accustomed places' as used in the Medicine Creek Treaty, securing to the Nisqually Indians their fishing station, would have included all of the areas that men could have fished on this trip to Neah Bay? . . .

Lane: I think the answer would be in the affirmative, that yes, those would be usual, accustomed places, even though . . . it might not be in the territory which was recognized as ceded by that particular group or have to do with the treaty that covered the group that particular Indian belonged to. (Transcripts of Trial Record 1973, 1940–41)

Again in this segment of testimony, the strategy was self-defeating because the defense attorney facilitated Lane's process of triangulating the cultural evidence she had presented, a questioning strategy typical of ethnography but atypical for cross-examination. This cross-examination strategy strengthened the plaintiffs' argument about the meaning of the disputed words of the treaty and compromised the defense's argument that these terms had a restricted legal meaning.

Apparently, this testimony persuaded Boldt that the plaintiffs had a right to many traditional fishing sites. Judge Boldt's opinion concluded:

Dr. Lane's opinions, inferences, and conclusions based upon the information stated in detail and well documented in her reports, appeared to the court to be well taken, sound and reasonable. In summary, the court finds that where their testimony differs in any significant particular, the testimony of Dr. Lane is more credible and satisfactory than that of Dr. Riley and is accepted as such except as otherwise specified. (*U.S. v. Washington* 1974, 350)

In the many cases involving Indian treaties, the fishing trials as well as the Indian Claims Commission cases, the principal focus of the trial testimony was on the natives' culture. To bring out the cultural issues, attorneys and witnesses used ethnography to emphasize the ideational content of witnesses' insider information. After eliciting inductive narrative from witnesses, attorneys validated the evidence by comparing it to other similar testimony, a comparative approach characteristic of ethnological triangulation.

JUDGE BOLDT AS ETHNOGRAPHIC INTERPRETER

Judge Boldt's interpretation of the ethnographic testimony reflected another method common to ethnographers. First, he called attention to his nonjudgmental status by accepting cultural and personal testimony from witnesses that presented a self-interested point of view. He also recognized the value of the personal diaries of observers such as ethnologist George Gibbs. In ways similar to other ethnographic interpreters, Boldt tried to view the cultural practices objectively without imposing his own viewpoint (Fetterman 1989, 33). His 1974 opinion consolidated the reports of Lane and her anthropological sources with the recollections of the living elders. An example of his process of constructing meaning appeared in this segment of his opinion:

At the time of the treaties, non-Indian commercial fishing enterprises were rudimentary and largely unsuccessful. . . . The Gibbs-Stevens census of 1854 shows a total of 7,559 Indians for all of Western Washington. A decline in population continued during the decades following the signing of the treaties, due in large part to diseases introduced by non-Indians. . . . The Northwest Indians developed and utilized a wide variety of fishing methods which enabled them to take fish from nearly every type of location at which fish were present. . . . Aboriginal Indian fishing was not limited to any species. They took whatever species that were available at the particular season and location. . . . Although there are extensive records and oral history from which many specific fishing locations can be pinpointed, it would be impossible to compile a complete inventory of any tribe's usual and accustomed grounds and stations. (*U.S. v. Washington* 1974, 352–53)

In this excerpt, Boldt reported what others had said in the trial, and he referred to cultural documents. By reporting the information as fact, he certified it as the truth as it best could be determined nearly 125 years after the treaty was signed.

Second, Boldt adopted the ethnographer's viewpoint when he looked for symbols that identified the culture of the witnesses. One significant symbol shared by the tribes was the salmon ceremony. Identifying significant symbols helps interpreters classify and categorize their understanding of cultural values (Fetterman 1989, 37). Ritualistic symbols give clues about what members of a culture value the most highly. The exhibits of the plaintiffs, Lane's explanations, and the oral traditions of the Indian elders called attention to the value the Indians placed on the salmon ceremony. Boldt's opinion verified the existence of the salmon ceremony, suggesting it symbolized the importance of fishing to the plaintiff tribes. He noted:

The first-salmon ceremony, which with local differences in detail was general through most of the area, was essentially a religious right to ensure the continued return of salmon. The symbolic acts, attitudes of respect and reverence, and concern for the salmon reflected a ritualistic conception of the interdependence and relatedness of all living things which was a dominant feature of the native Indian world view. Religious attitudes and rites insured that salmon were never wantonly wasted and that water pollution was not permitted during the salmon season. (*U.S. v. Washington* 1974, 351)

Drawing on the testimony of more than thirty elders, the ethnographic works written at the time of the treaty, and the testimony of Lane, Boldt concluded: "The fish were vital to the Indian diet, played an important role in their religious life, and constituted a major element of their trade and economy" (*U.S. v. Washington* 1974, 350).

Third, Boldt met standards for ethnographic interpretation when he made sense of a huge amount of cultural and legal information through a clearly structured argument. His method of argumentation mirrored the method of triangulation used by ethnographic interpreters. Boldt's opinion suggested that he compared the cultural data presented by the plaintiffs, selected the data he found most reliable, excluded the information he found unreliable, and integrated this information with the legal precedents. An example of Boldt's process of triangulation occurred when he evaluated the use of Chinook jargon in Stevens' treaty negotiations. He concluded:

The vast majority of Indians at the treaty councils did not speak or understand English. The treaty provisions and the remarks of the treaty commissioners were interpreted by Colonel Shaw to the Indians in the Chinook jargon and then translated into native language by Indian interpreters. Chinook jargon, a trade medium of limited vocabulary and simple grammar, was inadequate to express precisely the legal effects of the treaties, although the general meaning of treaty language could be explained. Many of those present did not understand the Chinook jargon. . . . A dictionary of the Chinook jargon, prepared by George Gibbs, indicates that the jargon contains no words or expressions that would describe any limiting interpretation on the right of taking fish. (*U.S. v. Washington* 1974, 356)

This conclusion included the testimony common to both anthropological experts—Lane and Riley. He compared the testimony to the comments made in George Gibbs' diaries, the treaty council minutes, and Gibbs' dictionary. The segment of the opinion on Chinook jargon appears to validate all sources and to acknowledge the segments of testimony where both experts agree about the limitations of the Chinook jargon. Lane had testified:

In a general way, I believe the terms of the treaty could be explained in Chinook jargon. As to the legal entailments of the language in the treaties, I do not believe this could be conveyed in the jargon. I believe I am in complete concurrence with Dr. Riley in that portion of his direct testimony in which he says . . . "if all parties had spoken fluent Makah or fluent English, there still would have been problems in communicating the meaning of the language of the treaty, because people were operating from two different approaches with different kinds of understandings about property rights, et cetera, and this would make for difficulties at least in that area." . . . I find myself in complete agreement with Dr. Riley at this point. (Transcripts of Trial Record 1973, 1886–87)

These direct connections between the judicial opinion and the testimony show that Judge Boldt interpreted evidence based on the method of triangulation in which he integrated cultural testimony with legal principles.

Finally, Boldt showed the implications of the cultural testimony for the law in particular and for the fishing industry in general. In doing so, he engaged in what Janice Schuetz and Kathryn Snedaker (1988) refer to as the law-development function of the courts; he developed a new understanding of the common law and accommodated it to the demands of individuals and institutions (182). In this case, Boldt focused on enforcing the laws of the treaties and protecting the rights of the Indian tribes who were parties to these treaties. Since the early 1960s, the state of Washington had created laws that in Boldt's opinion had violated those treaties. He opined:

Therefore, the court finds and holds that every fishing location where members of a tribe customarily fished from time to time at and before treaty times, however distant from the then usual habitat of the tribe, and whether or not other tribes then also fished in the same waters, is a usual and accustomed ground or station at which the treaty tribe reserved, and its members presently have, the right to take fish. (*U.S. v. Washington* 1974, 332)

He further argued that the state laws permitting the departments of fisheries and game to regulate Indian fishing off-reservation "have not been established as reasonable and necessary for conservation and the application thereof to plaintiff tribes is unlawful" (334).

In addition to making new law or at least clarifying the legal power of treaty law, Boldt's opinion made policy for the Indian tribes, state and federal agencies, and commercial fishermen. He declared that the Indian tribes should create maps of their usual and accustomed fishing grounds, update tribal membership, improve fishing methods, participate in an Indian Fisheries Commission representing the tribes covered by the decision, provide fishing regulations, develop methods of tribal fishery management, and produce scientific studies of the size of fish runs. He also created policies for the state by advising the Departments of Fisheries and Game to continue to monitor the amount of fish taken by state-licensed fishermen, to engage in reasonable conservation practices, to cease seizures of Indian nets and fishing gear, to continue the work of the hatcheries, to allow Indians to catch 50 percent of available fish, and to release fishing gear previously seized from the Indians. Additionally, Boldt voided fourteen state regulations and statutes concerning Indian fishing. In this way, Boldt's opinion developed law and prescribed public policy; in doing so, it had an immense effect on Puget Sound fishing practices.

IMPLICATIONS

The effects of the Boldt decision continue in the lessons learned about Puget Sound Indian culture, continuing political disputes, subsequent legal decisions, and evolving economic outcomes for the fisheries industry.

Cultural Lessons

The extensive use of cultural testimony in the 1973 trial broke new ground for civil trials. First, the rhetoric surrounding the Treaty of Medicine Creek revealed the government's economic and political motives. The treaty diminished the economic base of the Indian tribes and amplified the power of the government over land and resources. The failure of the treaty to gain compliance from the Puget Sound tribes resulted in regional Indian wars in the 1850s, eventuated the fishing conflicts of the 1960s, led to the 1973 trial, and produced Boldt's 1974 opinion. The main purpose of the trial was to reconstruct the meaning of the treaty and to determine the meaning of "usual and accustomed" fishing sites. The cultural reconstruction of facts that occurred in the trial was atypical of evidence gathering processes in most civil cases.

Plaintiffs and defense attorneys employed ethnographic methods. For example, attorneys acted as ethnographers by seeking the records and interpretations of anthropologists and by allowing elders from many of the fourteen tribes who brought the lawsuit to testify. Instead of acting as adversaries, defense attorneys responded by validating the testimony of anthropologists and listening to Indian elders testify about their experiences, traditions, and religion. Throughout the trial, witnesses acted in ways similar to cultural insiders in ethnographic interviews; they presented their ideational views and expressed values and traditions through inductive narratives about their relationships to one another, the Great Spirit, and the environment. Attorneys for both sides of the case encouraged anthropologists to triangulate data so that their information reconstructed the facts and related it to the behaviors that had occurred during treaty times.

The opinion of Judge Boldt demonstrated understanding and sensitivity to cultural issues. He accepted personal stories told by Indians from their self-interested points of view. He recognized salmon as a key symbol of the Puget Sound tribes by acknowledging the ceremonial importance of the first salmon ceremony. He interpreted the cultural testimony, using his own kind of triangulation; he compared history, ethnography, and the reports of elders before drawing conclusions about "the usual and accustomed fishing locations." Even though his opinion continues to be controversial, his lengthy decision permitted cultural interpretations of law in a carefully argued opinion. Boldt's decision changed government-Indian relations in the

Puget Sound region of the country and created extensive new legal initiatives for fishing and hunting among other tribes.

Political Implications

Despite the complexity of the trial, the thoroughness of the legal clarification, and the establishment of policy regarding fishing, the non-Indian fishing entities expressed strong dissatisfaction with the opinion. Washington State Attorney General Slade Gorton fought the decision. First, Gorton appealed the decision to the 9th Circuit Court in 1975, but the opinion was affirmed. In 1976, he appealed the opinion to the U.S. Supreme Court, but this court refused to hear the case. After commercial fishermen sued the state without success, non-Indian fishing interests reduced the size of their fleets but then tried without success to sue the state Department of Fisheries for damages. Although the Thurston County Court made rulings that conflicted with the 1974 decision, Boldt forbid this court from carrying out its rulings.

Illegal fishing continued until violent conflicts erupted between Indians and commercial fishermen. To remedy this problem, Boldt set up a mediation board to try to resolve disputes called the Indian Fisheries Advisory Board (Cohen 1986, 84–87; Wilkinson 2000). Even today illegal fishing occurs. As recently as September 1997, a non-Indian, Mark Stangler, was caught stealing salmon from an Indian gillnet on Hood Canal (Williams 1997a, 10). Harassment of Indian fishermen has taken new forms. Mel Elofson, a Klallam tribal member explains:

They used to leave our nets alone during the daytime and vandalize them at night. Then a couple of guys got brave enough to start vandalizing them in the daytime. . . . They would cut up the nets and dump the fish. Some guys would steal the fish and reset the nets. (Williams 1997b, 8)

Despite the attempts by tribal law enforcement officers the conflicts among fishermen frequently erupt.

Congressmen from Washington continue to fight against the fishing rights guaranteed by Boldt. Washington Congressman John E. Cunningham introduced legislation to abrogate Indian treaties in 1977 and 1978 with no success (Prucha 1994, 424). As recently as 1997, Slade Gorton, now a U.S. Senator, attached legislation to an appropriations bill to rescind tribal sovereignty in an attempt to reduce Indian fishing rights. His amendment to an Interior appropriations bill failed (Frank 1997, November, 2).

Legal Implications

The immediate legal impact of the Boldt decision was detailed in the petitioner's brief for the Puget Sound Gilnetters case (*Puget Sound Gilnetters v. Moos* 1977, 677):

On February 12, 1974, the District Court . . . appointed a master, a "fishing expert" and a "fisheries advisory board" to apply the decision. Since that time nearly "two-hundred subsequent orders and . . . more than five thousand" complaints have been issued, twenty appeals have been submitted to the Ninth Circuit Court in which non-Indian and Indian fishermen were defendants. In 1992, the Court permitted tribes to take herring at all of its usual and accustomed places. (*U.S. v. Washington* 1049)

In 1994, U.S. District Court Judge Edward Rafeedie extended the Boldt decision by ruling that tribes can take 50 percent of the harvestable shellfish on western Washington beaches (1422). In 1995, the court ruled that if a dispute arises between a property owner and a treaty fisherman concerning the exercise of the right to gather shellfish, the matter is to be decided by a special master (*U.S. v. Washington* 787). In 1998, the Ninth Circuit Court upheld the right of tribes to harvest shellfish in natural beds but limited their right to commercial shellfish (*U.S. v. Washington* 630). In fact, a current assistant attorney general for the Departments of Game and Fisheries, Fronda Woods, told me in an interview (1998, September 10) that the Boldt decision appears to be "conservative when viewed in the context of contemporary legal decisions."

The Boldt decision represented a major achievement for Indians. It clarified and upheld Indian treaties and returned rights to Indians that they believed had been taken away by state laws favoring commercial and sports fishermen. In doing so, the decision gave new responsibilities to Indian fishermen. It also laid the groundwork for Indians gaining rights to other wildlife harvests, including gray whales (Anderson 1998, October 8, B10).

Economic Impact

In addition to the legal impact, the immediate economic effect was also negative. Barsh (1979) claimed that the decision changed income distribution, decreased the value of Puget Sound salmon, and failed to deal with industrial development problems that reduced the salmon run (76–79). However, twelve years later when Barsh (1991) looked at the effects of Boldt's decision, he observed a positive long-term impact from the decision. He explained that Native American fishing has expanded in terms of numbers of fishermen and aggregate harvests, and it has shifted from riparian to marine areas, "from relatively inexpensive gear to large vessels, and from a predominantly subsistence level to large-scale commercial objectives" (99).

By 1997, salmon and steelhead fish harvests had significantly decreased due to hydro power, irrigation operations, and industrial development. Despite an aggressive effort on the part of Washington Department of Fish and Wildlife to protect native fish, costing approximately $300 million, the number of anadromous fish continues to decline as does the amount of money for fish hatcheries (Williams 1997b, 7, 10).

At the same time the 1973 trial and the Boldt decision paved the way for additional rights and resources for Indian fishermen, it limited the access of sports and commercial fishermen and thereby changed the economic beneficiaries of the fishing industry. The trial and resulting judicial opinion were then and continue to be a source of controversy about fishing rights in the Northwest.

Chapter 10

Lamentation and Agitation at Wounded Knee, 1890 and 1973

The coming of the circle, according to Oglala religious leaders, refers to an understanding of the present time in terms of the past (Ortiz 1977, 183). Perhaps this is the reason why the public knows more about the cultural struggles of the Sioux people than any other group of Indians. The 1862 wars between the Santee Sioux and Minnesota settlers and the ensuing Mankato trials gained the attention of Congress and the president. Later, the stories of Indian captives and the powerful oratory of Chief Red Cloud created notoriety for the Teton Sioux.

The struggles of the Sioux loomed large on the public agenda for 150 years for several reasons. The Sioux, one of the most populous tribes of the Plains Indians, consisted of powerful warriors who repeatedly resisted government control. By voicing their opposition to the Treaty of Fort Laramie (1868) and insisting on the rights of the bands they represented, several traditional chiefs earned reputations as effective oratorical advocates. Moreover, Man Afraid of His Horse, Red Cloud, Sitting Bull, and Crazy Horse were legendary Indian warriors. Additionally, medicine man Black Elk shared Teton Sioux visions and religious beliefs with the public. AIM leaders Russell Means, Leonard Peltier, Leonard Crow Dog, Ellen Moves Camp, and Gladys Bissonette focused national attention on Sioux history during their trials in the mid-1970s. Widely circulated research by noted Oglala historian Vine Deloria Jr. also gave insight into Sioux history and law. Other information about Custer's last stand in 1876, the massacre of Wounded Knee in 1890, and the government standoff in 1973 appeared in numerous American history books. All of these factors combine to place the Sioux more in the historical spotlight than the other Indian groups discussed in this volume.

The goal of this chapter is to analyze the rhetoric during the cultural struggles between the Teton Sioux and the government, focusing first on the stories and lamentations about the Wounded Knee Massacre in 1890 and then on the agitation and control strategies used in the 1973 negotiations between Sioux leaders, AIM advocates, and the government. For each episode, the chapter traces the historical context and then identifies key rhetorical features to explain the impact of the events on the cultural identity of the Teton Sioux residing at the Pine Ridge Reservation.

CULTURAL OPPOSITION: 1868–1890

The struggles between minority groups and government colonizers constitute key sources of cultural history. Simon Ortiz (1977) emphasizes the value of history for all Indians. He concludes:

Indian people must value their history. Recognition of this oral history is the truest affirmation of the moral value of our lives. This history contains within it all the struggles that our people have gone through. Therefore, its continuance means the continuance of our current struggles and our lives. (14)

Ortiz's conclusions apply to the Teton Sioux and their struggles at Wounded Knee. Their oral histories about warriors, government deception, and Indian suffering offer clues about Sioux identity and the sources of cultural opposition. These histories emphasize the primacy of the Treaty of Fort Laramie of 1868 and the Sioux's view of themselves as a chosen people.

Primacy of Treaty of Fort Laramie

Intracultural and intercultural opposition between the Sioux and the government began before the Treaty of Fort Laramie. Chapter 5 explains the reluctance of Red Cloud to sign the treaty. But Red Cloud was not alone, he was part of what Catherine Price (1991) calls the "war faction" along with Man Afraid of His Horse, Iron Shell, and Red Leaf. These chiefs, representing 11,000 warriors, initially opposed the treaty, refused to accept gifts from the negotiators, and withdrew from the treaty negotiations. The war faction opposed the peace faction, consisting of the bands of Little Wound, Bad Wound, Pawnee Killer, Spotted Tail, Swift Bear, Man That Walks Under The Ground, and Standing Elk (60). After the government abandoned the Bozeman Trail, some of the war factions eventually signed the Fort Laramie Treaty even though they later claimed they did not understand what it meant.

The treaty had two major effects on the Teton Sioux's cultural identity. First, the treaty created intracultural tensions that divided the Sioux people into factions called pure bloods and mixed bloods or traditionalists and progressives. Second, the treaty provided 60 million acres to the Sioux that included the sacred Black Hills. Edward Lazarus (1991) emphasizes the Black Hills always held special meaning because this land contained fresh mountain water, lodge poles to build tepees, medicine plants for curing ceremonies, and holy places for vision quests. It was also the home of the Great Spirit, Wakan Takan. For this reason, the Black Hills "were sacred, powerful, and full of mystery" (7). The traditional Sioux demanded the Black Hills land area be retained, but the progressives agreed to relinquish part of it.

Irreconcilable Values

The treaties tried to reconcile incompatible differences between government and Indian values. At the root of the value conflict was the Sioux's belief in "their special creation," that is, "the Great Spirit had made the whites to farm and build cities and the Indians to hunt and live in harmony with the natural world" (Lazarus 1991, 52). To the Sioux, the Black Hills were a spiritual place; for the government, the Black Hills were a source of material wealth to be used for economic gain. Additionally, the treaties forced the Teton Sioux onto reservations and demanded they farm and convert to Christianity even though the traditional Sioux wanted to remain free and practice their traditional ceremonies of purification, vision quest, and the Sun Dance.

After the 1868 treaty placed the Black Hills under Sioux jurisdiction, the government continued making expeditions to investigate the gold and mineral deposits and plotted to get the Sioux to sell the land. As part of the government's plan to secure the Black Hills, Generals George Custer and George Crook moved their soldiers into Sioux country to force the Indians into designated reserves. They failed to round up the Indians and instead suffered a massive defeat in 1876 at the Battle of the Little Big Horn led by Crazy Horse and Sitting Bull. Ralph K. Andrist (1964) explains,

Thousands of Indians had left the agencies, determined to fight after having seen their protests against the rape of the Black Hills ignored. All had joined together, ready for any soldiers who might come, and certain they could whip them. (274)

Custer's loss was the biggest defeat ever suffered by American troops at the hands of the Indians, with an estimated 269 U.S. soldiers dead (Lazarus 1991, 94).

The defeat at Little Big Horn affirmed the Sioux's sense of themselves as a chosen people and increased their pride in warrior culture. The material ambitions of the government, however, continued to erode treaty promises. The increasing migration of settlers into the rich Black Hills country put

pressure on government leaders to obtain Sioux land for mining and development, resulting in the 1876 agreement which reduced the 60 million
acres allocated to the Sioux in the Treaty of Fort Laramie to 22 million
acres and gave control of the Black Hills to the government. A subsequent
agreement in 1889 further reduced the Sioux reservation to 12.6 million
acres (Hoover 1989, 58; Prucha 1994, 388). Furthermore the new agreements demanded the Sioux settle on designated reservations and fueled the
factionalism between Sioux leaders. Even though Red Cloud eventually
complied by settling at the Pine Ridge Agency, Sitting Bull and Crazy Horse
and their bands refused to recognize the agreements and for a time remained free.

Eventually the disappearance of the buffalo, the requirements of the
Sioux agreements, and the surrender of Sitting Bull and Crazy Horse resulted in the Teton Sioux settling on reservations, abandoning their lives
as warriors, accepting government annuities, attending Christian services,
and sending their children to school. By 1880, the government demanded
even further compliance with government-imposed white Christian values,
by forbidding the Sun Dance and altering the Indians' traditional diet,
clothing, and lodging (Utley 1974, 22). In one sense, the government succeeded in imposing its values on the Teton Sioux. But in another sense,
Gordon Macgregor (1970) notes, the dependence on the government was
"intolerable" for the Sioux. Many Indians responded by manipulating the
government services to maintain their culture; they gave public assent to
federal demands but continued their religious practices in private. By 1889,
many Sioux publicly participated in the Ghost Dance based on the predictions of Indian prophet Wovoka (Mooney [1896] 1974). The ecstatic ceremony accompanying the Ghost Dance created panic among government
officials who immediately ordered military troops to bring the Indians under their control. However, General L. W. Colby concluded that the Ghost
Dance was not the cause of the Wounded Knee Massacre, it was only a
symptom of the deep-seated differences in values between the Sioux and
the government (Mooney [1896] 1974, 180).

The Sioux eventually realized they had been duped into parting with the
Black Hills. From this time forward the Indians viewed themselves as victims of government deception. Sources describe the condition of the Sioux
in various ways: "confined and prisoners of war" (Nurge 1970), "subjects
of conquest" (Lazarus 1991), people "enslaved in concentration camps"
(*Voices* 1974), and victims of "a trail of broken treaties" (Deloria [1974]
1985). These potent labels show how the history of government-Teton
Sioux relations negated positive tribal identity and transformed their view
of themselves from being a chosen people to being an oppressed and victimized minority group. The Wounded Knee Massacre epitomized this oppression.

LAMENTATION AND STORIES OF THE WOUNDED KNEE MASSACRE

After they were disarmed and surrounded by military troops in 1890, more than 300 Teton Sioux, mostly from Big Foot's and Sitting Bull's bands, were killed en route to Wounded Knee. The story of the battle was told and retold many times. Eventually stories of the massacre became a tribal lamentation, featuring rhetorical repetitions of cultural mourning and suffering that reinforced the Teton Sioux's view of themselves as victims of government oppression.

The oral record of the massacre surfaced in several sources. Shortly after the massacre in 1891, army officials retold the story to vindicate themselves from charges they had massacred the Indians (*Annual Report of the Commissioner of Indian Affairs*, 1891; Hawthorne 1896, 185–87). In the early 1900s, Eli S. Ricker collected stories for a proposed book (Danker 1981). In hopes of gaining monetary reparations from the government, survivors told their stories to congressional hearings in 1938 and 1939 (McGregor 1940). Stories of the massacre, reconstituted by Indian leaders, lawyers, politicians, and relatives of victims and survivors, continue to be told as evidence for the travesties committed against the Sioux (*Voices* 1974; Lazarus 1991; Gonzales & Cook-Lynn 1999).

Stories of the massacre resemble other kinds of legal stories because they are social constructions that recall a sequence of events, express a distinct point of view based on the presuppositions of the storyteller, and provide graphic images about events that permit the audience to judge the facticity of the stories (Bennett & Feldman 1981; Fisher 1987; Delgado 1989; Schuetz 1994). Teton Sioux stories, however, have had a more lasting impact than most legal stories because they were told and retold as cultural lamentations that connected Sioux suffering to failed government polices and unkept promises.

Stories, then and now, constitute a persuasive rhetorical form. First, stories are social reconstructions. Elizabeth Loftus and Katherine Ketcham (1991) explain that people reconstruct stories from bits and pieces of information in memory. After selecting relevant fragments of information, storytellers then fill in the gaps to make sense out of their memories (22). Story reconstructions may add information from succeeding and subsequent events as well as from other people's versions of an event (20). Eyewitnesses recollected all the massacre events after the fact, reconstructing their different stories according to diverse perceptions and points of view.

Second, stories express a point of view based on the presuppositions of the storyteller. A storyteller's point of view accounts for unique perspectives about the events by revealing certain features relevant to a theme and hiding other less salient traits (McCall 1990, 147). The themes of the stories of people from oral cultures are told in "fixed thematic and formulary patterns" that repeat recognizable epithets or morals (Ong 1973, 34–36). In this case, the Indian victims constructed the theme of the massacre as a narrative about the government oppression of helpless people. In contrast, government storytellers claimed that Indian savagery and misbehavior caused the massacre. Stories told about the massacre came from victims, military men, and neutral parties with differing presumptions about whether the government or the Indians were responsible.

Finally, stories provide persuasive images about the event. Ong (1973) characterizes the images of oral cultures as polemic reflections of the struggle between the forces of good and evil. Some massacre stories depicted images of brutal warfare between Indians and soldiers, and others portrayed an unfortunate battle between military heroes and Indian aggressors. In contrast to the stories of government sympathizers, the imagery of the oral stories emphasizes motion and a "swirl of exciting activity," showing configurations of causal forces operating at the same time (37). In a similar way, Indian storytellers depict their struggle in a context of rapid unexplainable actions. Storytellers, however, do not state what meaning their audiences should attribute to the imagery and action, but instead they persuade using enthymemes, emotional imagery that serves as premises for conclusions that audiences draw. In this way, the audience and the storytellers together construct the themes and thereby create shared meanings for the stories (Schuetz 1994, 178–79).

This section of the chapter examines four postmassacre stories told from different points of view about the events at Wounded Knee in 1890. These stories evolved in ways similar to how rumors evolve in other social systems. Rumor occurs when people pass information from one individual to another without official validation or denial. When this happens, the storyteller *levels* the information by leaving out details during transmission, *sharpens* the information by exaggerating or expanding facts and events, and *assimilates* by contrasting and sometimes distorting the information so that it fits with the storyteller's beliefs (Bowers et al. 1993, 16–17). After providing an example of a massacre story, the chapter analyzes each short narrative according to its social reconstructions, points of view and theme, and imagery and action.

The first story comes from Turning Hawk, a government sympathizer working at the Pine Ridge Agency, who was not an eyewitness to the events (*Annual Report of the Commissioner of Indian Affairs* 1891). Turning Hawk reported the massacre in this way:

These people were coming toward the Pine Ridge Agency, and when they were almost on the agency, they were met by the soldiers and surrounded and taken to the Wounded Knee Creek, and there at a given time, their guns were demanded. When they had delivered them up, the men were separated from their families, from their tipis [*sic*], and taken to a certain spot. When the guns were thus taken, . . . a young man of very bad influence, and in fact, a nobody, among that bunch of Indians fired his gun, and of course the firing of a gun must have been the breaking of a military rule of sort, because immediately the soldiers returned fire and indiscriminate killing followed. (180)

The importance of the account is that it came from stenographic reports taken shortly after the massacre and therefore was less tainted by subsequent events than other narratives. Since Turning Hawk was not an eyewitness, he reconstructed his story from fragments of information he had heard from others, probably Captain George Sword and other friendly Indians with whom he worked at the Pine Ridge Agency. His story exemplified leveling since he left out many of the details of the battle known to eyewitnesses. The theme of his story was that the massacre occurred because of an unfortunate accident that got out of control because of a bad person. The story reflected a military point of view since Turning Hawk justified the shooting of the Indians because of "the breaking of some rule." However, he regretted the indiscriminate killing that followed. By characterizing the perpetrator as a "person of bad influence" and "a nobody," he diminished the responsibility of the Indians. Because the story lacked the vivid imagery and excited action typical of eyewitness accounts, audiences likely viewed the story as hearsay.

Another story comes from Indian survivor Dewey Beard. Through the interpretive pen of Ricker, Beard recollected events in this way:

There was a deaf Indian named Black Coyote who did not want to give up his gun; he did not understand what they were giving up their arms for. . . . While two or three sergeants came to the deaf man and were struggling with him for possession of the gun, Dewey heard something on the west side and looked that way and saw the Indians were all excited and afraid, their faces changed as if they were wild with fear; he saw that the guns of the soldiers were pointed at the council [of assembled Indians]. . . . The struggle for the gun was short, the muzzle pointed upward toward the east and the gun was discharged. In an instant a volley followed as one shot, and the people began falling. He saw everybody was rolling and kicking on the ground. (Danker 1981, 91–92)

In contrast to the story of Turning Hawk, Beard gave an eyewitness account many years after the massacre that sharpened events by adding details. Both stories concluded the massacre was an accident that turned into a tragedy. Beard's story added specific details not known to Turning Hawk. For example, the Indian with the gun was named "Black Coyote," he was not crazy but was deaf, and he would not relinquish his gun because he did not hear the instructions from the officers. Beard's story implied that the first shot was an accident because Black Coyote's deafness combined with the soldiers' aggressiveness forced the gun to go off. Typical of storytellers from oral culture, Beard's story contained imagery that conveyed the chaos of the situation. Once the shot went off, he said, chaos ensued and victims fell to the ground. An interesting feature of Beard's account was his use of passive tense to show the gunfire was unintentional and to hide the identity of the agents of the action; the "gun went off" and the "volleys followed." This account presented an Indian point of view similar to the one that has been repeated for decades by Teton Sioux.

Louie Mousseau, a mixed-blood who owned the trading post at Wounded Knee, gave a third story. When Ricker recorded his story in 1907, he identified Mousseau as the chairman of the progressive class of Indians who "doesn't do much work since the people are so disheartened." Mousseau remembered the event in this way:

Somebody went up to him [Wallace, a military man] and a couple of orderlies and an interpreter [were] with him. He opened the blanket of one who had a Winchester and the Indian turned it over to him. The second one did not have any gun that Louie saw. When he went to the third, the Indian would not give his up, but he brought it up to arm's port and Wallace had hold of it, and they swung it and fired one way and then the other; and when the muzzle was up, it was discharged. . . . After this gun was discharged, there was a pause of perhaps half a minute, maybe not so long, two more shots were fired and he saw Wallace [a soldier] fall. Then the Indians broke for the guns in the piles. Then the soldiers fired a sudden volley. (Danker 1981, 230)

Mousseau's version of events showed sharpening by his addition of new details about the action. His theme emphasized the deliberate, measured response of soldiers in contrast to the hasty, impulsive responses of the Indians. Mousseau's story took the point of view of the military when he named the officer (Wallace), emphasized the fairness of the situation because interpreters were present, and noted the correct procedural moves Wallace made when taking the weapons. In contrast to these deliberate military actions, Mousseau stressed that the Indian's resistance caused the gun to go off, a soldier to fall, and the rest of the Indians to retrieve the guns they had already relinquished. In Mousseau's story, the responsibility for the massacre rested with the Indians. Unlike the rest of the accounts, Mousseau identified a sequence of struggles and gunfire by Indians that left the military with no choice except to return fire. He provided no name, identity, or extenuating circumstances to absolve the Indians of guilt, but he did emphasize the soldiers seemed to be following military procedures for disarming aggressors. His story replicated the military position and tried to absolve them of guilt. His story resembled the one presented by the soldiers participating in the massacre who received Congressional Medals of Honor for killing the Indians (Dewing 1995, 11).

In hopes of receiving financial reparations for massacre victims, a fourth story was given in the 1930s by Mrs. Rough Feather as part of the testimony to a congressional hearing. This story appears in a work by James McGregor (1940). Rough Feather recalled the event in this way:

The next morning we were getting ready to break camp when the Indian men were ordered by the soldiers to come to the center of the camp and bring all their guns. After they did this, the soldiers came to where the Indian women were and searched the tents and the wagons for arms. They made us give up axes, crowbars, knives, awls, etc. About this time an awful noise was heard and I was paralyzed for a time. Then my head cleared and I saw nearly all the people on the ground bleeding. I could move some now, so I ran to a cutback and lay down there. I saw some of the other Indians running up the coulee so I ran with them, but the soldiers kept shooting at us and bullets flew all around us. (128)

Rough Feather observed the initial shot and perceived the event through her lens as a woman victim. She assimilated her story according to personal beliefs and memory. Rough Feather viewed the military as aggressors that forced the Indians to comply with their demands. The important point of her story was her personal suffering; she was struck by a bullet, recovered her senses enough to run for cover, and dodged subsequent bullets. By describing the scene as a mayhem resulting from unarmed victims fleeing indiscriminate military gunfire, Rough Feather established her theme that unarmed women were innocent victims of military aggression. Because her story corroborated many other Indian accounts, she added further evidence to support the claim that the military killed and injured innocent people.

Many others have reconstructed massacre stories. For example, influential white historian, Robert M. Utley (1974), purported to give the most authentic account of the massacre. His version merged several different points of view into a single story. For example, Utley claimed that Yellow Bird, dressed in a Ghost Dance costume was "gyrating" and "muttering incantations" and encouraging people to join in the dance. He said that Black Coyote was both the crazy and deaf man who waived his rifle and caused an officer to struggle with him. Utley's story implicated the Ghost Dance and an irrational Indian as the causes of the bullet going off, but he also incorporated other military points of view, stating that several other Indians fired their guns at soldiers forcing the military to return fire. Mirroring some of the victim's accounts, Utley concluded that soldiers then fired on women because they resisted military orders (210–15). Although Utley called the massacre "a regrettable tragic accident," his reconstruction supported the military story because he included the Indian accounts that fit with the government's version of the event.

Audiences reconstruct stories and make interpretive arguments by expressing new points of view, themes, and contexts. Stories persuade audiences to the extent that the assumptions of the storyteller fit with those of the audience. For example, Gonzales and Cook-Lynn (1999), proponents of the Indian viewpoint, fault Utley's implication of the Ghost Dance "as a rationale for the atrocity against families at Wounded Knee." They claim Utley's promilitary view reaffirms government values and actions (95). Other historians preferred the version passed down orally among the Indians. For example, British historian Alistair Cook interpreted the event in this way:

In the autumn of 1890 near the reservation town of Pine Ridge, South Dakota, the Seventh Cavalry, the same regiment chopped up at the Little Bighorn, mustered for kill. . . . Without a parley or any attempt to establish that this horde was a band of warriors, the Seventh annihilated them, and the next day they dug the bodies from the snow and buried them in a common grave. The wretched episode was known to the white man, and still is, as the "battle" of Wounded Knee. (Quoted in Gonzales & Cook-Lynn 1999, 242)

Cook concluded the Indians were victims of ruthless government aggression.

During the standoff, participants turned the Indian laments about the massacre into justifications for their militant activism. After one exchange of gunfire at the standoff, for example, a U.S. marshal told a church representative that one night "he kept hearing cries and screams and he thought the Indians were approaching his bunker. He shot at them and shot at them but they kept coming. They finally disappeared." Indians informed the church leader that the marshal's vision came from the spirits of victims of the Wounded Knee Massacre (*Voices* 1974, 188). During the standoff, the massacre gravesite, located close to bunkers of the dissidents, served as a potent religious and political symbol for the suffering that the Oglala historically had experienced at the hands of the government. The massacre is now and was then seen as an important source of the cultural identity of the Teton Sioux.

CULTURAL OPPOSITION FROM 1890 TO 1973

Contemporary Sioux identity depends on cultural history. Robert E. Daniels (1970) explains that

the Oglalas see their significance in American life from the point of view of history. They simplify and condense the key events—the Battle of the Little Big Horn, the treaties, and the Wounded Knee Massacre—and then use the past to explain current social divisions and government grievances. (233)

Historical events subsequent to the massacre contributed even further to the Oglalas' cultural identity. The massacre helped to explain long-standing struggles between tribal members and their leaders as well as animosity

between the government and the Indians. Some of the other historical grievances that the agitators used to justify the 1973 standoff at Wounded Knee
were the government's refusal to pay reparations to the massacre victims,
the failure of the allotment and reorganization programs, the negative consequences of the relocation of Indians to urban areas, and the suppression
of Indian activism and the AIM movement.

Unpaid Reparations

As early as 1893, some victims of the massacre asked for reparations
from the federal government of more than $200,000 based on the Sioux
Depredation Act of 1891 (26 Stat. 1002). After investigating the claims,
however, Special Agent James A. Cooper decided that nearly $111,000 was
due 744 claimants. Cooper made those payments, but Gonzales and Cook-
Lynn (1999) conclude, the claims were parceled out to friendly Indians,
churches, and white people, and no reparations were paid to survivors of
Chief Big Foot's band. Big Foot's survivors filed for reparations from the
government in 1938 and 1939, but again the government appropriated no
money to pay their claims.

It is not surprising that the massacre became a common lamentation of
the dissidents in the standoff. As a rhetorical strategy, lamentation repeats
stories about suffering and cultural mourning to affirm the tribal identity
of victims of government oppression. After the government failed to respond appropriately to the lamentation, the response continued to be repeated. For the Sioux, the lament was both a political and a religious
response because the massacre broke the circle of trust between them and
the government. For this reason, the Sioux invoked the lamentation over
and over again at the standoff and continued to do so in other resistance
against government policies. For example, Leola Hall, an Oglala, said in
1983, "The United States of America was built on the murder and genocide
of our people, and, unless people know that, believe it and act on it, our
lives will continue to be pitiful" (Quoted in Gonzales & Cook-Lynn 1999,
187). Since the government has failed to make a direct apology, pay reparations, or admit wrongdoing, the Teton Sioux continue to express their
lament about the massacre and argue that their identity has been perma-
nently scarred by an unjust government who has refused to acknowledge
its mistakes.

Allotment and Reorganization

Teton Sioux cultural identity further fractured when government programs depleted their land base, deprived them of traditional forms of
government, and forced them to act like their oppressors. The goal of
government programs was to assimilate the Teton Sioux; instead, these

programs forced the Indians into impossible double cultural binds that demanded compliance with policies that destroyed traditional culture. Double binds refer to conditions that place the Indians in an untenable position. If, on the one hand, the Teton Sioux agreed to assimilate, then they admitted their culture was inferior. If, on the other hand, they refused to assimilate, they lost the physical, psychological, and economic benefits that would permit them to retain traditional culture. These untenable situations produced both intracultural factionalism and cultural despair.

The double-bind inducing programs began with the Dawes Act (General Allotment Act) (1887), a law that permitted tribal members to own 160 acres of land or to sell or lease their land to others. At the time the act passed, American Indians held 138 million acres. However, by 1934 they had lost 60 million acres through allotment to white owners (Burnette & Koster 1974, 112). At the same time allotment diminished Indian land ownership, the BIA refused to recognize traditional chiefs and political systems, forced Indians to attend school often at long distances from their reservation, and demanded they change their appearance, give up their language, and practice the Christian religion. Instead of producing assimilation, these programs increased dependence on government annuities and initiated resistance from traditional Indians.

In an effort to correct the abuses of allotment, the government placed the Sioux and other tribes under the Indian Reorganization Act (1934). From the government's point of view, this program corrected the problems created by allotment by conserving land resources, giving Indians opportunities to form businesses, promoting home rule, providing industrial education, and restoring surplus lands to the tribe. Instead the act increased factionalism for Indians at the Pine Ridge Agency because the traditionalists viewed self-government as an erosion of treaty rights while progressives saw it as an opportunity to strengthen their allegiances to the government (Dewing 1995, 14–15).

Initiatives for self government fostered more cultural double binds and reopened old historical wounds. Roxanne Dunbar Ortiz (1977) explains:

[T]he American government imposed on the Sioux reservations a uniform governmental system, modeled not on traditional forms which would have been familiar to the Indians, but on the white man's own government—a system of tribal councils, headed by executive officials who were members of the tribes. . . . Since the Bureau of Indian Affairs gave up none of the important functions on the reservations—including that of veto power over all financial matters—the Indian tribal council governments were purely accommodating rubber stamps for white bosses. (26–27)

The early fears of the traditional Oglalas about reorganization proved accurate when the progressives, who dominated Pine Ridge administration before, during, and after Wounded Knee, took jobs and power away from the traditional Indians.

Eventually the traditionalists found themselves between another rock and a hard place. If they abandoned their traditional culture and sided with the progressives, they gained access to the power and economic resources needed to rule the tribe. If they retained traditional values, however, the tribal government would marginalize them and trivialize their way of life. These unresolved cultural grievances led to more cultural double binds that increased contempt and factionalism at Pine Ridge. By 1973, the intracultural infighting led to the impeachment trial of Dick Wilson and eventually to the standoff.

Urban Relocation

Other attempts by the government to assimilate the Teton Sioux justified further lamentation about government oppression and created even more cultural double binds. In the 1950s, the BIA urged 35,000 Indians to leave the reservations, relocate in cities, and raise their families in Metropolitan areas. As a result, many Indians moved to Denver, Phoenix, Los Angeles, Albuquerque, San Francisco, Dallas, Cleveland, and Chicago. Gordon Macgregor (1970) explained the problem in this way. On the one hand, the Sioux wanted to better themselves by receiving better salaries and finding more challenging jobs in urban settings; but, on the other hand, they desperately wanted to work on reservations where they could live between tribal kin and attend traditional ceremonies (92–106). Some tried without success to resolve this double bind by moving back and forth.

To encourage migration to urban areas, the government subsidized transportation, shipped household goods, and offered financial subsistence for families. But federal programs did not meet the simultaneous needs of many Indians who wanted both economic and cultural security. For example, many left the South Dakota reservations between 1952 and 1959, but many returned by the 1970s. As part of this migration, 4,000 Sioux moved to Rapid City, South Dakota, and separated into groups called "camp, transition, and middle-class Indians." "Camp" Indians just recreated a new kind of reservation in the city and provided an urban haven for reservation relatives. Rapid City leaders created a separate addition so the "camp" atmosphere would not adversely affect other city residents (White 1970, 182–83). Similar Indian communities sprang up in Denver, Minneapolis, and Los Angeles. But instead of creating more despair, some of these urban Indian settlements became centers for Indian activism in the 1970s.

Indian Activism

Several excellent studies (Deloria [1974] 1985; Churchill & Vander Wall 1990; Matthiessen [1980] 1991; Dewing 1995; Smith & Warrior 1996) chronicle the events that led to the activism at Wounded Knee in 1973. This section of the chapter describes the formation of AIM, the Indian activists' occupation of Alcatraz and the Bureau of Indian Affairs, and the local precipitating events prior to the standoff. For the Teton Sioux, Indian activism gave them hope for changing the conditions at the Pine Ridge Reservation.

Dennis Banks, George Mitchell, and Clyde Bellecourt organized the American Indian Movement (AIM) in Minneapolis in 1968. One of their early goals was to document incidences of police abuse of Indians in the Twin Cities. On the surface, AIM resembled other 1970s civil rights groups since its purpose was to create public awareness about ineffective government policies and to agitate the establishment for change. Additionally, AIM's rhetoric included phrases that mirrored the black movement: a rallying cry was "red power"; AIM labeled government sympathizers as "apples," red on the outside and white on the inside; and the organization referred to assimilated Indians as "Uncle Tomahawks" (Dewing 1995, 17). But beneath the surface AIM was distinctly Indian, expressing its resistance to "genocidal" government programs, calling attention to Indian sovereignty, and demanding the ouster of ineffective tribal leaders and their BIA supervisors (Lazarus 1991, 298).

AIM developed a reputation for militancy when 78 people took over Alcatraz in 1969 for nineteen months. The militant rhetoric of the occupiers concentrated on the need for the government to meet treaty obligations, the evil effects of relocation, and the inconsistencies in federal Indian policy. The militant rhetoric of dissidents featured potent emotional analogies comparing the government aggression against Indians to the ill-conceived intervention in Vietnam, demanded programs to propagate Indian identity, and claimed title to government property (Smith & Warrior 1996, 111).

The Trail of Broken Treaties in 1972 further empowered Indian activists to attract public attention to their grievances against the government. In its planning stage, Indian activists decided to present political petitions to the government and engage in nonviolent protest. But activists ended up participating in a spontaneous and destructive takeover of the headquarters of the Bureau of Indian Affairs in Washington, D.C. The event commenced in Seattle and San Francisco and proceeded to Minnesota where various caravans that had picked up Indians along the way gathered for a strategy meeting. At the time, dissidents drew up a twenty-point proposal they planned to deliver to the president. Eventually more than 2,000 Indians made their way to Washington, D.C. The activists' intention to engage in nonviolent protest changed after they arrived in the city and found their lodging inadequate and their plans for civil disobedience compromised by government regulations. At the instigation of Russell Means, the Indians demanded entry into the auditorium of the Bureau of Indian Affairs (BIA) building. After arming themselves with clubs and spears and painting themselves for battle, the dissidents took over the BIA offices (Churchill & Vander Wall 1988, 125). The takeover turned ugly when the activists trashed BIA offices and confiscated agency records. Despite this fact, Indian negotiators finally got an agreement from White House representatives to review their proposal for solving tribal grievances. To avoid any further disruptions, the government eventually paid the expenses for the Indians to return to their homes. The takeover cost the government $2.2 million, earned the Indian activists the reputation of "revolutionary hooligans," and attracted the FBI's attention to AIM's militancy (Smith & Warrior 1996, 167).

Although AIM participated in the takeovers of Alcatraz and the BIA, their leaders gained productive administrative experience by working in areas designated as "urban opportunity zones." For example, AIM flourished in Denver, Cleveland, and Minneapolis because of leaders' awareness of civil rights, their consciousness of tribal identity, the availability of government funds for their work, and their reputation for getting things done (Means 1995, 136–48).

The activist reputation of AIM fit the needs of Pine Ridge residents who were experiencing the ill effects of eighty years of ineffective government programs. At the time of the standoff, Pine Ridge residents suffered from poor health, 50 percent unemployment, high suicide rates, and the lowest per capita income in the nation (Dewing 1995, 38). In addition to poor living conditions, Dick Wilson, an unpopular mixed-blood tribal chair, had created his own tribal police force, called the "goons," to enforce police repression against traditional Indians. Wilson's heavy-handed leadership resulted in his acceptance of a number of murders, beatings, and rapes at the hands of his tribal police.

AIM leaders came to the Pine Ridge Reservation at the invitation of dissatisfied traditional Oglalas. When local police in Gordon, Nebraska, released five drunken white men who had killed Sioux cowboy Yellow Thunder, Dennis Banks and Russell Means organized more than 1,000 Pine Ridge residents to protest the police action. Shortly after the protest, some of these same residents approached AIM leaders to assist them with the impeachment of tribal chair Dick Wilson. Fearing trouble at Pine Ridge during the impeachment, President Richard Nixon sent 65 armed marshals to protect the BIA and Wilson from anticipated tribal violence. After the impeachment failed, 250 AIM members came to the village of Wounded Knee to protest. The standoff took place when the government forces failed to stop the residents, Indian "warriors," and AIM sympathizers from taking over the village of Wounded Knee. Instead of continuing their lamentations about oppression, the traditionalists at Pine Ridge mobilized forces to confront the government about their grievances.

AGITATION AND CONTROL AT WOUNDED KNEE

Research about the 1973 standoff analyzes the events from several different perspectives. For example, Smith and Warrior (1996) describe the standoff as part of a historical movement, Churchill and Vander Wall (1988) as a war caused by the FBI, Lazarus (1991) as part of an ongoing legal dispute over treaty land, Mary Crow Dog (1990) as an identity-changing experience, and Dewing (1995) as a regrettable historical event. Surprisingly, no substantive rhetorical studies exist even though the events constitute one of the most important Indian civil rights actions of the last century. This segment of the chapter analyzes the Wounded Knee standoff in several stages by identifying the American Indian Movement's (AIM's) agitation strategies in juxtaposition with the control strategies of the government. John W. Bowers et al. (1993) explain agitation as persuasion "characterized by highly emotional argument," presentation of grievances, and definitions of "violations of moral principles." Agitators are people from outside the system "who advocate social change" and "encounter resistance" from the establishment who controls the power in a given situation (3–4). In contrast, the establishment "exerts control" by virtue of its "wealth, power, status" and its ability to manipulate information. Because of its superior position in the social system, the establishment can define issues, infiltrate protest groups, and force agitators to fight among themselves (9–10).

Explanations of Indian agitation as a response to establishment control are complicated because so many advocates took part. The advocates included Oglala Russell Means and Chippewa Dennis Banks, primary AIM spokespersons; Carter Camp and Stan Holder, Indian Vietnam veterans from Oklahoma who set up the military operations; Leonard Crow Dog and Wallace Black Elk, Oglala medicine men who gave spiritual counsel; and traditional Oglala women, Ellen Moves Camp and Gladys Bissonette. John Adams from the National Council of Churches and some traditional chiefs, especially Fools Crow, helped broker the final agreement with the government. The government exercised its control through FBI agents, James Trimbach and Roy Moore; Justice Department officials, Ralph Erickson, Richard Hellstern, Kent Frizzell, and Harlington Wood; Marvin Franklin, assistant secretary for Indian affairs; and South Dakota Senator James Abourezk rendered significant input into some of the negotiations. A third faction, represented by tribal council president Dick Wilson and his goons, provoked violence against residents. Wilson, in one sense, was an advocate for the establishment since the Bureau of Indian Affairs supported his leadership and agreed that some traditional Oglalas were the enemy. In another sense, Wilson and his police represented a despised third party, who interfered both with the agitators and the establishment. The names listed here represent only a small group of the dozens of people on all sides of the conflict who participated in the long standoff at Wounded Knee on the Pine Ridge Reservation.

The rhetoric of the standoff, what Russell Means (1995) calls a "siege" (257–73), features some strategies typical of agitation and control (Bowers 1993 et al. 1993) as well as other unique methods of dissent. Four distinct rhetorical phases emerged, including intimidation, polarization, stalled negotiations, and abdication.

Intimidation

Between February 14 and March 5, a process of mutual intimidation took place at Wounded Knee. Intimidation refers to the ways that the advocates use threats and promises to inhibit each other's actions. Threats stipulate negotiators' preferences for action and impose sanctions for others not adhering to the conditions of the threat. Ultimatums are statements of either-or alternatives; they imply coercion or some other militant resistance if parties do not adhere to the requested alternative. Promises are expressions of mutual hope and reward that invite cooperation and concession-making between negotiators. Typically, intimidation consists of mutual threats and ultimatums between negotiators. Additionally intimidation creates "insurgent arguments" that permit agitators to define the establishment as "corrupt, mendacious, and exploitative" and to demand the establishment's accountability for the problems it has caused (Stewart et al. 1994, 228). The Wounded Knee agitators focused their insurgent arguments on the Pine Ridge council chair Dick Wilson and Superintendent Stanley Lynam, demanding that both men be dethroned from power and removed from the reservation.

The intimidation phase began with both sides defining their grievances. Gladys Bissonette identified the impeachment of Wilson as a necessary action for changing the unjust tribal government. She explained:

There was three council members who were impeaching him, for misuse of Tribal funds, and . . . [for] so many Tribal laws that he's broken. These three council members knew that he wasn't acting on behalf of his people, which he was supposed to have done. . . . Because he was for Dick and his family and his goons and his friends, he wasn't for the Oglala Sioux Tribe. . . . He didn't keep any books and didn't hold the tribal sessions like he was supposed to. (*Voices* 1974, 26)

For her, Wilson's acquittal of impeachment charges was a travesty of justice.

In contrast to the village residents, Superintendent Stanley Lynam viewed the impeachment as just another event in the cultural struggle:

The tribal council was a split between those of mixed-blood Sioux ancestry and those who were full-bloods. The full-bloods felt that those of mixed ancestry were too close to the white establishment and that basic Sioux interests and culture were compromised. (Lynam 1991)

For him, the impeachment was an illegitimate attempt of radical Indians to get rid of an effective tribal leader. These contrasting statements of grievances show the polarized positions of the factions in the conflict.

A second feature of the intimidation was the mobilization of forces to support the different factions. Mobilization refers to the persuasive effort of agitators to get others "to join together to bring about or to resist change." Those desiring change must gain support from legitimizers who are committed to the goals of the dissidents (Stewart et al. 1994, 60). Because the BIA expected trouble at Wilson's impeachment hearings on February 14, before the AIM activists arrived, they mobilized government resistance from seventy-five U.S. marshals, units called the Special Operations Group (SOG), and from FBI agents from Pierre, South Dakota (Smith & Warrior 1996, 192). After the impeachment proceedings failed, traditional Oglalas requested help from AIM even though Wilson had banned this group from the reservation.

Shortly after, fifty-five cars occupied by AIM leaders entered Wounded Knee, looted public buildings, and took over the homes of white merchants and church leaders and called them "hostages" (*Voices* 1974, 31). In response to the takeover, Wilson's goons, together with some progressive tribal members and fearful ranchers, gathered their arms and ammunition together, set up roadblocks, and lit grass fires to try to force the agitators to surrender. Afterwards government forces, Wilson sympathizers, and traditional Oglalas together with AIM members settled in for a long rhetorical and physical confrontation.

The standoff began with petitions, that is, the agitators identified unresolved grievances and asked the government to respond to their proposals for addressing these problems. Petitions are the typical strategy that agitators use to make demands (Bowers et al. 1993, 20). Specifically, the Indian agitators demanded that (1) the Senate Foreign Relations Committee conduct hearings on treaties made with Oglalas, (2) the White House investigate the Bureau of Indian Affairs and the Department of Interior, and (3) the government examine the work of its agents on all Sioux reservations in South Dakota. Furthermore, the agitators agreed to negotiate only with a few top level government leaders. The agitators delivered this ultimatum using these words: "[T]he only two options open to the United States of America are: They wipe out the old people, women, children, and men, by shooting and attacking us," or they negotiate our demands (*Voices* 1974, 50–51).

The intimidation created by the agitators' threats, ultimatums, petitions, and mobilization created a series of militant confrontational strategies. Charles J. Stewart et al. (1994) explain that militant confrontational strategies include verbal violence, destruction of property, and aggressive actions that "provoke the establishment into overreaction and violent suppressions" (139). In the standoff, the government and the agitators reacted as predicted. First, Trimbach created roadblocks and threatened to arrest anyone who was not a tourist (*Voices* 1974, 34). In turn the government establishment tried to maintain power by threatening to harm the agitators. When Trimbach approached Indian leaders for information about the hostages, Russell Means gave him a list of hostages. Then Means followed this good faith gesture by issuing another threat based on lamentations about the massacre. Means asserted that "many Indians were massacred at Wounded Knee years ago" and if the government came after him, "many others would die" (*Voices* 1974, 36). In an effort to legitimize his power, Trimbach made good on one of the Indian demands on March 1 when he brought Senators James Abourezk and George McGovern along with other senate staff to Wounded Knee to resolve the hostage situation. At the meeting, McGovern supported the establishment rhetoric, stating that "I deplore the tactics that have been used by AIM, tactics of violence," used to "disrupt orderly procedure. We can't tolerate that" (*Voices* 1974, 39). However, AIM got unexpected support when one of the so-called hostages said, "These Indians are here and they have legitimate grievances. You people—it's all your fault" (Means 1995, 267). This new found hostage ally forced the establishment to rethink their strategy. In this phase, the agitators achieved a desired effect because a hostage agreed that the government, not the agitators, were the aggressors in the standoff.

Polarization

The polarization phase occurred between March 5 and 11. Bowers et al. (1993) describe polarization as forcing "choices between the agitators and the establishment," clarifying contested issues, naming individuals worthy of attack, and using derogatory language to characterize adversaries (35–36). Instead of being just one phase of the conflict, some polarization strategies continued during the standoff. During this period, both sides established their incompatible positions by making ominous prophecies about the outcome of the standoff, using violence to back up their threats, and soliciting support from sympathizers. Additionally, when the agitators asserted their independence from the establishment by forming the Independent Oglala Nation, called ION, this action had two rhetorical effects. First, it gained symbolic power by asserting that the agitators were a nation of equal importance to the United States. Second, this act reinforced group cohesiveness by enabling the agitators to assert their independence from AIM.

The prophecies of death and doom came from both sides. For example, Dick Wilson told the media that "AIM will die at Wounded Knee." He further asserted that "I will not be responsible for holding my people back, if necessary, I will join them with my guns" (*Voices* 1974, 46). Oglala medicine man Leonard Crow Dog noted, "We're not going to massacre the white man, we're going to massacre his attitude and his government" (*Voices* 1974, 48). Russell Means reiterated the agitators' position: "We came here and bet our lives that there would be historic change for our Nation. The Government can massacre us, or it can meet our basic human demands. Either way, there will be historic change" (*Voices* 1974, 51).

Both sides validated their prophecies of doom using violence to emphasize their commitment to militant confrontation. Through their confrontations, the agitators "goaded the establishment" into more violence (Bowers et al. 1993, 44). Reverend John Adams, a Methodist clergyman representing the National Council of Churches, noted that both sides accused the other of firing first and therefore both continued pressing the other side for more extreme concessions. Adams eventually succeeded in getting a cease fire, but he was afraid of a war between the factions. Adams recalled, "It was a serious matter. And there were lives at stake. And if people thought that those who said they were ready to die were just playing, they were wrong. They were ready at that point . . . to let their deaths be as strategic as possible" (*Voices* 1974, 53). Clearly the government had the gun power advantage, spending more that $5 million on ammunition in contrast to the Indians, who had shotguns, hunting rifles, knives, and a few pistols (Means 1995, 270). During the standoff, however, Indians underestimated the firepower of the establishment, and the establishment overestimated the weapons and ammunition of the Indians resulting in the continuance of the standoff.

Both the agitators and the establishment accepted symbolic support from their allies in order to strengthen their bargaining position and show their resolve to continue the conflict (Stewart et al. 1994, 79). The government, working in consort with Wilson and his tribal police, got support from local cattlemen whose livestock AIM had stolen and butchered. The cattlemen responded by setting fire to the Wounded Knee trading post and shooting at AIM bunkers (*Voices* 1974, 54). AIM gained support from black civil rights leaders, prominent leftist attorneys, soldiers and citizens opposing Vietnam, and movie stars (Means 1995, 269). For both sides the involvement of outsiders added legitimacy and attracted verbal, social, and economic support.

During this polarization phase the agitators gained strategic advantage over the establishment by declaring they were an Independent Oglala Nation (ION) and a group equal in power and status to the establishment law givers and rule makers. This symbolic transformation of the power structure proved an effective rhetorical move. Although without legal standing, the declaration solidified the agitators in opposing the goals of the establishment and created a new collective name for the agitators. Rex Weyler (1984) describes the declaration in this way:

[In] a ceremony led by Chief Fools Crow, the community declared itself sovereign, [proclaiming an Independent Oglala Nation (ION)] and assigning a delegation to the United Nations. One hundred and eighty-two Oglala-Lakota people became citizens of the Independent Oglala Nation; in addition, 160 Indians of other tribes in the United States and Canada became dual citizens of both their home nation and the Oglala. . . . The Independent Oglala Nation requested other Indian nations to send delegations to Wounded Knee, and they established working committees on housing, medical care, food supplies, customs and immigration, internal security, information, and defense; daily spiritual ceremonies were [scheduled] as well as council meetings. (83)

This declaration outraged the establishment, who claimed ION was just a group run by media-hungry outsiders, not traditional Oglalas. This rhetorical declaration, however, showed the solidarity among Indian people and symbolized the agitators' strength. In one way this declaration gave voice and power to traditional values at the same time it allowed ION to act out the sovereign role it demanded in negotiations. An example of this symbolic enactment of power occurred when Russell Means, acting as a police agent of the new nation, held postal inspectors at gun point as ION prisoners when they came to the Wounded Knee Museum. This coercive action evidently demonstrated ION's power since afterward the government immediately reinstated blockades and reinforced its positions (Smith & Warrior 1996, 218–19).

Stalled Negotiations

The negotiation phase lasted from March 12 to March 30. The word negotiation may be misleading since the term means that parties agree to rules and procedures for exchanging proposals and making concessions in order to reach an agreement (Folger et al. 1993, 8). In the standoff, the communications between the agitators and the establishment did not proceed according to predetermined rules and procedures. Instead the most prevalent form of communication consisted of a series of rhetorical actions and military reactions. When parties finally gathered to talk with one another, the exchanges resumed the demands and threats that characterized the polarization phase. Stalemates occurred because of incompatible goals; the agitators demanded attention to historical grievances, and the establishment responded with denial of the agitators' demands. The establishment tactic did not succeed because the agitators considered this denial just another government method for oppressing them (Bowers et al. 1993, 57).

Often the negotiations consisted of mutual harassment. The agitators asserted their power by verbally maligning the government and Wilson. The government responded by defining themselves as a neutral third party wanting justice; but, at the same time, they initiated new prohibitions, set up roadblocks to prohibit food and supplies from coming into the area, and shot at Indian sympathizers trying to enter Wounded Knee.

Separate negotiations occurred on March 13 and 17 and again from April 1 through 5. The March 13 to 17 negotiations occurred between ION leaders and Marshal Colburn and Assistant Attorney General Wood. At this meeting, the agitators expanded their demands; they wanted food and medical supplies for the people at Wounded Knee, a meeting with the Department of Interior, reduction of excessive bail for Indian defendants, and the removal of tribal chairman Wilson (Dewing 1995, 87). Government negotiators ignored ION's specific demands and instead offered to investigate violations of the rights of traditional Oglalas living on the reservation. An excerpt from the negotiations shows the contentious tone of the interaction.

Ramon Roubideaux, ION attorney: Why does the Government always get into the position of protecting a corrupt dictator like Wilson? . . .

Colburn: We have tried very hard to remain neutral. We were asked in here because the law enforcement in this agency was inadequate to cope with their problems. Mr. Wood has outlined a program that I think is very fair, and with his career on the line, I might add.

Dennis Banks: I realize his career is on the line. My life is on the line.

Colburn: We must defuse this situation. We must bring in civil rights, bring in the HEW [Heath, Education, and Welfare] people. Let's saturate this area and see if we can come up with a viable plan that will satisfy everybody. . . .

Roubideaux: We want these petitions acted upon, and an election called. . . .

Wood: Well, I think we can expose that—

Roubideaux: Well, you better expose that now, or you're going to have Wounded Knees all over the country. You better understand that. (*Voices* 1974, 113)

Following the stalemate, both sides started to make concessions by incorporating some of the "personnel of the agitative movement" and acknowledging part of their ideology. Such a strategy can be risky unless the establishment selects personnel willing to make concessions and accept ideology that does not threaten their power base (Bowers et al. 1993, 63).

The initial government attempt at concessions stalled. Assistant Secretary of Indian Affairs Franklin made what he called a final government offer; he promised to arrange a meeting with a civil rights representative if the agitators would give up their weapons and submit to arrest. He also offered to protect Wounded Knee residents by having federal marshals remain on the reservation after the Indians disarmed. This deal offended ION leaders who wanted the government to disarm and expected ION leaders to receive amnesty.

Although the government thought they had gained concessions, forces outside the negotiation again escalated the conflict. For example Superintendent Lynam immediately approved Wilson's request to evict all non-Oglalas and National Council of Churches' representatives from Wounded Knee, tightened media access, and prohibited outsiders from bringing in food and supplies (Dewing 1995, 88; *Voices* 1974, 123–24). Acting out of frustration over the erratic actions of Wilson and the BIA, government negotiators lashed out at the agitators. Interior Secretary Rogers Morton, for example, characterized the agitators' demands as blackmail, saying, "You cannot run this Government or find equitable solutions with a gun at your head. . . . These are criminal operations and should be dealt with accordingly" (*Voices* 1974, 114).

To bolster its militant rhetoric, the government issued verbal threats and engaged in aggressive warfare. Smith and Warrior (1996) report that the result was "one of the heaviest fire fights to date." They noted that "[t]racer bullets lit up the sky. Warriors answered with hunting rifles." They compared the battle to the use of Hotchkiss guns by the Seventh Cavalry that killed and wounded Indians at the Wounded Knee Massacre in 1890 (225). These coercive tactics had the effect predicted by Stewart et al. (1994, 155). Government intimidation strategies created fear among the agitators and forced them to comply with establishment demands. The coercion backfired when Wilson and his goons again got involved; they called the agitators "agents of the Communist Party" and then set up more roadblocks to prohibit the agitators from getting needed food and medical supplies. Both coercive strategies prolonged the conflict. In fact, Trimbach threatened even more severe measures, claiming he would gas the agitators if necessary (Dewing 1995, 98).

Abdication

By the beginning of April, the agitators' depleted resources made the continuation of the standoff unlikely. At this time, agitators were hampered by a lack of food, limited ammunition, and physical fatigue from their long periods of isolation. When the situation became almost unbearable, Senator James Abourezk initiated new negotiations that marked the beginning of the end of the standoff. Abdication means the act of relinquishing position or giving up control. For the agitators their road to abdication began with negotiations on March 31 and ended with treaty meetings at Kyle, South Dakota, on May 17 and congressional hearings in mid-June. Just as in previous stalled negotiations, when the meetings began, neither side agreed on rules and procedures ahead of time.

Two factors, however, seemed to push the settlement to completion. First, a change in negotiators added enthusiasm and commitment to the process. The new personnel negotiating on behalf of the agitators included defense lawyers, Oglala citizens, and traditional chiefs aided by AIM activists. To energize the establishment, Frizzell and Hellstern solicited assistance from the Community Relations Service and the Justice Department. Despite some hopeful signs, negotiations moved slowly because the agitators reasserted old grievances and the government made new demands. Second, the Sioux religious leaders continued to bring agitators together through prayer, ceremonies, and even a reenactment of the Ghost Dance. These traditional rituals reinforced cultural identity and transformed some of the agitators' anger and fear into spiritual petitions and cultural commitments (*Voices* 1974, 146–47, 164, 182).

Between March 31 and April 5, the agitators made a series of demands, including a thirty-day moratorium on arrests of Oglalas, government actions to prevent Wilson's attacks on tribal residents, investigations of the tribal council, hearings on the 1868 treaty, guarantees that legal proceedings against agitators would be held outside of North and South Dakota, and resumption of deliveries of medical services and supplies (*Voices* 1974, 34–58). In return, the government agreed to bring agitators' demands to the attention of the executive branch.

Because agitators distrusted the government representatives, they demanded that some of the ION leaders be allowed to deliver Indian proposals to the White House before they would agree to disarm themselves. Emphasizing this distrust, ION leader Carter Camp said, "If Russ [Means] and Chiefs Bad Cob and Crow Dog go to Washington, D.C., and we have communication from them that things were proceeding at pace, then we would get together . . . and begin a complete and detailed system of standing down all the arms here" (*Voices* 1974, 143). Even though the government responded by accusing the agitators of reasoning in bad faith, they eventually agreed to listen to ION's demands. This first fragile agreement culminated in a pipe smoking ceremony between government and Indian negotiators (*Voices* 1974, 146–47).

By April 7, however, the agreement already had collapsed because the agitators understood that the agreement stipulated simultaneous disarmament, but the establishment said it meant unilateral disarmament of agitators. ION leader Stan Holder argued that "when my people are disarmed in Wounded Knee, I feel that a simultaneous disarming of your people [is required]. Colburn objected, "Now wait a minute! You don't want that to happen" (*Voices* 1974, 150). When this verbal bickering ended, Clyde Bellecourt again evoked the memory of the massacre as the justification for the Oglala refusing to accept unilateral disarmament. He reasoned, "The people are pretty uptight about the fact that there would be marshals coming in with handguns and they would be totally unarmed. And they still envision what happened to Big Foot and his band in 1890, and they totally distrust the United States government at this point" (*Voices* 1974, 151). It appears that the image of the massacre helped convince the Indians to reject the proposal.

Hopes for a settlement faded between April 10 and 17 when the cease fire ended and federal forces again attacked agitators. The April 10 gunfire continued after three airplanes dropped food for the agitators. The ability of Bill Zimmerman (1976) and other pilots to penetrate government surveillance angered the marshals and FBI so much they returned volleys of gunfire, killing AIM sympathizer Frank Clearwater and wounding three other Indians. While intermediate fire occurred until April 17, government negotiators pouted about their inability to control the agitators' allies and to gain concessions from the Indians. For example, Frizzell noted on April 20, "I am concerned that the option I represent—to negotiate a settlement not involving force—has come to an end. The U.S. is in control of the situation, but not in control of the people" (*Voices* 1974, 186). At this time, the agitators claimed they would not abdicate their position until the government ceased its overt warfare against them. Clearly the government was not in charge because Wilson's forces and dissident ranchers still continued firing at the Indians.

In one of many comparisons by the agitators to Vietnam, an Indian veteran claimed the government's military aggression against the Indians matched his warfare experiences in Vietnam. He noted, "The men carry the same weapons that are used in Vietnam—the M-16, the M-79 grenade launcher is here, they have starlight scopes that were used for spotting people in the jungle at night time, they have infra-red sensors, trip-flares out here in the woods to prevent our foot patrols from coming. They use helicopters" (*Voices* 1974, 195). While verbal comparisons to Vietnam infuriated government negotiators, who had been targets of public outrage for their support of what many Americans believed was an ill-conceived war, these comparisons evoked a sense of righteousness among agitators.

When Frizzell met with traditional Oglala leaders in Kyle, South Dakota, between April 25 and 29, traditional chiefs repeated their concern about the government's violations of the 1868 treaty and grieved about the recent death of Oglala resident Buddy Lamont from government sniper fire. In what appeared to be another example of government insensitivity to Indian lamentations, Frizzell ignored the incident and instead threatened the Oglalas with more military assaults (*Voices* 1974, 222). After the government readmitted Oglala leaders to Wounded Knee, negotiations continued on May 3. At this time, the establishment negotiators conceded that the White House would write a letter to the traditional chiefs promising a meeting about the 1868 treaty, and if agitators would lay down arms, road blocks would be lifted to permit Buddy Lamont's funeral. They further conceded that after seventy hours people with warrants against them would be arrested and treaty meetings would be held within the month at Chief Fools Crow's land (231).

While the government won the concessions it sought, the agitators seemed to lose most of their demands. Whether they made concessions to the establishment because they suffered from shortages of food and ammunition or because they thought they had successfully raised public consciousness about Indian grievances is difficult to determine. Whatever the case Indian agitators abdicated their position. As promised in the May 8 agreement, members of the Community Relations Service came into the siege area, collected weapons, and processed all of the permanent residents. Treaty meetings followed at Chief Fools Crow's camp in the third week of May. At these meetings, both sides squabbled over a reinstatement of the treaty of 1868, but government representatives said this was impossible because of more than 100 years of subsequent federal law. The Indian representatives then repeated their demands for the ouster of both the BIA and the current tribal government, but the government failed to act, claiming they lacked jurisdiction over this issue. After the meeting, a presidential representative delivered a letter reaffirming the fact that treaty reinstatement was out of the question. More hearings occurred in June under the sponsorship of Senator James Abourezk. After the completion of the scheduled meetings, legal action ensued against ION leaders. Sadly, conditions at Pine Ridge continued to deteriorate for the next several years.

After the agitators abdicated, some conceived of the event, not as an embarrassing surrender, but as an important episode in tribal identity transformation. For example, Gladys Bissonette explained:

They [the Oglala people] have finally opened their eyes to what corrupt governing bodies we have on the reservation and they have finally realized that they should stand up to intimidation and stand up for their rights, now. I do really think that we have brought a lot of people to sanity instead of letting everybody push them [sic] around. I hope the Indians, at least throughout the Pine Ridge Reservation, unite and stand up together, hold hands and never forget Wounded Knee. . . . We were all happy together[,] and it is kind of sad to see everyone leave[,] but we know we'll be together again soon. (*Voices* 1974, 244)

Bissonette's perception indicates that even though the Indians did not gain the concessions they sought, they, at least for a time, experienced restoration of traditional values and gained dignity by confronting both the tribal and federal governments. Perhaps, restoring cultural pride to the Oglalas during the seventy-one days was a more important outcome than obviating government control. The agitators' solidification strategies may have reinforced their cultural identity more than any of their militant rhetoric and military action could. Those living at Wounded Knee empowered themselves as a people by unifying themselves against a common government enemy, engaging in communal interactions, sharing historical lamentations, and participating in traditional prayer and rituals.

Unfortunately, the end of the standoff did not terminate the conflict for either the agitators or the establishment. In the next three years, Oglala residents, Wilson loyalists, and ION leaders died on the reservation, presumably because of factionalism and resentment over the siege. Wilson continued as tribal chairman, 400 agitators were arrested, and 100 indicted for crimes related to the standoff (Zimmerman 1976, 344; Dewing 1995, 145–66). The government never apologized for its roles either at the massacre in 1890 or for the deaths and suffering it caused at the standoff.

Further, intracultural tension did not abate until December 1990 when Oglalas rode for 150 miles on horseback in freezing temperatures to heal the wounds caused by factionalism and to recall their common historical heritage. At this time "former goons and AIM members sought common ground in their shared spirituality [by] forgiving each other for the pain of 1973" (Smith & Warrior 1996, 279). Reconciling with one another reaffirmed common history and began to reconnect the circle broken by decades of intratribal hatred.

The signs coming from the present situation at the Pine Ridge Reservation are mixed. In July 1999, President Bill Clinton seemed to acknowledge the continuing failure of assimilation programs when he designated Wounded Knee "an empowerment zone" and promised new programs to help the Oglalas gain access to economic prosperity and restore traditional culture (Clinton 1999). In April 2000, however, the Justice Department sent lawyers to investigate the misuse of tribal funds after a long occupation of tribal offices by a dissident group of Oglalas, called the Grass Roots Oyate. Whether either of these events signals a positive change or not to the continuing conflict at Pine Ridge remains to be seen.

Chapter 11

Indian Alcohol Abuse, Narrative Reasoning, and the Gordon House Case, 1992–2000

The use of alcohol in Indian communities has a controversial history. For 300 years, traders provided alcohol to Indians in exchange for food and animal skins. At many treaty signing ceremonies, the sharing of alcohol was an essential feature of the celebrations (Mancall 1995, 50–51). Even though many Indian leaders, including Chiefs Black Kettle and Red Cloud, complained to federal officials that Indian agents and traders promoted alcohol, existing laws often were not enforced. Traders created a demand for alcohol by offering it as a medium for exchange. From the point of view of the traders, drinking excessive amounts of alcohol and getting drunk was a norm, and trappers, miners, soldiers, and Indians drank large amounts without being subject to social sanctions or legal penalties (Rorabaugh 1979, 126–27). A double standard existed because many men on the frontier drank to excess, but it was Indians who gained the most public ridicule for this behavior (Mancall 1995). From the perspective of government officials, however, the traders deserved most of the blame since they took advantage of the Indians' desire for spirits. As a result, the federal government created many laws to regulate the sale and use of alcohol on reservations. After 200 years of regulation, alcohol use and abuse continues to be a problem in Indian communities just as it is among other populations.

Even though the frequency of alcohol use among most Indians is similar to the rest of the population, the public perceives that Indians have a worse problem than other communities. One reason for this perception may be that alcohol has a more severe effect on Indian users than on other populations. For example, Fred Beauvais (1998) reported that the rate of alcohol-related deaths was 5.6 times greater for Indians than for the general population. Additionally, chronic liver disease, alcohol-related automobile deaths, and suicide and homicides resulting from excessive drinking were greater for Indians than the general population (254).

Another reason the public perceives Indian drinking to be more problematic than it is in other populations is that Indian drinkers often consume large amounts of alcohol in a short time. For example, some researchers (Mail & McDonald 1980) note that Indian drinkers tend to engage in binge or recreational drinking; that is, they consume five or more drinks in a short time with a social group with the expressed purpose of getting drunk. Philip May (1996) concludes that recreational drinking is the source of most alcohol-related problems in Indian communities, including family violence. A third reason is that among the tribes with large populations, such as the Navajo and Sioux, alcohol dependency is much greater than the rest of the population (Kunitz & Levy 2000, 158).

The historical record of many of the Indian groups discussed in this book identifies alcohol as a significant problem. For example, Berthrong (1972) discusses the problem with Cheyenne and Arapaho after their resettlement in Oklahoma. Similarly, Lazarus (1991), Matthiessen ([1980] 1991), and Means (1995) document the problem of alcohol use and abuse among present day Sioux. Contemporary reports about problems on the northern and some of the southwest reservations point to large percentages of male adults who drink heavily (Beauvais 1998). Because alcohol abuse is so prevalent among the Navajos and some other Indian populations, the issue gets a great deal of attention. Even though the Navajos still prohibit the sale of alcohol on the reservation, this prohibition is not working. Michelle M. Taggart (1999) explains that because the Navajo Nation is dry, members often take long drives off the reservation to buy alcohol, drive drunk, and get involved in many accidents (26).

This chapter (1) chronicles a brief history of government regulations concerning Indian alcohol consumption, (2) explains the social causes of the alcohol problem in connection with Navajo Indians, (3) describes how the courts dealt with the 1992 drunk-driving case involving Navajo Gordon House, and (4) identifies the implications of the case.

GOVERNMENT REGULATION AND INDIAN ALCOHOL CONSUMPTION

Historians document alcohol use by Navajos. For example, the records of Indian agents from the period predating the Treaty of Fort Sumner suggest that Navajo Headmen Ganado Mucho and Manuelito both drank alcohol. Frank McNitt (1962) claims Ganado Mucho was a social drinker, but Manuelito drank excessively (60, 248). Jerrold E. Levy and Stephen J. Kunitz (1974) report that from the 1850s to the beginning of the twentieth century, drinking was common among the wealthy Navajos who could afford to buy or trade for alcohol in exchange for blankets and jewelry at Indian trade fairs (69–71). In 1901 the liquor trade was so out of control in Gallup, New Mexico, a city adjoining the Navajo reservation, that the grand jury indicted thirty people in one week for selling whiskey to Navajos. This same jury recognized the problem was so bad that they urged the judge to bring in a special U.S. marshal to deal with it (McNitt 1962, 54).

Contemporary Navajos have an especially high rate of arrest for alcohol-related offenses because the tribal police make this a high priority. In addition to the efforts of Navajo police to deal with the problem, the tribe has made alcohol prevention and treatment a priority. Sobriety marches, treatment centers, and education about alcohol are common practices on the Navajo reservation. In fact, Gordon House, at the time of his arrest for drunk driving, was a counselor at an alcohol rehabilitation center.

Just as with other Indian tribes, the government historically viewed Navajo drinking in accordance with the "firewater myth"; that is, Indians were out-of-control drinkers who committed crimes when intoxicated. More specifically, Joy Leland (1976) defines "the firewater myth," as a belief that "Indians are constitutionally prone to develop an inordinate craving for liquor and to lose control over their behavior when they drink" (1). Although a number of studies (Dozier 1966; Levy & Kunitz 1974; McAndrew & Edgerton 1979; Mancall 1995) refute this myth, even today the government continues to struggle with the social problems created by Indians' use and abuse of alcohol. Sydney Harring (1994) explains, "Alcohol became a convenient, readily visible symbol of the impact of white society on the tribes, a symbol that deflected attention from the massive white theft of land and the herding of the tribes onto impoverished reservations" (278). It is not surprising that the Navajo Nation, the second largest American Indian tribe, has become a focal point of negative stereotypes and controversies involving alcohol use and abuse by Indians (Topper 1985; May 1996; Kunitz & Levy 2000).

For decades, treaties and statutes attempted to regulate Indian consumption of alcohol. Nearly all of the treaties with Indian tribes had provisions forbidding the use, sale, and distillation of liquor. The treaties for most of the tribes discussed in this volume contained prohibitions on alcohol. For example, such provisions appeared in the Treaty of Medicine Creek (1854), Treaty with the Sisseton and Wahpeton (1851, 1858), the Treaty with Mdewakanton and Wakpekute (1851, 1858), Treaty of Fort Lyon (1861), Treaty of Little Arkansas (1865), and Treaty of Medicine Lodge Creek (1870).

Surprisingly, the ratified treaties with the Navajos did not contain the standard section on alcohol prohibition. Although it was never ratified, the Articles of Agreement and Convention made with the Navajos in 1855 (Article 7) provided that "no spirituous liquors shall be made, sold or used on any of the lands herein set apart for the residence of the Indians; and the sale of same shall be prohibited" (Brugge & Correll 1971, 75). The 1868 Fort Sumner Treaty between the government and the Navajos contained no provisions concerning the use, sale, and trade of liquor although existing federal laws applied to them.

Despite treaty provisions, alcohol consumption continued among the tribe because of easy access and the lack of enforcement by government regulators. Traders supplied alcohol to Indians for trade goods, and many Indians accepted the alcohol as desirable payment. Navajos probably gained access to alcohol at annual trade fairs in Taos, New Mexico, a location where Mexicans traded alcohol for prized Navajo blankets (McNitt 1962, 53).

In addition to hard-to-enforce treaty stipulations, the U.S. Congress between 1832 and 1900 seemed adamant in its prohibition of alcohol procurement and use by Indians. As early as 1832, an act regulating trade with Indians stressed that merchants could be searched if the government had suspicions that they were trading "ardent spirits" to Indians. If this search resulted in the discovery of alcohol, then the traders would be forced to give up their trading license, forfeit all of their goods, and pay fines (*Indian Trade Regulations Act*, U.S. Stat. 3: 682–83). Just two years later, the *Trade and Intercourse Act* (1832) emphasized a complete prohibition of liquor sales to Indians. Section 21 stipulated:

If any person whatever shall, within the limits of the Indian country, set up or continue any distillery for manufacturing ardent spirits, he shall forfeit and pay a penalty of one thousand dollars; and it shall be the duty of the superintendent of Indian affairs, Indian agent, or sub-agent, within the limits of whose agency the same shall be set up or continued, forthwith to destroy and break up the same; and it shall be lawful to employ the military force of the United States in executing that duty. (U.S. Stat. 4: 729–35)

Each new law attempted to improve upon the one preceding it. By 1847, the government tried to strengthen the *Trade and Intercourse Act* by adding penalties for the sale of alcohol. Section 2, "An Act to Provide Better Organization of the Department of Indian Affairs" (1847), stipulated penalties for "any person who shall sell, exchange or barter, give, or dispose of any spirituous liquor or wine to an Indian, in the Indian Country" except for supplies for officers and troops of the United States government stationed in there. The act further added that Indians would be considered competent witnesses in legal proceedings against alcohol providers (U.S. Stat. 9: 202–4). Since these stipulations also applied to Indian country in the territories, they had jurisdiction over Navajo lands from the time of U.S. conquest in 1854. This act apparently had little effect on the Navajos, however, because Agent Alexander Irvine wrote in 1877, "Whiskey is sold to the Navajos in large quantities at all settlements around the reservation" (*Annual Report of the Commissioner of Indian Affairs*, 1879).

In 1892, the legal sanctions moved from the federal government to the tribes themselves. For example, the Court of Indian Offenses assumed jurisdiction for dealing with "intoxication and the introduction of intoxicants" by Indians. This law forbid the selling, exchange, giving, bartering of liquor as well as the making of liquor and subjected Indians convicted of such offenses to a minimum jail sentence of thirty days or a fine of between twenty and one-hundred dollars (U.S. Stat. 27: 614). In 1892, Congress passed legislation prohibiting Indians serving in the armed forces from drinking even though no such provision applied to other military personnel. And again in 1897, Congress prohibited the sale of intoxicating beverages to Indians who had received land allotments. These laws were especially difficult to enforce against the Navajos because they inhabited a vast area of land that was subject to a limited amount of government supervision.

The nineteenth-century laws remained in effect until 1953. At that time, Congress passed Public Law 277, a bill that allowed Indians to drink legally off-reservation, but permitted the tribes to determine whether or not to legalize drinking on a particular reservation. Although many tribes legalized on-reservation drinking at the time, the Navajos continue to this day to prohibit alcohol sale on reservation lands.

ALCOHOL USE AMONG THE NAVAJOS

The contemporary problems with alcohol on the Navajo reservation may have their roots in cultural conflicts. Specifically, some Navajos may drink because of social disruption and lack of tribal sanctions. For example, James F. Downs (1964) claims that the four years of imprisonment at Bosque Redondo significantly changed the Navajo who experienced disruption of their social and political structure and the introduction of a new material culture (10). James Zion and Elsie B. Zion (1996) claim that alcohol is part of the general alienation of the Navajo brought about by the 1868 treaty in which the "United States imposed alien laws, authoritarian governmental forms, and paternalistic institutions on the Navajo" (97). They argue that the treaty initially caused the breakdown of "the traditional values of equality and harmony" which the government programs replaced with "loss of hope," "dependence," and "disharmony." Moreover, the Indians' "subjection to countless indignities and humiliating experiences may cause them to seek ways to dull their senses and forget their feelings of inadequacy" (Dozier 1966, 25). The federal program of livestock reduction in the 1930s further increased the feelings of helplessness among the Navajos and at that time alcohol dependence increased (Kunitz & Levy 1994, 19).

Another factor that contributes to alcohol abuse is the conflicting attitudes and expectations of residents of the reservation. For example, Spicer (1997) claims that Indians believe that drinking is a positive way of stimulating interaction between friends, but at the same time, they are aware that alcohol abusers destroy their families and bring shame to the community. Most Indians believe that as a group they are more susceptible to alcohol abuse because of their culture's long history of this kind of abuse (Mail & McDonald 1980). Moreover Indians understand they are often disenfranchised from their social communities if they become sober (Spicer 1997). These conflicting attitudes set up a type of double bind: if Indians drink, they can hurt others; but if they do not drink, they can be excluded from the community. Although the research does not deal explicitly with Navajos, other research indicates this is a common but conflictive expectation among Navajos (Topper 1985; Beauvais 1996).

Ironically the alcohol problem among Navajos may result from lack of access to alcohol caused by prohibition in the 1950s. Some research claims that prohibition actually encourages binge drinking among some Indian social groups. Since the courts often accepted binge drinking as a legitimate excuse for crime, Indians may have justified drinking as a motivation for violence. As early as 1910, Franciscan priests recorded that Navajos were fond of whiskey and after they procured it, they drank to excess. The priests noted that this type of drinking brought "disgrace" to the inebriated person, but the legal officials never punished offenses committed while Navajos were drunk (Franciscan Fathers 1910, 217, 239). Binge drinking off the reservation among the Navajos may result directly from prohibition on the reservation. For example, Henderson (2000) explains that contemporary binge drinking often occurs when small groups of men friends get together off the reservation to celebrate. After gaining access to large amounts of liquor in nearby towns, such as Gallup, many Navajos consume the alcohol before returning to the reservation (43–45). In this way reservation prohibition actually promotes binge drinking. In turn, binge drinking fosters excessive drunkenness associated with interpersonal violence and property crimes (Kunitz & Levy 2000, 164).

Present-day statistics show a strong relationship between crime, fatal accidents, and alcohol consumption. Alcohol use and misuse are "very high in the adult Navajo population, more so for men than women" (Kunitz et al. 2000, 84). The prevalence of alcohol dependence, Levy and Kunitz (1974) conclude, is responsible for the majority of crimes committed by Navajos. They note that the death rate per 100,000 from alcohol is 26.7 versus 12.1 in the general population. High homicide and suicide rates result from excessive drinking (2). In 1996, 75 percent of Navajo seventh and eighth graders reportedly used alcohol, contributing to high levels of intratribal homicide and drunk driving (Beauvais 1996, 91). The National Highway Traffic Safety Administration in 2000 reported that Native Americans have the highest percentage of alcohol-related fatalities (tbhonline.com/cns/9902). When these incidents occur on the reservation, they are dealt with by the Navajo tribal courts. Drunk driving–related deaths occurring off the reservation, however, are tried as felony cases in the state courts.

THE GORDON HOUSE CASE

After a tragic automobile accident in 1992, Gordon House became a symbol of Indian drinking problems. He fit the profile of a drunk Indian in several ways. He was a young male Navajo, and most Indian drinkers are male. He engaged in binge drinking before the accident by consuming at least six beers after a Christmas party at his workplace. He purchased the alcohol off the reservation and consumed some of it in his vehicle. He drove when he was intoxicated and caused an accident that killed four people. In many other ways, however, Gordon House bore little resemblance to Indian problem drinkers. His family and friends never saw him drunk. His graduate education in social work trained him to treat Indian alcohol problems. He was respected and admired by his coworkers. He was connected to his culture and participated in both Christian and Navajo religious ceremonies. Despite these two contrasting portraits, when he was brought to trial Gordon House admitted he engaged in binge drinking, drove while drunk, and killed four people. In the preliminary hearing and the three trials that followed, the prosecutors and the media characterized Gordon House as a reckless drunk Navajo who had engaged in binge drinking. Not only did the prosecutors characterize House in racial terms but in numerous appeals his defense attorney claimed that racial stereotyping prohibited the defendant from getting fair trials.

The 1992 drunk-driving homicide involving Navajo Gordon House called attention to the problem of Navajo Indian drinking and its ramifications in the New Mexico state legal system. The trial received national attention when *Court TV* broadcast the third trial live and when NBC's *Dateline* devoted an entire program to the case with a focus on racial stereotyping and Indian drinking ("The Trial of Gordon House" 1994). This segment of the paper (a) relates the facts of the incident that produced criminal charges; (b) analyzes four legal narratives used in Gordon House's preliminary hearing by identifying assumptions, methods of logical justification, uses of language, and patterns for attributing causality; and (c) interprets how the content of these narratives evolved and transformed the reasoning of the legal proceedings.

Case Facts

The Gordon House case provides one window for observing some of the cultural issues of Indian alcohol use that entered into a highly visible New

Mexico legal proceeding. The facts of the case outline the tragic story line. At 9:30 P.M. on Christmas eve of December 24, 1992, the pickup truck of Gordon House, going the wrong way on Interstate 25 at high speed, hit head-on an oncoming car driven by Paul Cravens. The accident killed four of the five occupants of the Cravens' car, including Melanie Cravens 31, Kandyce Woodard 9, Erin Woodard 8, and Kacee Woodard 5. The driver of the Cravens' car survived after a long stay in the hospital. At the scene of the crime, Gordon House told police that he had consumed three beers (in later trials the figure was changed to six or eight), and police said he refused to take a blood alcohol test. Five hours after the accident, the police recorded a .1 blood alcohol level, then the legal limit of intoxication in the state of New Mexico. On December 29, 1992, the state charged Gordon House with four counts of vehicular homicide. According to state law, vehicular homicide occurs when "a person . . . commits homicide by a vehicle or great bodily injury by a vehicle while under the influence of alcohol or drugs" (*New Mexico Criminal Code*, 1982, 66–68: 101). After these charges were filed, the media reported that House had a previous driving while intoxicated (DWI) conviction. This report implied that Gordon House had not learned from his first conviction and showed that he had a history of alcohol abuse.

The Preliminary Hearing

The discovery of a previous conviction of drunk driving probably affected the district attorney's decision to charge House with the most severe crime possible under state law. On March 12, 1993, the state claimed they had discovered new evidence and changed the charges against Gordon House to four counts of first degree depraved mind murder. New Mexico is the only state in the United States that allows this charge. Although the charge has been rarely used in this century, it has been part of the *New Mexico Criminal Code* since the mid-nineteenth century.[1] After several motions challenging the constitutionality of the depraved mind murder charges by House's defense attorney, Ray Twohig, Judge Frank Allen Jr. scheduled a preliminary hearing on September 27, 1993. The goal of the hearing was to consider the evidence from both the prosecution and the defense and to then determine the legitimacy of charges. After hearing testimony for nearly a month, Judge Allen concluded that the charge of first degree depraved mind murder was not justified (Allen 1993, October 28, 6).

The public hearing featured four diverse legal narratives that emerged in the legal proceedings and the press coverage of the case. During the three trials that followed the preliminary hearing, these narratives figured prominently in the trial evidence and in the press coverage of the trials.

Legal Narratives

Legal narratives resemble literary stories in that they have protagonist and antagonist characters, setting, dialogue, conflict, and resolution of conflict. Legal narratives differ from literary stories in several ways. They have many storytellers with different points of view. The narratives emerge through written briefs, oral arguments, depositions, interrogations, and press reports. The stories evolve over a long period of time and are pieced together by storytellers and audiences who seek to make sense out of the narrative explanations.

Analyzing the narratives in a law case is one method for understanding legal processes and outcomes. This method assumes that legal discourse is a story and that adjudicators "rely on the adaptation of a particular story," one that makes sense to them (Scheppele 1989, 2080). Narrative analysis has several advantages. First, it shows how attorneys, judges, defendants, and accusers represent their cultural knowledge in interpretations of the case in and outside of the legal proceedings (Winter 1989, 2270). Second, this analysis invites those who study legal processes to see how people socially construct arguments to represent their personal views about reality (Winter 1989, 2276). Third, this method shows how many cultural perspectives converge in a legal case and how each culture constructs and expresses its reasons in different ways. Fourth, legal narratives are neither true nor false. These stories consist of "self-believed descriptions" emanating from diverse viewpoints and informed by different assumptions about how to express and make sense out of events (Scheppele 1989, 2082). Legal narratives therefore are windows for viewing the convergence and transformation of the communication of different cultures. Culture refers to a system of values developed and shared by a group of people who establish norms or rules about how members should behave toward one another. The narratives of a culture reveal its values, show what counts as evidence, and indicate how reasons are constructed. Professional legal culture converges with Navajo ethnic culture, New Mexico political culture, and mass media culture in the Gordon House case.

Narratives in the House Case

The prosecution's story surfaced in the pretrial motions and the preliminary hearing. Gordon Rackstraw presented the case for the state. He claimed that since observers did not see the truck of House swerve or move from its course that House must have intended to kill his victims and therefore committed "an act greatly dangerous to the lives of others," indicating a depraved mind and a disregard for human life (Asher 1993, September 28, A1). The prosecution's witnesses claimed House knew he was driving on the wrong side of the freeway because he failed to respond to visual signs from other drivers.

The defense led by Ray Twohig countered, saying that charges of first degree depraved mind murder were based on racism and stereotyping of Navajos and that the prosecution was abusing its discretion (Twohig 1993, August 5, 2). In his closing argument at the preliminary hearing, Twohig explained that "someone got confused because of their intoxication, got turned around on the highway going the wrong way and was too intoxicated to appreciate his surroundings" (Linthicum 1993, October 15, A1, A4). Defense witnesses agreed that House was confused and unfamiliar with the freeway system, and they insisted that he did not intend to hurt anyone.

The third story portrayed Gordon House as a successful and respected young Navajo who was acting out of character when he drove drunk on Christmas eve. One newspaper provided a portrait of House as a successful man who made his way in the Anglo world and yet retained his Navajo values. Gordon House directed a drug and alcohol treatment center for troubled Navajos in Thoreau, New Mexico, in the eastern region of the Navajo reservation. House was a prominent leader in the community with a reputation for excellence at his job. He was married and the father of two children and practiced both Christian and Navajo religion (Linthicum 1993, February 10, A1). The newspaper told the story of Gordon House as if the accident was a mystery that his family and coworkers could not explain. Those closest to House had no idea how he could have killed Cravens and her children. In fact, several associates claimed that their introverted, private friend never drank (Thompson 1992, December 29, A1, A7). To show his caring nature, one reporter talked specifically about his concern for the environment. Davis (1993, January 2) noted that often Gordon House would hunt deer, but "a medicine man told him that the upcoming weather would be cold. . . . So House took a 10-day trip this fall to leave hay and other food for the animals. . . . He was very spiritual; he had a high regard for people" (A5). This version of House's story demonstrated both his success in his Navajo ethnic culture and his achievements in professional culture.

A fourth story surfaced from the grief of the victimized family; they vowed to reform drunk-driving laws. The family of Melanie Cravens, devout members of an Assembly of God church, established the theme of their story as a "crusade" against drunk driving. Their extroverted and public character emerged even before the funeral when Nadene Cravens, mother and grandmother of the victims, declared: "There is a reason this happened to us because we're going to pursue drunken driving in this city. I am going to scream and scream, 'How could this have happened to my babies? What right did he have?' " (Police Suspect Alcohol 1992, December 26, A8). To begin their crusade, the family invited all of the state legislators, the governor, and the attorney general to the funeral of the victims. At what the mortician called "the largest funeral ever to occur in Albuquerque," dozens of legislators heard Pastor Rod Carman's eulogy emphasizing political action against drunk drivers (Casuas 1992, December 30, A1, A5). The family, with the help of their pastor, spoke about their tragedy in media interviews, conducted public meetings, gathered petitions, and lobbied the legislature to change state laws concerning alcohol use, distribution, and abuse. Many of these changes finally occurred during eight years of legislation from 1992 to 2000.

Narratives as Exemplars of Legal Reasoning

The key figures in the Gordon House case presented distinctive exemplars of narrative reasoning. Exemplars exhibit the qualities and sum up the characteristics that distinguish one type of legal story from another. The exemplars presented here resemble legal approaches identified by Martha Minow (1990) as formalism, rights, and social relations. A fourth approach to the law, political action, also surfaced in the House case. My analysis of the House case shows how the narrative of the prosecution corresponded to legal formalism, the defense to rights, the defendant to social relations, and the victims' family to political action. My subsequent analysis contrasts these approaches according to different assumptions about the law, methods of logical justification, uses of language, and attributions of causality.

Formalist Narrative. The narrative of the prosecution typically proves the charges that a person has violated the provisions of the law as set forth in the language of the law. This kind of reasoning follows the exemplar of formalist reasoning (McDonald 1979, 36–45). Typically, one of the first audiences to hear the charges is the grand jury. In this case, however, the charges never were presented to a grand jury because the state changed the charges from vehicular homicide to first degree depraved mind murder. The controversy about the charges then led Judge Frank Allen Jr. to change the proceedings from a grand jury to a preliminary hearing. A grand jury hears evidence from the state and gains a judgment about the indictment from a publicly selected jury in a proceeding closed to the public. In contrast, a preliminary hearing considers evidence from both the state and the defense and seeks the judgment of a judge about the indictment in a proceeding that is open to the public. Although preliminary hearings are relatively rare in New Mexico, they are held in high publicity criminal cases with controversial legal issues, a description that fits the Gordon House case.

The formalist narrative tried to justify why the state brought first degree depraved mind murder against Gordon House. New Mexico Law (N.M. Stat. 1984, 30: 2) describes first degree depraved mind murder as an act "greatly dangerous to the lives of others." The New Mexico Court of Appeals interpreted this charge to require that the accused had "subjective knowledge" of the act, and that the alleged act was "greatly dangerous to life" (*State v. McCrary* 1984, 671). Leo Romero explains that an "act greatly dangerous" means an act creating "a strong probability of death." He further explains that New Mexico law requires that the danger be experienced by "more than one person" (Romero 1990, 81).

Legal formalism assumes the law has fixed categories that establish boundaries into which arguers fit the facts of the case (Minow 1990, 8). These categories distinguish what is right and wrong, what is normal and abnormal, and "act as given receptacles, ready to contain whatever new problem may arise" (Minow 1990, 8). The laws provide linguistic standards for the judge to use to compare the facts to the legal categories. Prosecutor Rackstraw claimed at the preliminary hearing that first degree depraved mind murder was a legitimate charge against Gordon House because he drove the wrong way for twelve miles without swerving and without paying attention to drivers who flashed their lights and tried to get him to turn around. Rackstraw's narrative claimed: "When you combine the intoxication level that we'll be talking about with the expert testimony about Mr. House and his ability and his education and his training, along with the testimony of Mr. Green, it is going to become abundantly clear that House is guilty of first degree depraved mind murder" (Preliminary Hearing Record 1993 [hereafter cited as PHR], CR93–16933: 4–5). To demonstrate that House's act was both dangerous and showed disregard for human life, Rackstraw featured the testimony of Officer Tom Green who testified that even after he flashed his lights and used his horn, House only responded by "looking up and speeding into the oncoming car" (PHR 73–80).

Formalist legal reasoning uses patterns of deductive logic. The major premise of the prosecution's case was that first degree depraved mind murder is a category of the law. The minor premise was House's behavior fit that category. The conclusion followed, therefore, that House should be indicted on this charge of first degree depraved mind murder.

In this type of reasoning, the language related abstract concepts of the law like "subjective knowledge" and "dangerous to human life" as if these phrases were "clear and definitive" categories that were not subject to multiple interpretations (Minow 1990, 10). Rackstraw argued that "Mr. House had the subjective knowledge that what he was doing was not just dangerous, it was crazy" (PHR 5). By repeating the words of the statute, Rackstraw gave the impression that House's behavior was the same as that stipulated by the law. By adding the term "crazy," Rackstraw additionally implied that House was reckless in his behavior.

Narratives can attribute causality in a variety of ways. Formalists explain the causes of a crime by making attributions about the power and motive of the accused who allegedly committed a crime. This approach assumes that the person had full control over "the whole course of events and actions" (Heider 1958, 107). Fritz Heider (1958) explains that attributions of power show that a person had the ability to perform an act, and attributions of motivation show that a person had the intention and the potential to commit an act (97–103). Prosecutors argued that House had sufficient knowledge of his vehicle and of the driving process so that he had the power, if he had heeded signs from others, to change the course of his driving. And prosecutors concluded that House did not use his power to change course even though he had numerous opportunities to do so. This was the reason, prosecutors argued, that House must have had the intention to "cause great bodily harm" to the people in the Cravens' car. Unlike the theory developed by Heider, prosecutors did not show that House had both the power and motivation to commit the act. Instead they argued more indirectly suggesting that knowledge was a source of power and that if that knowledge was not applied in the "normal and rational way," then House must have acted intentionally for evil. This type of reasoning does not make a direct connection between case facts and legal categories, but instead it relies on a sequence of inferences based on missing evidence and gives the impression to a judge that a direct fit exists between the evidence and the language of the legal category.

The weakness of this formalist narrative was that it reinforced the public's prejudice against the defendant as a drunk Indian driver, stressed the power of the state to label the action as murder, and validated abstract concepts, such as "reckless endangerment" and "subjective knowledge." The prosecution conceived of legal words as if they had clear referents in behavior (Minow 1990) when in fact the categories had multiple interpretations.

Rights Narrative. The rights narrative differs significantly with formalism. The rights approach assumes that the individual has unique rights that must be protected under the Constitution, that all persons "similarly situated" should be treated alike, and, at the same time, that each situation is unique (Minow 1990). When people are not treated alike, then they do not receive "justice." Defense attorney Ray Twohig argued House's unique situation in a motion to dismiss the depraved mind murder charge (Twohig 1993, August 5, 2). Twohig reasoned:

The state's selection of this native American defendant to charge with this most serious of all possible offenses, where intoxicated drivers of the other races have consistently been charged with offenses which carry substantially fewer penalties in similar circumstances, for many years during which the statute has been the law of New Mexico, violated House's right to equal protection of the law. (2)

Although Judge Allen did not support the motion, Twohig clearly identified his case as a rights story, implying that House's rights were violated.

The rights approach uses a method of justification called abduction

("Logical Terms" 1967, 5: 56). This way of justifying acts assumes that the major premise is true. Thus, the defense attorney agreed that while driving on the wrong side of the road, Gordon House did kill four people on December 24, 1992. But abduction recognizes that the minor premises are only hypotheses about why Gordon House killed members of the Cravens family. Since hypotheses are only perspectives, each unique situation has the potential of generating different hypothetical premises. Twohig argued that reckless behavior and disregard for human life were refutable, and so he offered an alternative minor premise or hypothesis that House was merely "confused" because he was intoxicated. He challenged the hypothesis of the prosecution, claiming instead that House was singled out for charges of first degree depraved mind murder because he was a Navajo, "the people that were killed were such appealing people," and the "accident happened on Christmas eve" (Linthicum 1993, October 15, A5).

The language of legal narratives shows that law is rhetorical and that each version of an act is a social and linguistic construction. Twohig argued that the language of the law does not consist of accurate and definitive categories, but instead legal categories are subjective and rhetorical. He reasoned that:

New Mexico is the only state with the offense of first degree depraved mind murder still on the books. This historical anachronism subjects the identical conduct which constitutes second degree murder and involuntary manslaughter to a penalty of life imprisonment. . . . It permits prosecutors to choose, without any objective criteria, which punishment to seek in a case. (Twohig 1993, August 5, 2–3)

The rights perspective challenges the formal language of the law and demands that the accused be treated the same in similar circumstances.

The rights approach often attributes causality based on the opportunity and chance that adhere in a situation. Opportunity means "environmental conditions, rather than the person, are primarily responsible for the outcome," whereas chance means the person perceives the situation as allowing for the act but does not necessarily encourage it (Heider 1958, 91). The defense showed through its witnesses' stories that environmental conditions were partially responsible for House's conduct. For example, accident reconstruction specialist Robert Bleyl noted that the signs for freeway access were unclear, the city lights prevented House from seeing the oncoming car lights, and the interstate highway had barricades preventing the defendant from crossing to the other side or turning round (Author's Notes 1993, October 15).

Defense hinted at a second type of causal attribution related to biological-psychological conditions. The defense emphasized that subjective knowledge was missing since House's blood alcohol level prohibited him from clear thinking. Gordon Hodge, a professor of pharmacology, claimed that a person with the blood alcohol level attributed to House by the police would not be able to appreciate the consequences or know the risks of his behavior (Author's Notes 1993, October 15).

For lawyers who accept the rights approach, attributing alcoholism to social and biological conditions is often considered a legitimate excuse. Minow (1990) claims that actions are legitimate legal excuses when society tolerates these acts "because [they perceive] the proper behavior was beyond the individual's capabilities" (126). Using the logic of abduction, the defense agreed to the major premise that the act occurred but used causal attributions about environment and biology to provide legal excuses. These excuses questioned the truth of the minor premises of the prosecution about the intent and motivation of the defendant and also provided alternative explanations for the behavior of Gordon House.

Social Relations Narrative. This type of narrative takes a perspective that differs both from formalism and rights. The defendant engaged in a social relations narrative. This approach assumes that people and their relationships are more important ways to explain acts than are legal categories or constitutional rights. Those who embrace the social relations view see each person as possessing a unique character and having distinctive relationships with other persons. Social relationship narratives call attention to the particularity and subjectivity of an act and question the general and the objective categories of the law. For those telling social relations narratives, the responsibility of the law is to people and to human values, not to artificial linguistic legal categories. When used in the courts as a defense, advocates try to influence public opinion about a case. Although Gordon House did not testify at his hearing, he gave extended interviews to local newspapers (Linthicum 1993, February 10, A1, A9). These narratives constructed accounts about House's character and his relationships to the community. He was class president at his high school, was a senior airman in the Air Force, received an M.A. degree in sociology, worked as a community college instructor of Navajo studies, directed a local treatment center for drug and alcohol, organized the community to give to Toys for Tots, and was a responsible and loving father and husband. These details centered on House's character and contrasted his story with other press and trial stories that had persuaded the public about his faults and condemned him as a person. House noted, "People are reading into this what they think is the case, and a drunken Indian is what they want to see" (Linthicum 1993, February 10, A9).

In addition to character, House's story emphasized his relationships to the family of the victims and to God. He stressed,

I have grieved and I have prayed and I have wanted to meet with the Cravens-Milford family from day one. We feel it is our responsibility to meet that family. We need to start somewhere to heal. . . . Both ideas have confronted me and told me "God is not through with you, Gordon. You need to continue your journey in life. This is what you stood for. Because of this incident or accident you need to continue your journey." (Linthicum 1993, February 10, A9)

Social relations narratives emphasize induction as a method of justification. Narratives of this type stress the particulars of the case and uniqueness of each act. The reasoning in this approach challenges "institutional practices" and addresses the inequalities of power in society (Minow 1990, 219). House remarked that he was shocked at the charges of depraved mind murder. He noted that he was a victim of "sadistic, odious racism," resulting from political pressure on the office of the district attorney. He faulted other institutional processes, claiming he was "physically and verbally abused" by an attendant at the hospital after the accident and that the news media "were overzealous" in reporting his case as compared to their reporting of cases involving Indian victims ("Racism a Factor" 1993, March 30, A1). Unlike the formalist approach that elevates the power of institutions and the rights approach that concentrates on constitutional rights, the social relations approach generalizes about institutional flaws and gives voice to the accused who may be a powerless outsider in legal culture.

In social relations narratives, advocates view the language of institutions as consisting of misleading stereotypes and labels. As a result, they challenge legal categories and offer alternative terms and labels to define themselves and their acts. This approach "emphasizes the responsibility of the community" for choosing labels and "assigning meaning" to those labels and observes the ways that labels "obscure difference" (Minow 1990, 176–77).

House's attorney incorporated the defendant's media story into his theory of the case. For example, Twohig reiterated House's interpretation of the case as an example of media stereotyping and as evidence of public racism (1993, August 5). He noted,

The charges of first degree depraved mind murder brought against the defendant, a Native American, constitute selective prosecution on the basis of an impermissible classification, his race. This is the only known prosecution for the first degree depraved mind murder in New Mexico arising out of a motor vehicle accident. (6)

House concluded that the media had stereotyped him as a drunk Indian. Subsequently, his attorney used this as an issue in the trials and appeals.

The process of attribution in the social relations approach stresses power and motivation, but instead of attributing these qualities directly to the defendant as the formalist approach does, it allows the defense to challenge the power and motive of the factions that brought actions against the defendant. Minow (1990) explains that reversing explanations of causality by blaming institutions is one way the powerless person redefines prejudice and resists institutional power (109).

Political Action Narrative. The final type of narrative, political action, may be unique to cases that involve socially salient public policies. The family of the victims, the Cravens and Milfords, used political action narratives to establish their position as political advocates outside of the courtroom. Political action advocates assume that legislative process is more likely to solve problems and prevent crime than judicial action and that responsible people should use their power as citizens to force legislators to take action to solve public problems. This approach seeks the support of lawmakers and uses the legal action as evidence of the need for new laws. This type of narrative occurs in cases where the penalty does not seem to fit the crime. Political action was one way that the family of the victims transcended the judiciary, addressed directly the source of a problem, and lamented the effects of a drunk-driving tragedy.

In this case, the Cravens-Milford family decided to transform the deaths of their loved ones at the hands of a drunk driver into a public campaign for changing laws affecting the sale, use, and abuse of alcohol. At the funeral of the victims, Rod Carman, the Cravens-Milford pastor, demanded "a complete overhaul of New Mexico's drunk-driving laws to stop these needless tragedies." Carman exhorted, "The families should not be victimized because someone refuses to have the backbone to pass legislation" (Rodriguez 1992, December 29, A7; Casuas 1992, December 30, A3). Dozens of lawmakers attended the funeral at the invitation of the family. The visibility of the issue, emphasized by the narratives of the victims' family and friends, led the state attorney general to make public a DWI reform package the day after the funeral (Dingman 1992, December 30, D1).

By January 1, 1993, Alan Granger, head of the Victory Love Fellowship congregations in New Mexico, the church attended by the victims and their family, offered a complete legislative platform calling for mandatory jail sentences for DWI offenders, lowering of the blood alcohol level to 0.8, seizing of the vehicles of offenders, initiating a local excise tax on liquor, making liquor establishments liable if they contributed to an accident or death, and automating reports of DWI offenders so that their records would be available statewide to the police (Snow 1993, January 1, D1). The Cravens-Milford family, together with members of their church, gathered petitions, wrote letters, lobbied the legislature, and even participated in national hearings on alcohol and driving. Unlike the formal legal categories emphasizing the constitutional guarantees for the accused, or those demonizing the character of the offender in social relations narratives, the victims concentrated on making a comprehensive plan for political change by exhorting public officials to pass new laws.

The logic of the political action narrative was an extensive case for reform that follows stock issues analysis; that is, their case defined the problem, showed why the problem adhered in the current laws and the attitudes of lawmakers, presented the significance of DWI deaths in the state, proposed specific policy changes, and showed the advantages of the proposed policies over the present system (Ehninger & Brockriede 1970, 211–28).

In building the case for political change, the Cravens-Milford family transformed their experience of tragedy into a potential political problem that legislators had to attempt to resolve. More specifically, they defined the problem as a public crisis, identified those who promulgated the crisis as the liquor lobbies and reluctant legislators, created anxiety about the problem, and demonstrated they had voters' support for their position.

The plea for political action was so effective that when Paul Cravens returned to give testimony at the Victory Love Fellowship Church immediately after he was released from the hospital in late January 1993, he was joined by Marshall Plummer, vice-president of the Navajo Nation. At the church service, Plummer spoke: "The Navajo Nation has been called by the Lord and so has the Cravens family . . . to change the laws that govern liquor and drugs. . . . the Navajo Nation supports a statewide ban on drive up windows and controls on liquor dealers" (King 1993, February 1, A5). Plummer's appearance implied his agreement that alcohol was a problem for Navajos and established common ground between the social relations narrative of the defendant and that of the victims' family. Plummer's remarks showed that the drunk-driving deaths caused by Gordon House were symptomatic of a significant problem for the Navajo Nation as well as for other alcohol users in the state.

Political action narratives label and categorize events and institutions using language that calls attention to public interests. This type of narrative politicizes issues by calling attention to laws and explaining their benefits. Political action narratives not only exhort lawmakers to change, but they also encourage the public to demand change. The style of political action advocacy is to repeat key phrases, challenge the motives of authority structures, and lament the consequences of not acting (Edelman 1977, 109–12). Just like formalist laws, language is important to political action. Language is not, however, just a receptacle for interpreting facts. Instead the language of political action seeks to influence public opinion and change policy. It moves the narrative of the victims from the law courts, into public consciousness, and then into the legislative assembly.

In political action stories, causal attributions place the blame for evil acts on institutional leaders. Political action advocates adopt this approach because they are convinced that political leaders have the power and responsibility to resolve problems by creating new laws. Additionally, supporters of political action demand attention to problems through petitions and public rituals that motivate legislators to act. This type of narrative seeks to influence the legal decision makers by shifting the attention of the prosecutors and judge from case facts to public opinion.

The success of the political action approach, according to defense attorney Twohig, was devastating to Gordon House, who was charged with first degree depraved mind murder on March 12, 1993, after extensive discussion of alcohol abuse in public forums and the state legislatures. Twohig claimed that this publicity forced the district attorney to overcharge House. Specifically, he noted that House "has been publicly vilified as the only and the ultimate culprit in this case, excoriated in the mass media as no other New Mexican in recent times." He noted that the Cravens-Milford family mounted a media campaign that resulted in an "overwhelming guilt trip" for the public, and House was the scapegoat chosen to exonerate legislators from their guilt (Linthicum 1993, March 21, A1).

Narrative Transformations

Law is a complex web of facts and issues into which the cultural values of the participants and the public are woven. Even though the amount of discourse about the House case as reflected in the press, the motions, and the preliminary hearing is small compared to that of legal processes, this media discourse about the trial process vividly shows how narrative transformations occur.

Narrative transformations refer to the way that narrators and their audiences make sense out of events as the legal case evolves. Symbolic transformations occur as part of the progression of an event; that is, an act passes from one thing to another to become something else (Heath 1986, 134). In its discursive categorization, the act on Christmas eve changed from an accident to vehicular homicide, to first degree depraved mind murder, and then returned to vehicular homicide. When the case came to trial, additional transformations occurred. For example, House claimed he ran into the Cravens-Milford family, not because of excessive drinking, but because he was experiencing a migraine headache at the time of the accident (Asher, 1994, June 14, A1, A10).

Kenneth Burke ([1950] 1969) views all human conflict as a series of transformations that occur when interpretations of events are placed in dialectical opposition to one another. This essay shows how legal narratives transform one another when placed in dialectical opposition during the legal proceedings.

The House case illuminates several transformations. First, the prosecution transformed its formalist conclusion about the legal charges following the traffic accident and deaths of the Cravens-Milford family from vehicular homicide to first degree depraved mind murder. Quite clearly, the change resulted when the Cravens-Milford narratives, urging stiffer penalties and victims' rights, dialectically opposed the presumption of the law and the policy of the district attorney to charge House with vehicular homicide. When the district attorney changed the charges against House to include evil intent with consequences of stiff penalties, the state showed the public that the justice system can adequately respond to the suffering of victims and to public opinion. Although Judge Allen disallowed these severe charges, the state continued to show in the next three trials that it was committed to try Gordon House on the maximum charges that the vehicular homicide law allowed. In doing so, the state transformed the case from a typical vehicular homicide trial to a political trial that showcased the state's laws against drunk drivers.

Second, the empathy House generated through media portraits changed Twohig's approach to the defense. After House's media interviews, the defense framed its theory by adding arguments about the ethnic and civil rights issues that the defendant had promoted. The actual words used by House in media narratives about violations of his rights and racism reappeared in motions, in the opening statement, and in the closing argument of the defense at the preliminary hearing. The defense adopted portions of these media narratives to modify its legal stories and to magnify media stories about the defendant. By adopting this strategy, the defense established the character and relationships of the defendant as central issues in the defense's theory of the case presented at the trials and in the appeals.

Third, the political action story of the victims showed their power to get the state to charge the defendant with first degree depraved mind murder, an approach that helped delineate issues for the rights story of the defense. These lines of refutation permeated the motions of the defense who sought a preliminary hearing rather than a grand jury. For example, Twohig claimed that the defendant was a victim of stereotyping, racism, and was a scapegoat for the alcohol problem in New Mexico. In reality, House was a religious family man who sought forgiveness from the victims' family. When juxtaposed in competing narratives, this potent dialectic about House's character showed possible political motives about why the state would charge him with depraved mind murder months after the accident and in violation of his civil rights. After Judge Allen's decision, Twohig's office concluded:

The accident drew unprecedented attention because House is Navajo and the victims were Anglo and the District Attorney's Office responded to a public lynch mob mentality by trying to bring murder charges. . . . [House] has prayed with all his strength and with deep faith that the judge, the family of Melanie Cravens and her daughters, and the public will see and understand that he is not a murderer. (Linthicum 1993, October 29, A10)

Each of the narratives transformed elements of other narratives. By doing so, the stories changed the legal process so that House would not receive the standard indictment from a grand jury. Even though the process underwent many changes from the day of the accident on December 24, 1992, until the opening of the preliminary hearing in September 27, 1993, Judge Allen's decision seemed to rest solely on the testimony given at the preliminary hearing. Judge Allen claimed: "The evidence presented has not established probable cause to believe that the defendant knew that his act was greatly dangerous to the lives of others" (Allen 1993, October 28, 5).

The stories of the expert witnesses were the focus of Allen's decision. In fact, Allen reported that defense witnesses called into question the veracity of those of the prosecution. He noted that the state's witness, James Standefer, claimed that House's tolerance for alcohol allowed him to know what he was doing, but defense witness Gordon Hodge claimed he was confused and not coherent. Similarly the testimony of accident reconstruction specialists was not compelling. State witness Parker Bell claimed House had many visual clues that he was going the wrong way, but defense expert Robert Bleyl noted there were no signs, the night was dark, and only light traffic occurred on the freeway. Allen seemed to balance the evidence of witnesses in his decision. His opinion indicated he wanted to maintain the formalist perspective, to stick to the facts and the evidence within the case, and to keep the testimony separate from the rhetoric of relations, rights, and political activism.

Narratives about law transform legal proceedings in ways not reflected by judicial decisions. These transformations show how the professional and legal cultures alter the evidence and justifications of the narrators. After Judge Allen's decision, the victims acknowledged that their story had failed to influence the courts as they hoped it would. Bob Milford, father of Melanie Cravens, said:

I think Judge Allen caved in. I feel he had his chance to speak out and have the guts to represent the people who are in there helping to fight DWI and he let us all down—and he knows in his heart that he did. (Linthicum 1993, October 29, A1, A10)

The Milford-Cravens family did lobby the legislature to pass stiffer penalties for drunk drivers and restrictions for alcohol vendors, laws that affected how future DWI cases will be tried. They generated bicultural support for political action when officials of the Navajo nation joined together with them in seeking change in laws related to the distribution, use, and abuse of alcohol. Additionally, their political action narratives seemed directly to influence the district attorney to charge Gordon House with the most severe crime possible. In turn, these new charges resulted in new motions and a public preliminary hearing that gave their cause even more publicity.

The defense gained advantage from the Cravens-Milford activism, from the state's change in charges, and from House's media stories. The defense marshaled evidence from these political actions to claim the rights of the defendant for due process had been violated and that the state was abusing prosecutorial discretion. Additionally, the defense borrowed from House's stories in the media and accommodated the evidence about his character and relationships into its case and thereby strengthened its rights approach by permitting the cultural background of the defendant to enter into the legal discourse, giving power to his minority status and voice to his cultural values. Eventually, the defense won the first stage of its legal fights against the state by getting Judge Allen to throw out first degree depraved mind murder in the preliminary hearing. This action was an important first step in a long and complicated litigation process.

IMPLICATIONS OF THE CASE

The case had significant legal, political, and social effects. First, the Gordon House case showed how cultural issues related to drunk-driving homicides are played out in and outside of the courtroom. Second, the case contributed to the public discussion about the interface between politics and law in government-Indian relations. Finally, the case brought public attention to the problem of Navajo drinking and to the methods used by the state, the tribe, and the courts to deal with the problem and its consequences.

Legal Effects

After the preliminary hearing, House was tried on one count of driving while intoxicated, four counts of vehicular homicide, one count of causing great bodily harm, and one count of reckless driving. It took three trials to secure convictions on all three charges. To mitigate pretrial publicity, the first two trials held in 1994 were moved to Taos, a town about 150 miles north of the Albuquerque location of the vehicular homicide and a jurisdiction that had a significant number of Indians in the jury pool. The first two trials resulted in a conviction on driving while intoxicated, but the jury deadlocked on other charges. Media interviews with the jurors in the first two trials indicated that jury members failed to convict House on the most severe charges because they had sympathy for the House family and felt that the defendant had much to offer society (Asher 1994, June 20, A1; Asher 1994, November 7, A6). In the posttrial interviews, some jurors indicated they were persuaded more by the social relations narrative than by the formalist narrative of the prosecution.

A third trial took place in 1995 in Las Cruces, 250 miles south of Albuquerque, a jurisdiction with few Indians in the jury pool. This trial had almost identical content to the two that preceded it. One difference was that the trial was broadcast live on *Court TV*. Another difference was the trial took place in a location in which many citizens were sympathetic to the Cravens-Milford family. This trial resulted in a conviction on four charges of vehicular homicide and a twenty-two-year prison sentence for House. Just as in the other trials, this one concentrated on two issues: the problem of liberal alcohol laws in New Mexico, the issue raised by the victims' family, and the likelihood of racial stereotyping, the issue raised by the defense. What the third trial added to the public conversation about the case was an emphasis on cultural approaches to reconciliation. For example, the defense emphasized that the defendant sought forgiveness from the family of the victims and healing from traditional Navajo medicine men ("The Trial of Gordon House" 1994). In ways similar to previous newspaper accounts, the national television story of the Gordon House case promoted the social relationship narrative by showing that Gordon House was a spiritual person who sought reconciliation. In contrast to the narrative emphasis of the televised version of the case, the jurors viewed the case from the point of view of the formalist theory of the prosecution. They believed that Gordon House violated the law and should receive the maximum punishment available for the four vehicular homicides that he committed while driving drunk.

After House's conviction in his third trial, defense attorney Twohig appealed the case to the New Mexico Court of Appeals on the grounds that the trial was unfair because the Las Cruces jurisdiction was predisposed to convict an Indian. The court of appeals overturned the verdict in 1997. However, in 1999, the New Mexico Supreme Court reinstated House's conviction. Later that year Twohig appealed the case to the U.S. Supreme Court, but the Court declined to hear the case. Currently, Gordon House is serving his twenty-two-year sentence in a New Mexico prison. Under New Mexico law, if he earns every day of eligible "good time," he will be released in 2009.

Political Effects

The case had some positive long-term consequences for the prosecution, the defense, the New Mexico judiciary, the defendant, and the public political agenda. The rhetorical discourse about the case and the political actions of the victims' family produced significant political change. From the perspective of the prosecution, the case called attention to the problems of Indians and others who drive while intoxicated, motivated the passage of several new strict laws, and gave a potent public voice to the victims. By calling a Navajo medicine man and featuring testimony about Navajo methods of reconciliation, the defense also achieved some victories. The defense showed that cultural testimony provides important evidence in a criminal trial. Additionally, the defense's legal stories exposed the depraved mind statute as an outdated and potentially racist law. From the point of view of some of the judges in the case, the eventual incarceration of Gordon

House proved that everyone should be treated according to the formal meaning of the law. From the perspective of Gordon House, the case showed that racist stereotyping may indeed impact the way vehicular homicide cases involving Indians are tried. From the perspective of the family and friends of the victims, the trials helped call public attention to drunk driving in general. This attention created public support for their lobbying for changes in laws regarding the sale, use, distribution of alcohol and for punishment of drunk drivers. The result was extensive legislation that substantively changed state laws.

Indian Drinking

The Gordon House case highlights the continuing problem that the government and the tribal government has in their efforts to sanction alcohol sale and to reduce alcohol use and binge drinking among Navajos. Both the government treaties that prohibited the sale of alcohol to Indians and the subsequent statutes that modified the prohibition have not solved the problem of alcohol consumption on or off the reservation. The tribal police take legal action against those abusing alcohol by levying large fines and putting drunks in jail. Current legal measures often fail to deal with the root causes of the problem, such as off-reservation liquor sales, binge drinking, and the social and economic causes of alcohol problems. The case did then and continues now to figure into public discussion about drunk driving, Indian alcohol use, and the need for more education and stricter enforcement of laws against all people who drink when they drive. In one sense, House's attorney was correct; Gordon House was a scapegoat for the drunk-driving problems in the state. In the sense of Kenneth Burke ([1950] 1969, 12–13), he was a perfect scapegoat because his conviction succeeded to some extent in restoring the social order by calling attention to Indian binge drinking and by creating new policies that restricted driving while intoxicated on and off the reservation. The narrative presented in the preliminary hearing shows that law is not always a simple matter of comparing the facts to the language of a statute in the way that formalist narratives do. Rights narratives at times persuade more than other narratives as they did in defense's successful appeal to the New Mexico Court of Appeals. Social relations narratives prevail as they did in the minds of some jurors in House's first two trials. Formalist narratives persuade some juries as they did in House's third trial. Political action narratives in the end may have more impact than any of the other narratives do when it comes to social change.

Additionally, the case focused the state's attention on the firewater myth, Navajo alcohol abuse, binge drinking, and an individual's responsibilities for driving while drunk. Since tribes other than Navajos have a significant problem with alcohol dependency, it would not be difficult to find cases similar to that of Gordon House close to the reservations of the Puget Sound Indians in Washington, the Santee Sioux in Nebraska, the Southern Arapaho and Cheyenne in Oklahoma, or the Oglalas at Pine Ridge, South Dakota. The difference might be that the legal advocates, judges, media, voters, and legislators in different jurisdictions might treat Indian defendants and vehicular homicide differently than they did in this high profile case in New Mexico. Even though differences might exist, the importance of this case likely will not be diminished in impact by other similar cases.

NOTE

1. The New Mexico legal documents show that this law first appeared in 1865, but that it was not part of the original constitution drafted in 1849. Other states, such as New York and Arizona, have depraved mind and depraved heart murder statutes, but neither state uses these charges for murder nor for maximum criminal penalties in the same way that New Mexico law does.

Bibliography

Abel, Annie H. 1915. *The Official Correspondence of James S. Calhoun.* Washington, D.C.: Government Printing Office.

Abert, James J. 1962. *Aberts's New Mexico Report 1846–'47.* Albuquerque: Horn and Wallace.

Abrams, M. H. 1971. *A Glossary of Literary Terms.* New York: Holt, Rinehart and Winston.

"Account of George Quinn." 1962. "A Red Man's View of It: Three Indian Accounts of the Uprising." Edited by Kenneth Carley. *Minnesota History* 38: 147–48.

"Alcohol Use." 1892. U.S. Stat. 27: 614.

Allen, Frank. 1993, October 28. "Bind over Order after Preliminary Hearing." Albuquerque: New Mexico State District Court.

Altheide, David and John Johnson. 1980. *Bureaucratic Propaganda.* Boston: Allyn & Bacon.

American Friends Service Committee. 1970. *Uncommon Controversy: Fishing Rights of the Muckleshoot, Puyallup, and Nisqually.* Seattle: University of Washington Press.

Anderson, Gary Clayton. 1986a. "Introduction." In *The Dakota or Sioux in Minnesota as They Were in 1834.* Edited by Samuel W. Pond, xii–xxi. St Paul: Minnesota Historical Society Press.

———. 1986b. *Little Crow: Spokesman for the Sioux.* St. Paul: Minnesota Historical Society Press.

Anderson, Gary Clayton and Alan R. Woolworth. 1988. *Through Dakota Eyes: Narrative Accounts of the Minnesota Indian War of 1862.* St. Paul: Minnesota Historical Society Press.

Anderson, Peggy. 1998. "Northwest Tribe Ready for 1st Gray Whale Hunt in 70 Years." *Albuquerque Journal,* October 8, B10.

Andrist, Ralph K. 1964. *The Long Death: The Last Days of the Plains Indians.* New York: Collier Books.

Annual Report of the Commissioner of Indian Affairs [Zuni Pueblo]. 1850. House Executive Documents, 31st Cong., 2d Sess., 593: 128–43.

———. [Southern Cheyenne and Arapaho]. 1861. Washington, D.C.: Government Printing Office, 709.

———. [Minnesota Uprising]. 1863. Washington, D.C.: Government Printing Office.

———. [Red Cloud]. 1868. Washington, D.C.: Government Printing Office, 21–24.

———. [Navajo Warfare]. 1877a. Washington, D.C.: Government Printing Office.

———. [Red Cloud]. 1877b. Washington, D.C.: Government Printing Office.

———. [Navajo Depredations]. 1879. Washington, D.C.: Government Printing Office.

———. [Zuni Witchcraft]. 1889. House Executive Documents. 53rd Cong., 3d Sess., 3306: 209–15.

———. [Sioux Massacre]. 1891. Washington, D.C.: Government Printing Office, 179–811.

———. [Zuni Witchcraft]. 1892. Report to Office of Indian Affairs, 52nd Cong., 2d Sess., 3088: 548–63.

———. [Southern Cheyenne and Arapaho]. 1895. Washington, D.C.: Government Printing Office, 87, 221.

———. [Zuni Witchcraft]. 1897. 50th Cong., 2d Sess., House of Representatives, 361: 199–200, 213, 315.

Archibeck, Ronald P. 1972. *Taos Indians and the Blue Lake Controversy.* M.A. Thesis. Albuquerque: University of New Mexico.

Armstrong, Virginia I. 1971. *I Have Spoken: American History through the Voices of the Indians.* Chicago: The Swallow Press.

Arnold, Frazier. 1934. "The Ghost Dance and Wounded Knee." *Cavalry Journal* 43: 18–20.

"Articles of Agreement and Convention" (Navajo). 1855. In *The Story of Navajo Treaties.* Edited by David Brugge and Cornell J. Lee, 73–78. Window Rock, Ariz.: Navajo Historical Publications.

Asher, Ed. 1993. "Gordon House Knew What He Was Doing." *Albuquerque Tribune*, March 30, A1, A8.

———. 1993. "Christmas Eve a Blank for Dad." *Albuquerque Tribune*, September 28, A1, A8.

———. 1993. "House Meant to Go Wrong Way." *Albuquerque Tribune*, September 29, A3.

———. 1993. "Lawyer: House Was Too Drunk." *Albuquerque Tribune*, October 15, A1.

———. 1993. "4 Murder Charges Dropped in DWI Case." *Albuquerque Tribune*, October 28, A1.

———. 1994. "Migraine Defense Raised in Crash Trial." *Albuquerque Tribune*, June 14, A1, A10.

———. 1994. "House's Wrong to Blame Migraine, Expert Testifies." *Albuquerque Tribune*, June 16, A1, A10.

———. 1994. "House DWI Jurors Were Torn Apart Emotionally." *Albuquerque Tribune*, June 20, A1.

———. 1994. "Gordon House's First Jurors Sympathize with Next Panel's Task." *Albuquerque Tribune*, November 7, A6.

———. 1994. "House: I Know You're Crying." *Albuquerque Tribune*, November 19, A1.

———. 1994. "Behind Closed Doors." *Albuquerque Tribune*, November 25, D1, D7.

Atlas Video. 1992. *The Dakota Conflict*. St. Paul: KTCA, Minnesota Public Broadcasting.

Author's Notes. 1993. Albuquerque: New Mexico State District Court, October 15.

Bailey, L. R., ed. 1964. *The Navajo Reconnaissance*. Los Angeles: Westernlore Press.

———. 1973. *Indian Slave Trade in the Southwest*. Los Angeles: Westernlore Press.

Bakhtin, Mikhail M. 1986. *Speech Genres: The Late Essays*. Translated by Vern W. McGee. Edited by Caryl Emerson and Micheal Holquist. Austin: University of Texas Press.

Bandelier, Adolph. 1890–1892. "Final Report of Investigations among the Indians of the Southwestern United States, 1880–85." Archeological Institute of America Papers. Cambridge, Mass.: John Wilson and Sons.

Barker, Rodney. 1992. *The Broken Circle*. New York: Simon & Schuster.

Barney, Ralph A. 1955. "Legal Problems Peculiar to Indian Claims Litigation." *Ethnohistory* 2: 315–25.

———. 1974. "Arapaho-Cheyenne Indians." In *Indian Claims Commission Cases 329a and 329b*. Edited by Norman A. Ross, 13–17. New York: Clearwater Microfilm.

Bartlett, F. C. 1973. *Political Propaganda*. New York: Octagon.

Barsh, Russell L. 1979. *The Washington Fishing Rights Controversy: An Economic Critique*. Seattle: University of Washington, Graduate School of Business.

———. 1991. "Backfire from Boldt: The Judicial Transformation of Coastal Salish Propriety Fisheries in Common." *Western Legal History* 4: 85–97.

Barton, Winifred W. 1919. *John P. Williamson: A Brother to the Sioux*. New York: Fleming H. Revel.

Baxter, John O. 1995. "Problems of Land Use within a Portion of the Zuni Land Claim Area." In *Zuni and the Courts*. Edited by Richard Hart, 121–36. Lawrence: University of Kansas Press.

Beardsley, A. S. and Donald A. McDonald. 1942. "The Courts and the Early Bar of Washington Territory." *Washington Law Review and State Bar Journal* 17: 57–82.

Beauvais, Fred. 1996. "Trends in Indian Adolescent Drug and Alcohol Use." In *Native Americans, Crime, and Justice*. Edited by Marianne O. Nielsen and Robert A. Silverman, 89–95. Boulder, Colo.: Westview Press.

———. 1998. "American Indians and Alcohol." *Alcohol Health & Research World* 22: 253–60.

Bender, Norman J. 1984. *Missionaries, Outlaws, and Indians*. Albuquerque: University of New Mexico Press.

Benedek, Emily. 1992. *The Wind Won't Know Me: A History of the Navajo-Hopi Land Dispute*. New York: Vintage.

Bennett, William L. and Martha S. Feldman. 1981. *Reconstructing Reality in the Courtroom*. New Brunswick, N.J.: Rutgers University Press.

Benoit, William I. 1995. *Accounts, Excuses, and Apologies: A Theory of Image Restoration Strategies*. Albany: State University of New York Press.

Berkhofer, Robert F., Jr. 1979. *The White Man's Indian: Images of the American Indian from Columbus to the Present*. New York: Vintage.

Bernal Papers. Santa Fe: New Mexico State Historical Archives.

Berthong, Donald J. 1971. "White Neighbors Come among the Southern Cheyenne and Arapaho." *Kansas Quarterly* 3: 105–15.

———. [1963] 1972. *The Southern Cheyennes*. Norman: University of Oklahoma Press.

Biolosi, Thomas and Larry J. Zimmerman. 1997. *Indians and Anthropologists*. Tucson: University of Arizona Press.

Bohannan, Paul, ed. 1967. *Law and Warfare*. Garden City, N.Y.: The Natural History Press.

Bordewich, Fergus, M. 1996. *Killing the White Man's Indian: Reinventing Native Americans at the End of the Twentieth Century*. New York: Doubleday.

Bourdieu, Pierre. 1984. *Distinction: A Social Critique of the Judgment of Taste*. London: Routledge.

Bowers, John W., Donovan J. Ochs, and Richard J. Jensen. 1993. *The Rhetoric of Agitation and Control*. Prospect Heights, Ill.: Waveland Press.

Brayer, Herbert O. 1939. "Pueblo Indian Land Grants of the Rio Abajo, New Mexico." *University of New Mexico Bulletin* 434. Albuquerque: University of New Mexico Press.

Brown, Dee. 1970. *Bury My Heart at Wounded Knee: An Indian History of the American West*. New York: Holt, Rinehart, and Winston.

Brown, J.A.C. 1963. *Techniques of Persuasion: From Propaganda to Brainwashing*. Baltimore: Penguin.

Brown, Samuel. 1988. "Samuel J. Brown's Recollections." In *Through Dakota Eyes*. Edited by Gary Clayton Anderson and Alan R. Woolworth, 169–76, 222–28, 271–72. St. Paul: Minnesota Historical Society Press.

Brugge, David M. 1985. *Navajos in the Catholic Church Records of New Mexico 1694–1875*. Tsaile, Ariz.: Navajo Community College Press.

Brugge, David M. and Correll J. Lee. 1971. *The Story of Navajo Treaties*. Window Rock, Ariz.: Navajo Historical Publications.

Brummett, Barry. 1984. "The Representative Anecdote as a Burkean Method Applied to Evangelical Rhetoric." *The Southern Speech Communication Journal* 50: 1–23.

Bruner, Edward M. 1986. "Ethnography as Narrative." In *The Anthropology of Experience*. Edited by Edward M. Bruner and Victor W. Turner, 139–55. Urbana: University of Illinois Press.

Bryant, Charles S. 1864. *A History of the Great Massacre by the Sioux Indians in Minnesota, Including the Personal Narratives of Many Who Escaped*. Cincinnati: Richey & Carroll.

Bunzel, Ruth L. 1929–1930. *Introduction to Zuni Ceremonialism*. Washington, D.C: Bureau of Ethnology.

Burke, Kenneth. [1935] 1965. *Permanence and Change*. Indianapolis: Bobbs-Merrill.

———. [1931] 1968. *Counter-Statement*. Berkeley: University of California Press.

———. [1950] 1969. *A Grammar of Motives*. Berkeley: University of California Press.

———. 1970. *Rhetoric of Religion*. Berkeley: University of California Press.

———. [1937] 1971. *Attitudes toward History*. Boston: Beacon Press.

———. [1941] 1973. *The Philosophy of Literary Form*. Berkeley: University of California Press.

———. 1979. *A Rhetoric of Motives*. Berkeley: University of California Press.

———. 1986. *Language as Symbolic Action*. Berkeley: University of California Press.

Burnette, Robert and John Koster. 1974. *The Road to Wounded Knee*. New York: Bantam.

Campbell, John A. 1990. "Between the Fragment and the Icon: Prospect for a Rhetorical House of the Middle Way." *Western Journal of Speech Communication* 54: 346–47.

Campbell, Joseph. [1949] 1960. *The Hero with a Thousand Faces*. New York: Pantheum.

Carey, Raymond G. 1964. "The Puzzle at Sand Creek." *Colorado Magazine* 41: 279–98.

Carleton, Philips D. 1943. "The Indian Captivity Narrative." *American Literature* 14: 169–80.

Carley, Kenneth. 1962a. "A Red Man's View of It: Three Indian Accounts of the Uprising." *Minnesota History* 38: 126–49.

———. 1962b. "The Sioux Campaign of 1863: Sibley's Letters to His Wife." *Minnesota History* 38: 99–114.

———. 1976. *The Sioux Uprising of 1862*. St. Paul: Minnesota Historical Society Press.

Carlson, Leonard A. 1985. "What Was It Worth: Economic and Historical Aspects of Determining Awards in Indian Land Claims Cases?" In *Irredeemable America: The Indian's Estate and Land Claims*. Edited by Irma Sutton, 87–109. Albuquerque: University of New Mexico Press.

Carpenter, Cecelia Svinth. 1976. *Leschi: Last Chief of the Nisquallies*. Ortig, Wash.: Heritage Quest.

———. 1996. *Tears of Internment: The Indian History of Fox Island and the Puget Sound Indian War*. Tacoma, Wash.: Tacoma Research Service.

Carr, David. 1986. *Time, Narrative and History*. Bloomington: Indiana University Press.

Casuas, Phil. 1992. "Mourners Shed Countless Tears." *Albuquerque Journal*, December 30, A1, A3.

Cathcart, Robert. 1978. "Movements: Confrontations as Rhetorical Form." *Central States Speech Journal* 31: 233–47.

Chaput, Donald. 1972. "Generals, Indian Agents, Politicians: The Doolittle Survey of 1865." *Western Historical Quarterly* 3: 269–82.

Cherokee Nation v. Georgia. 1831. 30 U.S. 1.

Cheyenne-Arapaho v. United States. 10 Ind. Cl. Comm. 1, 1961 and 16 Ind. Cl. Comm. 162, 1965. All materials including the plaintiffs' brief, defendant's

brief, testimony, and commissioner's opinion are taken from the microfilm
collection of the Indian Claims Commission, Cases 329a and 329b. 1973.
Edited by Norman A. Ross. New York: Clearwater Publishing.

"Chief Big Eagle's Story." 1962. In "A Red Man's View of It: Three Indian Accounts of the Uprising." Edited by Kenneth Carley. *Minnesota History* 38:
129–43.

Churchill, Ward and Jim Vander Wall. 1990. *Agents of Repression*. Boston: South
End Press.

"Claims for Depredations by the Santee Sioux." House of Representatives, 38th
Cong. Ex. Doc. 58, Serial 1189, 1–23.

Clair, Robin Patric. 1997. "Organizing Silence: Silence as Voice and Voice as Silence in the Narrative Exploration of the Treaty of New Echota." *Western
Journal of Communication* 61: 315–37.

Clinton, Bill. 1999. Remarks by the President to the Pine Ridge Reservation Community (www.pitt.edu/-lmitten/clinton).

Clodfelter, Michael. 1988. *The Dakota War: The United States Army Versus the
Sioux, 1862–1865*. Jefferson, N.C.: McFarland & Co.

Cobb, Roger W. and Charles D. Elder. 1981. "Communication and Public Policy."
In *Handbook of Political Communication*. Edited by Dan D. Nimmo and
Keith R. Sanders, 391–416. Beverly Hills, Calif.: Sage Publications.

Coel, Margaret. 1981. *Chief Left Hand: Southern Arapaho*. Norman: University of
Oklahoma Press.

Cohen, Fay G. 1986. *Treaties on Trial*. Seattle: University of Washington Press.

Colby, General L. W. 1892. "The Sioux Indian War 1890–91." *Transactions and
Reports of the Nebraska State Historical Society* 3: 176–80.

"Colorado Indian Massacre Location to Become National Historic Site." 2000,
November 12 (cnn.com/2000/US/11/12/sandcreekmassacre.ap).

Collier, John. 1923. "Our Indian Policy." *Sunset* 50 (March): 93.

———. 1924a. "Persecuting the Pueblos." *Sunset* 52 (July): 50.

———. 1924b. *The Indian and Religious Freedom* (pamphlet). Collier Papers. New
Haven, Conn.: Yale University Americana Collection.

———. 1925. "Do Indians Have Rights of Conscience?" *Christian Century* 42
(March 13): 346–49.

Collier Papers. 1920–1930. New Haven, Conn.: Yale University Americana Collection, Boxes 1–20.

Collins, Dabney O. 1971. "Battle for Blue Lake." *The American West* 8: 32–37.

Condit, Celeste. 1990. "Rhetorical Criticism and Audiences: The Extremes of
McGee and Leff." *Western Journal of Speech Communication* 54: 330–45.

"Condition of the Indian Tribes." (1866–1867). Senate Report. U.S. Congress, 2d
Sess., 1279: 156.

Conley, John M. and William O'Barr. 1990. *Rules Versus Relationships: The Ethnography of Legal Discourse*. Chicago: University of Chicago Press.

Congressional Record—House. 1968. June 18, 5055–59.

Congressional Record—Senate. 1970. December 1, 19157–66.

———. 1970. December 2, 19226–44.

Court of Indian Offenses Act. 1892. U.S. Stat. 27: 614.

Cox, J. Robert. 1981. "Investigating Policy Argument as a Field." In *Dimensions of Argument.* Edited by George Ziegelmuller and Jack Rhodes, 126–42. Annandale, Va.: Speech Communication Association.

Craig, Reginald S. [1959] 1994. *The Fighting Parson: The Biography of Colonel John Chivington.* Tucson, Ariz.: Westernlore Press.

Crampton, C. Gregory (1977). *The Zunis of Cibola.* Salt Lake City: University of Utah Press.

Crow Dog, Mary (with Richard Erdoes). 1990. *Lakota Woman.* New York: HarperCollins.

Cushing, Frank Hamilton. 1979. "My Adventures at Zuni." In *Zuni: Selected Writings of Frank Hamilton Cushing.* Edited by Jesse Green. Lincoln: University of Nebraska Press.

———. [1882] 1990. "Killing Sorcerers: Remarkable Customs of the Zuni Indians of New Mexico." In *Cushing at Zuni.* Edited by Jesse Green, 340–42. Albuquerque: University of New Mexico Press.

Danforth, Sandra C. 1973. "Repaying Historical Debts: The Indian Claims Commission." *North Dakota Law Review* 49: 359–403.

Danker, Donald F. 1981. "The Wounded Knee Interviews of Eli S. Ricker." *Nebraska History* 2: 151–243.

Daniels, Robert E. 1970. "Cultural Identities among the Oglala Sioux." In *The Modern Sioux.* Edited by Ethel Nurge, 198–245. Lincoln: University of Nebraska Press.

Davis, Tim. 1993. "Heartsick Thoreau Tries to Fathom Tragedy." *Albuquerque Tribune,* January 2, A1, A5.

Dawes Act. (General Allotment Act). 1887. 25 U.S.C.A. 331.

de Certeau, Michel. 1984. *The Practice of Everyday Life.* Translated by Steven Randall. Berkeley: University of California Press.

Decker, Craig A. 1977. "The Construction of Indian Treaties, Agreements, and Statutes." *American Indian Law Review* 5: 299–311.

Defendant's Brief. 1974. In *Indian Claims Commission Cases 329a and 329b.* Edited by Norman A. Ross, 1–120. New York: Clearwater Microfilm.

Delgado, Richard. 1989. "Storytelling for Oppositionists and Others." *Michigan Law Review* 87: 2411–40.

Deloria, Vine, Jr. [1969] 1970. *Custer Died for Your Sins: An Indian Manifesto.* New York: Avon Books.

———. 1970. *We Talk You Listen: New Tribes, New Turf.* New York: Macmillan.

———. 1973. *God Is Red: A Native View of Religion.* New York: Grosset and Dunlap.

———. [1974] 1985. *Behind the Trail of Broken Treaties: An Indian Declaration of Independence.* Austin: University of Texas Press.

Deloria, Vine, Jr. and Clifford M. Lytle. 1983. *American Indians, American Justice.* Austin: University of Texas Press.

DeMallie, Raymond J. 1977. "American Indian Treaty Making: Motives and Meaning." *American Indian Journal* 3: 2–10.

———. 1984. *The Sixth Grandfather: Black Elk's Teachings Given to John G. Niehardt.* Lincoln: University of Nebraska Press.

Denton, Robert E. and Gary C. Woodward. 1985. *Political Communication in America.* New York: Praeger.

Department of Game v. Puyallup Tribe, Inc. 1973. 414 U.S. 44.

Derounian-Stodola, Katherine and James Arthur Levernier. 1993. *The Indian Captivity Narrative, 1550–1900*. New York: Twayne.

Dewing, Rolland. 1995. *Wounded Knee II*. Chadron, Nebr.: Great Plains Network.

Diedrich, Mark. 1989. *Dakota Oratory*. Rochester, Minn.: Coyote Books.

Dingman, Tracy. 1992. "Lawmakers to Propose DWI Reform." *Albuquerque Journal*, December 30, D1.

"Doniphans's Expedition." 1846. Senate Executive Document, 30th Cong., 1st Sess., 503: 1.

Downs, James F. 1964. *Animal Husbandry in Navajo Society and Culture*. Berkeley: University of California Press.

Dozier, Edward P. 1966. "Problem Drinking among American Indians: The Role of Socio-cultural Deprivation." *Quarterly Journal Studies of Alcoholism* 27: 72–87.

Dunham, Harold H. 1974. "Spanish and Mexican Land Policies and Grants." In *The Taos Pueblo Region, New Mexico*. Edited by D. A. Hoor, 152–312. New York: Garland Publishing.

Dunn, J. P. [1886] 1969. *Massacres of the Mountains*. New York: Capricorn Books.

Eastlick, L. [1863] 1959. *Personal Narrative of the Indian Massacres of 1862*. St. Paul: Minnesota Historical Society Press.

Edelman, Murray. 1977. *Political Language: Words That Succeed and Policies That Fail*. New York: Academic Press.

———. [1964] 1980. *The Symbolic Uses of Politics*. Urbana: University of Illinois Press.

———. 1995. *Constructing the Political Spectacle*. Chicago: University of Chicago Press.

Ehninger, Douglas, Bruce E. Gronbeck, Ray E. McKerrow, and Alan H. Monroe. 1986. *Principles and Types of Speech Communication*. Glenview, Ill.: Scott, Foresman.

Ehninger, Douglas and Wayne Brockriede. 1970. *Decision by Debate*. New York: Dodd, Mead.

Ehrenfeld, Alice. 1946. Legislative Material on the Indian Claims Commission Act of 1946. Washington, D.C.: Riegelman, Strasser, Schwarz and Spegelber Law Firm.

Ellis, Florence Hawley. 1974. "Anthropological Data Pertaining to Taos in Land Claim." In *Pueblo Indians* I: 1–150. Edited by D. A. Hoor. New York: Garland Publishing.

———. 1989. "Southwest: Pueblo." In *Witchcraft and Sorcery of the Native American Peoples*. Edited by Deward E. Walker, 191–222. Moscow: University of Idaho Press.

Emmons, Della G. 1965. *Leschi of the Nisquallies*. Minneapolis: T. S. Denison.

"Evidence and Proceeding in the Case of Leschi." 1857. *Pioneer and Democrat*, March 27, 2.

Fanon, Fritz. 1994. "On National Culture." In *Colonial Discourse and Post Colonial Theory*. Edited by Patrick William and Laura Chrisman, 36–52. New York: Columbia University Press.

Fay, George E., ed. 1982. "Indian Agency Reports: Zuni Indian Pueblo, New Mexico, 1887–1967." Ethnology Series, No. 20. Greeley: University of Northern Colorado.

Ferguson, T. J. 1995. "Zuni Archeology and Culture History." In *Zuni and the Courts.* Edited by E. Richard Hart, 3–7. Lawrence: University of Kansas Press.

Ferry, Barbara. 1996. "Senate Approves Transferring Ceremonial Land." *Santa Fe New Mexican,* April 3, B4.

Fetterman, David M. 1989. *Ethnography: Applied Social Research.* Newbury Park, Calif.: Sage Publications.

Fewkes, Walter J. 1891. "A Few Summer Ceremonials at Zuni Pueblo." *Journal of American Ethnology and Archeology* 1: 2–62.

Fisher, Walter R. 1987. *Human Communication as Narration.* Columbia: University of South Carolina Press.

Fitzpatrick, Thomas. 1847–1848. "Report on New Mexico." Senate Executive Document, No. 1. 30th Cong., 1st Sess.

Folger, Joseph P., Marshall Scott Poole, and Randall K. Stutman. 1993. *Working Through Conflict.* New York: HarperCollins.

Folwell, William Watts. 1961. *A History of Minnesota,* Vol. 2. St. Paul: Minnesota Historical Society Press.

Fowler, Loretta. 1982. *Arapahoe [sic] Politics, 1851–1978: Symbols in Crises of Authority.* Lincoln: University of Nebraska Press.

Francis, Lee. 1985. *Native Time: A Historical Time Line of Native America.* New York: St. Martin's Press.

Franciscan Fathers. 1910. *An Ethnologic Dictionary of the Navajo Language.* St. Michael's, Ariz.: St. Michael's Press.

Frank, Billy, Jr. 1997. "Congress, Get to Know Us." *Northwest Indian Fisheries Commission News* 17 (Summer): 2.

Frank, Maurice. 1968. *Fort Defiance and the Navajos.* Boulder, Colo.: Pruett Press.

Frazer, Robert W., ed., 1968. *New Mexico in 1850: A Military View.* Norman: University of Oklahoma Press.

Fridley, Russell L. 1962. "Charles E. Flandrau: Attorney at War." *Minnesota History* 38: 116–25.

Friedman, Lawrence. 1973. *A History of American Law.* New York: Simon & Schuster.

Frug, John. 1988. "Argument as Character." *Stanford Law Review* 40: 869–97.

"Gabriel Renville's Memoir." 1988. In *Through Dakota Eyes.* Edited by Gary Clayton Anderson and Alan R. Woolworth, 186–91, 230–33, 273–74. St. Paul: Minnesota Historical Society Press.

General Allotment Act. 1887. 25 U.S.C.A. 3.

Gibbs, George. 1877. "Tribes of Western Washington and Northwestern Oregon." *Contributions in American Ethnology,* Vol. 1. Washington, D.C.: Bureau of Ethnology.

Glassley, Ray H. [1953] 1972. *Indian Wars of the Pacific Northwest.* Portland, Ore.: Binfords and Mort.

Goffman, Erving. 1971. *Relations in Public.* New York: Harper & Row.

Gonzales, Mario and Elizabeth Cook-Lynn. 1999. *The Politics of Hallowed Ground.* Urbana: University of Illinois Press.

Goodnight, G. Thomas and John Poulakos. 1981. "Conspiracy Rhetoric: From Pragmatism to Fantasy in Public Discourse." *Western Journal of Speech Communication* 45: 299–316.

Gordon-McCutchan, Robert C. 1995. *The Taos Indians and the Battle for Blue Lake*. Santa Fe, N.Mex.: Red Crane Books.

Gosnell, Wesley B. [1856] 1926. "Reprint of Letter From W. B. Gosnell to Governor Isaac Stevens, Concerning the Indian War in Washington Territory." *Pacific Northwest Quarterly* 17: 289–99.

Graber, Doris A. 1981. "Political Language." In *Handbook of Political Communication*. Edited by Dan D. Nimmo and Keith R. Sanders, 195–223. Beverly Hills, Calif.: Sage Publications.

Grass Roots Oyate. 2000. (www.elementalpathways.com/pineridge).

Green, Jesse, ed. 1979. *Zuni: Selected Writings of Frank Hamilton Cushing*. Albuquerque: University of New Mexico Press.

———. [1882] 1990. *Cushing at Zuni: The Correspondence and Journal of Frank Hamilton Cushing, 1879–1884*. Albuquerque: University of New Mexico Press.

Gregg, Richard B. 1971. "The Ego Function of the Rhetoric of Protest." *Philosophy and Rhetoric* 2: 71–91.

Griffith, Leland. 1966. "A Dramatistic Theory of the History of Movements." In *Critical Responses to Kenneth Burke*. Edited by William H. Rueckert, 456–78. Minneapolis: University of Minnesota Press.

Grinnell, George Bird. [1923] 1972. *Cheyenne Indians: Their History and Ways of Life*, Vol. 1. Lincoln: University of Nebraska Press.

———. [1915] 1985. *The Fighting Cheyennes*. Norman: University of Oklahoma Press.

Gunther, Erma. 1928. *A Further Analysis of the First Salmon Ceremony*. Seattle: University of Washington Publications in Anthropology.

Haeberlin, Herman and Erma Gunther. 1930. *The Indians of the Puget Sound*. Seattle: University of Washington Publications in Anthropology.

Hafen, Leroy F. 1974. "Historical Development of the Arapaho-Cheyenne Land Area." In *Arapaho-Cheyenne Indians*. Edited by Norman A. Ross, 97–174. New York: Garland Publishing.

Hammond, George P. and Agapita A. Rey, eds. 1953. *Onatè, Colonizer of New Mexico, 1598–1628*, Vol. 6. Albuquerque, N.Mex.: Coronado Cuarto Centennial Publications.

Hariman, Robert. 1986. "Status, Marginality and Rhetorical Theory." *Quarterly Journal of Speech* 72: 38–54.

Harmon, Alexandra. 1998. *Indians in the Making: Ethnic Relations and Indian Identities around the Puget Sound*. Berkeley: University of California Press.

Harring, Sidney L. 1994. *Crow Dog's Case: American Indian Sovereignty, Tribal Law, and the United States Law in the Nineteenth Century*. Cambridge: Cambridge University Press.

Hart, E. Richard, ed. 1995. *Zuni and the Courts*. Lawrence: University of Kansas Press.

Hassrick, Royal B. 1964. *The Sioux: Life and Customs of a Warrior Society*. Norman: University of Oklahoma Press.

Hawthorne, Harry L. 1896. "The Sioux Campaign of 1890–91." *Journal of the Military Service Institution of the United States* 29: 185–87.

Heard, Isaac V. D. 1864. *History of the Sioux War and Massacres of 1862 and 1863*. New York: Harper and Brothers.

Hearings before the House Committee on Interior and Insular Affairs in the House of Representatives on H.R. 3306. 1969, 90th Cong., 2d Sess., 1–38.

Hearings before the Subcommittee on Indian Affairs of the Committee on Interior and Insular Affairs of the United States Senate on H.R. 3306 and S. 1624 and S. 1625. 1968. 90th Cong., 2d Sess.

Hearings before the Subcommittee on Indian Affairs of the Committee on Interior and Insular Affairs of the United States Senate on S. 750 and H.R. 471. 1970. 91st Cong., 2d Sess.

Heath, Robert L. 1986. *Realism and Relativism: A Perspective on Kenneth Burke.* Macon, Ga.: Mercer University Press.

Hebard, Grace and E. A. Bininstool. 1922. *The Bozeman Trail,* Vol. 1. Cleveland: Arthur Clark.

Heider, Fritz. 1958. *The Psychology of Interpersonal Relations.* New York: John Wiley & Sons.

Heilbron, Bertha L. 1941. "Frank Mayer and the Treaties of 1851." *Minnesota History* 22: 133–56.

Henderson, L. N. 1987. "Legality and Empathy." *Michigan Law Review* 85: 1574–1610.

Hodge, Fredrick West, ed. 1971. *Handbook of American Indians North of Mexico,* 4 vols. New York: Roman & Littlefield.

Hoebel, E. Adamson. 1978. *The Cheyennes: Indians of the Great Plains,* 2d ed. New York: Holt, Rinehart & Winston.

Hoig, Stan. 1961. *The Sand Creek Massacre.* Norman: University of Oklahoma Press.

Holcombe, Return I. 1894. "A Sioux Story of the War." *Minnesota Historical Collections* 6: 382–400.

Hoover, Herbert T. 1989. "The Sioux Agreement of 1889 and Its Aftermath." *South Dakota History* 19: 56–94.

Horr, David Agee. 1974. *Pueblo Indians I.* New York: Garland Publishing.

House Conference Committee Creating Indian Claims Commission. 1946. House of Representatives Conference Report, 92d Cong. 10403: 2643, 4497.

House Committee on Interior and Insular Affairs. 1967. House of Representatives, 90th Cong., 1st Sess., 53–69.

House [Gordon] Case, CR93–16933. Public Hearing Record (PHR). Albuquerque: Ray Twohig Law Office.

Hunt, Aurora. 1958. *General James Henry Carleton.* Glendale, N.Y.: Arthur H. Clarke.

Hyde, George E. 1968. *Life of George Bent Written From His Letters.* Norman: University of Oklahoma Press.

———. [1937] 1976. *Red Cloud's Folks: A History of the Oglala Sioux Indians.* Norman: University of Oklahoma Press.

"The Indian and Religious Freedom." 1922–1924. Collier Papers. New Haven, Conn.: Yale University Library.

Indian Civil Rights Act. 1968. 25 U.S.C.A. 1326.

Indian Claims Commission Act. 1946. 60 Stat. 1049.

Indian Depredation Files. Santa Fe: New Mexico State Archives, Box 114, Files 1–10.

"Indian Hostilities in New Mexico." House of Representatives Exec. Doc. 36th Cong., 1st Sess., No. 69, Serial 1274.

"Indian Massacre and the War of 1862." 1863. *Harper's* (June) 27: 1–24.

Indian Reorganization Act. 1934. 25 U.S.C.A. 461.

Indian Trade Regulation Act. 1832. U.S. Stat. 3: 682–83.

Institute for the Development of Indian Law. 1974. *Treaties & Agreements and the Proceeding of Treaties and Agreements of the Tribes and Bands of Sioux.* Washington, D.C.: Institute for Indian Law.

James, George Wharton. 1920. *New Mexico: The Land of the Delight Makers.* Boston: The Page Company.

Jamieson, Kathleen Hall and Karlyn Kohrs Campbell. 1990. "The Generic Approach: Introduction to Form and Genre." In *Methods of Rhetorical Criticism: A Twentieth-Century Perspective.* Edited by Bernard L. Brock, Robert L. Scott, and James W. Chesebro, 331–42. Detroit: Wayne State University Press.

Jasinski, James. 1990. "An Exploration of Form and Force in Rhetoric and Argumentation." In *Argumentation Theory and the Rhetoric of Assent.* Edited by D. C. Williams and M. Hazen, 53–68. Tuscaloosa: University of Alabama Press.

Jennings, Francis. 1976. *The Invasion of America: Indians, Colonialism, and Conquest.* New York: W. W. Norton.

Jensen, J. Vernon. 1981. *Argumentation: Reasoning in Communication.* New York: Van Nostrand.

Jensen, Richard E. 1990. "Big Foot's Followers at Wounded Knee." *Nebraska History* 71: 194–212.

Jett, Stephen C. 1974. "The Destruction of the Navajo Orchards in 1864: John Thompson's Report." *Arizona and the West* 14: 365–78.

Johnson, Andrew. 1865. "Message on Slavery." In New Mexico Superintendency Records, T21–6, Delgado to Dole, June 9.

Johnson, Ralph. 1972. "The State Versus Indian Off-Reservation Fishing: A United States Supreme Court Error." *Washington Law Review* 47: 207–36.

Jones, Douglas C. 1966. *The Treaty of Medicine Lodge Creek: The Story of the Great Treaty Council as Told by Eyewitnesses.* Norman: University of Oklahoma Press.

Jones, J. A. 1955. "Problems, Opportunities and Recommendations." *Ethnohistory* 2: 347–56.

Josephy, Alvin M. 1971. *Red Power: American Indian's Fight for Freedom.* New York: McGraw-Hill.

Kamberelis, George. 1995. "Genre as Institutionally Informed Social Practice." *Journal of Contemporary Legal Issues* 6: 115–71.

Kappler, Charles J. 1904. *Indian Affairs, Laws and Treaties.* 2 vols. Washington, D.C.: Government Printing Office.

Keleher, William. 1952. *Turmoil in New Mexico, 1846–1868.* Santa Fe, N.Mex.: Rydal Press.

Kelley, Dean M. 1967. "The Impairment of the Religious Liberty of the Taos Pueblo Indians by the United States Government." *Journal of Church and State* 9: 161–64.

Kelly, Fanny. [1871] 1993. *Narrative of My Captivity among the Sioux Indians.* Hartford, Conn.: Mutual Publishing Company.

Kenner, Charles L. 1969. *A History of New Mexican–Plains Indian Relations.* Norman: University of Oklahoma Press.

Kessell, John L. 1979. *Kiva, Cross and Crown.* Washington, D.C.: National Park Service, Department of Interior.

Kestler, Frances Roe. 1990. *The Indian Captivity Narrative: A Woman's View.* New York: Garland Publishing.

King, John. 1993. "Cravens Prays for Man Accused in Family Deaths." *Albuquerque Journal,* February 1, A1, A5.

Kluckholm, Clyde. 1962. *Navajo Witchcraft.* Boston: Beacon Press.

Kluckholm, Clyde and Dorothea Leighton. 1946. *The Navaho.* Cambridge, Mass.: Harvard University Press.

Kroeber, Adamson L. 1955. "The Nature of the Land-Holding Group." *Ethnohistory* 2: 303–14.

Krupat, Arnold. 1992. *Ethnocriticism.* Berkeley: University of California Press.

Kunitz, Stephen J. and Jerrold E. Levy. 1994. *Drinking Careers: A Twenty-Five Year Follow-up of Three Navaho Populations.* New Haven, Conn.: Yale University Press.

———. 2000. "Conclusions." In *Drinking, Conduct Disorder, and Social Change.* Edited by Stephen J. Kunitz and Jerrold E. Levy, 155–78. New York: Oxford University Press.

———, eds. 2000. *Drinking, Conduct Disorder, and Social Change: Navajo Experience.* New York: Oxford University Press.

Kunitz, Stephen J., K. Ruben Gabriel, and Jerrold E. Levy. 2000. "Alcohol Dependence: Definition, Prevalence, and Risk Factors." In *Drinking, Conduct Disorder, and Social Change.* Edited by Stephen J. Kunitz and Jerrold E. Levy, 54–85. New York: Oxford University Press.

Labat, Joseph. 1988. "Noble Savage." In *Dictionary of Literary Themes and Motifs L–Z.* Edited by Jean Charles Seigneuret, 918–28. Westport, Conn.: Greenwood Press.

LaDuc, Thomas. 1957. "The Work of the Indian Claims Commission." *Pacific Historical Review* 26: 1–16.

Lake, Randall A. 1983. "Enacting Red Power: The Consummatory Function in Native American Protest Rhetoric." *Quarterly Journal of Speech* 69: 127–42.

———. 1991. "Between Myth and History: Enacting Time in Native American Protest Rhetoric." *Quarterly Journal of Speech* 77: 123–51.

Lane, Barbara. 1977. "Background of Treaty Making in Western Washington." *American Indian Journal* 3: 2–11.

Larson, Charles. 1994. *Persuasion.* Belmont, Calif.: Wadsworth.

Larson, Robert L. 1997. *Red Cloud: Warrior-Statesman of the Oglala Sioux.* Norman: University of Oklahoma Press.

Lass, William E. 1963. "The Removal From Minnesota of the Sioux and Winnebago Indians." *Minnesota History* 38: 353–64.

"Last Appeal of Red Cloud." 1870. *New York Times,* June 17, 4.

Lavender, David. 1954. *Bent's Fort.* Garden City, N.Y.: Doubleday & Company.

Lazarus, Edward. 1991. *Black Hills, White Justice.* New York: HarperCollins.

League of Women Voters. 1980. *Washington State and Indian Treaty Rights*. Seattle: League of Women Voters Educational Fund.

LeDuc, William G. 1852. *Minnesota Yearbook for 1852*. St. Paul, Minn.: W. G. LeDuc.

Leff, Michael and Andrew Sachs. 1990. "Words the Most Like Things: Iconicity and the Rhetorical Text." *Western Journal of Speech Communication* 54: 252–73.

Leland, Joy. 1976. *Firewater Myths*. New Brunswick, N.J.: Rutgers Center of Alcohol Studies.

Leschi v. Washington Territory. 1857. Appeal Briefs. Olympia: Washington State Archives, Leschi File.

"*Leschi v. Washington Territory*." 1857. *Washington Territorial Court Reporter* 13: 1–15.

Leupp, Francis E. 1910. *The Indian and His Problem*. New York: Charles Scribner's Sons.

Levin, Murray B. 1971. *Political Hysteria in America: The Democratic Capacity for Repression*. New York: Basic Books.

Levy, Jerrold E. and Stephen Kunitz. 1974. *Indian Drinking: Navajo Practices and Anglo-American Theories*. New York: Wiley.

Lezon, Dale. 1997. "Taos Pueblo Salutes Return of Blue Lake." *Albuquerque Journal North*, January 4, 1, 3.

Lieder, Michael and Jake Page. 1997. *Wild Justice: The People of Geronimo v. The United States*. New York: Random House.

"Lightning Blanket's Story." 1862. In "A Red Man's View of It: Three Indian Accounts of the Uprising." Edited by Kenneth Carley. *Minnesota History* 38: 144–76.

Limerick, Patricia Nelson. 1987. *The Legacy of Conquest*. New York: W. W. Norton.

Lingren, Raymond E. 1946. "A Diary of Kit Carson's Navajo Campaign 1863–64." *New Mexico Historical Review* 22: 226–46.

Linquist, General E. E. 1948. "Indian Treaty Making." *Chronicles of Oklahoma* 25: 416–48.

Linthicum, Leslie. 1993. "House Gives Glimpse of Life." *Albuquerque Journal*, February 10, A1, A9.

———. 1993. "House May Face Murder Charges." *Albuquerque Journal*, March 21, A1.

———. 1993. "House Too Drunk to Reason." *Albuquerque Journal*, October 15, A1, A5.

———. 1993. "No Murder Charges for House." *Albuquerque Journal*, October 29, A1, A10.

———. 1994. "A Trying Case." *Albuquerque Journal*, November 5, C1, C5.

Llewellyn, K. N. and E. Adamson Hoebel. 1941. *The Cheyenne Way: Conflict and Case Law in Primitive Jurisprudence*. Norman: University of Oklahoma Press.

Loftus, Elizabeth and Katherine Ketcham. 1991. *Witness for the Defense*. New York: St. Martin's Press.

"Logical Terms." 1967. *Encyclopedia of Philosophy*. New York: Macmillan.

Loh, Jules. 1971. "Blue Lake Ally's Role Is Appraised." *Albuquerque Journal*, August 16, A1, A10.

Lokken, Ray N. 1952. "The Martial Law Controversy in Washington Territory, 1856." *Pacific Northwest Quarterly* 43: 91–119.

Long, Anton. 1949. *Senator Bursum and the Pueblo Lands Act of 1924*. M.A. Thesis. Albuquerque: University of New Mexico.

Longmire, James. 1985. "Reminiscences." *A Small World of Our Own*. Edited by Robert A. Bennett, 173–92. Walla Walla, Wash.: Pioneer Press Books.

Lurie, Nancy Oestreich. 1955. "Problems, Opportunities and Recommendations." *Ethnohistory* 2: 357–75.

———. 1957. "The Indian Claims Commission Act." *Annals of the American Academy of Political and Social Science* 311: 56–70.

Lynam, Stanley David. 1991. *Wounded Knee 1973*. Lincoln: University of Nebraska Press.

MacAndrew, Craig and Robert B. Edgerton. 1979. *Drunken Comportment: A Social Explanation*. Chicago: Aldine.

Macgregor, Gordon. 1970. "Changing Society: The Teton Dakota." In *The Modern Sioux*. Edited by Ethel Nurge, 92–106. Lincoln: University of Nebraska Press.

Maestas, John R. 1976. *Contemporary Native American Address*. Provo, Utah: Brigham Young University Publications.

Mail, Patricia D. and Robert B. McDonald. 1980. *Tulapia to Tokay: A Bibliography of Alcohol Use and Abuse among Native Americans of North America*. New Haven, Conn.: HRAT Press.

Major Crimes Act. 1885. 18 U.S.C.A. 1153. 23 Stat. 363.

Mancall, Peter C. 1995. *Deadly Medicine: Indians and Alcohol in Early America*. Ithaca, N.Y.: Cornell University Press.

"Mankato Trials." 1862. *St. Paul Pioneer Press*, December 1, 2.

Manners, Robert A. 1957. "The Land Claims Cases: Anthropologists in Conflict." *Ethnohistory* 3: 72–81.

Marino, Cesare. 1990. "History of Western Washington since 1845." In *Handbook of the North American Indian*, Vol. 3. Edited by William C. Sturtevant, 160–69. Washington, D.C.: Smithsonian Institution.

Martin, Calvin. 1987. *The American Indian and the Problem of History*. New York: Oxford University Press.

"Mass Meeting of the Citizens of Washington Territory." 1858. *Pioneer and Democrat*, January 29, 2–3.

"Massacre of Cheyenne Indians." 1864–1865. Report of the Joint Committee on the Conduct of the War. Senate Report 142, 38th Cong., 1st Sess.

Matthiessen, Peter. [1980] 1991. *In the Spirit of Crazy Horse*. New York: Penguin Books.

May, Phillip. 1996. "Overview of Alcohol Abuse: Epidemiology for American Indians." In *Changing Numbers, Changing Needs: American Indian Demography and Public Health*. Edited by Gary Sandefur, Ronald Rinfuss, and Barbara Cohen, 235–61. Washington, D.C.: National Academic Press.

McBride, Delbert J. 1970. "Governor Isaac Ingalls Stevens and the Treaties with the Nisqually Indians: An Examination of Promises Made to the Indians in

December 1854, and the Manner in Which They Were Kept." Olympia: Washington State Library File.

McCall, Michel M. 1990. "Significance of Storytelling." *Studies in Symbolic Interaction* 11: 145–61.

McConkey, Harriett E. B. [1889] 1970. *Dakota War Whoop: Indian Massacres and the War in Minnesota of 1862–1863*. Minneapolis: Ross & Haines.

McDonald, William F. 1979. *The Prosecutors*. Beverly Hills, Calif.: Sage Publications.

McGee, Michael C. 1990. "Text, Context, and Fragmentation of Contemporary Culture." *Western Journal of Speech Communication* 54: 274–89.

McGregor, James H. 1940. *The Wounded Knee Massacre from the Viewpoint of the Sioux*. Minneapolis: The Lund Press.

McKerrow, Raymie E. 1989. "Critical Rhetoric: Theory and Praxis." *Communication Monographs* 56: 91–111.

McKerrow, Raymie and Michael Bruner. 1997. "Argument and Multiple Identities: Contemporary European Nationalism and Environmentalism." *Argumentation and Advocacy* 34: 51–65.

McNickle, D'Arcy. 1971. *Indian Man: A Life of Oliver LaFarge*. Bloomington: University of Indiana Press.

McNitt, Frank. 1962. *Indian Traders*. Norman: University of Oklahoma Press.

———. 1964. *Navaho Expedition Journal of a Military Reconnaissance from Santa Fe, New Mexico, made in 1849 by Lieutenant James A. Simpson*. Norman: University of Oklahoma Press.

———. 1972. *Navajo Wars: Military Campaigns, Slave Raids and Reprisals*. Albuquerque: University of New Mexico Press.

McNitt Papers. n.d. Sante Fe: New Mexico State Historical Society.

Means, Russell (with Marvin J. Wolf). 1995. *Where White Men Fear to Tread*. New York: St. Martin's Press.

Medicine Creek Treaty. 1858. 10 U.S. Stat. 1132.

Medicine Lodge Creek Treaty. 1867. 11 U.S. Stat. 785.

Meeker Papers. n.d. Olympia: Washington Historical Society.

Meeker, Ezra [1905] 1980. *The Tragedy of Leschi*. Everett, Wash.: The Historical Society of Seattle and King County.

Memmi, Albert. 1965. *The Colonizer and the Colonized*. New York: Orion Press.

Mendoza, Patrick W. 1993. *Song of Massacre at Sand Creek Sorrow*. Denver: Willow Wind Publishing.

Meyer, Roy V. 1993. *History of the Santee Sioux: United States Indian Policy on Trial*. Lincoln: University of Nebraska Press.

Minow, Martha. 1990. *Making All the Difference: Inclusion, Exclusion, and American Law*. Ithaca, N.Y.: Cornell University Press.

Minutes of the Treaty Councils. 1854. In Trial Record, *U.S. v. Washington*. 1973. Olympia, Wash.: Attorney General's Office.

Mitchell, Maria. 1973. *The Navajo Peace Treaty of 1868*. New York: Mason & Lipscomb.

Mooney, James. [1896] 1974. *The Ghost Dance Religion and Wounded Knee*. New York: Dover Books.

Moquin, Wayne and Charles Van Doren. 1995. *Great Documents in American Indian History*. New York: Da Capo Press.

Morris, Richard and Philip Wander. 1990. "Native American Rhetoric: Dancing in the Shadows of the Ghost Dance," *Quarterly Journal of Speech* 76: 164–91.

Nabokov, Peter. 1991. *Native American Testimony: A Chronicle of Indian-White Relations from Prophecy to the Present.* New York: Penguin Books.

Namias, June. 1993. *White Captives: Gender and Ethnicity on the American Frontier.* Chapel Hill: University of North Carolina Press.

"Nancy McClure Fairbault Huggan's Account." (1988). In *Through Dakota Eyes.* Edited by Gary Clayton Anderson and Alan R. Woolworth, 80–84, 138–40, 244–48. St. Paul: Minnesota Historical Society Press.

National Highway Safety Administration. 2000. (tbhonline.com/cns/9902).

Navajo Depredations Cases. Santa Fe: New Mexico State Archives, Box 1, Files 1–14.

Navajo Nation Home Page. 2000. (www.navajo.org).

Neilsen, Marianne O. and Robert A. Silverman. 1996. *Native Americans, Crime, and Justice.* Boulder, Colo.: Westview Press.

Nelson, Blake. 1995. *Rhetoric and Law: Understanding the Difference among Supreme Court Decisions.* M.A. Thesis. Minneapolis: University of Minnesota.

New Mexico Criminal Code. 1982. 66–68: 101.

New Mexico Statutes. 1984. 30: 2.

New York Times (Indians). 1870. June 1, 1.

———. 1870. June 4, 1.

———. 1870. June 8, 1.

———. 1870. June 11, 1.

———. 1870. June 12, 1.

———. 1870. June 13, 1.

———. 1870. June 14, 1.

———. 1870. June 15, 8.

———. 1870. June 17, 1.

Nisqually v. United States. 1971. 29 Ind. Cl. Comm. 432.

Nix, L. Jacob. [1887] 1994. "The Sioux Uprising in Minnesota, 1862." In *Jacob Nix's Eyewitness History.* Translated by G. Steinhauser, D. H. Tolzmann, and E. Reichmann. Edited by D. H. Tolzmann. Nashville: Indiana University German-American Heritage Society.

NMS (New Mexico Superintendency). 1824–1881, 1849–1853, 1849–1880. Washington, D.C.: National Archives.

Nurge, Ethel. 1970. *The Modern Sioux.* Lincoln: University of Nebraska Press.

O'Brian, Sharon. 1996. "A Legal Analysis of the American Indian Religious Freedom Act." In *Handbook of American Indian Religious Freedom.* Edited by Christopher Vecsey, 27–43. New York: Crossroads Publishing.

Oehler, Chester M. 1959. *The Great Sioux Uprising.* New York: Oxford University Press.

Olson, James C. 1965. *Red Cloud and the Sioux Problem.* Lincoln: University of Nebraska Press.

Ong, Walter J. 1973. "World as View and World as Event." In *Intercommunication among Nations and Peoples.* Edited by Michael H. Prosser, 27–44. New York: Harper & Row.

Ortiz, Roxanne Dunbar. 1977. *The Great Sioux Nation.* Berkeley, Calif.: Moon Books.

Otero Slave Code. 1861. Territorial Law Archives. Santa Fe: New Mexico State Archives.

Paisley, William. "Public Communication Campaigns: The American Experience." In *Public Communication Campaigns.* Edited by R. E. Rice and C. E. Aiken, 15–38. Newbury Park, Calif.: Sage Publications.

Pandey, Triloki Nath. 1967. *Factionalism in a Southwestern Pueblo.* Ph.D. Dissertation. Chicago: University of Chicago.

Parsons, Elsie Clews. 1917. "Notes on Zuni." *The American Anthropological Association Memoirs* 4: 151–327. Lancaster, Pa.: The American Anthropological Association.

———. 1927. "Witchcraft among the Pueblos: Indian or Spanish." *Man* 27: 106–12, 125–28.

———. 1936. *Taos Pueblo.* Menasha, Wis.: G. Banta Publications.

Pennington, William D. 1979. "Government Policy and Indian Farming on the Cheyenne and Arapaho Reservation: 1869–1880." *Chronicles of Oklahoma* 55: 171–89.

Perelman, Chaim, and Lucie Olbrechts-Tyteca. 1969. *The New Rhetoric: A Treatise on Argumentation.* Translated by J. Wilkinson and P. Weaver. Notre Dame, Ind.: University of Notre Dame Press.

Petitioner's Brief. 1974. In *Indian Claims Commission Cases 329a and 329b.* Edited by Norman A. Ross, 1–130. New York: Clearwater Microfilm.

Pevar, Stephen. 1992. *The Rights of Indians and Tribes.* Carbondale: Southern Illinois University Press.

Philp, Kenneth R. [1977] 1981. *John Collier's Crusade for Indian Reform 1920–1954.* Tucson: University of Arizona Press.

Plamenatz, J. 1970. *Ideology.* New York: Praeger.

"Police Suspect Alcoholism in Christmas Eve Wreck." 1992. *Albuquerque Journal,* December 26, A1, A2.

Pond, Samuel W. [1908] 1986. *The Dakota or Sioux in Minnesota As They Were in 1834.* St. Paul: Minnesota Historical Society.

Pospisil, Leopold. 1967. "The Attitudes of Law." In *Law and Warfare.* Edited by Paul Bohannon, 25–42. Garden City, N.Y.: National History Press.

Preliminary Hearing Record (PHR). 1993. Gordon House Case, CR93–16933. Albuquerque, N.Mex.: Ray Twohig Office.

Preston, P. W. 1997. *Political/Cultural Identity.* London: Sage Publications.

Price, Catherine. 1996. *The Oglala People, 1841–1879.* Lincoln: University of Nebraska Press.

Proclamation of New Mexico Citizens. 1860. Santa Fe: New Mexico State Archives, Box 114, File 11.

Prosch, Thomas W. 1915. "The Indian War in Washington Territory." *The Quarterly of the Oregon Historical Society* 16: 1–23.

Prucha, Francis P. 1984. *The Great Father: The United States Government and the American Indians.* 2 vols. Lincoln: University of Nebraska Press.

———. 1990. *Documents of the United States Indian Policy,* 2d ed. Lincoln: University of Nebraska Press.

———. 1994. *American Indian Treaties: The History of a Political Anomaly.* Berkeley: University of California Press.

Pueblo Lands Act. 1924. U.S. Stat. 43: 639–42.

Pueblo of Taos v. United States. 1965. 15 Ind. Cl. Comm. 666.

Pueblo Relief Bill. 1938. U.S. Stat. 68: 108–11.

Puget Sound Gilnetters v. Moos. 1997. 88 Wn. 2d. 667.

Puyallup Tribe of Indians v. Department of Game. 1968. 391 U.S. 392.

"Racism a Factor." 1993. *Albuquerque Journal*, March 30, A1.

Red Cloud Chief of the Sioux 1909. Compiled by Addison E. Sheldon. Manuscript. Lincoln: State Historical Society of Nebraska.

Redfield, Robert. 1967. "Primitive Law." In *Law and Warfare.* Edited by Paul Bohannan, 3–24. Garden City, N.Y.: The Natural History Press.

Reichard, Gladys A. 1929. *Social Life of the Navajo Indians.* New York: Columbia University Press.

Reid, T. R. 1980. *Congressional Odyssey in the Saga of a Senate Bill.* San Francisco: W. H. Freeman.

Reike, Richard and Malcolm O. Sillars. 1984. *Argumentation and the Decision-Making Process.* Glenview, Ill.: Scott, Foresman and Company.

Richards, Kent D. 1991. "Historical Antecedents to the Boldt Decision." *Washington Legal History* 4: 69–84.

———. [1979] 1993. *Isaac I. Stevens: Young Man in a Hurry.* Pullman: Washington State University Press.

Riggs, Stephen R. [1880] 1969. *Mary and I: Forty Years with the Sioux.* Minneapolis: Ross & Haines.

Rister, Carl Coke. 1931. "Harmful Practices of Indian Traders in the Southwest." *New Mexico Historical Review* (July) 6: 228–45.

Roddis, Louis H. 1956. *The Indian Wars of Minnesota.* Cedar Rapids, Iowa: Torch Press.

Rodriguez, Richard. 1992. "Man Charged in Fatal Christmas Eve Crash." *Albuquerque Journal*, December 29, A1, A7.

Roessel, Ruth. 1973. *Navajo Stories of the Long Walk Period.* Chinle, Ariz.: Navajo Community College Press.

Romero, Leo M. 1990. "Unintentional Homicides Caused by Risk-Creating Conduct: Problems in Distinguishing Depraved Mind Murder, Second Degree Murder, Involuntary Manslaughter and Non-Criminal Homicide." *New Mexico Law Review* 20: 55–86.

Rorabaugh, William J. 1979. *The Alcoholic Republic: The American Tradition.* New York: Oxford University Press.

Rosenthal, Harvey D. 1990. *Their Day in Court: A History of the Indian Claims Commission.* New York: Garland Publishing.

Ross, Norman A. 1973. Indian Claims Commission, Microfilm, Cases 329a and 329b. New York: Clearwater Microfilm.

"Sand Creek Massacre." 1867. Report of the Secretary of War. Senate Executive Document 26. 39th Cong., 2d Sess.

Sando, Joe S. [1976] 1982. *The Pueblo Indians.* San Francisco: The Indian Historian Press.

Satterlee, Marion P. 1909–1914. "Narratives of the Sioux Wars." *Minnesota History* 15: 349–70.

————. 1923. *A Detailed Account of the Massacre of the Dakota Indians of Minnesota in 1862.* Minneapolis: Marion Satterlee.

————. 1927. *The Court Proceedings in the Trial of Dakota Indians.* Minneapolis: Marion Satterlee.

"Savages at the White House." 1870. *New York Times,* June 8, 1.

Sayer, John William. 1997. *Ghostdancing the Law: The Wounded Knee Trials.* Cambridge, Mass.: Harvard University Press.

Scheppele, Kim L. 1989. "Telling Stories." *Michigan Law Review* 87: 2073–97.

Schmidt, Joel J. 1966. "Until the Mothers Are Reached: Field Matrons on the Cheyenne and Arapaho Reservation." *Chronicles of Oklahoma* 74: 436–45.

Schmitt, Martin. 1949. "The Execution of Leschi and the 'Truth Teller'." *Oregon Historical Quarterly* 10: 30–39.

Schuetz, Janice. 1986. "Overlays of Argument in Legislative Process." *Journal of the American Forensic Association* 23: 223–34.

————. 1994. *The Logic of Women on Trial: Case Studies of Popular American Trials.* Carbondale: Southern Illinois University Press.

Schuetz, Janice and Janet Shiver. 2000. *Teams: An Approach to Business and Professional Speaking.* New York: McGraw-Hill Custom Publishing.

Scott, Bob. 1994. *Blood at Sand Creek: The Massacre Revisited.* Caldwell, Idaho: Caxton Printers.

Seger, John H. 1956. *Early Days among the Cheyenne and Arapaho.* Norman: University of Oklahoma Press.

Seigneuret, Jean-Charles, ed. 1988. *Dictionary of Literary Themes and Motifs: A–J.* Westport, Conn.: Greenwood Press.

Senate Report. [Red Cloud] 1870. Report 68, 41st Cong., 2d Sess., 1409: 1.

————. [Red Cloud]. 1871. Report 348, 41st Cong., 3d Sess., 1443: 1.

————. [Fanny Kelly] 1872. Report 79, 42nd Cong., 2d Sess., 14: 50–51.

Sergeant, Elizabeth Shapley. 1922. "Big Pow Wow of Pueblos." *New York Times,* November 26, 6, 14.

Shattuck, Petra T. and Jill Norgren. 1990. *Partial Justice: Federal Indian Law in a Liberal Constitutional System.* New York: Berg Press.

Shaw, B. F. 1903. "Medicine Creek Treaty." *Oregon Historical Society* 4: 24–32.

Shinkle, James D. 1965. *Fort Sumner and the Bosque Redondo Indian Reservation.* Roswell, N.Mex.: Hall Poobaugh Press.

Shotter, John and Kenneth J. Gergen. 1989. *Texts of Identity.* Newbury Park, Calif.: Sage Publications.

Silverman, Robert A. 1996. "Patterns of Native American Crime." In *Native Americans, Crime, and Justice.* Edited by Marianne O. Nielsen and Robert A. Silverman, 58–74. Boulder, Colo.: Westview Press.

Simmons, Marc. 1974. *Witchcraft in the Southwest: Spanish and Indian Supernaturalism on the Rio Grande.* Lincoln: University of Nebraska Press.

Simons, Herbert W. and Elizabeth W. Mechling. 1981. "The Rhetoric of Political Movements." In *Communication and Public Policy.* Edited by Dan M. Nimmo and Charles Elder, 417–44. Beverly Hills, Calif.: Sage Publications.

Sioux Depredation Act. 1891. 26 Stat. 1002.

"Sioux Indians, Wounded Knee Massacre." 1938. Subcommittee on Indian Affairs, 75th Cong., 3d Sess., HR 2535.

Sioux Tribe of Indians v. U.S. 1956. 146 F. Supp. 229.

Sisseton & Wahpeton Indians v. United States. 1923. 58 C. Cla. 302.

"Slavery in the Territory of New Mexico." 1861. House Exec. Document. 36th Cong., 1st Sess., 1051: 508.

Smith, E. B., ed. 1976. *Indian Tribal Claims Decided in the Court of Claims of the United States: Briefed and Compiled to June 30, 1947.* Arlington, Va.: University Publications of America.

Smith, Marian W. [1940] 1969. "The Puyallup-Nisqually," no. 32. *Contributions to Anthropology.* New York: AMA Inc.

Smith, Paul Chaat and Robert Allen Warrior. 1996. *Like a Hurricane: The Indian Movement from Alcatraz to Wounded Knee.* New York: New Press.

Smith, Sherry L. 1990. *The View from Officers' Row.* Tucson: University of Arizona Press.

Smith, Watson and John M. Roberts. 1954. *Zuni Law: A Field of Values,* Vol. 43. Cambridge, Mass.: Papers of the Peabody Museum of American Archeology and Ethnology, Harvard University.

Snow, P. C. 1993. "DWI Crusade Grips Church Congregation." *Albuquerque Journal,* January 1, D1.

Sohappy v. Smith. 1969. 302 F. Supp. 899.

Spicer, Carl. 1997. "Toward a (dys)Functional Anthropology of Drinking Ambivalence and the American Indian Experience with Alcohol." *Medical Anthropology Quarterly* 5, 11: 306–22.

Spivak, Gayatri Chakravorty. (1994). "Can the Subaltern Speak?" In *Colonial Discourse and Post Colonial Theory.* Edited by Patrick Williams and Laura Chrisman, 66–110. New York: Columbia University Press.

Spurr, David. 1993. *The Rhetoric of the Empire: Colonial Discourse in Journalism Travel Writing and Imperial Administration.* Durham, N.C.: Duke University Press.

State v. McCrary. 1984. 100 N.M. 671.

Stevens, Hazard. 1901. *The Life of Isaac Ingalls Stevens.* 2 vols. Boston: Houghton Mifflin.

Stevenson, Matilda Coxe. 1904. *The Zuni Indians: Twenty-Third Annual Report.* Washington, D.C.: The Bureau of American Ethnology.

Stevenson, Shanna. 1999. Interview conducted by the author, Olympia, Washington.

Steward, Julian H. 1955. "Theory and Application in a Social Science." *Ethnohistory* 2: 292–302.

Stewart, Charles J., Craig Allen Smith, and Robert E. Denton, Jr. 1994. *Persuasion and Social Movements.* Prospect Heights, Ill.: Waveland Press.

Strickland, Rennard. 1997. *Tonto's Revenge: Reflections on American Indian Culture and Policy.* Albuquerque: University of New Mexico Press.

Sutton, Irma. 1985. *Irredeemable America: The Indians' Estate and Land Claims.* Albuquerque: University of New Mexico Press.

Svaldi, David. 1989. *Sand Creek and the Rhetoric of Extermination.* New York: University Press of America.

Sweezy, Carl. 1966. *The Arapaho Way.* New York: Clarkson N. Potter.

Taggert, Michelle M. 1999. "Just Say 'To'd, Thit Donda." *American Indian Reports,* July, 26–28.

Talbot, Steve. [1981] 1985. *Roots of Oppression.* New York: International Publishers.

Taos Pueblo Indian Council. 1968. *The Blue Lake Area: An Appeal from Taos Pueblo.* Taos, N.Mex.: Tribal Council.

"Telecast Details Taos of Blue Lake Fight." 1966. *Albuquerque Journal,* n.d. In the clipping file entitled "Blue Lake Controversy." Santa Fe: New Mexico State Library.

Territory of New Mexico v. Nyuche, Hatotsi, Nourmasi, Napthlu, and Keeasi. 1899. Territorial Law Records for Valencia County, New Mexico, Criminal Case 511. Santa Fe: New Mexico State Archives.

Territory of Washington v. Leschi. 1856. True Bill. Trial Transcripts. Olympia: Washington State Archives, Leschi File.

———. 1857. Trial Motions. Olympia: Washington State Archives, Leschi File.

———. 1857. Trial Transcripts. Olympia: Washington State Archives, Leschi File.

Thompson, Frank. 1992. "Driver's Friends Mystified and Shocked." *Albuquerque Journal,* December 29, A1, A7.

Thompson, Gerald. 1976. *The Army and the Navajo.* Tucson: University of Arizona Press.

Toch, Hans. 1965. *The Social Psychology of Movements.* Indianapolis, Ind.: Bobbs-Merrill Company.

Tolmie, William T. 1857. "Letter to the Editor." *Pioneer and Democrat,* March 27, 2.

———. 1858. "Letter Supporting Pardon of Leschi." *Pioneer and Democrat,* February 5, 2.

Topper, Martin D. 1985. "Navajo Alcoholism: Drinking, Alcohol Abuse and Treatment in a Changing Cultural Environment." In *The American Experience with Alcohol.* Edited by L. A. Bennett and C. J. Ames, 227–51. New York: Plenum.

Trade and Intercourse Act. 1832. U.S. Stat. 4: 729–35.

———. 1847. U.S. Stat. 9: 202–4.

Transcripts of the Records of Trials of Certain Indians Charged with Barbarities in the State of Minnesota. 1862. Washington, D.C.: National Archives, Senate Records Box 37A, File 2.

Transcripts of Trial Record. *U.S. v. Washington.* 1973. Case #9213. Tacoma, Wash.: U.S. District Court.

Treaty of Fort Laramie. 1851. 11 Stat. 949.

Treaty of Fort Laramie. 1868. 15 Stat. 635–47.

Treaty of Fort Sumner. 1868. 15 Stat. 667–72.

Treaty of Little Arkansas. 1865. 14 Stat. 703–11.

Treaty of Medicine Creek. 1854. 10 Stat. 1132–37.

Treaty of Medicine Lodge Creek. 1867. 15 Stat. 593–99.

Treaty with Mdewakanton and Wapekute. 1851. 10 Stat. 954–59.

Treaty with Mdewakanton and Wapekute. 1858. 12 Stat. 1031–36.

Treaty with Sisseton and Wahpeton [Traverse des Sioux]. 1851. 10 Stat. 949–53.

Treaty with Sisseton and Wahpeton. 1858. 12 Stat. 1037–41.

Treaty with Sisseton and Wahpeton. 1867. 15 Stat. 505–11.

Trenholm, Virginia Cole. 1970. *The Arapahoes, Our People.* Norman: University of Oklahoma Press.

"Trial and Conviction of Leschi." 1857. *Pioneer and Democrat*, March 20, 2.

"The Trial of Gordon House." 1994. *Dateline*. New York: NBC Productions.

Truth Teller. 1858. February 3, 2. Available in Olympia, Washington State Archives.

Turner, Katharine C. 1951. *Red Men Calling on the Great White Father*. Norman: University of Oklahoma Press.

Turner, Victor. 1974. *Dramas, Fields, and Metaphors: Symbolic Action in Society*. Ithaca, N.Y.: Cornell University Press.

————. [1969] 1977. *The Ritual Process*. Ithaca, N.Y.: Cornell University Press.

————, 1982. *From Ritual to Theatre*. New York: PAJ Publications.

————. 1988. *The Anthropology of Performance*. New York: PAJ Publications.

Twitchell, Ralph Emerson. [1900] 1963. *The History of the Military Occupation of the Territory of New Mexico 1846–51*. Denver: Smith Brooks.

Twohig, Ray. 1993, August 5. Motion to Dismiss. Albuquerque: Twohig Law Office.

————. 1993, September 23. Motion to Stop Proceeding. Albuquerque: Twohig Law Office.

Underhill, Ruth. 1945. *Indians of the Pacific Northwest*. Riverside, Calif.: Sherman Institute Press.

————. 1956. *The Navajos*. Norman: University of Oklahoma Press.

United States War Department. 1880–1890. (R.R. Records of Rebellion). *The War of the Rebellion: A Compilation of the Official Records of the Union and Confederate Armies*, Vols. 31, 35, 51. Washington, D.C.: Government Printing Office.

U.S. Statutes at Large [Taos Pueblo]. 1933. 68 U.S. Stat. 108.

U.S. v. Washington. 1974. 384 F. Supp. 312.

————. 1988. 135 F.3d. 618 (9th Cir).

————. 1992. 873 F. Supp. 1492.

————. 1994. 898 F. Supp. 1453.

————. 1995. 909 F. Supp. 787.

————. 1998. 157 F.3d 630 (9th Cir).

Usher, John P. 1865. Report on the Navajo Indians. House Exec. Document, 38th Cong., 1st Sess., No. 65, 1193.

Utley, Robert M. 1974. *The Last Days of the Sioux Nation*. New Haven, Conn.: Yale University Press.

————. 1984. *The Indian Frontier of the American West 1846–1890*. Albuquerque: University of New Mexico Press.

Van Der Beets, Richard. 1972. "The Indian Captivity Narrative as Ritual." *American Literature* 43 (January): 548–62.

van Eemeren, Frans H. and Rob Grootendorst. 1990. "Analyzing Argumentative Discourse." In *Perspectives on Argument*. Edited by Robert Trapp and Janice Schuetz, 88–106. Prospect Heights, Ill.: Waveland Press.

Viola, Herman J. 1981. *Diplomats in Buckskins: A History of Indian Delegations in Washington*. Washington, D.C.: Smithsonian Institution Press.

Voices from Wounded Knee, 1973. 1974. Roosevelt, N.Y.: Akwesasne Notes, Mohawk Nation.

Wakefield, Sarah F. [1864] 1976. *Six Weeks in Sioux Tepees: A Narrative of Indian Captivity*. New York: Garland Publishing.

Walker, Deward, ed. 1989. *Witchcraft and Sorcery of the American Native Peoples*. Moscow: University of Idaho Press.

War of Rebellion: A Compilation of the Official Records of the Union and Confederate Armies. 1880–1901, 128 vols. Washington, D.C.: U.S. War Department.

Washburn, Wilcomb E. 1971. *Red Man's Land: White Man's Law*. New York: Scribner.

Watson, Adam. 1983. *Diplomacy*. Philadelphia: ISHI Publications.

Watts, John S. 1858. *Indian Depredations in New Mexico*. Washington, D.C.: Gideon Press.

Weyler, Rex. 1984. *Blood of the Land: The Government and the Corporate War against the American Indian Movement*. New York: Vintage Press.

Whately, John T. 1968. "The Saga of Blue Lake." *The Indian Historian* 2: 22–28.

Whipple, Henry P. 1864. "Clemency Appeal." In *History of the Sioux Wars and Massacres of 1862 and 1863*. Edited by Isaac V. D. Heard, 343–48. New York: Harper and Brothers.

———. 1899. *Lights and Shadows of a Long Episcopate*. New York: Macmillan.

White, James Boyd. 1984. *When Words Lose Their Meaning*. Chicago: University of Chicago Press.

———. 1985. *Heracles' Bow: Essays on the Rhetoric and Poetics of Law*. Madison: University of Wisconsin Press.

White, Lonnie J. 1969. "White Women Captives of the Southern Plains: 1866–1875." *Journal of the West* 8: 327–54.

White, Robert A. 1970. "The Lower-Class 'Culture of Excitement,' among the Contemporary Sioux." In *The Modern Sioux*. Edited by Ethel Nurge, 175–93. Lincoln: University of Nebraska Press.

Wickersham, James. 1893. "The Indian Side of the Puget Sound Indian War." Lecture presented at the State Historical Society Meeting. Olympia: Washington State Archives.

Wiley, J. W. 1855. "The Militia." *Pioneer and Democrat*, October 30, 2.

———. 1855. "The Puget Sound Rangers." *Pioneer and Democrat*, November 9, 2.

———. 1856. "Leschi, Quiemuth, etc." *Pioneer and Democrat*, November 28, 2.

Wiley, J. W. and E. Furste. 1858. "Execution of Leschi." *Pioneer and Democrat*, February 26, 2.

Wilkins, David E. 1997. *American Indian Sovereignty and the U.S. Supreme Court*. Austin: University of Texas Press.

Wilkinson, Charles F. 1987. *American Indians, Time and the Law*. New Haven, Conn.: Yale University Press.

———. 2000. *Messages from Frank's Landing: A Story of Salmon, Treaties, and the Indian Way*. Seattle: University of Washington Press.

Wilkinson, Glen A. 1966. "Indian Tribal Claims before the Court of Claims." *Georgetown Law Journal* 55: 511–28.

Williams, D. 1997a. "Non-Indians Caught Stealing Salmon." *Northwest Indian Fisheries Commission News* 17 (Fall): 10.

———. 1997b. "Tribal Fisheries Still Facing Harassment." *Northwest Indian Fisheries Commission News* 17 (Winter): 7–10.

Williams, Patrick and Laura Chrisman, eds. 1994. *Colonial Discourse and Post Colonial Theory.* New York: Columbia University Press.

Wilson, Raymond. 1981. "Forty Years to Judgment." *Minnesota History* 51: 284–91.

Winter, Steven L. 1989. "The Cognitive Dimension of the Agon Between Legal Power and Narrative Meaning." *Michigan Law Review* 87: 2225–75.

Woloch, Nancy. 1984. *Women and the American Experience.* New York: Alfred Knopf.

Woods, Fronda. 1998. Interview conducted by the author, Olympia, Washington.

Worchester, Donald E. 1951. "The Navajo During the Spanish Regime in New Mexico." *New Mexico Historical Review* 26: 101–18.

Work, Hubert. 1924. "Our American Indians." *Saturday Evening Post*, May 3, 92.

Young, Robert. 1990. *White Mythologies: Writing History and the West.* New York: Routledge.

Zimmerman, Bill. 1976. *Airlift to Wounded Knee.* Chicago: Swallow Press.

Zion, James and Elsie B. Zion. 1996. "Hazho's Sokee—Stay Together Nicely: Domestic Violence Under Navajo Common Law." In *Native Americans, Crime, and Justice.* Edited by Marianne O. Nielsen and Robert A. Silverman, 96–113. Boulder, Colo.: Westview Press.

Zuni Informant. 1994. Interview conducted by the author, September 10, Albuquerque, New Mexico.

Index

About the Author

JANICE SCHUETZ is a Professor of Communication at the University of New Mexico. She is the author of *The Logic of Women on Trial* and more than 60 articles and book chapters, and co-author of, among other books, *Communication and Litigation*, *The O.J. Simpson Trials*, and *Perspectives on Argumentation*.